Environmental Philosophy in Asian Traditions of Thought

Environmental Philosophy in Asian Traditions of Thought

EDITED BY

J. Baird Callicott
and James McRae

Published by State University of New York Press, Albany

© 2014 State University of New York

For information, contact State University of New York Press, Albany, NY
www.sunypress.edu

Production by Diane Ganeles
Marketing by Fran Keneston

Library of Congress Cataloging-in-Publication Data

Environmental philosophy in Asian traditions of thought/edited by J. Baird Callicott and James McRae.
        pages cm
"Conceived as a sequel to Nature in Asian traditions of thought"—Preface.
Includes bibliographical references and index.
ISBN 978-1-4384-5201-2 (hardcover : alk. paper) ISBN 978-1-4384-5200-5 (pbk. : alk. paper) 1. Environmental sciences—Asia—Philosophy. 2. Environmentalism—Asia—Philosophy. 3. Environmental ethics—Asia. 4. Philosophy, Asian. I. Callicott, J. Baird, editor of collaboration. II. McRae, James, editor of collaboration. III. James, George Alfred. Environment and environmental philosophy in India. IV. Nature in Asian traditions of thought. Sequel to:
GE40.E57 2014
179'.1095—dc23

2013028378

10 9 8 7 6 5 4 3 2 1

We dedicate this book to Roger T. Ames:
A gifted scholar, a trusted friend, and an exemplar of Confucian virtue.
Mahalo nui loa.

Contents

Preface

Nature in Asian Traditions of Thought, edited by J. Baird Callicott and Roger T. Ames, was published by SUNY Press in 1989. It remains in print more than twenty years later. In the two decades that have since elapsed, the field of "comparative environmental philosophy," which *Nature in Asian Traditions of Thought* inaugurated, has expanded and matured. *Environmental Philosophy in Asian Traditions of Thought* is conceived as a sequel to *Nature in Asian Traditions of Thought*. All eighteen papers included in this volume were written after 1989. All but four were originally published in widely scattered venues; those four exceptions appear here for the first time.

The idea for this book was conceived during September, 2007 in Fulton, Missouri at Westminster College's second Annual Symposium on Democracy—which was focused, that year, on the theme of "The Environment: Prospects for Sustainability." J. Baird Callicott was a speaker at the symposium. James McRae, a member of Westminster College's Department of Classics, Philosophy, and Religious Studies, introduced Callicott and his talk for the symposium. After Callicott's talk, McRae mentioned that he used *Nature in Asian Traditions of Thought* as a textbook in his environmental ethics course. He also mentioned that he had written his doctoral dissertation under the direction of its co-editor, Roger Ames. Callicott was pleased to hear that. It's always good to know that one's books are taught in the classroom. And McRae's personal connection with Callicott's good friend and colleague was a pleasant surprise.

Personal pleasantries aside, Callicott thought that a companion volume to *Nature in Asian Traditions of Thought*, representing newer work in the field, would also be useful to students and their instructors. Just as important, it could synergistically juxtapose the best new work in comparative environmental philosophy and thus stimulate further development of the field. McRae's doctorate is from the world's premier program in comparative philosophy at the University of Hawai'i, where students receive rigorous training, including language training, in various traditions of Asian thought. Callicott believed that he had found in McRae the perfect co-editor for this volume. Callicott could bring his up-to-date expertise in environmental philosophy to the project, McRae could bring his in comparative philosophy. Moreover, for a second-generation book—the son of *Nature in Asian Traditions of Thought*, as it were—what could be better than for one of the editors to be a member of the second generation of comparative environmental philosophers? In subsequent correspondence, Callicott proposed the project and McRae agreed to be his co-editor.

We, Callicott and McRae, the aspiring editors of what would become this book, then began to look for work of exemplary quality by gifted and expert scholars. Of course, there was an embarrassment of riches and the hardest part of the editorial process was to boil down the list of potential items for inclusion. Those included would have to fit into a single volume and it was imperative that we make sure that those that made their way into the volume were the best of the lot. In the meantime, another one of Callicott's books, *Earth's Insights: A Multicultural Survey of Ecological Ethics from the Mediterranean Basin to the Australian Outback*, was in process of being translated into Japanese. That book, first published in 1994, is based in part on the work of the scholars in *Nature in Asian Traditions of Thought*. The translation project introduced us to Tomosaburō Yamauchi and Hiroshi Abe, two Japanese philosophers, who enthusiastically agreed to contribute essays to the collection. Yamauchi's is published here for the first time.

Once we had made our selections, we organized them into a table of contents, drafted a prospectus, and sent both to Jane Bunker, then the Associate Director and Editor-in-Chief of the State University of New York Press, the publisher of *Nature in Asian Traditions of Thought*. She immediately saw the value of our proposed sequel and turned the project over to Nancy Ellegate, SUNY Press's acquisitions editor for Asian studies. We thank Ms. Bunker for her support for the project and Ms. Ellegate for her expert assistance in seeing the book through the process of production. In the meanwhile, Jane Bunker took a job at another press and was succeeded by co-Directors Donna Dixon and James Peltz, who generously helped move the project through the review process.

This anthology, as noted, contains both new articles and essays that were previously published in leading journals in the fields of environmental ethics and Asian and comparative philosophy:

1. George Alfred James's "Environment and Environmental Philosophy in India" appears for the first time in this collection.
2. Christopher Framarin's "Ātman, Identity, and Emanation: Arguments for a Hindu Environmental Ethic" was first published in *Comparative Philosophy* 2.1 (2011): 3–24.

3. "Gandhi's Contributions to Environmental Thought and Action" by Bart Gruzalski was first published in *Environmental Ethics* 24 (2002): 227–42.

4. Stephanie Kaza's "Acting With Compassion: Buddhism, Feminism and the Environmental Crisis" was first published in *Ecotheology* No 1 (July 1996): 71–98.

5. "Against Holism: Rethinking Buddhist Environmental Ethics" by Simon P. James was first published in *Environmental Values* 16 (2007): 447–61.

6. "Causation and 'Telos': The Problem of Buddhist Environmental Ethics" by Ian Harris was first published in the *Journal of Buddhist Ethics* 1 (1994): 46–59.

7. "The Relevance of Chinese Neo-Confucianism for the Reverence of Nature" by Mary Evelyn Tucker originally appeared in *Environmental History Review*, vol. 15, no. 2, Summer 1991.

8. "Beyond Naturalism: A Reconstruction of Daoist Environmental Ethics" by R.P. Peerenboom originally appeared in *Environmental Ethics* 13 (1991): 3–22.

9. "Conceptual Foundations for Environmental Ethics: A Daoist Perspective" by Karyn Lai first appeared in *Environmental Ethics* 25 (2003): 247–66.

10. "Process Ecology and the 'Ideal' Dao" by Alan Fox was originally published in the *Journal of Chinese Philosophy* 32, no. 1 (2005): 47–57.

11. "The Viability (Dao) and Virtuosity (De) of Daoist Ecology: Reversion (Fu) as Renewal by Sandra Wawrytko was first published in *The Journal of Chinese Philosophy* 32, no. 1 (2005): 89–103.

12. James Miller's chapter, "Ecology, Aesthetics and Daoist Body Cultivation," appears in print here for the first time.

13. "The Japanese Concept of Nature in Relation to the Environmental Ethics and Conservation Aesthetics of Aldo Leopold" by Steve Odin was first published in *Environmental Ethics* 13 (1991): 345–60. It has also appeared in Mary Evelyn Tucker and Duncan Ryūken Williams' anthology, *Buddhism and Ecology* (Harvard University Press, 1997).

14. "Dōgen, Deep Ecology, and the Ecological Self" by Deane Curtin first appeared in *Environmental Ethics* 16 (1994): 195–213.

15. "Conservation Ethics and the Japanese Intellectual Tradition" by David Shaner and R. Shannon Duval first appeared in *Environmental Ethics* 11 (1989): 197–214.

16. "From Symbiosis (*Kyōsei*) to the Ontology of 'Arising Both from Oneself and from Another'" Gūshō by Hiroshi Abe first appeared in *Interdisziplinäre Phänomenologie* 4 (2007): 109–129.

17. Tomosaburō Yamauchi's chapter, "The Confucian Environmental Ethics of Ogyū Sorai," appears in print for the first time in this volume.

18. James McRae's "Triple-Negation: Watsuji Tetsurō on the Sustain-ability of Ecosystems, Economies, and International Peace" was presented at the Tenth East-West Philosophers' Conference in 2011 and appears in Roger T. Ames and Peter Hershock's anthology, *Value and Values: Economics and Justice in an Age of Global Interdependence* (University of Hawai'i Press, 2014).

Acknowledgments

J. Baird Callicott: I would like to thank James McRae, who, if truth be told, did the bulk of the work on this project, but who, true to his adopted cultural manners, insisted that I should be the first (senior citizen) editor and who even insists to this day on calling me "Professor Callicott" (which I have grown to find endearing). I would also like to thank Priscilla Solis Ybarra for all the positive changes her association over sixteen years has induced in both my thinking and (I hope) in my character. And like Sly Stone sang back in 1969, I would like to say to everyone I know "Thank You Falettinme Be Mice Elf Agin."

James McRae: I would like to humbly thank Professor Baird Callicott for kindly inviting me to work with him on this project and for being such a fine friend and mentor to me. As always, I am indebted to my wife, Heather McRae, for her steadfast support and constant inspiration. I thank my parents, John and Derrill, and my grandmother, Marguerite, who taught me to cherish the natural world. Many thanks go to my research assistants, Thanh Ha, Graeme Cave, Geneva Steck, Andrew Robertson, and Katie McMurtrey, for their tireless work on this project. I sincerely thank Ron and Dianne Winney for their generous support of my research. I am also grateful to Rob Arp and Adam Barkman for their understanding and friendship as I worked to finish two books simultaneously. Finally, I offer my gratitude to the staff at SUNY Press, with whom it has been my distinct pleasure to work. Mahalo nui loa and aloha!

Introduction

As noted in the Preface, this book, *Environmental Philosophy in Asian Traditions of Thought*, is a sequel to its predecessor, *Nature in Asian Traditions of Thought: Essays in Environmental Philosophy*. The first volume represented the debut of a new field: comparative environmental philosophy. This second volume contains the best essays published in the field during the subsequent two decades.

Comparative environmental philosophy is the intersection of two previously existing, but relatively new fields: comparative philosophy and environmental philosophy. As the name suggests, comparative philosophy compares—and contrasts—philosophies derived from widely differing intellectual traditions, which emerged and evolved independently of one another. Comparative philosophy was first engaged on an east-west axis, comparing philosophies of "oriental" and "occidental" provenance. As comparative philosophy matured, comparison of philosophies was also engaged on a north-south axis. Nevertheless, in part due to the weight of tradition, the main axis of comparison remains east-west.

Environmental philosophy was also at first more narrowly conceived—as environmental ethics. The central problematique of environmental philosophy, as initially conceived, was to bring the natural environment into the purview of ethics as a direct beneficiary of "moral considerability." As environmental philosophy matured, its compass was broadened to the metaphysical and epistemological issues raised by emergent environmental concerns. In addition, environmental philosophy was broadened by its affiliation with various political movements, such as feminism (eco-feminism) and social justice (social ecology and now, more recently, environmental justice).

Comparative philosophy is the senior field, datable to the first East-West Philosophy Conference, organized by Charles A. Moore at the University of Hawai'i in 1939. Moore went on to found, in 1951, *Philosophy East and West*, the principal journal in the field, which he edited until 1967, the same year that the Society for Asian and Comparative Philosophy was chartered. Eliot Deutsch then edited the journal until 1988, when Roger T. Ames assumed the editorship and continued in that capacity until the present.

The first course in environmental ethics was offered at the University of Wisconsin-Stevens Point in 1971. The first published papers by nascent environmental philosophers—Arne Naess, Richard Routley (later Sylvan), and Holmes Rolston III—appeared between 1973 and 1975. The first monograph in environmental ethics, *Man's Responsibility for Nature*, by John Passmore, was published in 1974. The first anthology, *Philosophy and Environmental Crisis*, edited by William T. Blackstone appeared in 1975. *Environmental Ethics*, the principal journal in its field, was founded in 1979 by Eugene C. Hargrove, who continues to edit it. Several other journals devoted to the field have since been established. The International Society for Environmental Ethics was established in 1990 and the International Association of Environmental Philosophy was established in 1997. An *Encyclopedia of Environmental Ethics and Philosophy* was published by Macmillan in 2009. Both comparative philosophy and environmental philosophy are robust and growing. Comparative *environmental* philosophy is also robust and growing, and this book, as noted, represents some of the best of the recent work in the area.

Comparative environmental philosophy was conceived in the summer of 1984 at the Institute for Comparative Philosophy convened on the University of Hawai'i campus in Honolulu. Summer institutes, such as this one, are sponsored by the National Endowment for the Humanities principally to introduce college teachers to new areas of study that they could integrate into their courses. One of us, J. Baird Callicott, was a Fellow (participant). Callicott wanted to get something more out of the Institute of Comparative Philosophy than syllabi material for a couple of new courses. He wanted to convince the comparative philosophers staffing the institute that they had something of unique importance to contribute to environmental philosophy.

More than any other one text, "The Historical Roots of Our Ecologic Crisis" by Lynn White Jr., published in *Science* in 1967, stimulated the development of environmental philosophy and also *comparative* environmental philosophy. An "environmental crisis" was then rising to acute public concern in the United States and much of the rest of the world. Notoriously, White laid the blame for it at the doorstep of the Judeo-Christian worldview that had, for so long, dominated thought in the West. In barest outline, White's argument is this: The twentieth-century environmental crisis (which is only growing more serious in the twenty-first century) is a byproduct of "modern technology." What makes modern technology modern is the marriage of technology to science. Until the emergence of democratic societies, science and technology had been pursued separately— science by aristocrats seeking knowledge for knowledge's sake, technology by yeomen for purely practical purposes. Modern technology, according to White, is, in short, technology informed by science. Science and the aggressive development of aggressive technologies are both "Occidental" in provenance—a debatable point, we might note, parenthetically. Their emergence in the West was fostered by the Judeo-Christian worldview, according to White. For in Genesis, God created "man" in His own image and gave him dominion over and commanded him to subdue the rest of creation. If man is created in the image of God—and what could that mean except in the image of God's mind, for surely God has no body?— then it might be possible for man to understand the product of God's mind, His creation. It might be possible to "think God's thoughts after him" as the "natural theologians" (among them Isaac Newton) claimed—or as we might say today, it might be possible to "reverse engineer" God's creation. That fostered the development of science. And it is only too obvious and needs no explanation how believing that man was given dominion over creation and commanded to subdue it might have fostered the aggressive development of aggressive technologies.

It was less the lurid and cavalier "text"—that linking the Judeo-Christian worldview to the environmental crisis—than the "subtext," repeated in White's well-orchestrated and beautifully crafted essay like a refrain, that sparked the development of environmental philosophy. That subtext was this: *What we do* in and to the natural environment depends on *what we think* about the natural environment and our human relationship to it. As White put it, "What we do about our ecology depends on our ideas of the man-nature relationship. More science and more technology are not going to get us out of the present ecologic crisis until we find a new religion, or rethink our old one." The business of philosophers is to bring to light and critically engage what we think about things. Bringing to light and critically engaging what we think about the natural environment and our human relationship to it became the business of a new breed of *environmental* philosophers. Thus did environmental philosophy come into being.

In the hands of environmental philosophers, finding a new religion or rethinking our old one was soon generalized and transformed into finding a new metaphysics—a new worldview—or rethinking our old one. The Western worldview, after all, was shaped as much or more by Pythagoras, Democritus, Plato, and Aristotle as by the authors of Genesis. Copernicus, Galileo, and Newton may have been inspired by the Bible, as White claims, "to think God's thoughts after Him," but the thoughts they turned to as a starting point for their own thinking were those of the ancient Greeks, not those of the ancient Hebrews. The first generation of environmental philosophers took both the paths suggested by White. Some attempted to rethink our old Western worldview—that is, they revisited the Western philosophical canon and attempted to recover various metaphysics that might, if revived, provide us with a more environmentally benign worldview. White himself took this option and suggested a revival and reinvigoration of the theology of St. Francis of Assisi. For his part, Arne Naess recommended Spinoza's metaphysics, somewhat implausibly, as a basis for a more environmentally benign Western worldview. Until his affiliation with the Nazi's came to light, the philosophy of Martin Heidegger enjoyed popularity with some prominent environmental philosophers, as did that of Alfred North Whitehead. Others looked eastward for a new metaphysics, following up on another path also suggested by White.

Here is how White also stimulated the development of comparative environmental philosophy. He suggested that Zen Buddhism is, point for point, the inverse of the Judeo-Christian worldview: "The beatniks, who are the basic revolutionaries of our time, show a sound instinct in their affinity for Zen Buddhism, which conceives of the man-nature relationship as very nearly the mirror image of the Christian view." (*Beatnik* was a popular derogatory term for those influenced by the Beat Generation genre of literature, notably represented by poets Allen Ginsberg and Gary Snyder and novelist Jack Kerouac. The *nik* suffix was derived from *sputnik*, the name of the world's first artificial orbital satellite, launched by the Soviets in 1957. The term insinuated that the beat-generation counterculture was pink if not flaming red.)

White, however, went on, straightaway, to express skepticism about looking for a new worldview for the Occident in the Orient: "Zen, however, is as deeply conditioned by Asian history as Christianity is by the experience of the West, and I am dubious of its viability among us." But that did not deter a number of scholars from trying to sell Eastern worldviews to Western customers. Huston Smith, for example, wrote an oft-reprinted piece titled "Tao Now: An Ecological Testament" and Gary Snyder wrote a poem titled "Smoky the Bear Sutra."

By 1984, Callicott had become painfully aware that sorties into Asian traditions of thought by newly minted environmental philosophers were, for the most part, amateurish and naïve. He managed to convince Ames, Deutsch, and some of the other faculty of the Institute of Comparative Philosophy (one such represented here is Steve Odin) that they had something vital to contribute to environmental philosophy: professional and sophisticated explorations of the environmental attitudes and values in various Asian traditions of thought. Ames and Callicott organized several sessions at professional conferences on "Conceptual Resources for Environmental Philosophy in Asian Traditions of Thought." The best papers from those sessions were published in special issues of *Philosophy East and West* and *Environmental Ethics*. And the best of those articles and articles from other sources were collected in *Nature in Asian Traditions of Thought*. Thus, did a more formal and sophisticated comparative environmental philosophy come into being.

If White is right—and we think he is—that the viability of any Asian worldview in the West is dubious, what is the point of comparative environmental philosophy? As any philosophical endeavor, it is a study that is worth pursuing for its inherent fascination and charm. But environmental philosophy and its subfield, comparative environmental philosophy, have had a higher and, dare we say, a nobler calling: to help address environmental concerns, to help save the world. If Buddhism and other Asian traditions of thought are not generally viable in Western culture and civilization, they are certainly viable in their own cultural and historical contexts. And Asian cultures and civilizations need an environment-friendly worldview and an environmental ethic quite as much as these are needed in Western culture and civilization. So exploring the potential for environmental ethics in Asian traditions of thought for the purpose of helping develop environmental ethics viable in Asian cultures and civilizations is one important point of comparative environmental philosophy.

There is also another, more subtle reason for the pursuit of comparative environmental philosophy. The comparative study of very different ways of viewing the world and different values concerning the world can reveal deep assumptions that might escape critical reflection in the absence of *alternative* assumptions. For example, one might be tempted to think that there simply is a self that one "has"—until confronted with the Buddhist doctrines of *śūnyatā* (the emptiness at the core of all things) and *anātman* or *anattā* (non-self).

The very existence of a self is problematized by studying the Buddhist worldview; oneself may be less a fact of human existence than a socially constructed belief, a cultural artifact. More to the point of comparative *environmental* philosophy, while most Asian traditions of thought recognize the existence of mountains and waterfalls and rivers and oceans, an East-West comparison shows that belief in the existence of "wilderness" is peculiar to the Western environmental worldview. Mountains and waterfalls, rivers, and oceans are part of the common reality that all human beings inhabit. Wilderness, to the contrary, is an element of the cultural "reality" that only Westerners (and indeed not even all of us) inhabit.

Finally as to the point of comparative environmental philosophy— indeed as to the point of environmental philosophy per se, whether comparative or intracultural—White's subtext should be as critically scrutinized as his text.

As to the text: Does Genesis give "man" license to exploit and destroy nature, as White argued? It does not, according to Jewish and Christian apologists, who have countered White's interpretation with a "stewardship" reading (among them the aforementioned Pass- more in *Man's Responsibility for Nature*). In Genesis, after each day of His creative efforts, God declares what he created to be "good." Doesn't this invest the creation with what environmental philoso- phers call "intrinsic value?" And just whose creation is it, after all? Surely it remains God's, not man's. And what does "dominion" mean? As Genesis goes on to clarify, it does not mean despotic rule, but benign stewardship. Adam, the first man, was put in the Garden of Eden—that is, nature in the language of metaphor—to "dress and keep it." The Bible may be read to say that humans should manage God's creation as caretaker, not as a despotic tyrant.

And as to the subtext, does what we do in and to the natural environment really depend on what we think about it? We believe that it does. But we do not believe that what we do in and to the natural environment is *wholly determined* by what we think about it. Obviously, there are other causal factors contributing to what we do. From a biological point of view, we humans are one species. However contested, there is a human nature, which is a platform, as it were, on which various human cultures construct their various beliefs about what sort of world we live in and what it means to be a human being. Because all humans have hands, all humans tend to be manipulative. (The word *manipulative* is derived from the Latin, *manus*, meaning hand. Thus the claim that all humans have hands and thus tend to be manipulative is true almost by definition.) Cultural worldviews can justify, encourage, and thus accelerate the universal human tendency to manipulate the natural environment. Indeed, we can read White's text as claiming that this is just what the Judeo-Christian worldview does. Whether it does or not, the Daoist concept of *wu-wei* (not doing) may have the opposite effect; it may problematize, discourage, and deflect the universal human tendency to manipulate the environment. What we think about the natural environment is not the be all and end all of what we do in and to the natural environment, but what we think about the natural environment does have considerable influence on what we do in and to the natural environment.

Since *Nature in Asian Traditions of Thought* was released, much has been written and published about the conceptual resources for environmental ethics in world *religions*, including those whose home is Asia. In the mid-1990s, a series of ten conferences was held at the Harvard Center for the Study of World Religions, featuring papers by leading thinkers in various religious traditions from all over the world. The best of those papers were published in ten volumes, each devoted to one religious tradition, by Harvard University Press. By contrast, no volumes devoted to environmental *philosophy* from an Asian perspective have been published since the publication of *Nature in Asian Traditions of Thought*. The papers included in this volume were selected for their distinctly *philosophical* orientation. And while each may be intellectually located in the context of an associated religious tradition, they all bear the hallmark of philosophy: they present an individualized point of view; they have a critical, often polemical, edge; and they are more speculative than doctrinal.

The two main geographical sources of Asian philosophy are found in South Asia (India) and East Asia (formerly the "Far East," more particularly China and Japan). Asian traditions of philosophy are closely associated with Asian religions, just as, for many centuries, European (or "Western") traditions of philosophy were closely associated with Western religions, especially Judaism and Christianity. The Asian religions with which Asian traditions of philosophy are associated are Hinduism in South Asia; Buddhism (which originated in India but all but died out there) in China and Japan; Confucianism and Daoism, which are indigenous to China; and Shintō, which is indigenous to Japan. In addition, Islamic philosophy, which originated in Western Asia (formerly the "Near East" and presently often the "Middle East"), has now become accepted as the fourth major focus of comparative philosophy. Islam, however, is regarded by both secular and Muslim scholars as a religion of The Book, closely related to its predecessors Judaism and Christianity. Moreover, during the European Medieval Period, the philosophical achievements of the ancient Greeks were conserved, elaborated, and developed in the Islamic World. As Christendom began to recover its intellectual heritage in the late Middle Ages, it did so through the lens of earlier Muslim scholarship. Thus, at the level of generality typical of philosophical discussion, Islamic environmental philosophy is more closely affiliated with occidental than with oriental traditions of thought.

The essays in *Environmental Philosophy in Asian Traditions of Thought* are, accordingly, organized into three sections, each corresponding to a major area of Asian philosophy: Indian, Chinese, and Japanese. The first three articles in Section I deal with the contributions of Hinduism to Indian environmental philosophy.

In "Environment and Environmental Philosophy in India," George Alfred James provides an overview of India's biogeophysical endowments and its environmental problems. He aptly characterizes the kind of Hindu philosophy that has been recognized in mainstream environmental philosophy—and also, importantly, the kind that has not. James provides a sweeping history of the centrality of nature in Hindu thought beginning with that which may be inferred from ancient artifacts, moving on to that which is recorded in the Rig Veda, and that which culminates in the philosophy of Mohandas Gandhi.

In "Ātman, Identity, and Emanation: Arguments for a Hindu Environmental Ethic," Christopher Framarin explores the philosophical basis for environmental ethics within the Hindu tradition. Hindu environmental ethics are typically based on the following argument: since all living things are part of Brahman (Ultimate Reality or God), they are all worthy of moral consideration. In this chapter, Framarin refutes three variations of this view, arguing each fails to provide a satisfactory environmental ethic because it does not attribute intrinsic value and moral standing to non-sentient beings. He then offers an alternative Hindu environmental ethic that grants both intrinsic value and direct moral standing to plants and animals by virtue of the fact that these entities have a good.

Picking up on and expanding one theme in James's essay, the third article to address Hindu philosophy is Bart Gruzalski's "Gandhi's Contributions to Environmental Thought and Action." In this essay, Gruzalski responds to Vinay Lal's critique of Gandhi's environmental philosophy (see Lal's "Gandhi and the Ecological Vision of Life: Thinking beyond Deep Ecology" in *Environmental Ethics* 22 (2000): 149–68). Lal argues that while Gandhi held an ecological worldview, he cannot be understood as an environmentalist because he would reject many of the claims made by deep ecology, social ecology, and ecofeminism. Gruzalski's paper is an attempt to defend Gandhi's environmental philosophy against these claims and elucidate those aspects of Gandhian thought that resonate with and have even influenced today's environmental philosophy and activism. He argues that Gandhi took a biocentric approach to ethics that emphasized non-injury toward all sentient beings, which directly influenced his non-violent approach to activism of all kinds, including environmental issues. Gandhi endorsed a simple, sustainable manner of living that favored independent local economies over globalization, a philosophy that ultimately inspired the Chipko Movement of the 1970s that strove to preserve the forests of India. Gandhi argued that if human beings were to live in small, self-reliant communities, we could reduce the consumerism that has generated so many of the world's environmental problems.

The second half of Section I deals with Buddhist environmental philosophy in the Indian tradition.

The Buddhist half of Section I begins with Stephanie Kaza's chapter, "Acting With Compassion: Buddhism, Feminism and the Environmental Crisis." Kaza explores six areas of confluence between American Buddhism and feminist philosophy: experiential knowing, examination of the conditioned mind, the truth of interrelatedness, emotional energy as a source of healing, and the role of the community. She uses these areas of convergence to develop a normative environmental ethic grounded in the feminist concept of relationality, which is analogous to the Buddhist notion of dependent co-arising, but which avoids some of the philosophical pitfalls of traditional Buddhist thinking. Kaza then offers several cases that illustrate the practical application of Buddhist feminist thought to environmental education and activism.

Simon P. James offers a contrarian perspective on Buddhism in his article, "Against Holism: Rethinking Buddhist Environmental Ethics." James begins this paper by summarizing "The Unity Thesis," a common misconception of Buddhist environmental ethics, in three propositions: (1) Buddhism takes a holistic worldview that views humans as one with nature, which produces ethical concern toward the environment on the part of human beings; (2) Proposition 1 is grounded in the Buddhist teaching of emptiness; therefore

(3) Buddhism is a philosophy that is inherently friendly toward the environment. James rejects the first proposition because the fact that human beings are one with nature does not necessarily imply that we are in harmony with it. He further argues that the second proposition is false because Buddhists do not intend for the notion of emptiness to produce an ecological worldview, but rather one of non-attachment to all things, including the environment. Since 2 does not entail 1, 3 cannot follow. Nonetheless, James argues that the conclusion is true for a different reason: the virtues of compassion, gentleness, humility, and mindfulness are necessary components of a well-ordered human being and represent dispositions to treat the environment responsibly.

Ian Harris' article, "Causation and 'Telos': The Problem of Buddhist Environmental Ethics," offers an even stronger critique of Buddhist environmental philosophy. He articulates the proposition that any authentic ethical system must understand causation in a manner that allows for goal-directed activity: specifically, it must be able to draw a distinction between the way the world is and the way it ought to be. This depends upon a chronological understanding of causation that supports the notion that the world has an end or purpose, yet it is not clear that Buddhism endorses such a notion of causation. Harris concludes that since Buddhist philosophy is inherently dysteleological, it is a problematic basis for environmental ethics that can do little more than borrow arguments from those contemporary environmental philosophies that do not contradict its foundational principles.

Section II focuses on environmental philosophy in Chinese traditions of thought. In this section Daoism garners more attention than Confucianism, an emphasis that reflects the prevailing assumption by comparative environmental philosophers that core Daoist concepts, especially the concepts of the *dao* itself and *wu-wei*, represent an almost ready-made environmental ethics, with which many of the essays in this section engage. Though less immediately obvious, Confucianism also represents a rich source of ideas from which an environmental ethics might be constructed. The first essay in this section explores that source.

The second section begins with Mary Evelyn Tucker's "The Relevance of Chinese Neo-Confucianism for the Reverence of Nature." While much has been written about Daoist perspectives on the environment, articles that explore Confucian environmental philosophy are comparatively rare, and Tucker's paper offers an excellent summary of Confucian approaches to environmental ethics. Tucker argues that the industrial processes that have brought about our modern world have come at a terrible price to the environment, and we must seek a balance between the practical concerns of economic growth and the overall good of the ecosystems that sustain us. Such sustainability will only come as the result of a philosophical shift from anthropocentrism to ecocentrism, the latter of which is epitomized by Chinese Neo-Confucian thought. This article offers an intellectual history of Neo-Confucian environmental philosophy, focusing on the work of Chu Hsi, who understands the universe as an organic, holistic process in which human self-cultivation is contingent upon one's harmonious interrelation with the natural world.

The second article in this section is Karyn Lai's "Conceptual Foundations for Environmental Ethics: A Daoist Perspective." Here, Lai argues that the philosophy of the *Daodejing* supports a notion of environmental holism that can be used as the basis of a sound environmental ethic. While the term *dao* describes the totality of particulars, their interrelation, and the roles they play within the whole, the concept of *de* refers to the distinctive nature of each particular as manifested through interdependent relationships with other particulars. Lai pays particular attention to the role that spontaneous action (evident in the concepts of *wu-wei* and *ziran*) plays in maintaining both interdependence and integrity in these associations. Taken together, these ideas support a non-anthropocentric, non-hierarchical philosophy that promotes symbiotic relationships in which individuals interact to mutually benefit one another rather than sacrificing each other for either personal gain or the sake of the environment as a whole.

In "Process Ecology and the 'Ideal' Dao," Alan Fox uses Roger Ames and David Hall's process-philosophy interpretation of Daoism to analyze the implications of key Daoist concepts for environmental ethics. In particular, Fox explores the meaning of *wu-wei*, which has been traditionally interpreted as "non-interference." This understanding of *wu-wei*, when grounded in a metaphysical interpretation of *dao*, yields for human beings a tension between submission to the natural order and the intentional pursuit of one's goals. By understanding *dao* as a dynamic process rather than an abstract, metaphysical entity, human beings can understand themselves as *daos* that are constantly changing in response to their interrelation with other *daos* in the environment. This leads to a reinterpretation of *de* as a type of "virtuosity" by which individuals can prosper through minimal interference with other processes. This understanding of *dao* can inform environmental ethics by stressing that human beings can only interfere with the environment within certain tolerance limits if we wish to maintain prosperous, harmonious relationships with the natural world.

R. P. Peerenboom continues this discussion of the proper interpretation of *wu-wei* in "Beyond Naturalism: A Reconstruction of Daoist Environmental Ethics." In this essay, he challenges the traditional, naturalistic reading of Daoism that understands *wu-wei* as "acting naturally." He argues that this interpretation is of little use to environmental ethicists since humans must be either natural beings (who cannot possibly act unnaturally) or not part of nature (in which case they can only act humanly). Peerenboom proceeds to examine and reject four interpretations of what "natural" means, concluding that environmental ethics should be an attempt to determine not what is natural but rather what an intelligent person would deem normatively best in a particular situation. In this non-naturalist approach to Daoist philosophy, critical thinking about environmental ethics issues becomes a pragmatic process of balancing competing interests to achieve a state of harmony that is beneficial to all.

Sandra A. Wawrytko's paper, "The Viability (*Dao*) and Virtuosity (*De*) of Daoist Ecology: Reversion (*Fu*) as Renewal," challenges the claim that Daoist philosophy is impractical when applied to contemporary environmental problems. In an effort to repudiate contemporary commonsensical attitudes toward the environment, she examines key concepts in Laozi's *Dao De Jing*: *dao* (viability), *de* (virtuosity), *fu* (reversion or return), *wei-wu-wei* (action without artificial action), and *zi-ran* (natural flow). Wawrytko uses numerous examples of how contemporary humans' attempts to control the environment have violated the Daoist concept of *wei-wu-wei*. In contrast, she describes sustainable activities such as China's Dujiangyan Irrigation System that are consonant with the principles of Daoism and represent a way of interacting with nature without disrupting natural processes.

Section II concludes with James Miller's "Ecology, Aesthetics and Daoist Body Cultivation." The Daoist religious tradition offers a wide repertoire of body cultivation practices that focus on generating a phenomenological sensitivity to the inner body and its location within the world. These practices can be understood from the contemporary Western theoretical perspectives developed by Maurice Merleau-Ponty and Richard Shusterman. Merleau-Ponty proposed that the body constitutes the basis for phenomenological experience but did not develop the idea of the experience of the inner body that is so vital to Indian and Chinese body cultivation traditions. Richard Shusterman proposed the concept of "somaesthetics" or methods of training the body's experience of the world, but did not consider the value of this from an ecophenomenological point of view. Extending these theoretical perspectives to interpret Daoist cultivation methods reveals that Daoists aim to dissolve the experiential boundary between the body and the world and create an experience of the mutual interpenetration of the body and the world. Such an experience can form the aesthetic basis for cultivating ecological sensitivity.

Section III is dedicated to the exploration of environmental philosophy in Japanese traditions of thought.

The first chapter in this section is Steve Odin's "The Japanese Concept of Nature in Relation to the Environmental Ethics and Conservation Aesthetics of Aldo Leopold." Odin argues that Japanese Buddhism is characterized by a religio-aesthetic understanding of nature that views the natural world as a continuum of events that are co-dependently related as a network of interpenetrating fields. This view of nature is echoed in the works of twentieth century philosophers Nishida Kitarō and Watsuji Tetsurō, and extends ethics beyond the anthopocentric to include the moral relationship between human beings and the environment. This environmental philosophy closely resembles the land ethic of Aldo Leopold, in which normative values are hierarchically grounded in an aesthetic that stresses the intrinsic value of nature and views human beings as plain citizens of a larger biotic community. For Japanese Buddhism, the relationship between humans and the natural environment has soteriological value in the sense that nature is the ultimate locus for the realization of enlightenment.

In "Dōgen, Deep Ecology, and the Ecological Self," Deane Curtin argues that according to deep ecology, contemporary problems in environmental ethics can only be solved through a reevaluation of the Cartesian notion of self that understands human beings as something fundamentally separate from nature. Deep ecologists have often appealed to the work of Dōgen, the thirteenth-century Japanese Zen philosopher, for a more inclusive interpretation of the self. However, Curtin contends that while Dōgen's philosophical anthropology parallels deep ecology in its non-dualistic and non-anthropocentric nature, he would reject the expanded Self of deep ecology for the same reasons that Buddhism rejects the Hindu notion of *ātman*. If Dōgen's self is to be compared to any contemporary environmental ethic, it is most consonant with the notion of self that is articulated by ecofeminism.

The third article in this section is "Conservation Ethics and the Japanese Intellectual Tradition" by David Shaner and R. Shannon Duval. They argue that Japanese philosophical and religious traditions have traditionally advocated the type of ecocentric worldview that is most useful for dealing with contemporary problems in environmental ethics. This is particularly true of the philosophy of Nishida Kitarō, who is arguably the most important and influential Japanese philosopher of the twentieth century. The authors use the philosophy of William James as a tool for investigating philosophical parallels between the early works of Nishida and the naturalist philosophy of Louis Agassiz, a nineteenth-century biologist. Since James was a student of Agassiz and James' concept of pure experience influenced Nishida's early masterwork, *Zen No Kenkyū*, studying the relationship between these thinkers' ideas can help to elucidate Nishida's environmental philosophy.

In the essay, "From Symbiosis (Kyōsei) to the Ontology of 'Arising Both from Oneself and from Another'," Hiroshi Abe explores the Japanese ethical concept of *kyōsei*. Typically translated as "symbiosis" or "mutual benefit," *kyōsei* was first articulated in 1991 by Ryūzaburō Kaku, the Chairman of Canon, Inc. Though it has been used as a central paradigm in international business ethics, it has until now received little treatment in the field of environmental ethics. In this article, Abe calls for a reevaluation of human nature in terms of "human ecology," which understands humans as defined by their relationships with the environment. To do this, he first examines the notion of symbiosis in biology and ecology, critiquing the prevailing, dualistic logic that understands species interaction as *either* mutualism *or* competition. Abe then draws from Tokuryū Yamanouchi's interpretation of Nāgārjuna's *Treatise Concerning the Middle* to develop a new understanding of symbiosis based upon *gūshō* ("arising both from oneself and another"), which understands relationships between species as an interdependent process in which every species affects and is affected by every other, either directly or indirectly.[1]

Tomosaburō Yamauchi explores the philosophy of a key Japanese thinker who is largely unknown to the West in his essay, "The Confucian Environmental Ethics of Ogyū Sorai." Sorai was a Japanese Confucian philosopher and one of the most influential scholars of the Edo period of Japanese history (also known as the Tokugawa Era, from 1603–1868 CE). In this article, Yamauchi draws upon Sorai's philosophy to develop a normative environmental ethic capable of dealing with the contemporary environmental problems that have been caused by anthropocentric worldviews. He explains how Sorai's utilitarian system of ethics can be used to reconcile competing moral claims without having to appeal to an absolutist metaethical framework. Sorai endorses a three-level system of social ethics grounded in a Confucian ecological worldview that understands human virtues as habits that promote eco-holistic welfare rather than purely anthropocentric interests.

Section III concludes with James McRae's chapter, "Triple-Negation: Watsuji Tetsurō on the Sustainability of Ecosystems, Economies, and International Peace." Environmental security is a relatively new branch of environmental studies that explores how national security issues are affected by ecosystem sustainability and the demands placed upon the natural world by human populations. The pursuit of consumer interests can often place stress on the environment, which can lead to a collapse of both ecosystems and economies, which in turn promotes political instability. For this reason, the fields of environmental ethics, business ethics, and international relations are ultimately intertwined. This essay draws from the philosophical anthropology of Watsuji Tetsurō's *Fūdo* to explain why human culture, economics, and the politics of warfare are so intimately tied to sustainability issues. The ethical principles of Watsuji's *Rinrigaku* are then used to articulate a normative framework that could be used to promote sustainability—and thereby maintain peace—on an international scale. By developing a relational understanding of environmental and business ethics that emphasizes roles and responsibilities over individual autonomy and rights, we can regulate business practices in a manner that is both environmentally and socially conscious. Because mismanagement of the environment leads to socio-economic problems that provoke global conflicts, the promotion of sustainability according to Watsuji's ethics can contribute to both a healthy economy and international security.

The editors of this anthology have done their best to keep each article as close as possible to the format of its original publication. Since there are multiple forms of transliteration used for non-Western languages, terms will sometimes be written differently depending on the article. In Section I, Sanskrit and Pali terms are sometimes transliterated with diacritical markers (e.g., "*śūnyatā*"), while other authors prefer to drop the diacriticals and use Romanized spellings (e.g., "*shunyata*"). In Section II, some articles use the older Wade Giles spellings (e.g., "Taoism"), while others use the newer Pinyin system (e.g., "Daoism"). Section III uses standard Hepburn Romanization throughout, with long vowels indicated by macrons (e.g., "Dōgen"). Also, the original authors use different forms of citation depending on the requirements of the journals in which they were originally published. Thus, some articles feature footnotes while others use in-text citations. Some prefer MLA citation, while others use CMA or APA. The editors believe that reconciling these discrepancies would add little to clarify their content while doing a great deal to undermine the intent of their original authors. Thus, these works are presented in their original formats.

NOTES

1. Though Yamanouchi is a Nagarjuna scholar, the focus of Abe's article is on the concept of *kyōsei* (symbiosis), which is a distinctly Japanese philosophical notion. Since Nagarjuna's philosophy is used to clarify the meaning of *kyōsei*, we believe this is a work of Japanese philosophy more so than it is a work of Indian philosophy, which is why it is included in this section of the anthology.

SECTION I

Environmental Philosophy in Indian Traditions of Thought

Chapter 1

Environment and Environmental Philosophy in India

George Alfred James

As a region, India contains more biological diversity than perhaps any other landmass of a similar size in the world. With only 2.5 percent of the world's land area, India possesses 7.8 percent of the world's recorded species.[1] Its diverse environments stretch from the peaks of the world's highest mountain range, the Himalayas, to the tropical coastal estuaries of Kerala, and from the world's richest rain forests in the northeast region to the arid Thar Desert of Rajasthan, with a multitude of bioregions between. India is also a country of enormous cultural and religious diversity. Many of the religious and cultural traditions of India have supported strategies of resource use that have helped sustain India's biological diversity, and the ways of life that have depended upon it over a vast period of time.[2]

India is also a country in which colossal environmental damage has been done and continues to occur. The *First Citizen's Report* on the Indian environment of 1982 indicated that according to unofficial estimates, a million hectares of India's forests are cut down every year.[3] Depletion of native forests has led to soil erosion, causing floods and landslides that devastate villages and farmlands. Without adequate forest cover the rain of the monsoon (the rainy season) carries off valuable topsoil, depleting the land of nutrients. Overuse of chemical fertilizers is further depleting soil fertility. More than one third of India's land area has now been classed as unproductive.[4] Half of India's energy consumption is devoted to cooking. But, with steadily diminishing forest resources, women in villages are required to walk ever further to bring back firewood sufficient for domestic needs.[5] The uncontrolled exploitation of groundwater has resulted in an alarming drop in the water table and the seepage of ocean water into freshwater aquifers, leading to a scarcity of potable water. Forms of livelihood that have depended upon the bounty of nature—fishing, sheep rearing, basket weaving—are being abandoned in many parts of India. People who once subsisted on these activities are joining the surging wave of ecological refugees moving to the cities in search of employment.[6] Between the years 1951 and 1981, the population of Calcutta (now Kolkata) and Hyderabad doubled. In the same period, that of Bombay (now Mumbai), Madras (now Chennai), and Ahmedabad tripled, and that of Delhi and Bangalore quadrupled.[7] These cities have seen acute shortages of water and other resources. A third of the urban population of India has no access to sanitary facilities of any kind. When the Yamuna River enters the city of Delhi its water contains about 7,500 coliform organisms per 100 milliliters.[8] As it proceeds south from the city on its way toward Vrindavan, the mythical birthplace of Lord Kṛṣṇa, the coliform count is 24,000,000 per 100 milliliters. Seventy percent of all the fresh water available in India is polluted. Its consumption accounts for the continuous epidemic of diarrhea that takes the lives of over a million children every year.[9] With the proliferation of transportation by diesel and petrol vehicles, sulfur dioxide and particulate matter in these cities far exceeds the limits set by the World Health Organization.[10] Dangerous levels of pesticide residues are being recorded in foodstuffs, and in animal and human tissues.[11] Today, the pressure of human activity upon India's forests and land threatens many of the 15,000 plant species and the 75,000 animal species found in India. A flourishing illegal trade in wildlife products such as tiger bones and skins, many exported to China for traditional medicines, poses a further threat to India's biodiversity.[12] These conditions have laid an especially heavy burden upon pastoral nomads and the tribal peoples of India who have often been required to relinquish their habitat, heritage, and history, to make way for projects to preserve biodiversity or for the construction of hydroelectric power projects to feed the energy needs of the burgeoning cities.[13]

In 1962, the publication of the book *Silent Spring* by Rachel Carson brought widespread American public attention, perhaps for the first time, to the extent of ecological damage wrought by human intervention in nature.[14] Interest in the preservation of nature, however, goes back to an appreciation of natural beauty sparked in large measure by the Romantic Movement of the nineteenth century in Europe and the United States. It is perhaps a paradox, then, that the Romantic philosophy of writers like Emerson and Thoreau was inspired in no small measure by their encounter with some of first philosophical and religious writings of India available in the West.[15] Emerson's exploration of some of the sacred writings of India led him to reject the Western notion of deity as a Supreme Being that stands over nature, and to accept of the idea of divinity in nature itself. This led him eventually to the view that nature ought to be protected not just for what it can provide for human beings, but for its own intrinsic worth. This irony raises the question of the relevance of India's philosophical traditions to the environmental crisis that country faces.

In what follows, I first examine the understanding of India that has been a part of the development of contemporary environmental philosophy in the West. I then examine some of the most pervasive values concerning nature that we find in Hindu philosophical traditions, and the questions they raise. Finally, I examine the significance of some of these ideas in the thought of Mohandas Gandhi and some of his followers, and indicate their environmental relevance.

INDIA IN WESTERN ENVIRONMENTAL THOUGHT

In the 1960s, the growing awareness of the global environmental crisis and the recognition that Western ways of thinking had not provided a solution provoked renewed interest in the religious ideas of non-Western civilizations and in the religions of India in particular. In 1967, in the famous essay titled "The Historical Roots of Our Ecologic Crisis," the renowned environmental historian Lynn White Jr. argued that the environmental crisis was rooted in attitudes deeply embedded in Western religious traditions.[16] The idea that human beings were created uniquely in the image of God, that God had given human beings dominion over the created order, and that God had created the world for the use of human beings, had fostered attitudes hostile to the environment. This, he said, was an anthropocentric, or man-centered religion, the most anthropocentric religion to appear in human history (except perhaps, he averred, Zoroastrianism). In some non-Western religions he found an attitude toward nature completely opposite that of the West. Other scholars joined White and affirmed that in non-Western traditions, nature is not the inert and spiritless product of a craftsman-like God who stands above it. Rather, it is the very essence of divinity, to be adored, venerated, and cared for.[17] Hinduism, with its doctrine of the divine Spirit that pervades all of reality, its teaching of reincarnation that makes a family of all living species, and its doctrine of non-injury to all living things, seemed to provide an attractive alternative to the Western preoccupation with humanity as a special creation whose sense of privilege seemed to have put nature out of balance.

Not all writers concerned with the environment were so enthusiastic about Indian religious thought. Some were reluctant to forsake the religious and intellectual history of Western civilization for ways of thinking very different from their own. The Australian philosopher John Passmore argued that the doctrine of the sacredness of nature and the claim that all living things are entitled to protection is fundamentally flawed. He held that the more reasonable teaching of stewardship towards nature is the unique product of Western religious and philosophical traditions.[18]

Writings that draw such a stark contrast between non-Western traditions like those of India and the traditions of the West reflect the influence of what has been called orientalist discourse.[19] In such writing, the traditions of India are seen as either (a) an ancient ecological wisdom that provides an alternative to modern exploitative Western attitudes towards nature, or (b) a primitive and irrational response to contemporary environmental problems. More recent research recognizes that neither of these views is accurate.[20] Unlike the predominant religious traditions of the West, the Hindu religious tradition does not have a single doctrinal viewpoint. It is a living tradition in which differing viewpoints concerning the divine, concerning nature, and concerning the nature and destiny of the human person have been negotiated over an enormous period of time. The Hindu religious tradition has not just one but a great variety of views and attitudes toward nature.

NATURE IN THE HINDU RELIGIOUS TRADITIONS

A strong interest in nature is evident from the very earliest sources of Indian culture. Among the remains of the Indus Valley Civilization, which flourished between 2800 and 1800 BCE, small, mostly square steatite seals (measuring 1 ½ to 3 inches across) depict trees, water, and a goddess figure, standing in close relation with one another. Some of them seem to depict the earth as a mother giving birth to a tree, and scenes composed of animals, trees, and human beings are usually interpreted as revealing the common rhythm in human, animal, and vegetative life. The relationship of trees, water, and the goddess found in the remains of the Indus Valley Civilization bear a striking resemblance to later Hindu images of the Ganges River as a goddess pictured beneath a tree.[21]

In the *Rig Veda*, (composed ca. 1800–800 BCE) the earliest literary source of the Hindu religious tradition, hymns of praise and adoration are directed to a number of the phenomena of nature depicted as deities. Indra is the seasonal monsoon rain, pictured as a colossal male figure destroying the demon that is holding back the waters from the thirsty land. Sūrya is the sun, the Maruts are the storm spirits, and Āpas is the waters. Pṛthvi is the Earth, praised as sustaining the world and all that dwells upon her:

Thou bearest truly, Pṛthvi,
The burden of the mountains' weight;
With might, O thou of many streams,
Thou quickenest, potent one, the soil.
With flowers of speech our songs of praise
Resound to thee, far spreading one,
Who sendeth forth the swelling cloud,
O bright one, like propelling speed;
Who, steadfast, holdest with thy might,
The forest-trees upon the ground,
When, from the lightenings of thy cloud,
The rain-floods of the sky pour down. (*Rig Veda* 5: 84)[22]

The *Rig Veda* and other ancient Vedic (or wisdom) collections also lavish praise on such rivers as the Yamunā, the Saraswatī, the Indus, and the Ganges. Indian religious traditions regard all rivers as sacred, and on the banks of such rivers we still find ancient temples in which a deep piety toward the river is expressed. In the Vedas we also find the origin of the idea of the universe as an organic whole, an idea that is developed more thoroughly in later Indian philosophy. In one of the hymns of the *Rig Veda*, the origin of the universe is depicted as the sacrifice of a colossal anthropomorphic deity known as Puruṣa, in which all of the elements of the natural world are related:

The moon was born from his spirit (*manas*), from his eye was born the sun, from his mouth Indra and Agni, from his breath Vāyu (wind) was born.
From his navel arose the middle sky, from his head the heaven originated, from his feet the earth, the quarters from his ear.
Thus did they fashion the worlds. (*Rig Veda* 10: 90)[23]

Many scholars have observed that the universe is understood here as a living organism in which every part is related to the life of the whole. Later there develops the idea that all of life is sacred because all living beings reflect the One divine reality from which all of life has come, and the ethical injunction against injury to living things.

In the Upaniṣads (composed ca. 800–600 BCE), philosophical supplements to the Vedic hymns, the attitude of admiration for the natural world is retained. But here, alongside of that admiration a new understanding of nature is expressed. The result is that the overall attitude towards nature in the Upaniṣads is less consistent than it is in the hymns of the *Rig Veda* and other Vedic collections. There are over two hundred *upaniṣads*, often portrayed as dialogues between a teacher and a student of sacred knowledge. Their subject matter centers upon such topics as the ultimate ground and source of the visible world, the nature of the true Self that resides within the depths of the human person and all other living creatures, the condition of the embodied Self in the visible world, and the path that leads to knowledge that liberates the embodied Self from its condition of bondage and rebirth in the visible world called *samsāra*. Despite the great variety of figures and analogies employed to express the insights of the Upaniṣads, their attitude toward the natural world can be gathered together in terms of two diverging tendencies. On the one hand the natural world and all that it contains, all that has being at all, is nothing other than *Brahman*, the Ultimate Reality. Sometimes phenomena of nature are presented as analogies upon which to recognize the true relationship of the visible world to its ultimate but not evident ground.

> As birds resort to a tree for a resting-place, even so, O friend, it is to the supreme Self (Ātman) that everything here resorts. (*Praśna Upaniṣad*)[24]

> As herbs rise upon the earth,
> As the hairs of the head and body from a living person,
> So from the Imperishable arises everything here. (Muṇḍaka Upaniṣad)[25]

> As, from a well-blazing fire, sparks
> By the thousand issue forth of like forms,
> So from the Imperishable, my friend, beings manifold
> Are produced, and thither also go. (Muṇḍaka Upaniṣad)[26]

From this viewpoint, the world of nature is supremely valuable because it is the visible manifestation of the ultimate divine reality. On the other hand, some passages emphasize that while the Supreme Self dwells in all things, it is also other than all things, the unseen seer, the unheard hearer, the unthought thinker. In some places, this reality is to be sought not in the outer world, but by means of reflection upon the depths of the inner Self. And while the Upaniṣads do not all agree upon a single method for the pursuit of the knowledge of this ultimate reality, many of the most influential of the Upaniṣads recommend a method that entails the renunciation of the material world, seen now as a provisional and transitory reality. There is, for this reason, a tendency in some of the Upaniṣads to minimize the importance of the material world and enjoyments available within the human body, in which the embodied soul is condemned to repeated lives. It is perhaps in the *Maitri Upaniṣad* that this attitude towards the material world is most forcefully expressed:

> In this ill-smelling, unsubstantial body, which is a conglomerate of bone, skin, muscle, marrow, flesh, semen, blood, mucus, tears, rheum, feces, urine, wind, bile, and phlegm, what is the good of the enjoyment of desires? . . . . In this sort of cycle of existence (saṁsāra) what is the good of the enjoyment of desires, when after a man has fed on them there is seen repeatedly his return to this earth? . . . In this cycle of existence I am like a frog in a waterless well. (*Maitri Upaniṣad* I: 3–4)[27]

Later Hindu tradition sought to mediate between these opposing tendencies by articulating four ends or purposes to human existence (*puruṣārthas*). They consist of the pursuit of (1) *kāma*, or sensuous and aesthetic pleasure, (2) *dharma*, or the demands of moral life, (3) *artha*, or political and economic well-being, and (4) *mokṣa*, or release, the final and spiritual end that culminates in *mukti* or liberation from the cycle of rebirth. For later Hinduism as well, the human life is understood to be laid out in terms of four *āśramas* or stages: that of the student (*brahmacarya*), the householder (*gṛhastha*), the forest dweller (*vānaprastha*), and the renounced (*sannyāsin*). While the pursuit of pleasure as well as economic and political gain is always mitigated by considerations of morality (*dharma*) and while the final goal of liberation remains on the horizon of every stage of earthly life, the four ends of life are not seen to be of equal relevance to all the stages of life. The life of the householder consists largely of the pursuit of the pleasures of intimacy, the responsibilities of raising children, and of material and economic welfare for the family and society. When such responsibilities are fulfilled, this stage is (or may be) followed by that of withdrawal from material and economic life. Then at the stage of renunciation (*sannyāsin*), a stage but rarely put into practice, the most relevant pursuit is the mastery of those religious texts that focus upon final end of release (*mokṣa*) from the cycle of rebirth. It is at this last stage of life that all privileges and responsibilities associated with material and economic life come finally to an end.[28]

While support for the care of nature can be found even in those texts that recommend renunciation of the visible world, it is in the writings or *Śāstras* concerned with *dharma* or moral virtue and *artha* or economic and political well-being that the most explicit guidance concerning the treatment of the natural world is can be found. One of the most important sources for the understanding of economic and political value is the *Arthaśāstra* (321–296 BCE), attributed to Kautilya, a minister of the first ruler of the Mauryan Empire. For Kautilya, *artha* is not limited to what we today would associate with economics and politics. What he calls *arthaśāstra* is an account of the views of the ancient teachers concerning the acquisition and maintenance of the earth. The earth, however, means both the material source of the life and welfare of the community *and* the society that is dependent upon it. It is Kautilya's view that a large part of the responsibility for maintenance of the earth falls upon government. Kautilya believes that a competent monarchy is the form of government most likely to protect the weak from the strong and maintain the welfare of the people. For this to work, much depends upon the character and competence of the sovereign.

As guardian of the social and ecological order, the sovereign understands, supports, and enforces all duties (*dharmas*) distributed among the various classes (*varṇas*) and stages of life (*āśramas*), into which the society is divided. He also supports the duties that pertain to all persons regardless of their social class or stage in life: non-violence, truthfulness, purity, compassion, and forgiveness.

Much of what we today would call agricultural administration, disaster management, and environmental policy falls, in Kautilya's view, within the purview of the King. He is expected to establish policies for the proper maintenance of pastures and forests, and enforce the laws that protect the environment. When appropriate, he is expected to undertake agrarian reforms.[29] The attention of this ancient authority to matters of environmental concern is indicated by specific fines he advocates for such offenses as disposing of dust on roads, urinating or defecating near a well, pond, or temple, and for inappropriately disposing of a dead animal. A striking example of his concern for forest resources is the specific schedule of sanctions he imposes upon those who destroy trees, groves, or forests. Here he recommends fines of varying severity corresponding to the damage done. For the cutting off of the tender sprouts of fruit trees, flowering trees, or shade trees in parks near a city he recommends a fine of six *panas*. For the cutting of the minor branches of such trees the fine is twelve *panas*, and for the cutting of the large branches of such trees, the fine is twenty-four *panas*. For the cutting of the trunk of such trees the fine is forty-eight to ninety-six *panas*, and for the felling of such trees the fine is 200–500 *panas*. And for trees that mark boundaries or are worshipped the sanctions are doubled.[30] While it is nearly impossible to know precisely what a *pana* would be worth in terms of today's dollars, it significant that offenses that result in damage to forest resources were taken seriously enough that a fine would have been imposed. Moreover, the fact that the gradations of the fines increase geometrically with the size of the damaged branches strongly suggests that trees were objects of value. And the fact that damage to a tree that has religious significance has especially severe penalties indicates not only that trees were objects of worship, but that provisions of law supported the worship of trees. Another ancient legal document is the sacred law proclaimed by Manu (ca. 100 BCE). Widely considered the most authoritative of the ancient treatments of *dharma* or duty, it states specifically that poisonous substances or impure objects like urine, feces, spit, or anything that contains blood are never to be disposed of in water.[31]

While ancient legal writings take specific measures for the protection of nature, attitudes toward nature are also reflected in the great literary narratives of the tradition: the Rāmāyaṇa (composed ca. 500–100 BCE), and the Mahābhārata (composed ca. 400–100 BCE), as well as the *purāṇas* (composed ca. 300–1000 CE). It was in the great forests of India that Lord Rāma and Sītā spent the years of their exile from Ayodhyā, and it was with the help of the forest animals, especially the monkeys, that Rāma succeeded in the rescue of Sītā from the demon Rāvana. It was in the forest that the five sons of Pāṇḍu spent the exile in the years that led up to the great battle that was the climax of the *Mahābhārata*. In the Bhagavad Gītā, a book of religious teaching that constitutes one of the key episodes of the *Mahābhārata*, Kṛṣṇa as the Supreme Lord of the universe proclaims:

I am the taste in the waters . . . the light of the sun and moon. I am the pure fragrance in earth and brightness in fire. I am the life in all beings (7: 8–9).[32]

The *Bhāgavada Purāṇa* tells the story of the birth and childhood of Lord Kṛṣṇa as he grows up in the twelve forests of Vṛndavan on the banks of the Yamunā River. It is here that the stories are told of his miraculous birth and escape from the evil king who had intended to take his life. The forest is the context of the stories of his miraculous childhood pranks, his play with the gopis, and the story of his love for Rādhā. The forests are valued in such literature as the context of the many stories in which his teachings are set.[33]

In the *Matsya Purāṇa* (composed fifth to tenth century CE) the goddess Pārvatī plants an Ashoka tree and cares for it. As the tree prospers and the other deities and sages observe her attention to this tree they begin to question her. They point out that people desire children and feel they have been successful in life when they have seen them grow up and become the parents of another generation. Pārvatī replies that a person who digs a well in a place where water is scarce lives in heaven for as many years as there are drops of water in the well. And she states that a large reservoir is worth ten wells, and that one son is like ten reservoirs. She goes on to say, however that one tree is equal to ten sons. "This," she says, "is my standard." The same *Purāṇa* describes a festival for the planting of trees, indicating that in the context in which they were originally written the planting of trees was an activity that had strong religious support. Another document of the period, the *Viṣṇudharmottara*, states that one who plants a single tree will never fall into hell.[34]

In many of the narratives in the *purāṇas* animals are often symbols of the deities. They are the *vāhanas* or vehicles and therefore the representatives of the gods. They are also featured among the characters in the narratives in which the stories of the gods are told: the bull is the *vāhana* of Lord Śiva, the cow is the *vāhana* of Lord Kṛṣṇa, the elephant of Indra, the peacock of Pārvatī. Often a particular animal gains religious significance because of its significance in the narrative. The monkey, among the most ubiquitous of Indian fauna, is the living representation of Hanūmān, the monkey God who, in the *Rāmāyaṇa*, rendered assistance to Lord Rāma, when his wife, the goddess Sītā, was abducted by the demon, Rāvaṇa. Today these animals appear prominently in Indian religious life.

We observed earlier that as compared with the *Rig Veda* and other Vedic collections, the attitude towards nature in the Upaniṣads was more ambivalent. This ambivalence is closely related to the quest in the Upaniṣads for liberation from the cycle of rebirth, what becomes in later Hinduism the final purpose of human existence. In the philosophical traditions that are based upon the Upaniṣads, this ambivalence emerges again. Contemporary with many of the narratives that extol the value and virtue of nature, India has produced philosophers and philosophical texts that tended to look upon the visible world and its engaging variety and biodiversity with suspicion. One of the most influential of the philosophers of India is Śaṅkara. Although he lived a mere 32 years sometime in the eighth or ninth centuries of the Common Era, he became the principal exponent of a school of Indian philosophy known as unqualified non-dualism (*Advaita Vedānta*), what Western scholars have sometimes called monism. On the basis of the Upaniṣads and other ancient texts, Śaṅkara developed the view that in truth there is but one reality. It is known in the Upaniṣads as *Brahman*, The Ultimate. He held that the world that is experienced in everyday life as a world of infinite diversity is the world of mere appearance. While he did not precisely argue that the visible world is pure illusion, he maintained that it is not reality either. The visible world, for Śaṅkara, is an appearance of the ultimate reality under the conditions of ignorance (*avidyā*), the condition of the self that is embodied in temporal existence. Because Śaṅkara was committed to the goal of *mokṣa*—and recommended this goal to his followers—he encouraged them to place as little value as possible upon the world of appearance. He argued that one should cultivate an attitude of indifference to the visible world, and direct one's affection toward the ultimate within, the true reality beyond appearance. Some of the passages in which Śaṅkara expresses these views evoke an attitude of disgust for the present natural world. It is described as a terrible ocean infested with monsters. Selves trapped in this world go from birth to birth without peace. Like worms caught in a river, they are swept from one whirlpool to the next. The person who is committed to the teachings of Śaṅkara and his followers should be possessed of the desire to escape the round of death and rebirth in the present world. Such a person is expected to be celibate and to renounce all attachment to the visible material world.

It is argued by some that Śaṅkara's understanding of the visible world encourages an attitude of indifference to environmental problems.[35] Some have even attributed the deplorable condition of the environment in India to the influence to such thinking.[36] While it is true that we are unlikely to find any sense of communion with nature or an understanding of nature as having intrinsic worth in the writings of Śaṅkara or his followers in the *Advaita Vedānta* tradition, it does not follow that this school of thought is completely at odds with environmental concerns. In the first place, while the Hindu tradition fully acknowledges the importance of Śaṅkara's thought, we have already seen that it did not commend his lifestyle as the social norm, and it seems unreasonable to assume that Śaṅkara himself did so. "Let the wise one," he says, "strive after freedom."[37] While Śaṅkara renounced the world at a young age, the most influential of the scriptures concerned with duty (dharmaśāstra) consider renunciation and the pursuit of mokṣa to be the goal of the last of the stages of life. Thus, as we saw above, while mokṣa remains the ultimate goal of life, the penultimate goals of material and economic well-being (artha) are governed by considerations of duty (dharma) that pertain to mundane conditions in the visible world. Secondly, while Śaṅkara and his followers frequently spoke disparagingly of the visible world, their purpose is clearly to oppose attachment to the material world. It is attachment that feeds ignorance of the true reality, and leads to continuous rebirth. Thirdly, having renounced the natural world, the follower of Śaṅkara has radically reduced his desire to exploit the earth's resources, or to consume the products generated from its exploitation. His existence has the lowest possible environmental impact. The earthly life of the sannyāsin is one of self-control, non-violence, simplicity, and frugality. Finally, it is precisely by the renunciation of worldly ambition that some leaders of environmental movements have achieved the moral authority to address abuses of power that profit from the exploitation and destruction of environments upon which the powerless and disenfranchised depend.

While the influence of Śaṅkara was great, his attitude concerning the visible world, and therefore the natural world, was not the only viewpoint of the time. Another influential philosopher of medieval India was Rāmānuja (1017–1137 CE), an exponent of what came to be known as "qualified non-dualism." Like Śaṅkara, he believed that reality is one, that Brahman is the only true Reality. But while Śaṅkara argued that reality was pure identity without difference, Rāmānuja held that reality was the unity of the differences within the visible world, including individual souls and the objects that constitute the empirical world.[38] Under the conditions of bondage and ignorance we fail to see this unity, but with attention to the scriptures, with meditation and devotion, with the achievement of true insight, this unity can be realized. For Rāmānuja the natural world is not simply an appearance to be dispelled by the higher knowledge of the One. Rather the sentient and non-sentient matter that forms the universe is the body of God. Just as the individual soul pervades the individual physical body so does Viṣṇu (God) pervade all souls, and the entire natural world. Rāmānuja's viewpoint is supported by those passages in the Vedas that describe the physical world as pervaded by the presence of divinity, and by the image in the Bhagavad Gītā and the Bhagavada Purāṇa of the universe as the body of Kṛṣṇa, as the Ultimate Reality incarnate. While Rāmānuja encouraged renunciation of material attachments as the practical path to liberation he also recognized virtue and devotion to God as the legitimate means to recognition of the presence of God in the natural world.

Gandhi on the Environment

Through the period of British rule in India these traditions of thought were largely marginalized. At end of the nineteenth and the beginning of the twentieth century, Indian philosophers came to recover them. They also came fully to recognize the centrality of the natural world in the principle sources of the Hindu religious tradition. Space does not permit an exploration of the impact upon this development of Ram Mohan Roy (1772–1833), Dayanand Sarasvati (1824–1883), or Ramakrishna Paramahamsa (1834–1886). Yet it is significant that the works of Swami Vivekananda (1862–1902) indirectly inspired, under the leadership of Anna Hazare, one of the most visible movements for ecological restoration in recent years, and that the teachings of Sri Aurobindo (1872–1950) inspired the founding of a community near Pondicherry in South India called Auroville in which ecological restoration and progress towards sustainability have been central goals.[39] Among these figures, however, the thought of Mohandas K. Gandhi (1869–1948) is of special significance. His thought has had a visible impact upon some of the most celebrated of contemporary environmental movements in India and on the Deep Ecology movement in the West.

Born the son of the Chief Minister of a small princely state in what is today the Indian state of Gujarat, Mohandas K. Gandhi was sent to England in his late teens to be educated in the field of law. Following his promise to his mother to remain a vegetarian he found himself in the company of a circle of friends in London who were interested in the philosophical traditions of India. With them, for the first time, he came to read the Bhagavad Gita as well as the Bible and the Qur'ān. On his return to India he accepted a job offer to do legal work in Natal, in South Africa. There he encountered the abysmal prejudice towards the Indian community that had been a part of the colonial

South African tradition for generations. There he quickly became involved in the struggle of Indians in South Africa for civil rights. During his years in South Africa, Gandhi rejected the self-image he had cultivated of an upwardly mobile English lawyer and instead recovered the ideals and values he had found through his study in London of Hindu philosophical and religious traditions. While he insisted that he was a practical man without interest in metaphysics or philosophical speculation, an analysis of the central features of his thought reveal a strong environmental ethic, grounded in the philosophical and religious thought of India.

A recent study of Gandhi's views concerning the environment suggest that his personal life and political vision reflected the influence of yoga, the ancient philosophical science of control of the body and mind that leads finally to the liberation of the human soul.[40] In 1914, when Gandhi returned to India, his rise to political influence placed him at the center of the independence movement. His vision for India entailed not only the independence of India from foreign control, but also economic and cultural liberation of India's people. "Real home-rule," he said, "is self-rule, or self-control."[41] As it was developed in classical Indian thought, the practice of yoga consisted of several stages of discipline, eight in all. The first two of these, known as the five *yamas* or abstentions and the five *niyamas* or injunctions, are the ethical foundation upon which the higher disciplines of posture, breath control, withdrawal of the senses, the fixing of attention, contemplation, and concentration all depend. Exponents of yoga hold that without them, further yogic practice is useless, and that if one proceeds no further, they constitute in themselves a firm grounding for ethical action in the world. Each of these steps had a critical place in Gandhi's life and thought. By appropriating them he was recovering his cultural roots. Several of them correspond directly to the eleven vows to which the participants in Gandhi's ashrams were committed, and have a direct bearing on the care of the environment.

The centerpiece of Gandhi's philosophy is the first of the five *yamas* called *ahiṃsā* or non-injury. Gandhi is widely recognized for having transformed the idea of non-injury from a personal code of behavior to a social, economic, and political force. Yet because he applied this doctrine to the entire world, it also had profound environmental significance. "It is an arrogant assumption," he said, "to say that human beings are lords and masters of the lower creatures." For Gandhi, the human being is not the master but the trustee of the lower animal kingdom. He argued that a society could be judged based on the manner it treats the animals in its care.[42] Gandhi's practice of non-injury, however, cannot be fully understood apart from his commitment to truth, the second of the five *yamas* in the philosophy of yoga. While most theologians would accept that God is truth, Gandhi took the decisive step of affirming that truth is God.[43] The implication is that commitment to God can never be used to stand in the way of truth or justify the repudiation or suppression of truth and it can never justify violence. Gandhi speaks frequently of truth and non-violence as being two sides of the same coin. Violence can never establish truth, and truth can never rely upon violence. Because his method of social and political change was based upon truth he called it *satyāgraha*, or persevering in the truth without recourse to violence of any kind.

The third of the five *yamas* called *asteya*, means abstention from stealing or the misappropriation of the possessions of others. When asked whether an independent India would achieve the standard of living of Britain, Gandhi replied that it took half the resources of the planet to achieve the prosperity that Britain enjoys. He then rhetorically inquired, "How many planets will a country like India require!" On another occasion he pointed out that the economic imperialism of a tiny island kingdom was keeping the world in chains. He suggested that if India were to follow Britain's example of industrial development and economic exploitation "it would strip the world bare like locusts."[44] Gandhi states that when fully and properly understood, the fourth of the five *yamas* called *brahmacarya* "means search for Brahma," or God, which for Gandhi is the search for Truth. In the classical context the student of sacred knowledge was expected to remain unmarried and celibate in order to devote full attention to study and discipline. For Gandhi, *brahmacarya* signified "control of all the senses at all times and all places in thought, word, and deed." While it includes sexual restraint it also embraces restraint of diet, emotions, and speech. It precludes violence, hate, anger, and any deviation from truth. Being without desire, it creates stability of mind leading to thoughtful and sound judgment.[45] *Brahmacarya* is closely related to the fifth and last of the *yamas* called *aparigraha*, the rejection of worldly possessions beyond one's requirements. For Gandhi, this meant casting off the symbols of wealth and status to which he had become accustomed in his days as a student in England. He laid aside the wardrobe of a young English gentleman for a plain *dhoti*, the garment worn in India by the common man. Beyond this he retained only those objects necessary for his life and work: spinning wheel, sandals, cap, staff, glasses, and a watch. "Man falls from the pursuit of the ideal of plain living and high thinking," he said, "the moment he wants to multiply his daily wants." Gandhi's future life would be a protest against the supposed needs of a consumer society and its unreasonable demands on the biosphere. His advice to the wealthy capitalists of his day was to undertake business with restraint so as not to exhaust the resources of the earth. "The earth," he said, "provides enough to satisfy every man's need, but not every man's greed."[46]

The *yamas* or restraints of the philosophy of yoga are followed by five positive injunctions called the *niyamas*. They begin with *saucha* or cleanliness. In the ashrams that Gandhi founded in South Africa and later in India, cleanliness was a paramount concern. Cleaning duties were distributed equally among all participants regardless of rank. Gandhi states that "anyone who fouls the air by spitting about carelessly, throwing refuse and rubbish, or otherwise dirtying the ground, sins against man and nature. Man's body is the temple of God. Anyone who fouls the air that is to enter that temple desecrates it."[47] One of Gandhi's most celebrated achievements was the elevation of the class of persons responsible for the cleaning of Indian streets from the status of untouchability to that of people of God, or *harijans*. The second of the five *niyamas* is *santosh* or contentment. The person who is discontented, says Gandhi, "however much he possesses, becomes a slave to his desires."[48] Yet the life of truth and non-violence must remain an empty dream, according to Gandhi, without the third of the five *niyamas* called *tapas*, meaning exertion toward self-purification. For Gandhi, fasting and prayer are the most powerful forms of *tapas*. "A genuine fast," he says, "cleanses the body mind and soul. It crucifies the flesh and to that extent it sets the soul free."[49] A sincere prayer, he says, "is an intense longing of the soul for its even greater purity." It is as indispensable to the soul as is food for the material body.[50] *Swādhyāya*, the fourth the five *niyamas* is the examination of oneself in the light of sacred scriptures. It is closely related to the last of the *niyamas* called *Ishvar pranidhān*, or devotion to God. An examination of one's self in the light of sacred scriptures dislodges the human person from the understanding of one's self as the master of creation. It locates the person within the larger web of life, and to its duties and responsibilities. Devotion to God supports this self-understanding. Gandhi acknowledges that there are innumerable definitions of God because of his innumerable manifestations. For this reason, he acknowledged the validity of the many images of God that the Hindu tradition has generated. Yet he points out that he, himself, worships God as truth alone. In the same place he points out that he has not found God, but is seeking after him.[51] When he states that he worships God as truth alone he points out that what he means by truth is not simply truthfulness in thought or assent to the relative truths of our experience but "the Absolute Truth, the Eternal Principle." While he speaks of having "faint glimpses of the Absolute Truth," he holds that we must constantly seek the approximations of truth that occur in daily life. "That relative truth," he says, "must, meanwhile, be my beacon, my shield and buckler."[52] In that daily life he found the Bhagavad Gītā to be his constant companion and guide. Its call to self-sacrifice and devotion to God engendered in him the conviction that non-violence was not just an effective strategy for social change but an eternal quality of truth or reality itself.

Towards the end of his life, Gandhi stated that while the Indian National Congress had won political freedom, he believed that economic, social, and moral freedom was yet to be attained. "Independence," he said, "must begin at the bottom." For this, his focus was upon rural and especially village development. He held that just as the whole of the universe is contained in the Self, so the whole of India is contained in her villages. He held that if the villages should perish, then India would perish as well. For this reason, he says, "Every village has to be self-sustained and capable of managing its own affairs."[53] He argued that it is in the simplicity of the village that India could fully realize truth and non-violence.[54] In the village setting, attending to real and not artificial needs, the human person can achieve *swadeshi*, or self-reliance, by means of true *swarāj*, or self-mastery. He explains that in the ideal village, people will not live in ignorance, darkness, or filth. Rather free, intelligent, and independent women and men will dwell neither in luxury nor indolence. Gandhi conceived of the future of India as a republic of independent self-reliant villages. He thought of circles of villages working collaboratively with one another, with other circles of villages, and with cities that served as clearing facilities of their products. He believed that the self-reliant village would be the heart of a self-reliant and truly independent India.

It was two female English disciples of Gandhi who took the message of village self-reliance to the western Himalayas. Having moved to India in 1925, Mira Behn (known in England as Madeleine Slade) quickly adjusted to life in the Sabarmati Ashram, where Gandhi was then residing, and in the course of time became one of Gandhi's closest associates. She accompanied him on many of his *khādi* tours, his tours to villages to instill the importance of village self-reliance including the spinning of home spun cloth called *khādi*. She was also his personal secretary when he went to England for the round table conference concerning India's independence.[55] After a term of imprisonment with Gandhi she moved to the hills to realize his vision for self-reliant villages and wrote extensively on the condition of the natural environment upon which the villages of the hills were dependent. Sarala Behn (Catherine Mary Heilemann) went to India in 1932 and also eventually moved to the western Himalayas where she established the Lakshmi Ashram for the education of village girls.[56] She also participated in the founding of an organization for the support of local sustainable forest industries to provide employment for village men. Both of them exerted a critical influence on the leadership of a grassroots environmental movement that raised a massive and protracted series of protests against the government policy of contract-felling of the Himalayan forests that endangered the mountain ecology and threatened the domestic economy of the local people. That movement was called Chipko, appropriating the word *chipko* (meaning "to hug") from their strategy of hugging the trees to shield them from the axe.[57] In the course of almost ten years of non-violent activism, the movement succeeded in bringing about decisive changes in forest policy, including a ban on the felling of green trees for commercial purposes above an altitude of 1,000 meters. When questioned about the inspiration and motivation behind the movement, Sunderlal Bahuguna, one of the most visible exponents of the Chipko Movement, refers to the religious and philosophical heritage of the people and especially to the philosophies of yoga and of *Vedānta*.[58] For him the essence of *Vedānta* is the conviction that the divine reality resides not only in temples and in images, but also in trees and in mountains, in rivers and in landscapes, in birds and in beasts, that the Divine Reality is embodied in the natural world.

Notes

1. Jairam Ramesh, "Forward," *India's Fourth National Report to the Convention on Biological Diversity* (New Delhi: Ministry of Environment and Forests, 2009). See also pp. 15–53.
2. Christopher Chapple and Mary Evelyn Tucker eds., *Hinduism and Ecology: The Intersection of Earth, Sky, and Water* (Cambridge MA: Harvard

University Press, 2000). Pankaj Jain, *Dharma and Ecology: Sustenance and Sustainability* (Burlington VT: Ashgate, 2010).

3. Anil Agarwal, Ravi Chopra, and Kalpana Sharma eds., *The State of India's Environment: The First Citizen's Report* (New Delhi: Centre For Science and Environment, 1982), p. 32.

4. Ibid., pp. 3–14.

5. Anil Agarwal, "Human-Nature Interactions in a Third World Country," in *Ethical Perspectives on Environmental Issues in India* ed. by George A. James (New Delhi: APH Publishing Corporation, 1999), pp. 42, 54–56.

6. Madhav Gadgil and Ramachandra Guha, *Ecology and Equity,* in *The Use and Abuse of Nature,* by Madhav Gadgil and Ramachandra Guha (New Delhi: Oxford University Press, 2000), pp. 3–5.

7. Anil Agarwal et al. *State of India's Environment: The First Citizen's Report,* pp. 92, 93–111.

8. Ibid., pp. 16, 17–30.

9. Ibid., pp. 16, 126.

10. Ibid., p. 72.

11. Ibid., p. 176.

12. Ibid., p. 164.

13. Ibid., pp. 63–66, 114, 119–24.

14. Rachel Carson, *Silent Spring* (New York: Houghton Mifflin Company 1962).

15. Ralph Waldo Emerson, *Nature and Selected Essays (1889)* (New York: Dover, 2003). Henry David Thoreau, *A Week on the Concord and Merrimack Rivers* (New York: Penguin Classics, 1998).

16. Lynn White, "The Historic Roots of our Ecologic Crisis," *Science* 155: 3767 (March 1967).

17. Roderick Nash, *Wilderness and the American Mind* (New Haven: Yale University Press, 1967), pp. 21–22.

18. John Passmore, *Man's Responsibility for Nature: Ecological Problems and Western Traditions,* Second Edition (London: Duckworth, 1980), pp. 28–40.

19. Edward Said, *Orientalism* (New York: Random House, 1979). Ronald Inden, "Orientalist Constructions of India," *Modern Asian Studies* 30 (3): 409–414.

20. George Alfred James, "The Construction of India in Some Recent Environmental Philosophy." *Worldviews: Environment, Culture, Religion* 2 (1): 3–20.

21. Steven G. Darian, *The Ganges in Myth and History,* Second Edition (Honolulu: The University of Hawaii Press, 1978), pp. 42–47.

22. Sarvepalli Radhakrishnan and Charles Moore eds., *A Sourcebook of Indian Philosophy* (Princeton, NJ: Princeton University Press, 1957), p. 11.

23. Ibid., p. 20.

24. Ibid., pp. 50.

25. Ibid., p. 51.

26. Ibid., p. 52.

27. Ibid., pp. 93–94.

28. Shanti Nath Gupta, *The Indian Concept of Values* (New Delhi: Manohar, 1977), pp. IX, I, 31ff, 146f.

29. Ibid., pp. 48–51.

30. *Kautiliya's Arthashastra,* trans. R. Shamasastry (Mysore: Mysore Printing and Publishing House, 1967), p. 225.

31. Manu Smriti, 2: 17–23 in George Buhler, *The Laws of Manu* (New Delhi: Motilal Banarsidass, 1964), quoted in Vasudha Narayanan, "'One Tree is Equal to Ten Sons:' Some Hindu Responses to the Problems of Ecology, Population and Consumption," *Journal of the American Academy of Religion* (June 1997) 65 (2): 291–332 and "Water, Wood, and Wisdom: Ecological Perspectives from the Hindu Traditions," *Daedalus* (Fall 2001) 130:4, pp. 188.

32. Radhakrishnan and Moore, p. 127.

33. Swami Venkatesananda, *The Concise Bhagavatam* (Albany: SUNY Press, 1989), pp. 235ff.

34. Vasudha Narayanan, "Water, Wood, and Wisdom," pp. 187.

35. J. Baird Callicott, *Earth's Insights: A Multicultural Survey of Ecological Ethics from the Mediterranean Basin to the Australian Outback* (Berkeley: University of California Press, 1994), pp. 47ff.

36. Lance E. Nelson, "The Dualism of Nondualism: Advaita Vedanta and the Irrelevance of Nature," in *Purifying the Earthly Body of God: Religion and Ecology in Hindu India*, ed. Lance E. Nelson (Albany, NY: SUNY 1998), pp. 61–88.

37. Sankaracharya, *The Crest-Jewel of Wisdom and other Writings of Sankaracharya,* trans. Charles Johnston (Covina CA: Theosophical University Press, 1946), pp. 9–10.

38. Ramakrishna Puligandla, *Fundamantals of Indian Philosophy* (New Delhi: D. K. Printworld, 1994) pp. 255–261.

39. Ganesh and Vasudha Pangare, *From Poverty to Plenty: the Story of Ralegan Siddhi*, Studies in Ecology and Sustainable Development 5 (New Delhi: Indian National Trust for Art and Cultural Heritage, 1992). W. M. Sullivan, *The Dawning of Auroville* (Auroville: Auroville Press, 1994).

40. T. N. Khoshoo, *Mahatma Gandhi: An Apostle of Applied Human Ecology* (New Delhi: Tata Energy Research Institute, 1995), pp. 1–9. T. N. Khoshoo, "Gandhian Environmentalism," in *Ethical Perspectives on Environmental Issues in India*, ed. George A. James (New Delhi: A.P.H Publishing Corporation, 1999), pp. 241–281. Larry D. Shinn, "The Inner Logic of Gandhian Ecology," in *Hinduism and Ecology*, ed. Christopher Key Chapple and Mary Evelyn Tucker (Cambridge MA: Harvard University Press, 2000), pp. 213–241.

41. Mohandas K. Gandhi, *Hind Swaraj or Indian Home Rule* (Ahmedabad: Navajivan Publishing House, 1938), p. 90.
42. Cited in T. N. Khoshoo, *Mahatma Gandhi*, p. 65.
43. M. K. Gandhi, *Autobiography: The Story of My Experiments with Truth*, trans. Mahadav Desai (Washington DC: Public affairs Press, 1948), pp. 6–7.
44. Cited in T. N. Khoshoo, *Mahatma Gandhi*, pp. 18, 33, 66.
45. Mohandas K. Gandhi, *Vows and Observances*, ed. John Strohmeier, (Berkeley: Berkeley Hills Books, 1999), pp. 78, 125–8.
46. Quoted in T. N. Khoshoo, *Mahatma Gandhi,* p. 69.
47. Quoted in T. N. Khoshoo, *Mahatma Gandhi,* p. 66.
48. Quoted in T. N. Khoshoo, *Mahatma Gandhi,* p. 68.
49. M. K. Gandhi, *Young India*, March 24, 1920.
50. M. K. Gandhi, *Young India*, Dec. 15, 1927.
51. M. K. Gandhi, *Autobiography*, p. 6.
52. Ibid.
53. Quoted in T. N. Khoshoo, *Mahatma Gandhi,* p. 40.
54. T. N. Khoshoo, *Mahatma Gandhi,* pp. 66–7, 36–44.
55. Mirabehn, *The Spirit's Pilgrimage: the Autobiography of Madeline Slade* (Arlington: Great Ocean Publishers, 1960), pp. 64ff.
56. Sarala Behn, *A Life in Two Worlds: Autobiography of Mahatma Gandhi's English Disciple*, trans. David Hopkins (Kausani: Lakshmi Ashram, 2010), pp. 193ff.
57. Thomas Weber, *Hugging the Trees: The Story of the Chipko Movement* (New Delhi: Viking, Penguin Books, 1987).
58. "Sunderlal Bahuguna's Crusade" (Interview with Madhu Kishwar), in *Fire in the Heart, Fire Wood on the Back: Writings on and by Himalayan Crusader Sunderlal Bahuguna*, ed. Tenzin Rigzin (Amritsar: All India Pingalwara Charitable Society, 2005), p. 72.

CHAPTER 2

Ātman, Identity, and Emanation: Arguments for a Hindu Environmental Ethic

CHRISTOPHER FRAMARIN

1. INTRODUCTION

Many contemporary authors argue that since certain Hindu texts and traditions claim that all living beings are fundamentally the same as *Brahman* (God), these texts and traditions provide the basis for an environmental ethic.[1] I outline three common versions of this argument, and argue that each fails to meet at least one criterion for an environmental ethic.

This doesn't mean, however, that certain Hindu texts and traditions do not provide the basis for an environmental ethic. In the last section of the paper I briefly outline and defend an alternative, according to which all plants and animals have intrinsic value and direct moral standing in virtue of having a good.

2. THREE ARGUMENTS FOR A HINDU ENVIRONMENTAL ETHIC

Most authors who write on Hindu environmental ethics offer a version of the following argument. Certain Hindu texts and traditions claim that all living beings are fundamentally the same as *Brahman*.[2] Therefore these texts and traditions provide the basis for an environmental ethic. The basic argument can be schematized in the following way:

(SA–1)
Premise: Certain Hindu texts and traditions claim that all living beings are fundamentally the same as *Brahman*.
Conclusion: Hence these texts and traditions provide the basis for an environmental ethic.

In order for a theory to count as an environmental ethic, it must ascribe both intrinsic value and direct moral standing to non-sentient entities in nature, such as so-called lower animals, plants, and so on (Regan 1981, 19–20, Thompson 1990, 148).[3] To say that something has intrinsic value is to say that it has value independent of further ends towards which it is a means, and independent of the evaluations of valuers. To say that an entity has direct moral standing is to say that there are possible circumstances in which an agent morally ought to consider the entity for its own sake in deciding what to do (Regan 1981, 19–20, Timmons 2007, 511). Hence the basic argument can be elaborated to read:

(SA–2)
Premise One: Certain Hindu texts and traditions claim that all living beings are fundamentally the same as *Brahman*.
Conclusion One/Premise Two: Hence these texts and traditions claim that non-sentient entities (such as so-called lower animals, plants, and so on) have intrinsic value and direct moral standing.
Conclusion Two: Hence these texts and traditions provide the basis for an environmental ethic.

Implicit in this argument are the claims that (1) *Brahman* has intrinsic value and direct moral standing and (2) if all living beings are fundamentally the same as *Brahman*, then all living beings—including non-sentient entities such as so-called lower animals, plants, and so on—are intrinsically valuable and have direct moral standing.[4] So the full argument reads:

(SA–3)
Premise One: Certain Hindu texts and traditions claim that all living beings are fundamentally the same as *Brahman*.
Premise Two: *Brahman* is intrinsically valuable and has direct moral standing.
Premise Three: If all living beings are fundamentally the same as *Brahman*, and if *Brahman* is intrinsically valuable and has direct

moral standing, then non-sentient entities (such as so-called lower animals, plants, and so on) are intrinsically valuable and have direct moral standing.

Conclusion One/Premise Four: Hence these texts and traditions claim that non-sentient entities (such as so-called lower animals, plants, and so on) have intrinsic value and direct moral standing.

Conclusion Two: Hence these texts and traditions provide the basis for an environmental ethic.

In what follows, I will refer to this as the "Sameness Argument" (SA). It is advanced in some form or another by Eliot Deutsch (1970 and 1986), Rajagopal Ryali (1973), S. Cromwell Crawford (1982), David Kinsley (1991), Klaus K. Klostermaier (1991), Lina Gupta (1993), Harold Coward (1998), O. P. Dwivedi (2000), and others.

These authors offer at least three versions of SA, depending in part on which text or tradition they emphasize. According to the first version, which I will refer to as the '*Ātman* Argument' (AA), certain Hindu texts and traditions claim that each living being is an embodied *ātman* (eternal self). Each *ātman* is identical with *Brahman*[5]—in some sense.[6] Since each *ātman* is identical with *Brahman*, each *ātman* has intrinsic value and direct moral standing. And since each living being is an embodied *ātman*, each living being—including non-sentient entities such as plants and so on—is intrinsically valuable and has direct moral standing. Hence certain Hindu texts and traditions provide the basis for an environmental ethic.

Crawford advances this version of the argument when he claims that "[t]he general idea behind [relevant passages in the *Bṛhadāraṇyaka Upaniṣad*] is that the individual *ātman* is one with the universal *Brahman* . . . This *Brahman* force is manifest uniformly in the divinities of heaven, and in human and animal and plant life on earth" (Crawford 1982, 150). Hence "Hindu philosophy can provide the basis for an environmental ethic" (Ibid., 149). Anantanand Rambachan, arguing that Advaita affirms the "[world's] value and the value of life in it" (Rambachan 1989, 289), advances the *Ātman* Argument as well. "As the all-pervasive reality, and as the axis of the universe which intersects all things, God, in *Advaita*, exists at the deepest levels . . . as the Self (*ātman*)" (Rambachan 1989, 294).[7]

The *Ātman* Argument can be schematized in the following way:
(AA)
Premise One: Certain Hindu texts and traditions claim that the *ātman* is identical with *Brahman* in some sense.

Premise Two: *Brahman* is intrinsically valuable and has direct moral standing.

Premise Three: If each *ātman* is identical with *Brahman*, and if *Brahman* is intrinsically valuable and has direct moral standing, then each *ātman* is intrinsically valuable and has direct moral standing.

Premise Four: If each *ātman* is intrinsically valuable and has direct moral standing, and if each living being is an embodied *ātman*, then non-sentient entities (such as so-called lower animals, plants, and so on) are intrinsically valuable and have direct moral standing.

Conclusion One/Premise Five: So according to certain Hindu texts and traditions, non-sentient entities (such as so-called lower animals, plants, and so on) are intrinsically valuable and have direct moral standing.

Conclusion Two: Hence these texts and traditions provide the basis for an environmental ethic.

According to the second version of SA, certain Hindu texts and traditions claim that the distinctions between people, animals, plants, and *Brahman* are finally unreal. Hence everything is ultimately numerically and qualitatively identical with *Brahman*.[8] Since everything is identical with *Brahman* in this sense, and since *Brahman* has intrinsic value and direct moral standing, everything—including non-sentient plants and so on—has intrinsic value and direct moral standing. Hence these Hindu texts and traditions provide the basis for an environmental ethic.

This seems to be the sense of at least one of Deutsch's arguments for a Hindu environmental ethic. He says, "Vedānta would maintain that . . . fundamentally all life is one . . . and that this oneness finds its natural expression in a *reverence* for all living things" (Deutsch 1970, 82).[9] In defense of the claim that Hinduism endorses "treating the creation with respect without harming and exploiting others," Dwivedi claims that "for the Hindus of the ancient period, God and nature were one and the same" (Dwivedi 2000, 5–6).[10]

This second version of the argument can be schematized as follows:
(IA)

Premise One: Certain Hindu texts and traditions claim that the distinction between living beings and *Brahman* is unreal.

Premise Two: *Brahman* is intrinsically valuable and has direct moral standing.

Premise Three: If the distinction between living beings and *Brahman* is unreal, and if *Brahman* is intrinsically valuable and has direct moral standing, then non-sentient entities (such as so-called lower

animals, plants, and so on) are intrinsically valuable and have direct
moral standing.

Conclusion One/Premise Four: So according to certain Hindu texts and
traditions, non-sentient entities (such as so-called lower animals,
plants, and so on) are intrinsically valuable and have direct moral
standing.

Conclusion Two: Hence these texts and traditions provide the basis for
an environmental ethic.

In what follows, I will refer to this argument as the "Identity
Argument" (IA).

According to the third version of SA, certain Hindu texts and
traditions claim that all of nature is a manifestation of *Brahman*.[11]
'Manifestation of *Brahman*' in this context means that *Brahman*
produces or creates nature from its own form, so that the substance
of nature is the same as that of *Brahman*.[12] Hence nature is identical
with *Brahman* in this sense.[13] Since all of nature is a manifestation of
Brahman, all of nature is intrinsically valuable and has direct moral
standing. Hence these texts and traditions provide the basis for an
environmental ethic.

This version of SA is the most popular. Coward, for example,
claims that

> Hindus speak of the cosmos (including the stars, the atmosphere, the
> earth, plants, animals, and humans) as God's body. Since everything
> is divine, an ethic of reverence and respect is demanded from humans
> toward all other manifestations of God's body (Coward 1998, 40).

Gupta argues that since "Hinduism speaks of . . . the essence
called 'Brahman' that manifests itself in manifolds of this
universe . . . all parts of this Nature have an intrinsic value" (Gupta
1993, 113). Dwivedi argues for an Indian environmental ethic by
citing the claim from *Bhāgavata Purāṇa* (2.2.41) that "ether, air,
fire, water, earth, planets, all creatures, directions, trees and plants,
rivers, and seas, they are all organs of God's body" (Dwivedi
2000, 5). Klostermaier and Patricia Y. Mumme defend this kind
of view as well. They explicitly associate it with Rāmānuja and
Viśiṣṭādvaita (qualified non-dualism), but point out that it has its
origins in earlier texts, such as the *Puruṣa Sukta, Śatapaṭha
Brāhmaṇa, Bṛhadāraṇyaka Upaniṣad, Muṇḍaka Upaniṣad,
Bhagavadgītā*, and *Bhāgavata Purāṇa* (Klostermaier 1991, 250-1
and Mumme 1998, 139).[14]

This third version of the argument, which I will call the "Emanation Argument" (EA), reads:

(EA)
Premise One: Certain Hindu texts and traditions claim that all living beings are a manifestation of *Brahman*.
Premise Two: *Brahman* is intrinsically valuable and has direct moral standing.
Premise Three: If each living being is a manifestation of *Brahman*, and if *Brahman* is intrinsically valuable and has direct moral standing, then non-sentient entities (such as so-called lower animals, plants, and so on) are intrinsically valuable and have direct moral standing.
Conclusion One/Premise Four: So according to certain Hindu texts and traditions, non-sentient entities (such as so-called lower animals, plants, and so on) are intrinsically valuable and have direct moral standing.
Conclusion Two: Hence these texts and traditions provide the basis for an environmental ethic.

As Klostermaier and Mumme point out, the Emanation Argument is most naturally associated with Viśiṣṭādvaita. The Identity Argument, in contrast, is most naturally associated with Advaita. These associations are helpful as a rule of thumb, but I want to avoid identifying these arguments with these traditions too strongly. Again, as is clear in Klostermaier and Mumme's accounts, these philosophical themes have their origin in texts that precede the distinction between Advaita and Viśiṣṭādvaita. Both Śaṅkara and Rāmānuja defend these systems with extensive references to texts that precede them.[15]

3. Objections to the *Ātman* Argument

The fourth premise of the *Ātman* Argument states that if each *ātman* is intrinsically valuable and has direct moral standing, and if each living being is an embodied *ātman*, then non-sentient entities (such as so-called lower animals, plants, and so on) are intrinsically valuable and have direct moral standing. At first this inference might seem puzzling. It's not clear how the intrinsic value of one item—in this case, the *ātman*—can transfer to another item—in this case, the living body. Indeed, many contemporary philosophers define intrinsic value in terms of the value an item or state of affairs has independent of its relations with other objects or states of affairs.

G. E. Moore's influential position is that a state of affairs has intrinsic value just in case it has value in complete isolation. Its value must persist even in the absence of everything else (Moore 1903, 187).[16]

The body component in the *ātman*/body composite does not have value in the absence of everything else, however, because it is valuable only in virtue of being inhabited by, or in some way connected with, an *ātman*. The claim that the living body is entirely without value, even though the *ātman* with which it is connected has great intrinsic value, seems consistent.

Indeed, the primary objection to a Hindu environmental ethic advanced by contemporary authors has been just this. Lance E. Nelson, for example, claims that according to the *Bhagavadgītā*, "*ātman* is what is important. The physical, on the other hand, is expendable, and certainly not worth any emotional distress" (Nelson 2000, 141). J. Baird Callicott (1987, 124) and Arvind Sharma (1998, 57–8), among others,[17] make the same claim.

Consider the following analogy. Assume that human beings are intrinsically valuable. A certain human being must spend the rest of her life in an Iron Lung. (Suppose it's 1930.) In this situation, it's clear that the Iron Lung has instrumental value, as a means of keeping the person alive. It does not come to have intrinsic value, however, merely because an intrinsically valuable person inhabits it for her entire life. Likewise, it seems, the material body does not come to have intrinsic value merely because an intrinsically valuable *ātman* inhabits it for a lifetime.

One might reply that the intrinsic value of the *ātman* need not establish the intrinsic value of the isolated body. All it must do is establish the intrinsic value of the *ātman*/body composite, and this it does. In the Iron Lung case, when an intrinsically valuable person occupies the Iron Lung, the person/Iron Lung composite is intrinsically valuable, even if the Iron Lung by itself is not, simply because the person is. This is all that is required for AA to succeed. The *ātman*/body composite is intrinsically valuable, even if the body is not, simply because the *ātman* is.

This kind of view, even if it technically succeeds at establishing the intrinsic value of the living being, seems at least to miss some of the spirit of the demands of an environmental ethic. Holmes Rolston III objects to a related argument by saying, "animals need to be valued . . . as biological agents . . ." (Rolston III 1987, 175). The word "agents" here is somewhat misleading in the present context, since an environmental ethic must attribute intrinsic value and direct moral standing to non-sentient entities in nature whether they are agents— that is, whether they are capable of intentional action—or not. So the objection can be revised to read: animals and plants need to be valued as biological entities—and not simply as biological containers for something else that has intrinsic value and direct moral standing. The most plausible version of AA, however, does not value animals or plants as biological entities, but as embodied *ātmans*.

The problem becomes more apparent if we consider the issue of moral standing. Even if living beings are intrinsically valuable, as a consequence of being constituted in part by the *ātman*, it is not clear that the direct moral standing of the *ātman* transfers to the living being that it inhabits.

In the most famous discussion of the topic within the Indian philosophical tradition, the *Bhagavadgītā* states that the *ātman* is not harmed by the destruction of the body. "Weapons do not cut [the *ātman*], fire does not burn it, waters do not wet it, the wind does not dessicate it . . . The body being killed, [the *ātman*] is not killed" (2.23, 2.20).[18] That we must, in deliberating over whether to perform a certain action, consider how the *ātman* will be affected does not entail that we must, in deliberating over whether to perform a certain action, consider how the body that is inhabited by the *ātman* will be affected, because the *ātman* is not affected by what happens to the body. As Nelson says with regard to the *Bhagavadgītā*, "physical harm—whether the destruction of war or, presumably, ecological devastation—however regrettable on the empirical level, does not affect what ultimately matters, namely spirit" (Nelson 2000, 142).[19]

So the first two objections to AA might be understood as two different versions of a similar transfer problem. The first objection is that the intrinsic value of the *ātman* does not transfer to the biological being. The second objection is that the direct moral standing of the *ātman* cannot transfer to the biological being.[20]

This second objection can be strengthened. It is not clear that *ātman* or *Brahman* has direct moral standing in the first place. In many classical texts, such as the *Yogasūtra*, the *Sāṃkhyakārika*, the *Gītā*, and various *Upaniṣads*, the *ātman* (or *puruṣa*) is typically characterized as an uninvolved and unaffected witness to the events of the world. In other texts, including some *Upaniṣads*, the *ātman* is described as the agent within the living being.[21] Nonetheless, the *ātman* is unchanging, and untouched by pain and pleasure. The same is true of *Brahman*.[22] In other words, neither *Brahman* nor *ātman* could be affected by any event whatsoever.[23]

If neither *Brahman* nor *ātman* could be affected by any event, then there is no possible set of circumstances in which a being must consider how *Brahman* or *ātman* will be affected by an action. If there is no possible set of circumstances in which a being must consider how *Brahman* or *ātman* will be affected by an action, then neither *Brahman* nor *ātman* has direct moral standing, since to say that a being has direct moral standing is to say that there are possible circumstances in which an agent morally ought to consider the entity for its own sake in deciding what to do. And if neither *Brahman* nor *ātman* has direct moral standing, the direct moral standing of the *ātman* cannot transfer to the body or the *ātman*/body composite.

The cogency of AA, however, depends on the truth of the claim that the *ātman* has direct moral standing. Since the *ātman* does not have direct moral standing, the argument is unconvincing. If the argument fails, then AA does not prove that certain Hindu texts and traditions provide the basis for an environmental ethic.

4. Objections to the Identity Argument

Both the Identity Argument and the Emanation Argument might be thought of as more robust versions of the *Ātman* Argument. AA states that every *ātman* is in some sense identical with *Brahman*. IA and EA state that everything—including every *ātman*—is in some sense identical with *Brahman*. Hence the failure of AA to establish a Hindu environmental ethic need not mean that IA and/or EA fail as well.

The Identity Argument certainly avoids the first objection to AA— the objection that the intrinsic value of the *ātman* does not transfer to the biological organism per se—because according to IA, the biological organism is identical with both *ātman* and *Brahman*. Hence the intrinsic value of the biological organism is not a result of the problematic transfer of intrinsic value from the *ātman* or *Brahman*. The biological organism's value just is the value of *Brahman*.

IA is equally vulnerable, however, to the second objection to AA. The cogency of IA depends essentially on the plausibility of the claim that *Brahman* has direct moral standing (Premise Two). If *Brahman* does not have direct moral standing—as I argue above—then the direct moral standing of *Brahman* cannot establish the direct moral standing of living beings, sentient or non-sentient. Hence IA fails to show that certain Indian texts and traditions (namely those that claim that all distinctions are illusory) provide the basis for an environmental ethic, because IA fails to show that living beings have direct moral standing.

My point here is not that since, according to IA, the living being is identical with *Brahman*, and since *Brahman* lacks direct moral standing, so does the living being. If this were the point, long digressions about the distinction between conventional and ultimate reality would be unavoidable. (See below.) My point is more modest. Since *Brahman* does not have direct moral standing to begin with, IA is unconvincing, because IA claims that the direct moral standing of *Brahman* is the basis for the direct moral standing of the living being. This is consistent, however, with the establishment of the direct moral standing of living beings by some other means. (See below.)

IA also faces an objection that AA avoids. Thus far, I have focused on two criteria for an environmental ethic. An environmental ethic must (1) attribute intrinsic value to non-sentient entities in nature, and (2) attribute direct moral standing to non-sentient entities in nature. These criteria are not exhaustive, however. Additionally, an environmental ethic must satisfy what Janna Thompson calls the "non-vacuity requirement" (Thompson 1990, 149). Thompson argues that

> [t]he criteria for determining what things or states of affairs are intrinsically valuable must not be such so that it turns out that every thing and every state of affairs counts as equally valuable. The reason why this requirement must be satisfied should be clear. An ethic is supposed to tell us what we ought or ought not to do; however, it cannot do so if it turns out that all things and states of affairs are equally valuable, for if they are, then there is no reason to do one thing rather than another, to bring about one state of affairs rather than another (Ibid.).

An ethic of any sort is supposed to be action-guiding. It is supposed to tell us what to do under certain circumstances. In order for an ethic to tell us what to do, it must be able to discriminate between what is good and bad. If a theory attributes equal value to everything,[24] however, then it cannot discriminate between good and bad, because everything is equally good or bad. Nothing is any better than anything else.[25]

Consider the example of murder. It might be thought that since a living person is intrinsically valuable, the person should not be harmed (all other things being equal). Hence killing is worse than avoiding killing. If, however, the value of the dead body is equal to the value of the living body, it is not clear why refraining from murder is preferable to murder. In both cases the outcome is equally valuable—a dead body is no less valuable than a living body. Even the sorrow of the friends and family of the murdered is equally valuable to the joy they might have felt if the murder had not occurred. Hence on this view, the distinctions between right and wrong, and good and bad, disappear.

IA, however, entails that everything has equal value. Notice first that Premise One of IA is unnecessarily narrow. If all distinctions are illusory, then the distinctions between *Brahman* and inanimate objects are illusory along with the distinctions between living beings and *Brahman*. Instead, Premise One should read: "Certain Indian texts and traditions claim that the distinctions between all things and *Brahman* are unreal." Premise Two states that *Brahman* has intrinsic value. When these premises are combined with Premise Three, which says that if the distinction between *Brahman* and X is illusory and *Brahman* has intrinsic value, then X has intrinsic value, they entail the conclusion "all things are intrinsically valuable." If their value derives exclusively from their identity with *Brahman*— and IA says nothing to suggest that this is not the case—then all things are equally intrinsically valuable. If all things are equally intrinsically valuable, then the distinctions between good and bad and/or right and wrong are lost. Hence IA cannot establish an environmental ethic.

Again, some distinction might be drawn here between ultimate and conventional reality. One might admit that Advaita (as an example) attributes equal value to all things at the ultimate level, but insist that at the conventional level Advaita accepts evaluative distinctions. At the conventional level, a living person, animal, or plant is more valuable than a dead one, and the act of protecting life is better (more right) than the act of killing. Since most human beings live life at the conventional level, it is this level that is relevant to environmental ethics.

The problem with this response is that the proponent of IA argues that the conventional conception of the value of things— according to which there are differences in the value of things, and so on—should be replaced by the ultimate conception of the value of things—according to which all things are identical, and therefore have equal value. The proponent cannot, then, cite aspects of the conventional conception as a means of avoiding the further implications of attributing equal value to all things. The proponent of IA says that we should see all things as identical with *Brahman*. The proponent cannot then reply to the vacuity objection by pointing out that ordinarily we do not see all things as *Brahman*.[26]

5. OBJECTIONS TO THE EMANATION ARGUMENT

Like the Identity Argument, the Emanation Argument entails that the biological entity has intrinsic value, since the biological entity, like the *ātman*, emanates from, and is constituted by *Brahman*. So EA avoids the first objection to the *Ātman* Argument.

EA is just as vulnerable, however, to the second objection to AA. Like IA, EA states that *Brahman* has direct moral standing (Premise Two of both arguments), and this premise is crucial to deriving the conclusion that each living being has direct moral standing. If *Brahman* does not have direct moral standing—as I argue above—then even if Premise Three is true—"If each living being is a manifestation of *Brahman*, and if *Brahman* is intrinsically valuable and has direct moral standing, then non-sentient entities (such as plants and so on) are intrinsically valuable and have direct moral standing"—it does not follow that all living beings have direct moral standing. Hence EA does not provide the basis for an environmental ethic.

Additionally, EA seems to face the vacuity objection. Again, Premise One is too narrow. Not only living beings, but non-living things are a manifestation of *Brahman*. Rāmānuja, for example, elaborates *Gītā* 10.8, which reads: "I am the creator of all"[27] as "I am the creator, the cause and origin, of the manifestation of all manifold [things], sentient and non-sentient."[28] Throughout his commentaries on the *Gītā* and the *Brahmasūtra*, Rāmānuja simply says that *Brahman* is the creator of all things, and that both eternal selves and matter constitute God's body (Carman 1974, 115). Likewise, none of the creation stories that Mumme or Klostermaier cite specify that Brahman only creates living beings. Mumme says, citing the best-known analogies for the emanationist perspective,

> [a]s a spider emits a thread (*Bṛhadāraṇyaka Up.* 2.1.20 and *Muṇḍaka Up.* 1.1.7) or as grass arises from the earth, or as hairs arise from the body, so too, from the Imperishable Lord, arises *all of creation* (*Muṇḍaka Up.* 1.1.7) (Mumme 1998, 139, emphasis added).

Hence Premise One of EA should instead read: "Certain Hindu texts and traditions claim that all things are a manifestation of *Brahman*."

Premise Two states that *Brahman* has intrinsic value. When these premises are combined with Premise Three—which says that if X is a manifestation of *Brahman*, and if *Brahman* is intrinsically valuable, then X is intrinsically valuable—they entail that all things are intrinsically valuable. If their value derives exclusively from being a manifestation of *Brahman*—and the argument says nothing to suggest otherwise—then EA entails that all things have equal intrinsic value. If a theory attributes equal intrinsic value to all things, however, it cannot discriminate between good and bad and/or right and wrong. It cannot be action-guiding, and therefore cannot be an ethic.[29]

Finally, EA faces an objection that IA does not. Premise Three of IA states, "If the distinction between living beings and *Brahman* is unreal, and if *Brahman* is intrinsically valuable and has direct moral standing, then non-sentient entities (such as so-called lower animals, plants, and so on) are intrinsically valuable and have direct moral standing." The premise seems plausible in part because if two items are identical, it is hard to see how one could have qualities that the other lacks. If the capital of Canada is Ottawa, then if Ottawa has over one million people, so does the capital of Canada. Likewise, if a living being is identical with *Brahman*, then if *Brahman* has intrinsic value and direct moral standing, then so does the living being.

Premise Three of EA, in contrast, states, "If each living being is a manifestation of *Brahman*, and if *Brahman* is intrinsically valuable and has direct moral standing, then non-sentient entities (such as so-called lower animals, plants, and so on) are intrinsically valuable and have direct moral standing." There is no corresponding platitude, however, to the effect that if one item is a manifestation of another, the former has all of the qualities that the latter possesses. Consider one of the analogies just mentioned. Assume that a human being is intrinsically valuable. The hair of a human being emanates from the human being. It might even be said to be of the same substance as a human being. From this it does not follow that the hair is also intrinsically valuable. Similarly, the fact that living beings emanate from *Brahman* does not obviously entail that they share in *Brahman's* intrinsic value.

Indeed, there is a precedent in Rāmānuja's work for denying that living beings possess the qualities of *Brahman*. *Brahman* is, among other things, infinite and eternal, unlike any of the entities he creates.[30] *Brahman* is often described as omniscient and perfectly blissful. Rocks, however, are incapable of knowledge or bliss, and even human beings are rarely perfectly knowledgeable or blissful. If a number of *Brahman's* qualities do not inhere in elements of his creation, despite these elements emanating from *Brahman*, then at the very least the proponent of EA must offer an argument for why the intrinsic value of *Brahman* does inhere in the elements of his creation, even though other qualities of *Brahman* do not.

Yet proponents of EA do not make this case. And even if there are arguments for the claim that certain qualities inhere in the elements of creation, there must be additional arguments for the claim that the qualities inhere only in certain entities. Again, proponents of EA do not make this case.

6. AN ALTERNATIVE TO THE *ĀTMAN*, IDENTITY, AND EMANATION ARGUMENTS

Arguments for an Indian environmental ethic that rely on some kind of identity between nature and God are unconvincing. It isn't clear, however, that this kind of argument is needed. R. W. Perrett argues that certain Indian texts and traditions ascribe direct moral standing to all sentient beings in virtue of their sentience. He offers the following argument:

> It is possible to construct arguments for our direct duty to animals . . . Thus, consider first the assumption that was erroneously supposed to support the indirect duty view: that we each ought to self-interestedly pursue our own liberation as our primary goal. But why should we pursue *mokṣa* [liberation] at all? Because, says the Indian tradition, life is essentially characterized by suffering and unsatisfactoriness (*duḥkha*). It is the elimination of this suffering that is intrinsically valuable, indeed the ultimate value . . . But if we admit these claims then we must also come to ask ourselves what is so special about our own suffering. What properties do I possess that make my suffering morally significant without it also being the case that others' suffering is equally morally significant? Rationally we are drawn towards a universal perspective on our own suffering (Perrett 1993, 94).

My attainment of *mokṣa* is intrinsically valuable (at least in part) because my avoidance of suffering is intrinsically valuable. There is nothing about me that distinguishes me in a relevant way from other sentient beings. Therefore the avoidance of suffering is intrinsically valuable regardless of whose suffering it is.

A parallel argument concludes that pleasure or happiness is intrinsically valuable regardless of whose it is: My attainment of *mokṣa* is intrinsically valuable (at least in part) because my happiness is intrinsically valuable. There is nothing about me that distinguishes me in a relevant way from other sentient beings. Therefore happiness is intrinsically valuable regardless of whose it is. Hence we have direct duties to sentient beings. If we have direct duties to sentient beings,

then sentient beings have direct moral standing, and presumably
intrinsic value.[31]

There is still some space between the conclusion of Perrett's argument and the criteria for an environmental ethic. If Perrett is right,
then we might conclude that all sentient beings have direct moral
standing and intrinsic value. In order for a theory to count as an environmental ethic, however, it must ascribe intrinsic value and direct
moral standing to non-sentient beings, like so-called lower animals,
plants and so on.

In a number of Hindu texts, however, lower animals and plants are
described as sentient as well.[32] *Manusmṛti* 1.49, for example, reads:

> Those [beings], enveloped by the *tamas* [one of three basic elements
> (*guṇas*) that constitute the material universe, characterized by dark-
> ness and ignorance] with many forms caused by [past] actions, are
> internally conscious, and fully endowed with [the capacity for] pleasure
> and pain.[33]

If Perrett's argument is convincing, and if all living beings are
sentient, then all living beings have direct moral standing and intrinsic
value. If all living beings have direct moral standing and intrinsic
value, then at least the first two criteria for an environmental ethic are
satisfied.[34] The non-vacuity requirement is also satisfied, since some
things are non-sentient, and hence devoid of direct moral standing and
intrinsic value. Hence, one might conclude, certain Indian texts and
traditions provide the basis for an environmental ethic.

There is little doubt that the Indian Law Books are concerned with
the matter of causing pain to plants and animals. One passage from
the *Manusmṛti* (8.286) advises rulers to punish in proportion to the
pain caused: "If a person strikes people or animals to pain [them], just
as great as the pain [caused], just that great should the punishment
be."[35] This suggests that the quantity of pain is the measure of the
wrongness of an action, and that the capacity for pleasure and pain
makes the well-being of sentient beings relevant.

In another important passage (5.49), Manu says, "having seen the
origin of meat and the binding and slaughter of embodied beings
(*dehinām*), [a person] turns away from eating all meat."[36] This might
be taken to imply that to the careful observer, the value of animals is
self-evident. One thing that is evident to anyone is that animals experience pain and pleasure. All of this implies that sentient beings have
direct moral standing and intrinsic value because they are capable of
experiencing pleasure and pain.

One obvious objection to this kind of view is that many animals, and all plants, are not in fact sentient. One way to avoid this problem is to argue that certain Indian texts and traditions attribute intrinsic value and direct moral standing to animals and plants because they are alive. Each of the passages cited above might be interpreted in accord with this claim, simply because pain is typically a consequence of harm, and harm often has the consequence of shortening life. The more severe the pain is, the more likely it is that the pain will have a negative consequence on the being's longevity. This is why, one might argue, the severity of the punishment tends to correspond with the severity of the pain.

The passage that states "having carefully considered the origin of meat and the tying up and slaughter of living beings [that is the source of meat], a person turns away from the eating of all meat," implies that the reason meat-eating is wrong is self-evident. Even more self-evident than the animal's pain as a result of slaughter, however, is the animal's death.

Elsewhere, Manu warns against hindering a calf from suckling (4.59). To merely hinder a calf's suckling might be painful to the calf and the mother, by producing hunger pangs and anxiety, but to preclude it altogether is deadly. Hence these passages support the view that the criterion of being alive is the basis of the intrinsic value and direct moral standing of plants and animals as well.

The criterion of being alive makes better sense, however, of those passages that describe punishments for killing. If all that is wrong with killing is that it tends to produce pain, killing an animal should be no worse than actions that cause equivalent pain. Yet the Law Books typically single out killing as a special kind of trespass.

The criterion of being alive also has the advantage of explaining why the painless killing of animals and plants is wrong—even if their lives, if spared, will not be more pleasurable than painful. Medhātithi, the most important commentator on the *Manusmṛti*, says clearly that plant life, in particular, is almost exclusively painful.

> Due to an abundance of *tamas*, tied to infidelity to the Vedas, pain, and so on, [plants] are experiencing the fruits of their *adharmic* [acts] for a very long time—[as if] eternally. And from the presence of *sattva* [another of the three *guṇas*, typically characterized in terms of lightness and knowledge] in them, under certain conditions, [plants] also enjoy a little pleasure as well (1.49).[37]

An animal birth, like a plant birth, is also on balance more painful than pleasurable. What could be the fault, then, in killing a sleeping animal, if only pain has disvalue?[38] If being alive is intrinsically valuable, however, then killing an animal is wrong whether it is asleep or awake.

So while the *Manusmṛti* is concerned with pleasure and pain, it is also concerned with killing. The concern with pleasure and pain is better explained by the concern with killing than the concern with killing is explained by the concern with pleasure and pain. Additionally, the criterion of being alive avoids two objections to the criterion of sentience. First, it is simply false that all plants and animals are sentient. It is true, however, that all plants and animals are alive (at least for as long as we want to attribute intrinsic value and direct moral standing to them). Second, the criterion of being alive explains the emphasis on the blameworthiness of killing, including killing that does not increase overall pain.

By itself, however, the criterion of being alive is problematic as well. One of the more obvious problems is that the reduction of the value and disvalue of pleasure and pain to the value and disvalue of life and death seems implausible. Suppose, for example, that a person has a chronic disease that causes a great deal of pain. Even if there's nothing we can do to prolong her life, we should minimize her pain. If all that matters is the avoidance of death, however, then attempts to minimize her pain should be abandoned with the attempts to prolong her life. Indeed, we should at no point bother to minimize her pain unless there is reason to think it will prolong her life.

Another way to put this point is to say that there's reason to think that pleasure and pain have value and disvalue in themselves, regardless of their contribution to the length of a person's life. This is Perrett's point in the quotation above. According to certain Indian texts and traditions, liberation is valuable in part because it is pleasurable and devoid of pain. Hence pleasure and the avoidance of pain are intrinsically valuable. The criterion of being alive, by itself, does not account for this.

So rather than choosing between the two criteria, both might be adopted. Certain Indian texts and traditions ascribe intrinsic value and direct moral standing to plants and animals both because they are sentient, and because they are alive. Hence certain Indian texts and traditions provide the basis for an environmental ethic.

There are still at least two problems with the combined account. The first is that since lower animals and plants are not in fact sentient, the account is implausible insofar as it attributes intrinsic value and direct moral standing to lower animals and plants because they are sentient. So on the combined account, lower animals and plants have intrinsic value and direct moral standing solely because they are alive. If this is right, then lower animals and plants can be treated in whatever way one chooses, so long as their lives are not shortened. If it turns out that fish are non-sentient, for example, then they provide no direct reason to leave salmon runs open, rather than round them up in pools, where they are fed and allowed to mate. The combined account offers no plausible explanation for the wrongness of such actions.

Second, the combined account cannot explain the intuition that sentient beings can be harmed even if neither their longevity nor their overall happiness is diminished. Imagine that lead poisoning will not compromise a child's longevity or overall happiness. The child will have a mild learning disability, but will be no less happy overall. The combined account has no resource for explaining why the diminution in the child's mental capacities is of disvalue. Yet it is.

A final alternative—and the one I favor—is to interpret these texts as attributing intrinsic value and direct moral standing to certain beings in virtue of their having a good.[39] Human beings, along with animals and plants, can either flourish or languish. If something can flourish or languish, then it must have some optimum state. Movement towards the optimum state amounts to flourishing, movement away from the optimum state amounts to languishing. This optimum state is the entity's good.[40]

The distinction between flourishing and languishing covers both the criterion of sentience and the criterion of being alive, since any plausible characterization of the distinction between flourishing and languishing will refer to longevity, and any plausible characterization of flourishing and languishing in sentient beings will refer to pleasure and pain. So the criterion of having a good exhibits the benefits of the combined account.

The criterion of having a good is also no more controversial than the combined account. While it covers both the criterion of sentience and the criterion of being alive, it leaves open the possibility that an entity's good is more complex than this, without asserting that it certainly is.

At the same time, it seems certain that the good of human beings is not reducible to being alive, avoiding pain, and experiencing pleasure. It also seems certain that the Hindu traditions acknowledge this. There is little reason to think that the *Manusmṛti's* prescriptions of Vedic studentship, monogamous marriage, the performance of rituals, dutiful childrearing, retirement to the forest, and so on can be explained entirely in terms of the longevity and balance of pleasure over pain to which these practices lead (other than the assumption at the outset that the worldview is hedonistic). A more plausible interpretation is that these practices lead to a human life of flourishing broadly construed; in raising children, a person flourishes, but not just by increasing his or her longevity and long-term balance of pleasure over pain. If a human being's good is not reducible to being alive, avoiding pain, and experiencing pleasure, then perhaps the goods of non-human beings are not reducible either.

Another benefit of this criterion is that it leaves open the question of what, other than being alive, avoiding pain, and experiencing pleasure, constitutes a specific entity's good—if anything does. This standpoint is appropriate, given the ongoing debate among philosophers of science, environmental ethicists, ecologists, and others over how to determine an entity's good. It is also appropriate given the relative infancy of the field of Hindu environmental ethics, which has yet to consider these questions carefully.

Additionally, the final account is well-supported by the nearly pan-Indian cardinal virtue of *ahiṃsā*. The term is usually translated as "non-violence" or "non-harm". The latter translation is often favored because of its breadth; the word "non-violence" often suggests physical or explicit harm, whereas *ahiṃsā* refers to the avoidance of any harm whatever—even if that harm is neither painful, nor life-shortening. Theft, for example, constitutes a harm even if it is never discovered, and even if the stolen item would never have benefited its original owner. The same is true for harms of deception, coercion, and so on. If an entity can be harmed without causing it pain or shortening its life, however, then its good is not exhausted by longevity, the avoidance of pain, and the experience of pleasure.

The criterion also avoids the objections mentioned above. Even harms that are neither painful nor life shortening have disvalue, simply in virtue of being harms that cause the being to languish rather than flourish in other ways. This is most obvious in the case of human beings.

Lastly, the criterion of having a good avoids the implication that all things are equally valuable. Anything that is not alive, and lacks a good, lacks intrinsic value and direct moral standing. Hence the account I outline avoids the vacuity objection. There might seem to be additional counter-intuitive consequences to this view, such as the equal intrinsic value and direct moral standing of all living beings (since all have a good). Nothing I have said here entails this, however. It might be, for example, that an entity has some amount of intrinsic value in virtue of having a good, but that the amount of intrinsic value nonetheless varies, as a result, for example, of varying capacities and potentials.[41]

If all living entities have a good, and if all entities that have a good have intrinsic value and direct moral standing, (and if the vacuity objection is avoided,) then certain Hindu texts and traditions—the *Manusmṛti* and many texts and traditions that share its views—do provide the basis for an environmental ethic.

7. Conclusion

Arguments that cite some kind of identity between nature and God in support of the conclusion that certain Hindu texts and traditions provide the basis for an environmental ethic are not convincing. Some of these texts and traditions do provide the basis for an environmental ethic, however. They ascribe intrinsic value and direct moral standing to all living beings, in virtue of their having a good.

Acknowledgments

My thanks to Mark Migotti, Elizabeth Brake, Dennis McKerlie, Sam Borsman, John Taber, Richard Hayes, Kelly Becker, Stephen Harris, Laura Guererro, Ethan Mills, three anonymous referees at *Comparative Philosophy*, and an anonymous reader of this volume for suggestions that improved the paper. The paper also benefited from input from students in my Environmental Ethics and Hinduism and the Environment courses.

References

Primary Sanskrit Sources

Bhagavadgītā in Sadhale, Shastri, G. S. (ed.) (2000a and 2000b).
Bṛhadāraṇyakopaniṣad in Sadanand, V. (ed.) (1981).
Manusmṛti in Jhā, Ganganatha (ed.) (1999a and 1999b).
Medhātithi, *Manubhāṣya* in Jha, Ganganatha (ed.) (1999a).
Rāmānuja, *Gītābhāṣya* in Sadhale, Shastri G. S. (ed.) (2000a).
Śaṅkara, *Gītābhāṣya* in Sadhale, Shastri G. S. (ed.) (2000a).

Edited Volumes of Sanskrit Texts

Jhā, Ganganatha (ed.) (1999a), Manusmṛti *with the* "Manubhāṣya" *of Medhātithi* vol. 1 (Delhi: Motilal Banarsidass).
———— (ed.) (1999b), Manusmṛti *with the* "Manubhāṣya" of Medhātithi vol. 2 (Delhi: Motilal Banarsidass).

Sadanand, V. (ed.) (1981), Bṛhadāraṇyakopaniṣad Bhāṣya (Chennai: All India Press).

Sadhale, Shastri G. S. (ed.) (2000a), *The* Bhagavad-Gītā *with Eleven Commentaries* vol. 1 (Delhi: Parimal Publications).

——— (ed.) (2000b), *The* Bhagavad-Gītā *with Eleven Commentaries* vol. 2 (Delhi: Parimal Publications).

——— (ed.) (2000c), *The* Bhagavad-Gītā *with Eleven Commentaries* vol. 3 (Delhi: Parimal Publications).

Secondary Sources

Callicott, J. Baird (1987), "Conceptual Resources for Environmental Ethics in Asian Traditions of Thought: A Propaedeutic", *Philosophy East and West* 37: 115–30.

Carman, John B. (1974), *The Theology of Rāmānuja: An Essay in Inter-religious Understanding* (New Haven, CT: Yale University Press).

Chapple, Christopher. K. (1993), *Non-Violence to Animals, Earth, and Self in Asian Traditions* (Albany: SUNY Press).

Coward, Harold G. (1998), "The Ecological Implications of Karma Theory", in Lance. E. Nelson (ed.) *Purifying the Earthly Body of God: Religion and Ecology in Hindu India*, ed. (Albany: SUNY Press), pp. 39–49.

Crawford, S. Cromwell (1982), *The Evolution of Hindu Ethical Ideals* (Honolulu: University of Hawaii Press).

Dasgupta Sherma, Rita (1998), "Sacred Immanence: Reflections of Ecofeminism in Hindu Tantra", in Lance. E. Nelson (ed.), *Purifying the Earthly Body of God: Religion and Ecology in Hindu India* (Albany: SUNY Press), pp. 89–132.

Deutsch, Eliot (1970), "Vedānta and Ecology", in *Indian Philosophical Annual* 7 (Madras: The Center for Advanced Study in Philosophy), pp. 79–88.

———. (1986), "A Metaphysical Grounding for Natural Reverence: East-West", *Environmental Ethics* 8: 293–9.

Dwivedi, O. P. (2000), "Dharmic Ecology", in C. K. Chapple and M. E. Tucker (eds.) *Hinduism and Ecology: The Intersection of Earth, Sky, and Water* (Cambridge, MA: Harvard University Press), pp. 3–22.

Gupta, Lina (1993), *Ecofeminism and the Sacred* (New York: Continuum Press).

Kinsley, David R. (1991), "Reflections on Ecological Themes in Hinduism", *Journal of Dharma* 16: 227–45.

Klostermaier, Klaus K. (1991), "*Bhakti, Ahimsa* and Ecology", *Journal of Dharma* 16: 246–254.

Lal, Basant K. (1986), "Hindu Perspectives on the Use of Animals in Science", in T. Regan (ed.) *Animal Sacrifices: Religious Perspectives on the Use of Animals in Science* (Philadelphia: Temple University Press), pp. 199–212.

Lee, Keekok (1996), "Source and Locus of Intrinsic Value: A Reexamination", *Environmental Ethics* 18: 297–309.

Lipner, Julius (1986), *The Face of Truth* (Albany: SUNY Press).

Lombardi, Louis G. (1983), "Inherent Worth, Respect, and Rights", *Environmental Ethics* 5: 257–270.

Moore, G. E. (1903), *Principia Ethica*. (Cambridge: Cambridge University Press).

Mumme, Patricia. Y. (1998), "Models and Images for a Vaisnava Environmental Theology: The Potential Contribution of Srivaisnavism", in Lance. E. Nelson (ed.) *Purifying the Earthly Body of God: Religion and Ecology in Hindu India* (Albany: SUNY Press), pp. 133–59.

Narayanan, Vasudha (1997), "One Tree is Equal to Ten Sons": Hindu Responses to the Problems of Ecology, Population, and Consumption", *Journal of the American Academy of Religion* 65: 291–332.

Nelson, Lance. E. (1998), "The Dualism of Nondualism: Advaita Vedānta and the Irrelevance of Nature", in L. E. Nelson (ed.) *Purifying the Earthly Body of God: Religion and Ecology in Hindu India* (Albany: SUNY Press), pp. 61–88.

———. (2000), "Reading the *Bhagavadgītā* from an Ecological Perspective", in Christopher. K. Chapple and Mary. E. Tucker (eds.) *Hinduism and Ecology: The Intersection of Earth, Sky, and Water* (Cambridge, MA: Harvard University Press), pp. 127–64.

Norton, Bryan G. (1984), "Environmental Ethics and Weak Anthropocentrism", *Environmental Ethics* 6: 131–48.

O'Neill, John (1992), "The Varieties of Intrinsic Value", *Monist* 75: 119–137.

Perrett, Roy. W. (1993), "Moral Vegetarianism and the Indian Tradition", in N. Smart and S. Thakur (eds.), *Ethical and Political Dilemmas of Modern India* (St. Martin's Press), pp. 82–99.

Rambachan, Anantanand (1989), "The Value of the World as the Mystery of God in Advaita Vedanta", *Journal of Dharma* 14: 287–97.

Regan, Tom (1981), "The Nature and Possibility of an Environmental Ethic", *Environmental Ethics* 3: 19–34.

Rolston Holmes, III. (1987), "Can the East Help the West to Value Nature?", *Philosophy East and West* 37: 172–90.

———. (1994), "Value in Nature and the Nature of Value", in Robin Attfield and Andrew Belsey (eds.) *Philosophy and the Natural Environment* (Cambridge: Cambridge Univerity Press), pp. 13–30.

Ryali, Rajagopal (1973), "Eastern-Mystical Perspectives on Environment", in David C. Steffenson, Walter J. Herrscher, and Robert S. Cook (eds.), *Ethics for Environment: Three Religious Strategies* (Green Bay, WI: UWGB Ecumentical Center), pp. 47–56.

Sharma, Arvind (1998), "Attitudes to Nature in the Early Upanisads", in L. E. Nelson (ed.), *Purifying the Earthly Body of God: Religion and Ecology in Hindu India* (Albany: SUNY Press), pp. 51–60.

Taylor, Paul W. (1986), *Respect for Nature: A Theory of Environmental Ethics* (Princeton, NJ: Princeton University Press)

Thompson, Janna (1990), "A Refutation of Environmental Ethics", *Environmental Ethics* 12: 147–160.

Timmons, Mark (2007), *Disputed Moral Issues* (Oxford: Oxford University Press).

Notes

1. The authors whose views I consider in sections 2 through 5 are often unclear about which Hindu texts and traditions they have in mind. Where they are explicit, they refer to Advaita Vedānta, Viśiṣṭādvaita Vedānta, and the *Upaniṣads*. In section 6, I focus primarily on the *Manusmṛti*, with the thought that its authority on matters of *dharma* is broadly accepted.

2. As I point out in my objections, two of the views that I consider imply not only that all living beings have intrinsic value and direct moral standing, but that everything—both living and non-living—does. This implication turns out to be problematic, however. See sections 4 and 5 below.

3. So 'environmenal ethic' should not be understood as a success term in this context, equivalent to "plausible ethic of the environment" or "adequate ethic of the environment", since authors disagree widely on what constitutes a plausible ethic of the environment. One justification for these criteria is that if non-sentient entities in nature do not have intrinsic value and/or direct moral standing, then environmental ethics is not really a distinct subdiscipline. It is simply one of many areas within the field of ethics (and/or animal ethics), much like medical ethics or business ethics, that deal fundamentally with the ways that human beings should treat one another (and perhaps other sentient entities) (Norton 1984, 131–2). This is why many of those who deny the plausibility of an environmental ethic still define an environmental ethic in this way (such as Thompson [1990]).

4. The argument also assumes, uncontroversially, that the relevant class of non-sentient entities—so-called lower animals, plants, and so on—are included in the class of living beings.

5. *Bhagavadgītā* 10.20, for example, reads, "I am the *ātman*, O Arjuna, that resides in the heart of all beings (*aham ātmā guḍākeśa sarvabhūtāśayasthitaḥ/*)" (Sadhale 2000b, 234).

6. I say "in some sense" in order to make the argument consistent with a variety of metaphysical pictures, including Advaita and Viśiṣṭādvaita. See below.

7. Ryali also mentions the correlation between *ātman* and *Brahman* in his analysis of Hinduism's conception of "man's relationship with nature" (Ryali 1973: 48). He says, "*Brahman* resides in *atman* and indeed *Brahman* is *atman*" (Ryali 1973, 49). His view, like Rambachan's, is

ambiguous—it is not clear if he takes the *ātman* to be identical with *Brahman*, or simply part of *Brahman*.

8. *Gītā* 11.20, for example, reads, "All space between heaven and earth is occupied by you [Kṛṣṇa] alone (*dyāvāpṛthivyor idam antaraṃ hi vyāptaṃ tvayaikena diśaś ca sarvāḥ'*)" (Sadhale 2000, 293). 18.20 states, "Know that knowledge to be sattvic by which [a person] sees the one eternal being in all beings, the undivided in the divided (*sarvabhūteṣu yenaikaṃ bhāvam avyayam īkṣate / avibhaktaṃ vibhakteṣu taj jñānaṃ viddhi sāttvikam //*)" (Sadhale 2000c, 330).

9. Vasudha Narayanan ascribes this view to Deutsch (Narayanan 1997, 298).

10. A number of authors outline the implications of Vedāntin "monism," such as Ryali (1973, 49), Kinsley (1991, 239), and Christopher Key Chapple (1993, 75). Presumably they have some version of IA in mind as well.

11. Gītā 10.8, for example, reads: "I am the source of all. From me all arises (*ahaṃ sarvasya prabhavo mattaḥ sarvaṃ pravartate /*)" (Sadhale 2000b, 218).

12. *Brahman*, on this view, is the material, or what Julius Lipner calls the "substantial cause" (*upādānakāraṇa*) of the world (Lipner 1986, 82).

13. Note that this sense of identity is different from the sense of identity in IA. One might say that a certain person, plant, or animal is God in the sense that they in part constitute God, without claiming that a certain person, plant, or animal is qualitatively and numerically identical with God.

14. David Kinsley also claims that everything is a manifestation of *Brahman* as part of an argument for a Hindu environmental ethic (Kinsley 1991, 239). Also see Deutsch (Deutsch 1970, 83).

15. It should be no surprise that many of these authors advance more than one version of SA. The *Ātman* Argument, after all, is entailed by IA and EA (so long as the identity cited in AA is qualified appropriately), but does not entail either.

16. I take Moore's formulation to be equivalent to the formulation of intrinsic value that I offer above, according to which intrinsic value is value independent of both means-end relations and what might be called "valued-valuer relations". John O'Neill offers what he takes to be examples of other types of relations that are excluded by Moore's formulation, but which do not reduce to either the means-end or valuer-valued relation. He offers the example of wilderness, and argues that it has value "because it is untouched by humans" (O'Neill: 1992, 125). Yet the relation of being untouched by humans does not reduce to the means-end or valuer-valued relation. The problem with the example is that it is not obvious that the value that wilderness has in virtue of being wilderness is intrinsic. If it is not, then the example does not demonstrate that intrinsic value excludes relations other than the means-end and valuer-valued relations. The same is true of O'Neill's example of rarity (O'Neill 1992, 124).

17. See also Basant K. Lal (1986, 200-1) and Rita DasGupta Sherma (1998, 95).

18. *nainaṃ chindanti śastrāṇi nainaṃ dahati pāvakaḥ | na cainaṃ kleday-anty āpo na śoṣayati mārutaḥ | . . . na hanyate hanyamāne śarīre ||* (Sadhale 2000a, 136 and 119). Both Śaṅkara and Rāmānuja interpret the verses straightforwardly.

19. See footnote 21 below for an objection and reply.

20. Each version of the transfer problem is unique to the present context. Intrinsic value cannot be transferred in the above way because intrinsic value is the value that an entity has independent of its relations to other things, and direct moral standing cannot be transferred in the above way because the initial entity from which direct moral standing is supposed to transfer (the *ātman*) does not have direct moral standing in the first place. I don't mean to say that there is a problem in transferring qualities from one entity to another more generally.

21. Neither Hindu traditions in general nor Vedāntin traditions are uniform in their characterization of the relations between *Brahman*, *ātman*, and the body, but these are the most dominant conceptions.

22. *Bṛhadāraṇyaka Upaniṣad* identifies both *Brahman* and *ātman* as the inner controller (*antaryāmiṇa*) of the body (BU 3.7.1), but also describes the *ātman* as free of hunger, thirst, pain, and delusion (BU 3.5.1).

23. This is surely the Sāṃkhyan and Yogic view, which the *Gītā*, Śaṅkara, Rāmānuja, and others generally adopt. There are some passages, however, such as *Gītā* 17.6, that suggest that both *ātman* and *Brahman* are indeed affected by the events of the body. The verse reads: "the mindless, causing harm to the body, [which is] the aggregate of physical elements, also [cause harm to] me within the body. Know them as demonic [in their] intentions (*karśayantaḥ śarīrasthaṃ bhūtagrāmam acetasaḥ māṃ caivāntaś śarīrasthaṃ tān viddhy āsuraniścayān ||*)" (Sadhale 2000c, 248). These kinds of passages are overshadowed by the more common and extensive claims to the contrary, which emphasize a radical dualism between *ātman/Brahman* and the body. The former are, however, quite promising as bases for the development of a Hindu environmental ethic. (My thanks to an anonymous referee at *Comparative Philosophy* for this point.)

24. By "equal value" I mean value that is both of the same kind and of the same quantity.

25. An objection might go as follows. An ethic is action guiding if it draws the distinction between right and wrong. The distinction between right and wrong, however, might not depend on the distinction between good and bad. This is what Kant, among others, asserts. Yet Kant's view also depends on ascribing intrinsic value to human beings (and denying it to other entities and things).

26. Nelson argues that Advaita and the *Bhagavadgītā* deny that the material world has intrinsic value (Nelson 1998, 2000). I don't think his

argument succeeds, but the distinction between conventional and ultimate reality cannot refute it, for the same reasons I outline here.

27. *aham sarvasya prabhavaḥ* . . . (Sadhale 2000b, 218).

28. *aham sarvasya vicitracidacitprapañcasya prabhava utpattikāraṇam* . . . (Sadhale 2000b, 219, lines 27–28).

29. It might be objected that according to some of the texts and systems that imply the Emanation Argument, different things instantiate Brahman to different degrees, and hence that different things have varying levels of intrinsic value and/or direct moral standing. Rāmānuja, for example, explains *Gītā* 2.16, which states, "Existence is not found among the unreal. Non-existence is not found among the real (*nāsato vidyate bhāvo nābhāvo vidyate sataḥ /*)" (Sadhale 2000a, 102), by quoting *Viṣṇu Purāṇa*: "Consciousness (*jñāna*) is real, whereas all else is unreal (*jñānam yathā satyam asatyam anyat*)" (Sadhale 2000a, 104, line 35). If consciousness is more real than non-consciousness, then perhaps conscious entities are more valuable, or have greater direct moral standing, than non-conscious entities. If this is right, then the vacuity objection might be avoided—a living body is more valuable than a dead body because the living body is conscious.

   If this is the argument, however, then proponents of the Emanation Argument must make this case explicitly, and presumably concede that it is not simply the fact that an entity emanates from Brahman that makes it valuable/worthy of consideration, but something more. Additionally, even if this case is made, the account faces some of the other problems I have raised above. In the same passage in which Rāmānuja states that consciousness is more real than non-consciousness, he says that "the real has the nature of indestructibility (*vināśasvabhāvo hy asattvam avināśasvabhāvaś ca sattvam*)" (Sadhale 2000a, 104, line 33). If consciousness is indestructible, then it is not clear that it can be harmed, and hence unclear how it can have direct moral standing. (This is not to say that it cannot be. But some case must be made that this is so.) Additionally, it seems to be the conscious entity that resides in the material body—and not the biological entity per se—that is truly real, and hence not the material body that has greater value or moral standing.

30. So long as "eternal" is taken to mean always existent in both the past and present.

31. If this argument succeeds, then it might be inferred from each of the classical Indian *darśanas*—including, with some modifications, Nyāya, which denies that liberation is pleasurable.

32. In what follows, I focus on the *Manusmṛti* in particular, although the views of the *Manusmṛti*—along with its authority—are accepted quite broadly. Perrett's argument above, for example, seems to come from Śaṅkara's *Gītābhāṣya* 6.32, which explains that the yogin knows, by analogy with himself, that pleasure is desirable and pain undesirable, no matter whose it is.

33. *tamasā bahurūpeṇa veṣṭitāḥ karmahetunā / antaḥsaṃjñā bhavanty ete sukhaduḥkhasamanvitāḥ //* (Jhā 1999a, 29).

34. One small oddity arises here. In order for a theory to count as an environmental ethic, it must ascribe intrinsic value and direct moral standing to non-sentient entities. If the *Manusmṛti* ascribes intrinsic value and direct moral standing to entities in virtue of their sentience, however, then it technically fails to ascribe intrinsic value and direct moral standing to non-sentient entities, even though it attributes sentience to plants and so-called lower animals. In order to avoid this counter-intuitive consequence, the criteria for an environmental ethic ought to be interpreted to read: in order for a theory to count as an environmental ethic, it must ascribe intrinsic value and direct moral standing to entities normally considered non-sentient, such as plants and lower animals.

35. *manuṣyāṇāṃ paśūnāṃ ca duḥkhāya prahṛte sati / yathā yathā mahadduḥkhaṃ daṇḍaṃ kuryāt tathā tathā //* (Jha 1999b, 196).

36. *samutpattiṃ ca māṃsasya vādhabandhau ca dehinām / prasamīkṣya nivarteta sarvamāṃsasya bhakṣaṇāt //* (Jhā 1999a, 441).

37. *atas tamobahulyān nityaṃ nirvedaduḥkhādiyuktā adharmaphalam anubhavantaḥ suciram āsate / sattvasyāpi tatra bhāvāt kasyāṃcid avasthāyāṃ sukhaleśam api bhuñjate /* (Jhā 1999a, 30, lines 2–3).

38. I don't mean to imply here that killing an entity allows it to avoid the suffering it would have experienced. A standard view is that this suffering is moral desert, and hence that the entity will experience it in the next life.

39. The word "good" here is shorthand for "good of its own". Taylor explains that the difference between living beings and artifacts is that the artifacts' goods "ultimately refer to the goals their human producers had in mind when they made [them]." (They might also simply refer to the goals that the artifacts' users ascribe to them.) The goods of living beings, in contrast, are "inherent to them," that is, they are independent of the intentions of other entities (Taylor 1986, 124).

40. This kind of argument is advanced by Taylor (1986), O'Neill (1992), Rolston (1994), Norton (1984), Lee (1996), and many others. The claim that certain living beings have a good is controversial, however. I deal with these issues in another paper in progress.

41. Louis G. Lombardi levels this criticism against Taylor, and offers a response like the one I have just outlined (Lombardi 1983).

CHAPTER 3

Gandhi's Contributions to Environmental Thought and Action

BART GRUZALSKI

LAL AND GANDHI'S ECOLOGICAL VISION OF LIFE

Many environmentalists consider Gandhi the father of the environmental movement in India, and environmentalists around the world celebrate his contributions to environmental thought and action. In a recent article in *Environmental Ethics*, Vinay Lal raised doubts about Gandhi's status as "the father of Indian environmentalism,"[1] but promised to provide an argument "for viewing Gandhi as a man with a profoundly ecological view of life."[2] In the first section of this paper, I briefly summarize Lal's reasons for thinking that Gandhi had a profoundly ecological view of life. I take issue with Lal's claims, for they would leave a reader, unfamiliar with Gandhi, with a distorted view of Gandhi's significant contributions to the environmental movement. In sections following my discussion of Lal's article, I describe these significant contributions.

Lal rejects the idea that Gandhi was an environmentalist,[3] but provides four reasons to support his thesis that "Gandhi's social practices and conduct is writ large in his ecological vision of life."[4] (1) "As nature provides for the largest animals as much as it provides for its smallest creations, so Gandhi allowed this principle to guide him in his political and social relations with all manner of women and men."[5] (2) "Gandhi was resolutely of the view that nature should be allowed to take its own course."[6] (3) "Gandhi transformed the idea of waste [undeveloped land] and rendered it pregnant with meanings that were the inverse of those meanings invested in it by European representational regimes."[7] In particular, Lal claims Gandhi "was inclined to the opposite view that man was prone to transform whatever he touched, however fertile, fecund, or productive, into waste."[8] (4) Lal's final support for Gandhi's "profoundly ecological view of life" is that "Gandhi did not make of his ecological sensitivities a cult or religion."[9] I assess in turn each of these alleged supports for Gandhi's ecological vision of life and show why these four supports fail.

1. Lal's first support for Gandhi's ecological vision of life is that "as nature provides for the largest animals as much as it provides for its smallest creations, so Gandhi allowed this principle to guide him in his political and social relations with all manner of women and men."[10] There is no evidence that Gandhi intentionally guided his conduct with a principle that nature provisions the smallest and largest animals equally. Furthermore, there is no such principle. Small mammals such as mice, snakes, small birds, and insects have a significantly higher rate of infant mortality than elephants, human beings, or whales. Gandhi practiced egalitarianism and firmly believed that all people were created equal.[11] Gandhi, in order to show his identity with the poorest in India, eventually dressed in the only clothes many of them could afford, a simple loincloth.

2. Lal's second support is that "Gandhi was resolutely of the view that nature should be allowed to take its own course."[12] The author cites several alleged examples of Gandhi exemplifying this view. One was Gandhi's use of "nature cures." The problem is that "allowing nature to take its own course" suggests no cures whatever. Lal also cites Gandhi's remark that flies causing his colleagues exasperation were only doing what he, Gandhi, would do were he a fly. For Gandhi to say that the flies were only doing what he would do were he a fly was plausibly one way that Gandhi tried to persuade his colleagues not to harm them. Another example Lal offers of letting nature take its course is that Gandhi didn't kill snakes. The most obvious explanation of Gandhi not killing snakes is Gandhi's commitment to *ahimsa* (non-violence). The author considers this possibility but rejects it because "such an interpretation ignores the critical primacy accorded to *satya* (truth) over *ahimsa* (non-violence) in Gandhian thinking, much

as it overlooks the fact that Gandhi was an advocate of the mercy killing of animals."[13] Lal never explains what the former clause means or how the idea that truth has primacy over non-violence supports the rejection of non-violence as the explanation of Gandhi's not killing (healthy) snakes. Lal also does not explain why the mercy killing of nonhuman animals who are suffering undermines non-violence as his rationale for not killing healthy snakes. More importantly, Gandhi's advocacy of mercy killing for nonhuman animals hardly shows a commitment to let nature take its course. Letting nature take its course, in the case of a dying animal, more plausibly is to let the animal die without any intervention.

3. Lal's third support for Gandhi's "profoundly ecological view of life" is that "Gandhi transformed the idea of waste and rendered it pregnant with meanings that were the inverse of those meanings invested in it by European representational regimes."[14] The author notes that "almost nothing was as much anathema to European colonizers as the idea that the vast lands [of India] . . . were entirely unproductive or certainly not as productive as they thought desirable."[15] The author uses this European idea as a contrast to Gandhi who "was inclined to the opposite view that man was prone to transform whatever he touched, however fertile, fecund, or productive, into waste."[16] One would expect that Lal would carefully document a claim that Gandhi held such a profoundly negative view of all human activity. Instead, the author cites two examples. In one, Gandhi criticized a colleague for taking a branch off of a plant rather than just the few leaves that he needed. In another example Gandhi expressed pain that people would pluck flowers for garlands or would throw flowers in his direction. We more accurately read these examples as illustrations of Gandhi's *ahimsa* and his respect for the sacredness of all life, not as a condemnation of all human activity as productive of waste. Gandhi was clear that he regarded even "the destruction of vegetable life as *himsa* [violence]."[17]

4. Lal's final support for Gandhi's "profoundly ecological view of life" is that "Gandhi did not make of his ecological sensitivities a cult or religion."[18] Lal illustrates this claim with Gandhi's tolerance toward those who ate meat and a similar comment about alcohol. However, Lal fails to note that Gandhi often had tolerance toward those committed to violence. Gandhi's tolerance was part of his *ahimsa* and his commitment to convert, persuade,

and transform those who were not vegetarians, drank alcohol, or were not committed to non-violence. He did not believe it would be useful to coerce meat eaters, drinkers, or those committed to using violence into an external mimicking of the actions he advocated. "All true change comes from within," Gandhi believed. "Any change brought about by pressure is worthless."[19] Even though being tolerant while trying to persuade others to adopt a perspective in which one believes is often taken as evidence of wisdom, it is not evidence or support for believing that the tolerant person has an ecological vision. Polluters can and do upon occasion tolerantly encourage others to adopt their perspective.

Lal's support for Gandhi's "ecological vision of life" distorts our view of Gandhi and fails to show how Gandhi could have become an inspiration for the environmental movement. In what follows, I develop several of Gandhi's contributions to environmental thought and action, beginning with his non-violence.[20]

Non-Violence and Non-Cooperation

Gandhi's non-violence is one of his most important contributions to environmentalism. For Gandhi, non-violence was both a means to an end as well as a constituent of the society toward which he struggled. Environmental activists worldwide today use non-violence to defend environmental values in the various arenas in which environmental activism is taking place. In addition, there is a convincing environmental rationale to strive for a nonviolent society. A nonviolent society would refrain from huge military expenditures that lead to emissions causing global warming, to resource depletion, and to waste generation. Finally, a non-violent society would renounce warfare, which, especially in modernity, is a cause of serious ecological damage.

While non-violence is both a means and an end from a Gandhian perspective, and while the implementation of both would produce a better environmental future, the idea of non-violence that most obviously informs environmentalism is non-violence as a technique for highlighting and preventing environmental harms. An important variety of this non-violence is noncooperation. Noncooperation can be as simple as being a vegetarian, thereby not contributing to the environmental degradation of factory farms, or using bicycles instead of motorized vehicles, and thereby not contributing to the emissions that are causing global warming and climate change. These and many other activities can become organized efforts to boycott practices that environmentalists claim cause ecological destruction. If consumers were to stop using the products produced by those industries that are degrading ecosystems, those destructive practices would soon cease. Of course, doing so would require consumers to begin to live more simply and more self-reliantly, two essential themes of Gandhi's thought.

SIMPLE LIVING IN PLACE OF CONSUMERISM

While non-violence and noncooperation have become the tools of environmental activists in India and around the globe, non-violence as a technique does not explicitly address the causes of the ecological crises that we and future generations face. According to the World Wide Fund for Nature, because human activities are already thirty percent above the Earth's carrying capacity, people in the developed world need to consider reducing their consumption.[21] The greenhouse effect and the resultant warming trend "that many scientists expect will characterize coming decades"[22] are now predicted to have dire consequences unprecedented since humans have been on the planet. Current predictions are for warming in the next ninety years in the United States greater than the warming we have experienced since the last ice age. The oceans are predicted to rise nineteen inches and perhaps as high as thirty-seven inches. Looking at the worldwide effects of global pollution and the greenhouse effect, it is predicted that, in the next twenty years, up to seventy-five percent of the world's people, most in poor countries, may be at risk from droughts and floods. A Christian Aid spokesperson claims that nine of the past eleven catastrophes to which Christian Aid responded were caused by extreme weather conditions that were produced by the pollution of the wealthiest countries.[23] Although there may not be consensus on these various claims and predictions, there is a near consensus on both the general effects of the greenhouse effect and one of its chief causes, overconsumption.

Gandhi emphasized what is the only clear antidote to overconsumption: simple living. Living simply, for Gandhi, means rejecting the "artificial increases in our wants" and rearranging our lives so that we will "refuse to have what millions cannot."[24] Gandhi believed that "insofar as we have made the modern materialistic craze our goal, in so far are we going downhill in the path of progress. I hold that economic progress in the sense I have put it [modern materialistic craze] is antagonistic to real progress."[25] Because progress lay in a different direction, whether individual, community-level, or national, Gandhi thought that simple living is worth the attempt "even though only an individual or a group makes the effort."[26]

Gandhi thought that we were seriously deceived when we thought that bigger, faster, and more are better. These are the "positive" goals of modern urban civilization, he wrote:

> Whose roadways are traversed by rushing engines, dragging numerous cars crowded with men who know not for the most part what they are after, who are often absentminded, and whose tempers do not improve by being uncomfortably packed like sardines in boxes and finding themselves in the midst of utter strangers who would oust them if they could and whom they would, in their turn, oust similarly. I refer to these things because they are held to be symbolical of material progress. But they add not an atom to our happiness.[27]

Contemporary environmentalists reiterate Gandhi's critique of our mesmerization with the goods of modernity and the notion of progress as "more," "bigger," and "faster." Maneka Gandhi, a former Indian Minister of State for Environment and Forestry, claims that the main cause of environmental degradation in India is "the constant brain-washing to the effect that ideal living, prosperity, means the Western way of life—more of everything, bigger, faster, more waste-gener-ating. This conception generates imitation and raises consumption levels of people who cannot afford it. It also destroys a biomass-based economy without replacing it with anything better."[28] Maneka Gandhi sees this "brainwashing" as involving the adoption of the economic orthodoxy of our time: "the greatest harm done to the environment by the West is through the spread of an ideology on growth which has taken firm roots among our third world elite. The axioms of this ideology are simple: more growth is good; less growth is worrying; negative growth is disastrous. The relationship between growth and welfare is ignored. Are the goods produced valuable? Are they benefi-cial? Have they been distributed to all?"[29]

It is clear that Gandhi's critique of the orthodox views of progress in the West has both supported and inspired current environmentalists in India and elsewhere. The foreseeable ecological crises that we face provide reasons to conclude that we need to think about changing our lives to a degree to which we would not have even thought about a few years ago. Economist Juliet Schor, in describing the growing movement that is "addressing the environmental, cultural, and social effects of the old American dream and trying to devise a new one," remains positive about our abilities to create a new future: "It can hardly be possible that the dumbing-down of America has proceeded so far that it's either consumerism or nothing. We remain a creative, resourceful, and caring nation. There's still time left to find our way out of the mall."[30]

INAPPROPRIATE PRODUCTION AND APPROPRIATE TECHNOLOGY

Gandhi's work for full employment led him to what today we call appropriate technology. He was critical of the use of machinery in mass production for several reasons. One involved his criticism of globalization and the fact that those who produce with machinery can control those who lack the machinery. Another was that the use of machinery created unemployment.[31] Objecting to "the craze for machinery, not machinery as such," he wrote:

> The craze is for what they call labour-saving machinery. Men go on 'saving labour' till thousands are without work and thrown on the open streets to die of starvation. I want to save time and labour, not for a fraction of mankind, but for all. I want the concentration of wealth, not in the hands of a few, but in the hands of all.[32]

Gandhi considered large-scale machinery destructive because it created unemployment, although he was not against "simple tools and instruments and such machines as saves individual labour and lightens the burden of the millions of cottages."[33] "My opposition to machinery is much misunderstood. I am not opposed to machinery as such. I am opposed to machinery which displaces labour and leaves it idle."[34]

Gandhi endorsed what today we would call "appropriate technology," that is, technology that is appropriate to the aim and goals and wherewithal of a people in a place. The aim was "not to produce village articles as cheap as possible; it [was] to provide the workless villagers with work at a living wage."[35] Given this aim, those technologies and social arrangements that would foster full employment were appropriate, whereas technologies of mass production that left people unemployed were not.[36]

The principal village industry is agriculture. Gandhi recommended intensive, small-scale farming, composting, and returning manure to the land—practices that would be essential in order not to degrade ecosystems for future generations. These practices would not suffice to create full employment. Gandhi knew that other village industries, consistent with agriculture, were needed to meet the goals of full employment. Gandhi believed that the spinning wheel would not only solve the problem of unemployment, but that its beneficial economic effects would radiate throughout the community:

> It is not merely the wages earned by the spinners that are to be counted but it is the whole reconstruction that follows in the wake of the spinning wheel. The village weaver, the village dyer, the village washerman, the village blacksmith, the village carpenter, all and many others will then find themselves reinstated in their ancient dignity, as is already happening wherever the spinning wheel has gained a footing.[37]

The spinning wheel would not only help create full employment, but by replacing polluting machinery and the need to transport goods great distances, its use would mitigate the environmental harm of other technologies and the transport of goods.

Today, in the West, we tend to emphasize the consequences to the environment as one of the criteria of appropriate technology. Bringing in the positive value of environmental protection broadens Gandhi's notion of appropriate technology to include solar power, compost toilets, and much more.

DECENTRALIZATION RATHER THAN GLOBALIZATION

Given that Gandhi was a critic of overconsumption, it is unsurprising that he was a critic of "industrialism" and "mass production," two terms that refer to what we currently call "globalization." Many environmentalists today consider globalization to be the mechanism for worldwide ecological degradation. Although neither Gandhi nor anyone in his time focused on worldwide environmental problems and their link to globalization, in one of Gandhi's many warnings about the spread of industrialism he used a metaphor that we would use today to express our concern for the ecological destruction caused by globalization: "God forbid that India should ever take to industrialism after the manner of the West. If an entire nation of 300 millions took to similar economic exploitation, it would strip the world bare like locusts."[38] If we focus on Gandhi's metaphor of people stripping "the world like locusts," the image is one of ecological disaster if India successfully followed the West. Eco-economist Herman Daly's warning about globalizing U.S. levels of consumption explicitly expresses a similar environmental concern: "Crises of depletion, pollution, and ecological breakdown would be the immediate consequences of generalizing U.S. resource consumption standards to the whole world."[39]

Gandhi's primary criticism of globalization was not environmental, but instead focused on the exploitation inherent in globalization. Gandhi saw mass production and industrialism as the vehicles for this exploitation, and saw the major world powers in Europe and America using these vehicles "to exploit the so-called weaker or unorganized races of the world."[40] He saw that globalization would be disastrous for the rural villager.

To clarify how globalization can exploit the villager, imagine a rural village economy that is self-reliant with respect to its agriculture. Suppose further that markets are opened and that large mechanized farms in another nation can import grain into the village area at a price significantly below that which the village farmer needs to continue production. The result is that the village farmer will go out of business and the people will begin relying on imported grain. The lower price for the imported product is a function of an economics of scale (large mechanized farms), new hybrids, pesticides, and inexpensive chemical fertilizers. While each of these cause ecological degradation, Gandhi's focus was on how they make agricultural products vulnerable to volatile price fluctuations. Whenever machinery or vehicles are used for production or transportation of grain, the price of the grain will partly depend on the price of fuels. Furthermore, if grain is imported across a national boundary, its cost will also be affected by currency speculation. As a result, a person's access to the very grain she needs for her family is dependent on causes beyond her control that had no affect on her at all when she produced her own grain.

To avoid this problem, which was affecting millions of people, Gandhi insisted on decentralization of the production of food and clothing.[41] His idea was that "every village has to be self-reliant. Things required in a village should be produced in the village itself."[42] Gandhi wanted each family, if possible, to grow its basic commodities because these were money crops "and, therefore, subject to the fluctuations of the market."[43] Gandhi believed that "the farmer needs to know that his first business is to grow for his own needs. When he does that, he will reduce the chance of a low market ruining him."[44]

Gandhi also believed that decentralized production in small villages resolves the problem of the distribution of goods and tends to solve the problem of overproduction: "When production and consumption both become localized, the temptation to speed up production, indefinitely and at any price, disappears."[45] This element of Gandhian thought also has powerful ecological implications.

When a people produce and consume within the same locality, they do not rely on the transportation that produces greenhouse gases and carcinogens. Furthermore, the localization of production and consumption within a locality allows people to experience firsthand the ecological benefits and costs of economic practices. As a result, they are more able to live in an ecologically responsible manner and even come to protect their local ecosystems. As Wendell Berry has pointed out, "When there is no reliable accounting and therefore no competent knowledge of the economic and ecological effects of our lives, we cannot live lives that are economically and ecologically responsible."[46] In the next section, I show one specific example of how Gandhi's emphasis on local, self-reliant economies brought about an environmental movement in India.[47]

FROM LOCAL ECONOMIES TO CHIPKO

The day before his assassination, in what has become known as his "last will and testament," Gandhi wrote that the Indian National Congress had achieved political independence and should disband. The goal was to "uplift" the rural villages. In 1956, Sunderlal Bahuguna, a Congress party leader in northern India, decided to follow Gandhi's last wish. Bahuguna inspired other idealistic youth, including Chandi Prasad Bhatt. New poverty in the hills had led to a migration of the men to the plains below in search of jobs. Bhatt wanted to find occupational alternatives so that the young men could stay in their own villages. Increased development in the village hill areas in 1962 did not help the young village men, since managerial, skilled and semiskilled jobs went to outside workers. Bhatt and his coworkers decided to organize the village men. Their mixed successes convinced them that the forests held the key to the economic vitality of the local people.[48] "The quest," explains Bahuguna, "was to find a solution to the problem of poverty."[49]

During this time there was little awareness of the fragility of the hill forest ecosystems and the impact of these ecosystems on the millions of people living in the northern plains. The manifesto issued by cooperative workers only a year before the 1970 floods reveals this lack of watershed and ecological consciousness:

> Since time immemorial, forests have remained the socioeconomic basis of our lives. Protection of trees is our main duty and we solicit our birthright to get our basic needs and employment in forests and forest products. To maintain a loving relationship with forests, the basis of

our happiness, it is essential that the treasure of the forests be used primarily for the needs of the inhabitants of this region. For this the material used in village industry and other daily needs should be made available to the common-folk and small industries should be set up in the vicinity of forest for the processing of raw materials obtained there. Cooperative societies of forest laborers should be established and the contractor system should be done away with.[50]

The 1970 monsoon rains changed these attitudes. The floods inundated the region, destroying bridges, buses, crops, and killing fifty people.[51] These floods created a new ecological consciousness among the cooperative workers who, organizing relief operations, came to see the connection between bad forest policy and floods they now knew to be man-made.

This new awareness, combined with the focus on local industries for village people, prepared the way for the emergence of the Chipko movement. In 1973 the cooperative workers faced another struggle over the government's allocating trees to a company that was not local. In Gandhian fashion, a public meeting was held to determine the form of direct action. After much discussion, those present endorsed the tactic that "when these people go to cut them, we cling to the trees and dare them to let their axes fall on our backs."[52] The group drafted a resolution to explain the proposed action to government and forestry department officials. When the loggers arrived to cut the trees, they met a hundred activists committed to stopping them. The movement India and the world knows as "Chipko" (a Hindi word roughly translated as "hug" and referring to tree-hugging tactics) had realized its first success.

The Chipko movement broadened its focus to include maintaining the forests as an ecological resource. As a result, Chipko became involved in reforestation. The average survival of Chipko plantings was eighty to ninety percent compared with a dismal ten percent survival rate of government reforestation projects.[53] Local involvement and awareness also filled the gap created by the ineffectiveness of a central government trying to prevent the illegal smuggling of forest products. A noteworthy example of the effectiveness of local guardianship occurred in India 1982 when unarmed Chipko women volunteers caught an armed battalion of timber smugglers in Kashmir.[54] These examples illustrate the ways in which Gandhi's emphasis on local self-reliant economies led to ecological awareness and a resultant reduction of ecologically destructive practices.

Gandhi's Proposal for Self-Reliant Villages

Perhaps Gandhi's most controversial proposal was for self-reliant villages. Gandhi's idea of the independent, self-reliant village was "a complete republic, independent of its neighbors for its own vital wants, and yet interdependent for many others [wants] in which dependence is a necessity. Thus every village's first concern will be to grow its own food crops and cotton for its cloth."[55] To support the self-reliant village, Gandhi encouraged urban consumers to purchase village products in order "to give the villages their proper place."[56] Everyone was to help "revive village industries by using the products thereof in place of things produced in city factories, foreign or indigenous."[57]

Gandhi's focus on self-reliant communities as an antidote to globalization has enormous ecological implications. Recent authors have criticized Gandhi's proposal for self-reliant communities and the localization of production and consumption as "naive," "unrealistic," "utopian," "pushing the clock back," and even "wooly minded."[58] Early in his struggles in India, Gandhi confronted similar criticisms. To one complaint that focused on the spinning wheel, Gandhi replied: "Is it such a visionary ideal—an attempt to revive an ancient occupation whose destruction has brought on slavery, pauperism, and the disappearance of inimitable artistic talent?"[59] To another, Gandhi asked rhetorically: "Why am I turning back the course of modern civilization, when I ask the villager to grind his own meal, eat it whole, including the nourishing bran, or when I ask him to turn his sugarcane into gur for his own requirements, if not for sale? Am I turning back the course of modern civilization when I ask the villagers not merely to grow raw produce, but to turn it into marketable products and thereby add a few more pies to their daily income?"[60] We now know that eating fresh, unprocessed food containing roughage is much healthier than eating the overly processed food that in colonized areas becomes a status symbol of wealth and prestige. We also know that, economically, a region is better off if its people export processed raw materials to which their own labor has added value.

Gandhi's responses pale in comparison to those we can make when we realize that Gandhi's proposal is a viable alternative to prevent or at least minimize as far as possible foreseeable ecological crises caused by overconsumption and the unnecessary transportation of goods. The consumer way of life requires each family and often each individual to have entertainment equipment, multiple changes of clothing, private bathroom facilities, private vehicles, a kitchen fully equipped with appliances, and, if there is a yard involved, lawnmower and garden equipment. These constitute the complete household "set" of indoor and outdoor equipment and the vehicle(s) necessary for transportation. In the United States, we have built infrastructures that force us to rely on motorized vehicles to get to work, for shopping, for school, and even for play. As a result, we pollute air and water and use land that otherwise might be left as green space or used for gardens and agriculture.

If we want to reduce the wastes generated and the resources extracted in the production of the standard set of household goods now thought the norm in the United States, an obvious change would be to share many of these goods. For example, a lawnmower is used only occasionally, so different people could use the same lawnmower. With significantly more effort put into coordination, people could share the same vehicles. If we are willing to rethink the standard single-family-home design and turn to Gandhi's model of a self-reliant village, the savings of time and effort are multiplied. For example, in a self-reliant community there would only need to be a few vehicles for an entire community. Taking Gandhi's own intentional community ashrams as a model for how people can live and rethinking them for other cultures and environments, we could develop ways of living that use significantly fewer resources.

Consider, for example, the intentional community of Twin Oaks in Louisa, Virginia. This community is not modeled on Gandhian principles but reflects a significant move away from the nuclear family style of living and in the direction of a Gandhian community model. There are public living rooms for every five to ten people, shared bathrooms, small kitchens available to every dozen or so people, while each person has his or her own private room. Community members prepare meals for the entire community three times a day in a central dining area. People work in the community, so there is no commuting. Through sharing tools, appliances, and space, individuals living at Twin Oaks consume significantly fewer resources than those living an equivalent life style elsewhere in North America.

When we consider the ecological harm of consumerism and the unnecessary duplication (hence production and eventual disposal) of machines and appliances that are underused or sit idle most of the time in North American homes, we see the promise of Gandhi's model of the rural self-reliant community and its variants. Intentional communities such as Twin Oaks, and others we could design and build, are workable alternatives that promise to minimize contributions to the looming ecological crises. As the ecological clocks tick and ecological conditions deteriorate, Gandhi seems much more farsighted than "wooly minded."

Gandhi's Biocentric Perspective

We have explored Gandhi's enormous contributions to the environmental movement of non-violence, decentralization, local self-reliant economies, and the self-reliant village. In addition to these contributions, Gandhi also had a remarkably biocentric perspective on the value of sentient life. Gandhi's view is that nonhuman animals have the same moral worth as human animals. "To my mind the life of a lamb is no less precious than that of a human being. I should be unwilling to take the life of a lamb for the sake of the human body. I hold that, the more helpless a creature, the more entitled it is to protection from the cruelty of man."[61]

This biocentric perspective reinforced Gandhi's vegetarianism. However, his view that all sentient life has equal worth did not lead to an implication that we should never kill nonhumans. For example, he claimed that he had an obligation to "kill a serpent threatening to bite a child under my protection, if I could not otherwise turn the reptile away."[62] He also thought that we should kill a nonhuman out of compassion to end its agony and discussed the case of a maimed calf in agony in the ashram. A physician was called and assessed that nothing could be done to help the calf. Gandhi wrote: "The suffering of the animal was so great that it could not even turn on its side without excruciating pain. In these circumstances I felt that *ahimsa*[63] demanded that the agony should be ended by ending life itself."[64]

Gandhi believed that some violence was unavoidable in the process of living, some was required by moral dilemmas, and some apparent violence (compassion from his perspective) was required in order to end the agony of a dying being whose agony could be relieved in no other way. As Gandhi summarizes his position and compares it with what then was the orthodox position in the West, he is recommending an alternative to the anthropocentric view of the value of nonhuman animals:

> The West (with the exception of a small school of thought) thinks that it is no sin to kill the lower animals for what it regards to be the benefit of man. It has, therefore, encouraged vivisection. The West does not think it wrong to commit violence of all kinds for the satisfaction of the palate. I do not subscribe to these views. According to Western standard[s], it is no sin, on the contrary it is a merit, to kill animals that are no longer useful. Whereas I recognize limits at every step.[65]

CONCLUSION

When we look at the focuses and aims of contemporary environmental spokespersons and activists, Gandhian themes are dominant. Gandhian biocentrism and his recommendations not to harm even nonsentient life unnecessarily are familiar in contemporary environmental thinking. Gandhian non-violence is both a technique of environmental activists and, for some, one of the constituents of the world for which they struggle. Gandhi emphasized simple living, an important theme for many who are concerned about looming ecological crises. Taking a broader perspective, Gandhi also criticized what we today call globalization and encouraged, in its place, the decentralization of economic activities. Gandhi's emphasis on decentralization and local economic self-reliance led to the Chipko movement in India, a nonviolent struggle to protect forests. Gandhi emphasized appropriate technologies, those technologies that were good for the people in a locality or a nation. Although today we broaden the meaning of "appropriate technologies" to include those technologies that are less harmful to the environment, Gandhi paved the way for our looking more closely at the appropriateness of our tools and machines and for favoring "small is beautiful."

One of the great strains on the carrying capacity of the planet is the consumption required by our individualistic/nuclear-family style of living. The pressures on local and global ecosystems require that we begin rethinking how we live in ways that we would not imagined a few years ago. Here, too, Gandhi seems to be more farsighted than we might have imagined, and those who wish to begin this rethinking process need to put Gandhi's model of the self-reliant village and its variants (including intentional communities) on the drawing board. While the proposal that we should live simply in self-reliant communities is a radical departure from our consumer way of life, it may be the only proposal that offers hope for significantly reducing the ecologically degrading consumption that is a major cause of looming ecological crises. The specific details of Gandhi's implementation of this way of life may not be replicable, but the general blueprint offers guidelines that can be used to make or to remake communities that are more self-reliant and ecologically sound. Although this approach may seem a drastic one, the ecological problems we face are drastic and unprecedented. Gandhi's reminder that "drastic diseases require drastic remedies"[66] is significant for us as we face a deteriorating ecological future unprecedented in the history of our species.

Notes

1. Vinay Lal, "Gandhi and the Ecological Vision of Life," *Environmental Ethics* 22 (2000): 151.
2. Ibid., p. 152.
3. Although Gandhi may not have been an environmentalist, why he might not have been can be naturally explained by the fact that there was no environmental movement during his life and no concern about global ecological degradation. Lal argues against this explanation claiming that "no one suspects that Gandhi was merely a man of his times: so it is not unlikely that Gandhi could have been an environmentalist and more, anticipating in this respect as in many others modern social and political movements" (ibid., p. 150). I see no plausibility to Lal's claim that Gandhi could have had foreknowledge of recent and current environmental concerns. Without any indication of a plausible source of such foreknowledge, it is more plausible to think that Gandhi was not an environmentalist in the same way that he was not concerned about cloning, bioengineering, or the disposal of spent nuclear fuel from nuclear reactors. Nonetheless, as I argue below, Gandhi's contributions to environmental thought and action are significant.
4. Lal, "Gandhi and the Ecological Vision of Life," p. 164.
5. Ibid.
6. Ibid., p. 165.
7. Ibid., p. 166.
8. Ibid., p. 167.
9. Ibid., p. 167.
10. Ibid., p. 164.
11. Mahatma Ghandi, *The Collected Works of Mahatma Ghandi* (Ahmedabad: Navajivan Trust, 1958), vol. 35, p. 1.
12. Lal, "Gandhi and the Ecological Vision of Life," p. 165.
13. Ibid., p. 166.
14. Ibid.
15. Ibid., pp. 166–67.
16. Ibid., p. 167.
17. Gandhi, *Collected Works,* vol. 32, p. 43.
18. Lal, "Gandhi and the Ecological Vision of Life," p. 167.
19. Gandhi, *Collected Works,* vol. 83, p. 317.
20. Lal also mentions Gandhi's nonviolence but does not attribute any ecological or environmental significance to it. Lal mentions that Gandhi was "a warrior who absolutely forsook arms" (Lal, "Gandhi and the Ecological Vision of Life," p. 152), but Lal only mentions this to reveal the "layers of the anomaly that one may see the environmentalist in him but it is difficult to describe him as an environmentalist" (ibid., p. 151). Lal notes that Gandhi "strikes a remarkable chord with all those who have . . . cherished the principles of non-violence" (ibid., p. 162), but Lal

fails to emphasize or develop this major contribution to the environmental movements. Instead, Lal holds that his account, summarized above in the text, is clearly superior to "the cliched observations that Gandhi was the 'prophet of non-violence' or an astute political campaigner unusually interested in moral questions, if we are to be fully cognizant of the profound manner in which Gandhi's entire life functioned much like an ecosystem" (ibid., p. 168). In none of these passages does Lal acknowledge the profound significance for environmental thought and action of Gandhian nonviolence as both a means and an end.

21. "WWF: Humans Pushing Planet Earth beyond Capacity," Reuters, 20 October 2000.

22. Andrew C. Revkin, "Warming Effects to be Widespread," *New York Times on the Web*, 12 June 2000.

23. Alex Kirby, "Disasters Blamed on Pollution," BBC News, 15 May 2000.

24. Gandhi, *Collected Works,* vol. 31, p. 45.

25. Ibid., vol. 13, p. 314.

26. Ibid., vol. 85, p. 206.

27. R. K. Prabhu and U. R. Rao, eds. *The Mind of Mahatma Ghandi* (Ahmedabad: Navajivan Publishing House, 1967), p. 232.

28. Maneka Gandhi, "Consumed with Rage," *Common Cause,* Autumn 1991, p. 25.

29. Ibid. She adds: "Fabric softeners? What a scam!"

30. Elizabeth Schor, *The Overspent American* (New York: Basic Books, 1997), p. 167.

31. Gandhi, *Collected Works,* vol. 87, p. 326.

32. Ibid., vol. 25, p. 251.

33. Ibid., vol. 31, p. 13.

34. Ibid., vol. 85, pp. 239–40.

35. Ibid., vol. 61, p. 250.

36. Given that our concerns are at least as ecological as they are labor-focused, today we also use this term to refer to technology that furthers ecological values. In Gandhi's time, there was almost no explicit worry about ecological destruction.

37. Gandhi, *Collected Works,* vol. 33, p. 151.

38. Ibid., vol. 38, p. 243.

39. Herman Daly, *Valuing the Earth* (Cambridge: Massachusetts Institute of Technology, 1993), p. 369.

40. Gandhi, *Collected Works,* vol. 48, p. 164.

41. Ibid., vol. 71, p. 56.

42. Ibid., vol. 87, p. 251.

43. Ibid., vol. 75, p. 151.

44. Ibid., vol. 75, p. 151.

45. Ibid., vol. 48, pp. 163–64.

46. Wendell Berry, "Back to the Land: the Radical Case for Local Economy," *The Steelhead*, no. 34 (Spring 2000): 29.

47. Gandhi acknowledged that not everything need be decentralized: "I detect no incompatibility in the idea of decentralizing, to the greatest extent possible, all industries and crafts, economically profitable in the villages of India, and centralizing or nationalizing the key and vital large industries required for India as a whole" (Gandhi, *Collected Works,* vol. 80, p. 352).

48. The material earlier in this paragraph is based on Anupam Mishra and Satyendra Tripathi, *Chipko Movement: Uttarakhand Women's Bid to Save Forest Wealth* (New Delhi: Radhakrishna, 1978), pp. 2–5; and Thomas Weber, *Hugging the Trees* (New Delhi: Penguin Books, 1987), p. 35.

49. Bahuguna, "CHIPKO: The Peoples Movement for the Protection of the Forests," in *Forests in India's Heritage,* ed. J. Bandyopadhyay and Vandana Shiva (Dehra Dun: Research Foundation for Science, Technology and Natural Resource Policy, 1985), p. 10.

50. Weber, *Hugging the Trees,* p. 34.

51. See Mishra and Tripathi, *Chipko Movement,* p. 4, and Anil Agarwal, "Gandhi's Ghost Saves the Himalayan Trees," *New Scientist,* 14 August 1975, p. 387.

52. Mishra and Tripathi, *Chipko Movement,* p. 9.

53. Irene Dankelman and Joan Davidson, *Women and Environment in the Third World* (London: Earthscan Publications, 1988), p. 50.

54. Vandana Shiva, J. Bandyopadhyay and N. D. Jayal, "Reforestation for Survival," in Bandyopadhyay and Shiva, *Forests in India's Heritage,* pp. 21–22.

55. Gandhi, *Collected Works,* vol. 76, p. 308.

56. Ibid., vol. 71, p. 103.

57. Ibid.

58. *Time,* 31 December 1999, p. 93.

59. *Young India,* 16 February 1921.

60. Gandhi, *Collected Works,* vol. 60, p. 54.

61. Mahatma Gandhi, *An Autobiography or The Story of My Experiments With Truth* (Ahmedabad: Navajivan Publishing House, 1927), pt. 3, sec. 18, p. 197.

62. Gandhi, *Collected Works,* vol. 32, p. 72.

63. The word *ahimsa* appears in the original Gujarati version in *Navajivan,* 30 September 1928. I substitute it for the word *humanity* that appears in the English text since I believe the original to be a clearer statement of Gandhi's position.

64. Gandhi, *Collected Works,* vol. 37, p. 310.

65. Ibid., vol. 32, p. 43.

66. Ibid., vol. 73, p. 108.

CHAPTER 4

Acting with Compassion: Buddhism, Feminism, and the Environmental Crisis

STEPHANIE KAZA

On my altar at home stands a small bronze casting of Kuan Yin (also known as Kannon Kanzeon in Japan), who serves to bless my meditation space and daily activity. Her robes are flowing and gracious, and in her hand she holds a vase of healing water. She stands ready to receive the suffering of the world with compassion and equanimity. Above the kitchen sink I have a picture of a carved jade Kuan Yin from China. She holds a rabbit on her arm, manifesting the spirit of harmony with life and all living beings. On my desk, covering the books and papers of my current work, is a prayer cloth of the Green Tara. She sits on a lotus dais; her aura and soft face radiate gentle and penetrating power.

I begin with Kuan Yin because she represents a feminine gender form of a realized Bodhisattva, known to many people for thousands of years as the embodiment of compassion for all beings in the vast interdependent mutually causal web. Sometimes depicted with a thousand arms, Kuan Yin reaches out to offer a thousand tools of compassion—a shovel, a flute, a blanket, a kind word. Kuan Yin is 'the Mahayana archetype of mutual support, giving life and fulfillment to the Sangha . . . of stones and clouds, of wild creatures and forests, of people . . . in the slums and prisons of our cities, not to mention our own families and friends'.[1] In the Tibetan tradition, the feminine form of the Green Tara serves as a reminder of the one who heals by her presence, serving countless beings. Her green color symbolizes the capacity to take action; her right hand forms the *mudra,* or gesture of calling forth awakening, and her left the gesture of refuge.[2]

As realized beings, Kuan Yin and Tara listen to *all* the cries of the world, not just those of people. This means they are also concerned with plants and animals, mountains and valleys, small creatures and large. The feminine compassionate presence has long been addressed by Buddhists of many cultures to relieve human sickness, grief, and poverty of spirit. In the current sweep of environmental destruction, it is Kanzeon and Tara who see and experience with us the pain and suffering of deserts, forests, soils, groundwater, oceans, and skies. They offer a model of radical presence in the world, of no separation between the one who suffers and the one who responds. The calls for action and healing arise spontaneously and naturally out of the cries of death and despair.

In this introductory work, I draw on the courage and inspiration of these Bodhisattvas to investigate the role of Buddhist practice and philosophy informed by feminist principles in support of work for the environment. As Buddhism and feminism gain strength and momentum in the Western world, the environmental crisis looms large on the horizon of our survival. I believe those trained in the self-discipline, analysis, and reflective processes of Buddhism and feminism have a powerful contribution to make in addressing the enormous challenges of environmental work. I encourage many more women and men to develop these tools for effective, grounded, sensitive, and nonviolent action on behalf of the earth.

I speak from my own perspective as a Buddhist, feminist, and environmentalist. I have been studying Zen Buddhism for sixteen years with Kobun Chino Roshi, practicing at Green Gulch and Jikogi Zen Centers in California, and serving as chair of the national Buddhist Peace Fellowship board. I have evolved as a feminist through my mother's example as a lawyer for the poor, through my experience of power relations in patriarchal workplaces and religious centers, and through examination of feminist discourse in theory, philosophy and morality. I am an environmentalist by profession, with academic training in both biology and social ethics. I have been working in the field of environmental education and conservation for twenty years and currently teach Environmental Ethics at the University of Vermont in Burlington.

I begin with principles held in common by Buddhism and feminism that are relevant to the environmental crisis. I then offer examples of these principles in action, of feminist women engaged in environmental work as Buddhist practice. This exploration is an introduction to a field of integrated perspectives which is just developing. I draw primarily on American Buddhism; the paper should not be construed to be internationally inclusive.

INTRODUCTION

When Buddhism arrived in the West, it encountered curious and bright minds of both sexes, eager for teachings and spiritual practices relevant to their lives. The search for spiritual foundation escalated in the 1960s and 1970s as sensitive men and women suffered through the paralyzing national pain of the civil rights movement and the Vietnam War. College students and activists scrutinized social values in depth and rejected much of the status quo parochialism that characterized American thinking. Spurred by their interest and, in the case of Tibet, cultural destruction, the most extensive wave of Buddhist teachers arrived in America from Tibet, Japan, Korea, Thailand, Sri Lanka, and Burma.[3]

At the same time, feminism was blossoming and gaining strength as a social movement. Women were waking up to the repressed and hidden cruelties of male domination in individual relationships as well as social institutions. In consciousness-raising groups across the United States, women examined issues of reproduction and health, power and sexual abuse, and outright misogyny. Feminist intellectuals took on the challenge of deconstructing gender-biased assumptions that underlay the foundations of Western language, politics, psychology, medicine, law, and philosophy. Feminist Buddhists questioned patriarchal Asian forms and inappropriate teacher-student conduct.[4]

Earth Day 1970 marked a watershed point in public concern for the environment. Widespread exposure to extensive environmental problems generated a wave of citizen action groups and environmental education programs. Activists pointed to the cumulative excesses of postwar industrialization and commercialization, along with skyrocketing human populations, as pressing the limits of the planet's carrying capacity. Doomsday predictions forecast large-scale environmental catastrophes long before Chernobyl, Love Canal, or the loss of the Black Forest. Antinuclear activism was a relatively new movement struggling against the enormous odds of a fearful Cold War nation.

In the two decades between Earth Day 1970 and Earth Day 1990, Buddhism, feminism, and concern for the environment in America grew and changed tremendously, reflecting a period of serious questioning of values and social structures. The maturation of understanding and insight over these two decades provides a significant setting for reviewing the role of Buddhism teachers of the 1960s and 1970s. Twenty years later, there were over 300 Buddhist centers across the country and a dozen major Buddhist publications.[5] In this period of growth, over twenty women gained recognition as formal Buddhist teachers.[6] In the 1960s, feminism was a little-known word, but by 1990, feminists had established hundreds of nonprofit organizations to support women's issues, from rape hotlines to women's history weeks. Retreats and conferences for women Buddhists were regular features on Western meditation calendars.

By Earth Day 1990, the proliferation of books, graduate programs, environmental careers, and by now well-established environmental lobbying groups was an indicator of the all-encompassing scale of the ecological situation. The environmental crisis had grown beyond local, state, national, and international capacity to handle it. Amidst the world context of North-South tension, over 1500 women from 84 countries stood in solidarity for women's environmental needs at the 1991 Women's World Congress for a Healthy Planet. One after another presented moving testimonies of economic injustice, forest degradation, loss of soil and farms, and frustration with political systems that systematically destroyed environmental resources.[7]

I believe there is a powerful confluence of thought, practice, commitment, and community in the lives of feminist Buddhists working for the environment who have lived through this history of startling change. In these two decades, leadership and participation of women in Buddhist practice have paralleled the rise in feminist theory research and explorations in conservation biology and restoration biology. A whole new generation of young people has been raised in families with feminist and/or Buddhist parents concerned about the environment. Feminists, Buddhist women practitioners, and environmental advocates are no longer isolated from one another.

The growth and maturation of these social and religious movements have come at a time when people are hungry for ethical response to the environmental problems they see around them. Yet most Americans lack the patience and moral reasoning skills to work through the complexities of environmental dilemmas. The discipline of Buddhist practice and the social analysis of feminism now bring a mature perspective to the endless suffering of the environment and a capacity to live with the tension of unresolved issues that will take more than several generations to correct.

Environmentally Relevant Principles of Buddhism and Feminism

The philosophical principles of Buddhism and feminism overlap and complement each other in a number of areas, mutually supporting an interdependent, systems-oriented view of the environment. There are also several areas in which one of these is under-developed in its traditions, practices, or teachings and is enhanced or influenced by exposure to the other. I outline here six areas of confluence, with some comments on differences that are not yet fully addressed.

Experiential Knowing

In contrast to much of Western philosophy and theology, Buddhism begins with the truth of personal experience. Experiential knowing in relationship to spiritual development is valued over textual, abstract, or other sources of knowing, which are distant from the individual.[8] The early canons of Buddha's teachings repeatedly urged the practitioner to thoroughly study his or her own experience and mental conditioning in order to break through the limitations of the falsely constructed self. The Buddha insisted his followers not take his authority as a final say on any matter, but rather sincerely investigate the teachings for themselves. Meditation practices aim to quiet and stabilize the mind so that it is capable of observing thoughts, sensations, and actions in great detail. One's own mind and experience are the places in which one learns to recognize the universal nature of suffering (the first of the Four Noble Truths in Buddhism).

Experiential knowing is based on embodied mindfulness practices that develop awareness of need and greed, the suffering of pleasure and pain, and the impermanent nature of things. The content for this learning is always one's own life. One's spiritual challenge is to investigate in depth the accumulated patterns of response to physical, social, mental, and psychological stimuli in order to liberate the practitioner from the suffering of unconsciousness. By shining the light of awareness on the nature of one's own conditioned reality, one finds the freedom to act effectively and skillfully, grounded in thorough self-knowledge. This experiential knowing or study of self in body, speech, and mind lies at the heart of all traditions of Buddhist teachings. Dogen Zenji, ninth-century Japanese Zen Master, expressed this:

> To study the buddha way is to study the self,
> To study the self is to forget the self.
> To forget the self is to be actualized by myriad things.[9]

Feminism is equally clear on the importance of experiential knowing as a foundation for social action and personal insight. The feminist movement in the United States, as well as in other countries, has consistently emphasized that women speak their own truths with their own voices. Feminists have encouraged women to reclaim the stories of their lives and speak what they know from direct experience. The personal is recognized as the political, for it is a genuine place of truth telling. This has meant speaking out about the painful suffering of sexual and environmental abuse, articulating the power of women's emotions, and hearing the realities of women's bodies and environmental health concerns. In feminist religious studies in Buddhist and other traditions, women struggle with the discontinuity between personal experience and patriarchal tradition, looking for new language, forms, and community that match women's religious experience.[10]

Feminists have validated the important realm of subjective knowing, acknowledging the inner experience of self that places the knower in an interior as well as exterior context.[11] Subjective knowing in women has been consistently denigrated by Western patriarchal cultures as self-centered, romantic, and distorted by emotionality. The scientific inquiry method, which insists on the necessity of an objective perspective, is the extreme opposite of subjective or interior knowing. It depends completely on the assumption that the actor can be separate from the object of one's actions.[12] This overlooks the critical discipline of subjective knowing that reveals the inner structure and conditioning of the individual mind. It is this built-in conditioning that limits accuracy and objectivity in perception. Integrated, experiential knowing, which includes both object of knowing and the knower herself, is necessary for understanding the complexities of the environmental crisis.

For many women, the experience of knowing in relation to the natural world develops the mind-body's response to other beings and to lunar and seasonal cycles, informed by kinesthetic and sensory awareness. Body rhythms and responses to the earth have long been celebrated in earth-based spiritual traditions such as the Goddess culture, not necessarily only by women. Among Buddhist cultures, the Japanese and others have cultivated an emotional and aesthetic attitude toward the natural world that represents intimate and prereflective encounter with the environment. In the Japanese view, nature is seen as the realm of 'spontaneous becoming'—a meeting ground for the dynamic unfolding of person, tree, rock and bird.[13]

The embodied knowing of child and mother can be a model for intimate relations with the earth.[14] The child in the womb knows only mother as earth; it is surrounded by, sustained by, and conditioned by the mother as context. Likewise, the earth is body to the woman, completely informing, conditioning, and nourishing her life. This metaphor does not imply that women have preferred access to these truths (the 'essentialist' position in feminist philosophy). Rather, embodied knowing for any person is a direct link to experience of relationship with the earth. The earth itself can be seen as Buddha's body, supporting all lives, being the Great Life.

Embodied knowing is a source of confidence for embodied spirituality and environmental political action. The Buddhist and feminist emphasis on direct experience of the environment is informed by the body as mind, rather than body and mind as separate. Through knowing based on experience, one becomes grounded in actual reality rather than in one's ideas of reality. Through this grounding, the practitioner gains a legitimate voice with which to speak personally and specifically of environmental relationships and how they are ignored, sabotaged, or otherwise denied.

Examining the Conditioned Mind

Central to Buddhist philosophy and meditation method is the practice of discriminating wisdom. This is the detailed study of how things work—both in external and internal realities and in the interaction and co-creation of the two. The purpose is to break through delusions that generate and perpetuate a sense of an independent and separately existing self. The discriminating mind can expose rationalized actions and mental-cultural-emotional habits that perceive beings as separate objects rather than as members of a web of relationships.

In the context of the environment, there are at least three prevalent patterns of thought that block relational perception.[15] One common thought habit is *stereotyping* of animals and ecosystems by describing them in oversimplified terms. People tend to lump the few characteristics they know of an organism or plant community into a generic representative that does not accurately reflect reality. For example, the generic whale is playful, altruistic, intelligent, large, and gentle—each characteristic fitting one species or another, but not existing anywhere in this combination in a real whale. Emotional responses to plant communities also lead to undifferentiated labeling. Deserts are viewed as wastelands, and all forests are seen as cool, dark places, despite the many differences in topography, climate, plant and animal inhabitants, and human history.

A second form of objectification is *projection,* in which the mind projects internalized ideas onto favored and unfavored elements of the environment. By reducing the reality of a forest to someone's idea of a forest, the community becomes objectified—seen as object with a convenient name and simplified description. 'Cute' or 'nice' animals, such as deer, rabbits, and songbirds, elicit more sympathetic responses than 'mean' animals, such as coyotes, spiders, and bats.[16] Likewise, good land is land that can be farmed or developed; bad land is what is too steep, dry, or impenetrable to be subdued.

A third prevalent thought habit is *dualistic thinking,* in which one object or idea is placed in opposition to another, often with the implication that one has power or superiority over the other. Self-other opposition forms the mental basis for anthropocentric relationships with plants and animals, as well as prejudice and racism. We-they conflicts, expressed in view of the environment as enemy, share the same mental polarizing structure as mind-body, creator-created, nature-culture dualisms.[17] The mind separates and distances one side of the polarity from the other, rather than seeing the opposites as complementary and inclusive, each arising in the context of the other.

Feminism has exposed a particular aspect of conditioned thinking generally overlooked in Buddhism: the influence of gender identity and cultural habits of objectifying women. Many writers have described in depth the suffering that has resulted from oppressive dualistic thinking, projection, and stereotyping of women. Ecofeminist philosopher Karen Warren suggests three features of oppressive conceptual frameworks that apply both to treatment of women and the environment.[18] The first, *value-hierarchical thinking* refers to placing value or giving preference to what is seen as being of higher status, as opposed to considering all things equally. The second, *value dualisms,* points to the typically Western pattern of viewing opposites as disjunct and exclusive, and then assigning moral superiority to one-half of the dualism, for example male-female, day-night, temperate-tropical, vertebrate-invertebrate.

The third feature is the *logic of domination,* the argument that justifies subordination of one opposite by the other. To uphold this logic requires considerable mental and social cooperation with oppressive cultural conditioning. One can see this logic at work in rationalizing intolerable conditions for laboratory and factory-farm animals.[19] The same dominating, objectifying mind that uses women for sex objects also justifies the use of land for strip-mining and forests for clear-cutting. Those with international power promote development projects for less industrialized nations that contribute not only to environmental degradation, but also to the oppression and further impoverishment of women.[20] In highly industrialized nations, women are subjected to aggressive domination by powerful market advertising that manipulates their desires for consumer products.

Both Buddhism and feminism provide critical tools for examining deeply the roots of antirelational thinking that support environmental destruction. Both insist on a thorough review of all aspects of the conditioned mind that perpetuate mental and physical patterns of domination. However, because Buddhism has been transmitted almost entirely through patriarchal cultures, its investigation of gender conditioning is underdeveloped. This weakens the Buddhist argument for ecological interdependence, because it misses the critical link between patterns of oppression of women and the environment. The feminist Buddhist position includes the connection, observing the nature of mind in women and men that sustains a separate self, capable of dominating humans and environment.

The Truth of Interrelatedness

The fundamental law in Buddhism is the Law of Dependent Co-Arising: that all events and beings are interdependent and interrelated. The universe is described as a mutually causal web of relationship, each action and individual contributing to the nature of many others.[21] The Pali word for this law, *Paticca-samuppada,* explains the truth in its literal meaning. *Patticca* means 'grounded on or on account of', *sam* is 'together', and *uppada* means 'arising'. Thus the whole phrase can be translated 'the being-on-account-of-arising-together'. Or in the text,

This being, that becomes:
from the arising of this, that arises;
this not being, that becomes not;
from the ceasing of this, that ceases.[22]

An image for this cosmology is the Jewel Net of Indra, from the Mahayana Buddhist tradition.[23] The multidimensional net stretches through all space and time, connecting an infinite number of jewels in the universe. Each jewel is infinitely multifaceted and reflects every other jewel in the net. There is nothing outside the Net and nothing which does not reverberate its presence throughout the web of relationships.

This law is one of the most obvious connections between Buddhism and the environment. As ecologists point out in example after example, ecological systems are connected through water, air, and soil pathways. Impacts of chemical pesticides on agricultural lands carry to adjacent wetlands; industrial carbon emissions affect global atmospheric climate patterns. Interdependence and interrelationship are central starting points for ecological research of food webs, nutrient cycles, and forest succession. Indra's Net, however, contains more than the ecological sum of biosphere, atmosphere, and lithosphere. The Buddhist principle of interdependence includes human thought, perception, and values, and their impacts on the ecological-evolutionary conversation. This critical difference is what makes it possible and necessary for people in the Net to act ethically out of regard for the other beings in the Net.

In the context of human relationship, feminist ethicist Mary Grey describes the metaphysic of connectedness as 'revelatory paradigm' and 'moral imperative'. She suggests that the ethics of care and responsibility develop from a person's experience 'trying to be faithful to relation or connection'.[24] A number of feminist ethicists and writers point to mutuality and solidarity as key values for the feminist movement.[25] These values spring from the need for sister bonding as a source of strength in facing the internalized pain of the victim of sexism and in organizing for institutional and social change. Full mutuality or interdependence is not possible for one dominated by the absolutizing, individualist 'I'. Thus to experience the richness of full mutuality, one must transcend or break through the limitations of the thought habit of individualism reinforced as the dominant ideology in the Western world.

For the woman who has suffered physical, economic, psychological, or spiritual oppression, freedom from the rigidity of the fixed 'I' / self and release into the web of relationships means the choice of many more nourishing options for growth and development. Because this maturation occurs in a shared context with others also suffering isolation, the feminist experience of interrelatedness is a process of mutual becoming, born out of mutual vulnerability. The joy and satisfaction of this experience may then be a foundation for 'passionate caring for the entirety of the relational nexus'.[26] A woman who uncovers her own capacity for mutuality can then (and often does) extend her efforts and empathy to the many other women in different cultures and places who also suffer from lack of freedom of choice.

For both Buddhism and feminism, the core truth of interrelationship or mutual becoming is central to individual liberation or freedom from false reification of an independent 'I'. Feminist Buddhists who understand this path of liberation can be extremely effective and compassionate participants in the struggle for environmental consciousness. Acting from deep-rooted experience in the freedom to choose options other than oppression, they can work creatively and skillfully to open up environmental conversations that have been frozen by loss of relationality.

Emotional Energy as Source of Healing

The Buddhist practice of investigating conditioned body, speech, and mind includes detailed observation of the nature of emotions. In the Sutra on the Four Establishments of Mindfulness, for example, the meditator is instructed to practice awareness of pleasant, painful, and neutral feelings as they arise in the mind and body. In Thich Nhat Hanh's modern-day commentary on this Sutra, he suggests exercises for identifying and acknowledging feelings and seeing the physical, physiological, or psychological roots of particular feelings.[27] By becoming fully familiar with the nature of anger, grief, fear, desire, denial, or the blocking of these feelings, a practitioner gains confidence in living through the sweep of emotional responses that naturally arise from moment to moment.

The first step of healing from the suffering of difficult emotions is to recognize and fully claim the rich information and energy response of the body/mind. In the investigation and mindfulness practice itself, energy is released and becomes available for healing through attention and understanding. Rather than suppressing deep emotions, Buddhist practice can help a person develop the capacity to consciously use this energy to relieve suffering. Much of the response to the current environmental crisis is an emotional response, filled with grief, fear, and anger at the loss and destruction of plants, animals, forests, and watersheds. The depth of response may be so overwhelming that people become immobilized and unable to act. Buddhist practices to validate and move through these waves of emotion can be extremely helpful in freeing up energy to take action on behalf of the environment.[28]

Western feminists also recognize the importance of emotional response in the process of awakening to oppression. Most Western white women have been conditioned not to express anger overtly. Strong displays of empassioned emotion have been marginalized and viewed as unacceptable by the ruling patriarchy and its male model of 'cool' and reserved emotions. Anger at sexual and environmental abuse qualifies as an 'outlaw emotion', invalidated by those who wish to avoid hearing other experiences.[29] Feminists, however, are well aware that social and gender conditioning can only be overthrown by a strong surge of energy and desire for change. Anger is very effective in marshaling the energy necessary to dismantle the structure that perpetrates violence against women and the environment.

If one begins with the fundamental truth of one's own experience, recognizing that perception and conception are intimately related, it becomes necessary to know how we feel in order to act morally. As feminist theologian Beverly Harrison asserts, 'The failure to live deeply in "our bodies, ourselves" destroys the possibility for moral relations between us.'[30] For Harrison, anger is a 'feeling-signal that all is not well in our relation to others or the world around us.'[31] Powerful emotion is a sign of resistance to the unsatisfactory moral quality of our social and environmental relationships. This signal is the wake-up call to look more deeply into the situation at hand. Harrison argues that the power to respond is the power to create a world of moral relations. This is the work of spiritual and religious practice, the transformative work that can serve to slow environmental destruction and heal the wounded biosphere.

The combination of Buddhist mindfulness practice and feminist moral response is a powerful antidote to widespread despair and depression over the possibility of nuclear annihilation, environmental catastrophe, or out-of-control corporate greed. This practice does not remove the threats or mitigate the devastating consequences of irresponsible actions, but it does help to generate the tremendous energy needed to address the complexities of the global environmental situation.[32] Anger, despair or other strong emotions alone are not enough to stop environmental tragedy, because they cause polarization and defensive reactions that block communication. Environmental activists already have a history and bad name in some circles for misusing emotions in the service of battle strategy.

Habitual unexamined anger can harden into ideology that further erodes opportunities for working together. By cultivating a deeper, more fully informed emotional response, one cultivates greater possibilities for a healing transformation of relationships between human beings and the environment.

Relational Ethics

Buddhist ethics are grounded firmly in the truth and experience of the Law of Dependent Co-Arising. *Sila,* or guidelines for moral action, are central to Buddhist practice in all traditions. The Three Pure Precepts are vows to refrain from actions that ignore interdependence, to make an effort to act out of understanding of interrelationship, and to serve all beings in the interdepending web.[33] The five (Theravada) prescriptive precepts to not kill, not lie, not steal, not abuse sexuality or intoxicants spring from a fundamental recognition of relationships. One aims to act as respectfully and inclusively as possible toward plant, animal, and human companions.

In the Mahayana traditions, the model of enlightenment is the Bodhisattva who gains awakening in order to serve all beings. This is in contrast to the Theravadan goal of achieving liberation to be freed from the cycle of endless suffering and rebirths in a human body. Buddhist or other religious beliefs that place emphasis on Otherworldliness, or some version of escaping from the drudgery of this world, are not helpful for responding to the escalating deterioration of the environment. Forests can only be replanted here on this earth by those who live here, not those who have transcended the world. The Bodhisattva model encourages the practices of compassion for all others as a means of accomplishing a profound sense of interrelatedness. One can specifically cultivate 'eco-bodhicitta' or the mind of enlightenment that serves all relations of the environment.[34]

The experience of compassion for others' suffering is what allows us to feel the connections with disturbed ecosystems and threatened species, distressing as they may be.[35] Sensitivity and moral concern for the health of human relationships can extend as well to plants, animals, forests, clouds, stone, and sacred places. Buddhist relational ethics are based on knowing that one cannot act without affecting other living beings, that it is impossible to live outside the web of interconnectedness. The beautiful Jewel Net of Indra is sustained and enhanced by the quality of moral intention and commitment to the many facets of the Net. To act from this sense of relatedness is deeply empowering, setting an ethical example for others to consider.

Compassion in Western culture, in contrast, is frequently associated with pity and powerlessness and relegated to the domain of women's nurturing.[36] In examining Western psychological values, feminist researchers have challenged the traditional stages of moral and psychological development based on male socialization, as described by Kohlberg.[37] In this model, moral maturity develops through increasing allegiance to universal rules or principles of justice and individual rights. Carol Gilligan's work, in contrast, suggests that women's moral development in the West is based on maturing responsiveness to relationships and consideration of others in moral choices.[38] Kohlberg's male model reinforces an environmental ethic oriented to rights and justice; Gilligan's alternative model supports an environmental ethic of care and responsibility.

Relational ethics as described by both Buddhist teachings and feminist writers might also be called contextual ethics. A contextual ethic, as I use the term, reflects both the diversity of human voices in a given place and time[39] and the specific environmental relationships in which the human dilemma is embedded.[40] Built into this approach to ethics is the rejection of any single authoritative ethical voice or posited human nature that exists independent of historical context. Abstract individualism is seen as ungrounded and relatively unhelpful in addressing the tensions of a specific environmental conflict.

Environmental moral dilemmas occur in a web of relationships. Each situation has a unique history, based on very particular causes and conditions. A contextual ethic represents a shift from emphasis on rights, rules, and predetermined principles to a conception of ethics grounded in specific relationships. Environmental actions based entirely on rules as moral guidelines inevitably leave out some aspect of the situation that is not included in the legal framework. Rules generalize; relationships are infinite and complex. A relational ethic calls for compassion for all the relationships involved in the situation—parent-child, tree-animal, bird-human, soil-rock. Relationships are not something outside of who we are; they, in fact, *define* who we are to a large extent as moral agents in a social and historical context. As Warren argues, 'Relationships of humans to the nonhuman environment are, in part, constitutive of what it is to be human'.[41]

Relational morality is not simple; it is extremely difficult to make sound environmental decisions when relatively little is known about ecological relationships. The stakes are often very high when the consequences of human actions mean the loss of millions of plant and animal lives. Trade-offs in tropical environments, for example, are almost a matter of triage today. The practices of compassion and contextual reflection generate a deep appreciation of biological and cultural complexity and of the long-standing ties between humans and all other members of the biotic community. I believe this is an essential foundation for critically needed re-evaluation of what we are doing on the planet and what is ethically acceptable and life-sustaining.

The Role of Community

All Buddhist traditions venerate the three Jewels—the Buddha, Dharma, and Sangha. In environmental terms, the Buddha can be interpreted as all beings who teach, or the teacher within, or the Buddha as environmental teacher. To see all beings as teachers means one can learn from wolf, redwood, buffalo, river, and mountain.[42] To see the Buddha as teacher within means one learns from one's own experience with the environment. The Buddha as environmental teacher is the one who points to the truth of interdependence and co-dependent arising of all life forms.

Dharma is the truth of the teachings in their many forms, perceptions, and experiences. Each plant and animal, as well as human, is an embodiment of evolutionary truth, a testimony to thousands of years of living more or less successfully in conversation with the environment. Each experience of connection with members of the environmental web is a taste of the deep truth of the nature of reality as mutually causal and interdependent.

The Third Jewel, the Sangha, is traditionally described in Buddhist literature as the monastic community, or those who practice within a retreat setting. Rules for Sangha behavior are extensive, numbering over 300 in some traditions, with specific rules for nuns, often in subordinate relationship to monks. For most American Buddhists, some of these rules are inappropriate because of cultural differences, but even more, they are not specific to lay or non-monastic practice, which is the prevalent form of practice in the United States. Deep ecologist Bill Devall proposes the concept of 'eco-sangha', in which people practice with all the members of their bioregion or watershed area and consciously identify with and include the environment as community.[43] One then sits in meditation not only with others in the human community, but also with the surrounding oaks, maples, jays, warblers, and wildflowers.

Feminist Buddhist Rita Gross suggests that Sangha is the 'indispensable matrix of spiritual existence' necessary for human liberation.[44] She critiques the historical tendency in Buddhism to emphasize the lonely path to freedom, suggesting that too much aloneness is not a good thing, for it is not, in itself, instructive in how to get along with others. Her feminist reconceptualization of Sangha rests on the values of community, nurturing, communication, and relationships, traditionally cared for by women in many cultures. With no theistic Ultimate Other in Buddhism to provide guaranteed relationship to the person experiencing isolation, there is no alternative but to provide relationship for one another. She suggests, 'It is necessary to create the social, communal, and compassionate matrix of a society in which friendship and relationship are taken as categories of utmost spiritual importance'.[45]

A feminist interpretation of Sangha validates and deepens the key feminist political and psychological values of solidarity and mutuality. Companionship and shared activities, including dialogue on environmental ethics, are then central to spiritual development and need to be cultivated as primary virtues. Women's friendships and love for each other and the mutual growth process may be threatening and confusing to some, because they challenge traditional ethics based in individualism. I believe that the friendship-Sangha model is a helpful and appropriate basis for refinding and redefining our human relationships with plants, animals, and ecological communities. It is both enjoyable and sustainable, and can serve as a significant counterpoint to the recent history of industrialized attack and plunder.

A Few Possible Limitations

These six areas of philosophical similarity or complementarity between Buddhism and feminism offer a solid foundation for a Buddhist feminist approach to environmental issues. I believe that the environmental ethics generated from such a position recommend restraint in human activities that cause destruction and loss of habitats, species, and ecosystems, with the aim of reducing suffering for many forms of life. However, for effective evaluation of these two approaches, it is necessary to keep in mind the historical traditions and limitations of each source philosophy. There are several potential weaknesses of traditional Buddhism that may serve either to limit Buddhist involvement with the environment or, through dialog and activity, may actually help define the evolutionary edge of American Buddhism.

Egocentrism as Central Concept

Buddhist philosophy and religious practice emphasize breaking through the limited perspective and conditioning of the small self or human ego, in order to experience the boundless interrelated nature of reality. The route to liberation assumes an overvaluation of self or ego, which distorts perception and perpetuates self-centeredness. This fundamental approach may not be as applicable for marginalized groups of people, including women. Teachings that point to the falsely constructed separate ego may be received as disconnected from the actual lived experience of oppression, or as a paternalistic strategy for pacification or assimilation.[46] For women and others experiencing social messages that continually devalue the self, the Buddhist emphasis on egolessness may only serve to further erode the not yet fully formed and validated person. Practices that suppress the ego may be misinterpreted as a denial of personhood which can be used as a method of subjugation and denigration of marginalized groups.

Feminism has taken a strong position on self-advocacy as a key principle in fighting abusive patterns of social conditioning, whether in marriage, work, or health matters. Self-advocacy is critical to women speaking up for their rights, their existence, and more human standards of behavior. The marginalized or oppressed woman is encouraged to find her voice, her dreams, her capabilities, her inner strength. This is essential spiritual work, the challenge of distinguishing the true self from the many layers of social and gender patterns that deny the self.

This critique of Buddhism is relevant to environmental work in at least two respects. One, in the realm of ecofeminist spirituality, there may be a tendency to overemphasize the subjective experience of environment as universal, in the enthusiasm for a women's nature-based religious practice. However, this may more accurately reflect the need to simply establish the existence and validity of women's personhood, long overlooked by many religions, including Buddhism. I suggest that Buddhist feminists seeking ecological spirituality examine the teachings in depth to recognize healthy aspects of self-development as well as the blocks to egolessness.

Secondly, recognition of the full 'personhood' or intrinsic existence of plants, animals, mountains, and rivers depends on one's capacity to fully recognize one's own personhood. For the Buddhist woman student, personhood may be displaced by the brilliant experience of boundarylessness before the self is fully developed. This then diminishes the person's capacity to deeply reflect and stand in solidarity with the full existence of any particular environmental other. Calling up the image of Indra's Net, this suggests that the reflective power of each jewel within the Net directly enhances the beauty and perception of all the other jewels. It is the quality of this reflection and existence that then guides our choice of environmental actions; an ethic of restraint expressing respect and appreciation for the beauty of the other members of the web is not possible if one does not first fully and deeply appreciate the self.

Power Relations Analysis

The social conditions of power, status, and privilege critically affect environmental decisions, law and treaty making, and natural resource negotiation. Social aspects of Buddhist religions are riddled with power, relations, as much as any other organized religion. The social glue of power roles determines the nature of attitudes and actions of those in power and those not in power. While Buddhist philosophy clearly includes the relevant tools for examining the nature of power relations and the abuse of power, this area of inquiry is not a central emphasis in American practice today. Gender power relations, in particular, are not generally addressed, most likely because Buddhist philosophy and practice forms have come through patriarchal cultures with primarily male teachers and leaders. In many schools of Buddhism, there is a strong emphasis on practice relationships with an authoritative teacher. This can be a relationship of respect, but it can also be a relationship of abuse, where power and status are used to gain sexual access to women students.[47]

Issues of power relations have been raised by American feminist Buddhists trying to correct for Asian cultural influence in the historical development of Buddhism.[48] This enquiry into gender conditioning is not widespread and not necessarily well received by American Buddhist centers or teachers. By broadening the field of inquiry to areas of hidden gender assumptions, feminists challenge the status of many of the governance and religious forms transferred to America from Asian patriarchal cultures. Those who hold religious or administrative power reinforced by Western male favoritism are generally not inclined to examine the language, behavior, and psychology of gender conditioning, despite feminist research showing the powerful capacity of gender conditioning to influence all other forms of conditioning.

This weakness in Buddhist philosophy as it has arrived in the Western world could have significant detrimental effects on the evolution of a Buddhist environmental ethic. The trust of interdependence, acknowledging the intrinsic value of each member of the web, is just a starting point for investigating the nature of specific relationships. The environmental crisis is driven by the complexities of power distribution, giving preference and status to some governments, some corporate ventures, some ecosystems, some species, some cultures over others. An effective Buddhist environmental ethic is strengthened by the dimension of power analysis presented by feminist theorists. Political, economic, and personal power can serve the environment, if illuminated by awareness and social consciousness of the logic of domination. Without this awareness, the critical role of power can be overlooked by the Buddhist practitioner focusing on the beauty and miracle of interdependence.

Social Ethics and Engaged Practice

Buddhist ethics traditionally emphasize behavior guidelines and liberation for the individual, rather than structural change of social systems. The current literature on Buddhism and social change is somewhat limited in covering the history of commitment to social issues.[49] In contrast, Christian social ethics trace their origin to the earliest stories of Jesus' suffering and compassion, developing principles of social justice as central to Christian religious practice. In some cases, Asian Buddhist cultures reinforce the acceptance of reality to the extreme of passivity. This can make it very difficult for Buddhist religious or social leaders to advocate social change.[50]

Feminism is fundamentally based in a need, desire, and strong motivation for social change. This drive for change might be seen as incompatible with Buddhism, presenting possible difficulty in merging these two approaches. The urgency and passion behind the feminist agenda may seem unmeditative to practicing Buddhists; the passive acceptance of Buddhist religious culture may seem unmotivated or apathetic to committed feminists. Yet each has something to gain from the other, particularly in developing a strong movement for environmental justice and a new code of environmental ethics.

Social environmental ethics are more than the sum of individual ethical practices regarding the environment. They are the ethics necessary for dealing with the whole systemic pattern of environmental destruction, which has a force and momentum of its own. A religious practice that only advocates individual improvement in environmental actions (such as recycling, vegetarianism, or birth control) does not go far enough in investigating the roots of socialized environmental destruction. The development of a social ethic to address the scale of environmental systemic disorder requires a motivation to work with the system as a whole and to uphold standards for the system as well as for the individual.[51] In this task, the commitment of feminism may be a useful catalyst for inspiring Buddhist dialogue and activity necessary to affect the environmental situation at any long-term meaningful level.

EXAMPLES OF BUDDHIST FEMINIST ENVIRONMENTAL WORK

Buddhist feminist activity on behalf of the environment is not yet very extensive, primarily because the number of people self-identified as Buddhist, feminist, and environmentalist is not large. However, examples of their environmental work are significant and are serving to inspire others around the world. These examples reflect primarily American Buddhist concern for the environment, though certainly there are women in other countries expressing their feminist and environmental concerns through Buddhist practice.

Research and Theory

Two examples of research carried out by Buddhist feminists concerned with the environment are the Perception of Nature Project undertaken by Chatsumarn Kabilsingh of Thailand and the comparative analysis of Buddhist philosophy and Western systems theory by Joanna Macy of the United States. Kabilsingh has reviewed the early Buddhist teachings of the Pali Canon to catalog specific references to the environment. Under the sponsorship of the World Wildlife Fund, a number of these teaching stories have been compiled and distributed throughout Southeast Asia.[52] Many of these early discourses cover the central points of Buddhist philosophy with specific references to refraining from harming others in the environment and specifically protecting trees, rivers, and animals of the forest.

Macy's work interprets the primary teaching of interrelationship in an environmental context, developing her ideas of 'the ecological self' based on analysis of the co-arising of knower and known, body and mind, doer and deed, and self and society.[53] Her careful review of the nature of causality lays an important foundation for a Buddhist analysis of environmental power relations. She bases her definition of mutual morality in the dialectics of personal and social transformation, laying out a Buddhist construction of an environmental philosophy that is appropriate for today's interdependently created ecological crisis. This work builds on her earlier theoretical writing, in which she develops the image/essence of the Perfection of Wisdom as a feminine form, as the pregnant point of potential action, light, space, and emptiness, calling this the author of the Tathagatas.[54] Macy's work is a major theoretical contribution to the evolution of an environmental ethic informed by Buddhist and feminist philosophy.

Environmental Activism

A second arena of Buddhist environmental activity lies in green politics and activism. The Buddhist Peace Fellowship (BPF) was founded in 1978 to bring a Buddhist perspective to the peace and environmental movements and to raise issues of social concern among Buddhist practitioners. In 1990, Doug Codiga, Margaret Howe, and I initiated a BPF campaign for environmental awareness by distributing to Buddhist centers and individuals over three hundred packets of materials and posters featuring the Buddha sitting in peaceful harmony surrounded by tigers, monkeys, tropical birds, and forest vines. The packets included suggested educational activities, a bibliography of readings, chants, and prayers, and ideas for environmentalizing local Buddhist centers.

The Berkeley BPF chapter has been actively engaged in Buddhist antinuclear environmental activism at the local Concord Naval Weapons base.[55] For the past five years they have led a half-day sitting meditation on the railroad tracks, blocking the passage of weapons out from the base. The protest is nonviolent and nonaggressive; it is meant as a statement of witness and solidarity, both with other non-Buddhist activists and with those who suffer from the threat or presence of nuclear weapons in their countries. Feminist and ordained Zen priest Maylie Scott has consistently promoted these sittings, serving as an inspiration to others by the strength of her practice and commitment to social change.

Another antinuclear effort, the Nuclear Guardianship project, protests the storage of nuclear waste underground, where problems are out of sight and difficult to manage. Joanna Macy, Charlotte Cooke, and others propose instead that waste be stored above ground, to be watched over by 'nuclear guardians' in monastery-like settings.[56] This radical solution draws on the Buddhist model of monastic life, where mindfulness is the central practice, developing consideration and consciousness for all beings in the nuclear-affected web of life.

The guiding ethic for the project reflects a deep sense of relationship with beings of the future who will inherit decaying nuclear isotopes in massive quantities.

Charlene Spretnak's work in green politics and spirituality reflects her belief that a spiritual infrastructure is essential for the successful transformation to a postmodern green society.[57] Spretnak draws on her Vipassana Buddhist practice to remain grounded and centered in the middle of inevitable political tension and strategizing. She has worked to incorporate principles of feminism and nonviolence in Green Party platforms in California. For Spretnak, environmental activism is a direct expression of Buddhist practice, an embodiment of her spiritual commitment to serve all beings.

Buddhists Concerned for Animals (BCA), founded in 1981, is an example of green Buddhist politics. This group is committed to stopping cruelty to animals, especially in the use of animals for scientific experimentation.[58] They were instrumental in pressuring the University of California at Berkeley to improve their animal research practices. As Buddhists, they urge vegetarian eating to protest the inhumane conditions of factory-farmed animals. BCA raises issues of domination by promoting cruelty-free cosmetics that do not depend on animal testing for safety checks.

Environmental Education

Among Buddhist feminists concerned with the environment, a number of women are professional teachers or writers associated with academic institutions or spiritual retreat centers. As a faculty in diverse departments or schools, they are building bridges between traditional subject areas and current environmental concerns. Buddhist feminists Lisa Faithhorn and Elizabeth Roberts teach Deep Ecology at California Institute of Integral Studies (CIIS) and Naropa Institute, respectively; Joanna Macy teaches systems theory, cross-cultural social activism, and spiritual practice in an environmental context at the Berkeley Graduate Theological Union, as well as at CIIS. I teach environmental ethics in the Environmental Studies program at the University of Vermont. For these educators, course design and content, as well as teaching style, reflect a grounding in Buddhist practice and philosophy and a feminist perspective on power and domination. Macy has led the way in working with the blocked energy of despair, grief, fear, and anger to enable people to transform and free this energy for the healing of the world. Her teaching content and style rest solidly on a feminist analysis of power and a Buddhist practice of compassion.[59]

Another group of Buddhist feminist teachers addresses environmental issues in retreat or workshop settings, where spiritual practice is the context for environmental understanding. For example, Wendy Johnson, head gardener at Green Gulch Zen Center since 1980, teaches classes in gardening and tree planting as mindfulness practice. Green Gulch, a well-established retreat center in central coastal California, supports both a garden and an organic farm, with over twenty acres in lettuce, potatoes, squash, and other kitchen vegetables.

Wendy sees tree planting as part of a long-term plan for restoration of the once forested hillside slopes. Joan Halifax combines Buddhist mindfulness practice with modern forms of shamanism, to evoke connection with the natural world.[60] Drawing on her background in anthropology, she leads workshops and trips to sacred sites to inspire spiritual grounding in the power of the earth itself.

Several writers also contribute to the educational literature, offering a Buddhist feminist perspective on the environment. Susan Griffin's book *Woman and Nature* is an American ecofeminist classic.[61] Griffin's Buddhist Vipassana practice informs her poetry and creative writing, allowing her to express in detail the illusory distinction between mind and body, mind and nature. She writes as a committed feminist, pointing directly and vividly to parallel examples of oppression of nature and woman. China Galland's work on women in wilderness settings, as well as her investigation of Tara and the Black Madonna, also reflect a serious commitment to Tibetan Buddhism and the importance of women's voices in reconnecting with the environment.[62]

Some Buddhist environmental education takes place through devotional practices or ceremonies. At Green Gulch Zen Center, Wendy Johnson and I designed a Buddhist Earth Day ceremony that included a morning lecture on the environment, animal memorial service, and taking of the precepts in the presence of the central oak tree.[63] Wendy and others have also organized a number of family practice days, in which children participate in harvesting vegetables and planting trees. Earth prayers and dedications have been collected by Elizabeth Roberts and Elias Amidon, subtly and skillfully reflecting an orientation to Buddhist mindfulness and a sense of the ecological self.[64] Mayumi Ada, Japanese Zen student, educates by painting large banners and silk screens of earth bodhisattvas surrounded by garden vegetables. She transforms traditional male figures such as Manjusri into female forms, cutting through delusion with spirited feminine energy.[65] Her feminist art has graced several conferences on Women and Buddhism held in the San Francisco Bay area; her drawings frequently appear in United States Buddhist publications.

This is only a sampling of examples of women engaged in environmental work based in Buddhist practice and feminist awareness. Certainly there are other examples from the wider international community. In contrast to so much feminist and environmental political work, which is combative in the desperate struggle for women's rights and environmental sustainability, a Buddhist nondualist and nonviolent viewpoint can make a very valuable contribution to the healing of the world. Women who are strong in their practice and understanding of Buddhism can bring a powerful intention to the difficult and sometimes overwhelming work of taking care of one another and the place where we are.

CONCLUSION

I believe these two streams of thought and activity-Buddhism and feminism-benefit from the insights and knowledge of each other in a way that can nourish and sustain the environment. The confluence of Buddhist and feminist thought, practice, commitment, and community in the 1990s offers a strong contribution to the healing of environmental loss and degradation. I opened this discussion in the context of the spiritual lineage of the feminine compassionate presence and the potential for healing she represents. By acknowledging Kuan Yin and Tara, I acknowledge all those who have drawn courage and inspiration from this aspect of their own Buddha natures in responding to the seemingly insurmountable suffering of the environment. Now, perhaps, these realized beings can be an inspiration and a source of guidance in taking care of the planet and each relationship in the complex biological and geophysical web of Indra's stunning Jewel net.

NOTES

1. R. Aitken, 'Kanzeon', in *Not Mixing up Buddhism: Essays on Women and Buddhist Practice* (Fredonia, NY: White Pine Press, 1986), pp. 24–29.

2. J. Blofeld, *Boddhisattva of Compassion: The Mystical Tradition of Kwan Yin* (Boulder, CO: Shambhala Books, 1978), and M. Wilson, *In Praise af Tara* (London: Wisdom Publications, 1986).

3. R. Fields, How the Swans Came to the Lake: A Narrative History of Buddhism (Boulder, Colorado: Shambhala Books, 1981).

4. S. Boucher, *Turning the Wheel: American Women Creating the New Buddhism* (San Francisco: Harper & Row, 1985).

5. D. Morreale, *Buddhist America* (Santa Fe: John Muir Publications, 1988).

6. L. Friedman, *Meetings with Remarkable Women* (Boston: Shambhala Books, 1987).

7. For further information on the Congress, or to obtain a copy of the Women's Action Agenda, contact Women's Environment and Development Organization, 845 Third Avenue, 15th Floor, New York, NY 10022.

8. D.T. Suzuki, *Practical Methods of Zen Instruction,* in *Essays in Zen Buddhism* (New York: Grove Press, 1949).

9. K. Tanahashi (ed.), *Moon in a Dewdrop: Writings of Zen Master Dogen* (San Francisco: North Point Press, 1985), p. 70.

10. J. Plaskow and C.P. Christ (eds.), *Weaving the Visions* (San Francisco: Harper & Row, 1989).

11. M.F. Belenky et al., *Women's Ways of Knowing: The Development of Self, Voice and Mind* (New York: Basic Books, 1986).

12. S. Harding. *The Science Question in Feminism* (Ithaca, NY: Cornell University Press, 1986).

13. H. Tellenbach and B. Kimura, 'The Japanese Concept of Nature', in J.B. Callicott and R.T. Ames (eds.), *Nature in Asian Traditions of Thought* (Albany, NY: State University of New York Press, 1989).

14. P. Levitt, 'An Intimate View', in A. Hunt-Badiner (ed.), *Dharma Gaia* (Berkeley: Parallax Press, 1990).

15. S. Kaza, 'Systems Thinking: Tools for Buddhist Restoration Ecology' (paper presented at the Society for Ecological Restoration and Management Annual Meeting, Oakland, California, 1989).

16. S. Kellert, 'Perceptions of Animals in America', in R.J. Hoage (ed.), *Perceptions of Animals in American Culture* (Washington, DC: Smithsonian Institution Press, 1989).

17. S. Keen, *Faces of the Enemy: Reflections of the Hostile Imagination* (San Francisco: Harper & Row, 1986).

18. K.J. Warren and J. Cheney, *Ecological Feminism: A Philosophical Perspective on What it Is and Why it Matters* (Boulder, CO: Westview Press, forthcoming).

19. M. Kheel, 'From Healing Herbs to Deadly Drugs', in J.Plant (ed.), *Healing the Wounds:* The *Promise of Ecofeminism* (Philadelphia: New Society Publishers, 1989).

20. V. Shiva, *Staying Alive: Women, Ecology, and Development* (London: Zed Press; New Delhi: Kali for Women, 1988).

21. D.J. Kalupahana, *The Principles of Buddhist Psychology* (Albany, NY: State University of New York Press, 1987), p. 26.

22. From the Pall Canon, Samyutta Nikaya II, 28,65, quoted and interpreted in S. Kaza, 'Towards a "Buddhist Environmental Ethic"', *Buddhism at the Crossroads* 1.1 (1985), pp. 22–25.

23. F.H. Cook, 'The Jewel Net of Indra', in Callicott and Ames (eds.), *Nature.*

24. M. Grey, 'Claiming Power in Relation: Exploring the Ethics of Connection', *JFSR* 7 (1991), pp. 7–18, p. 13.

25. M.A. Farley, *Personal Commitments* (San Francisco: Harper & Row, 1986). M. Daly, 'Be-Friending', in Plaskow and Christ (eds.), *Weaving the Visions,* pp. 199–207.

26. Grey, 'Claiming Power', 1991, p. 13.

27. T.N. Hanh, *Transformation and Healing* (Berkeley: Parallax Press, 1990).

28. Hanh, *Present Moment,* and J. Macy, *Despair and Personal Power in the Nuclear Age* (Philadelphia: New Society Publishers, 1983), pp. 158–61.

29. A.M. Jaggar and S. Bordo (eds.), *Love and Knowledge: Emotion in Feminist Epistemology, Gender/Body/Knowledge* (New Brunswick, NJ: Rutgers University Press, 1985).

30. B.W. Harrison, *Our Right to Choose: Toward a New Ethic of Abortion* (Boston: Beacon Press, 1983), p. 13.

31. B.W. Harrison, 'The Power of Anger in the Work of Love', in C.S. Robb (ed.), *Making the Connections* (Boston: Beacon Press, 1985), p. 14.

32. Macy, *Despair,* pp. 158–61.

33. I wrote this version of the Three Pure Precepts for the 1990 Earth Day ceremony at Green Gulch Zen Center. Much of the text is reprinted in the *Buddhist Peace Fellowship Newsletter* (Summer 1990), pp. 32–33.

34. A. Ross, Strange Weather: Culture, Science and Technology in the Age of Limits (New York: Verso, 1991).

35. J. Macy and J. Seed have developed a ritual Council of All Beings, designed to draw out these responses. Councils have been conducted all over the world, in a wide diversity of settings. The form is described in Seed et al., *Thinking Like a Mountain* (Philadelphia: New Society Publishers, 1988).

36. A. Klein, 'Compassion: Gain or Drain? Buddhist and Feminist Views on Compassion', *Spring Wind* 6.1, 2, 3 (1986), pp. 105–16.

37. L. Kohlberg, *The Philosophy of Moral Development* (San Francisco: Harper & Row, 1981).

38. C. Gilligan, *In a Different Voice* (Cambridge, MA: Harvard University Press, 1982).

39. K.J. Warren, 'The Power and the Promise of Ecological Feminism in Environmental Ethics', 12.3 (1990), p. 139.

40. J. Cheney, 'Eco-Feminism and Deep Ecology', *Environmental Ethics* 9.2 (Summer 1987), pp. 115–46.

41. Warren, 1990, *op. cit.,* p. 143.

42. D. Zenji, 'Mountains and Waters Sutra', in K. Tanahashi (ed.), *Moon in a Dewdrop* (San Francisco: North Point Press, 1985), pp. 97–127.

43. B. Devall and G. Sessions, *Deep Ecology: Living as if Nature Mattered* (Salt Lake City: Peregrine Smith Books, 1990).

44. R. Gross, 'Buddhism after Patriarchy', in P.M. Cooey, W.R. Eakin and J.B. McDaniel (eds.), *After Patriarchy* (Maryknoll, NY: Orbis Books, 1991), p. 78.

45. Gross, 'Buddhism', p. 78.

46. For an introduction to these ideas, see K. McCarthy, 'A Critique of Emptiness from the Margins' (paper presented at the Western Regional Meeting of the American Academy of Religion, March 1990, with additional comments from panel member Y. Vowels).

47. See *Turning Wheel: Journal of the Buddhist Peace Fellowship* (Summer 1991), pp. 22–29, with articles by J. Komfield and others and the formal statement of ethical guidelines by Second Generation Zen Teachers. See also Boucher, *Turning the Wheel.*

48. See Boucher, *Turning the Wheel;* R. Gross, 'Buddhism and Feminism: A Personal Synthesis', in *Not Mixing Up Buddhism: Essays on Women and Buddhist Practice* (Freedonia, NY: White Pine Press, 1986); and A. Karabinus, 'Women in North American Zen Buddhism' (unpublished, MA thesis).

49. S. Sivaksa, *Seeds of Peace* (Berkeley: Parallax Press, 1991), and K. Jones, *The Social Face of Buddhism* (Boston: Wisdom Publications, 1989).

50. This was a key topic at a social action training for Asian monks and other Buddhist activists I conducted with Paula Green in conjunction with the International Network of Engaged Buddhists meeting in Bangkok, February 1991.

51. G. Fourez, *Liberation Ethics* (Philadelphia: Temple University Press, 1982).

52. C. Kabilsingh, 'Early Buddhist Views on Nature', in A. Hunt-Badiner (ed.), *Dharma Gaia* (Berkeley: Parallax Press, 1990); and K. Davies, *Tree of Life: Buddhism and Protection of Nature* (Hong Kong: Buddhist Perception of Nature Project, 1987).

53. J. Macy, 'The Greening of the Self', *Common Boundary* July-August 1990), pp. 22–25; *idem, Mutual Causality in Buddhism and General Systems Theory: The Dharam of Natural Systems* (Albany, NY: State University of New York Press, 1991); *idem, World as Lover, World as Self* (San Francisco: Parallax Press, 1991).

54. J. Macy, 'Perfection Wisdom: Mother of All Buddhas', in R. Gross (ed.), *Beyond Androcentrism* (Missoula, MT: Scholars Press, 1977), pp. 315–17.

55. Regular updates of Berkeley chapter activities regarding the weapons base sitings are available through the Buddhist Peace Fellowship, PO Box 4650, Berkeley, CA, 94704

56. J. Macy, 'Guardians of the Future', *Context* 28 (Spring 1991), pp. 20–25.

57. C. Spretnak, *The Spiritual Dimensions of Green Politics* (Sante Fe: Bear & Company, 1986); and F. Capra and C. Spretnak, *Green Politics: The Global Promise* (New York: E.P. Dutton, 1984).

58. Boucher, *Turning the Wheel,* pp. 288–93.
59. See, for example, interviews of J. Macy in *Inquiring Mind* 5.2, pp. 1–3 and C. Ingram, *In the Footsteps of Gandhi* (Berkeley: Parallax Press, 1990), pp. 141–68.
60. J. Halifax, 'The Third Body: Buddhism, Shamanism, and Deep Ecology', in A. Hunt-Gadiner (ed.), *Dharma Gaia* (Berkeley: Parallax Press, 1990).
61. S. Griffin, *Woman and Nature: The Roaring inside Her* (San Francisco: Harper & Row, 1978).
62. C. Galland, *Longing for a Darkness: Tara and the Black Madonna* (New York: Viking, 1990).
63. Wendy Johnson's Earth Day talk, 'Sitting on Our Garbage', is reprinted in the *Buddhist Peace Fellowship Newsletter* (Summer 1990), along with the text of the Earth Day ceremonies.
64. E. Roberts and E. Amidon (eds.), *Earth Prayers from around the World* (San Francisco: Harper-Collins, 1991).
65. M. Oda, *Goddesses* (Volcano, CA: Volcano Press/Kazan Books, 1988).

CHAPTER 5

Against Holism: Rethinking Buddhist Environmental Ethics

SIMON P. JAMES

I.

Two assumptions are often made in studies of the environmental implications of Buddhism: (1) that Buddhism is an environmentally friendly religion, and (2) that this is because of the stress placed, in its teachings, on the 'oneness' of humans and nature. In this paper I argue that while (2) is false, (1) is true, that (to be more precise) Buddhism is environmentally friendly, not on account of its endorsing some notion of the 'oneness' of humans and nature (which it doesn't), but because of its distinctive conception of the good life.

Before setting out this argument, however, it is necessary both to clarify what it might mean to say that humans and nature are 'one' and to explain why anyone might think that Buddhists endorse such a view. A good place to begin in doing this is with the concept of nature, the realm that, according to (2), humans are supposed to be 'one' with. It might seem appropriate, then, to begin with a question such as the following:

Q1. What do Buddhists believe nature is?
   This, however, is a poorly formed question, and for several reasons. For one thing, it is not clear who the 'Buddhists' referred to are. Buddhism is, after all, a broad church, and Buddhists from different traditions often believe different things about nature.

Indeed it cannot be assumed at the outset of our inquiry that their comportment towards nature is best understood in terms of *belief*.[1] A further complication is that it is not obvious what, in this context, the term 'nature' means. It is not clear, for example, whether Q1 is meant to refer to nature-as-opposed-to-the-supernatural or to nature-as-a-realm-relatively-unaffected-by-human-activity, or to some other conception. Moreover, even if *we* can specify what we mean by nature in the present context, it is a further question whether any traditions of Buddhism have entertained such a conception. For instance, one would not be justified in assuming that Buddhists have subscribed to the notion that reality can be divided into two realms, the supernatural and the natural.

I will engage with some of these issues below. For the moment, however, I would like to consider one answer to Q1 that is often implied in discussions of the topic:

A1. Buddhists believe that all things are empty.
    The argument I intend to refute runs, therefore, as follows. Since they believe in the emptiness of all things, Buddhists are committed to the view that humans are in some sense 'one' with nature; moreover, it is because they believe this that they tend to act well in their relations with the natural world.

2.

Before considering the teaching of emptiness (Sanskrit: *śūnyatā*), some qualifications are in order. First, the teaching is understood in several different ways within the broad tradition of Buddhism, with the result that it can be misleading to speak of *the* teaching of emptiness at all (see, for instance, Harvey, 1990: 104–118). I will be treating the teaching of emptiness as it has been articulated in the Madhyamaka school of Mahayana Buddhism. Moreover, in the interests of keeping my account as accessible as possible, I will be presenting a very simplified account of that teaching.

Second, it must be borne in mind that, according to Buddhists, emptiness, whatever it is (and, indeed, regardless of whether it can properly be said to *be* anything at all), is not something that can be adequately understood in a merely intellectual way, but that it has rather to be experienced. So it is important at the outset that one be aware of how much—or rather, how little—any intellectual account of emptiness, such as the one I will be presenting below, might be able to achieve.

How, then, is one to understand the teaching of emptiness? As so often in the study of Buddhism, it is best to begin with the 'Noble Truths' identified by the Buddha. The first of these Truths states that our lives aren't as satisfying as they might be, are always marked, that is, by *duhkha* or suffering. The second identifies the cause of this disease, namely, our inveterate tendency to crave things, to lust after them or to seek obsessively to be rid of them.[2] Accordingly, the purpose of some of the most important Buddhist teachings is to undermine our attraction or attachment to the things we crave. And this, indeed, is the basic purpose of the teaching of emptiness: to loosen the hold things have upon us. As the Zen teacher Yasutani puts it, 'Once you realize the world of [emptiness] you will readily comprehend the nature of the phenomenal world and cease clinging to it' (quoted in Kapleau 1985: 79).

According to the emptiness teaching, we crave things (using this term in its widest sense) because we tend to see them as existing in themselves, independent both of their relations to other things and of their relation to us. This is not to say that the world is merely nothing, an absence of things. The claim is, rather, that whatever exists cannot do so on account of its possessing a non-relational essential nature: things, as Buddhists say, are empty (*śūnya*) of 'self-existence' or 'own-being' (*svabhāva*). Instead, it is said that any particular thing is what it is because of the coincidence of certain conditioning factors. So on this account, the mug of coffee on my desk, say, is the particular thing it is, not because it is imbued with an inherent nature, but because of the relations it bears both to other things and to me, the perceiver. If I could perceive it as such, if, that is, I could see it for what it is—conditioned, impermanent, a partial reflection of my own caffeine-addled mind—it, like anything, would have less of a hold on me.

3.

This is of course the barest sketch of the teaching of emptiness. I will have more to say about it below. For the moment, it will suffice to note that, condensed into such a brief summary, the teaching might seem to have something in common with the positions espoused by modern proponents of environmental holism ('ecological holists', as I shall refer to them).

The reasons for this conclusion are not hard to discern. Ecological holists such as Aldo Leopold and Arne Naess are defined as such on account of their commitment to a holistic conception of the natural world, according to which any element of that world can only be adequately understood in terms of its relations to other elements. And, in this, they would seem to be of a piece with Buddhist thinkers. For to say, with Naess for example, that organisms—or more generally, things—must be conceived as 'knots in the biospherical net or field of intrinsic relations' (1999: 3) is (one might suppose) to concur with the Buddhist's view that all things are what they are on account of certain conditioning factors. One might expect the ecological holist and the Buddhist to agree that a tree, say, is not a hard-edged, independent object but a nexus in a web of relations including, not just so many tons of wood and leaf, but the soil, sky, and sun—even, perhaps, the natural environment as a whole. More generally, one might conclude that Bill Devall is right in suggesting that 'Buddhist wisdom, including the awareness that everything is related to everything else . . . is echoed in the modern science of ecology' (1990: 161).

And one might, indeed, be tempted to go further. For if these conclusions are well taken, one might expect Buddhists to endorse what, for ecological holists, is often regarded as the central lesson of holism: that we—i.e., us humans—should be regarded as *one with* nature, not necessarily *in tune* with it, but *parts of* or even *identical with* it. One might therefore expect Buddhist thinkers to endorse the view here summarized by one ecological holist:

> [T]he central intuition of deep ecology . . . is the idea that there is no firm ontological divide in the field of existence. In other words, the world is simply not divided up into independently existing subjects and objects, nor is there any bifurcation in reality between the human and nonhuman realms. Rather all entities are constituted by their relationships. (Fox, 1999: 157: emphasis removed)

Furthermore, one might conclude that *this* is why Buddhism is an environmentally friendly religion: that the Buddhist, like the ecological holist, considers nature worthy of some kind of positive moral concern because she regards it as a holistic system with which she, and indeed all other natural things, are in some sense 'one'. Indeed one might be tempted to endorse the view espoused by one commentator, that the teaching of emptiness (interpreted as the view that 'nothing has a separate existence'), when internalized through practice, enables us humans to 'experience ourselves and nature as 'one' and so fosters 'respect for the beauty and power of nature' and the flowering of an innate 'biospirituality' (Badiner, 1990: xvi–xviii).

4.

The argument implied here (I will call it The Unity Thesis) runs roughly as follows:

- Premise 1. A holistic view of the world, according to which humans are regarded as being 'one' with nature, will necessarily engender environmental concern.
- Premise 2. The Buddhist teaching of emptiness represents just such a holistic view of the world.
- Therefore, Buddhism is an environmentally friendly religion.

The argument is valid (or rather, it could easily be made valid were it to be formulated in a more careful but more cumbersome manner). But is it sound?

Premise 1, for its part, is often assumed to be true, especially by writers towards the dark green pole of the environmental spectrum. And this assumption is also made in much of the literature devoted to 'Green Buddhism'. So, to give one of many examples, the Zen teacher Thich Nhat Hanh claims that since 'human beings and nature are inseparable', we should deal with nature the way we should deal with ourselves . . . we should not harm nature' (quoted in Harvey, 2000: 151). But this does not follow; indeed, Premise 1 is false.

Its falsity might not, however, be obvious. After all, there are no doubt some people, perhaps many, who believe that they and perhaps humans in general are in some sense one with nature, and who are thereby moved to act well in relation to the natural (roughly, non-artefactual) environment. But there is no reason to conclude that someone who subscribes to such a view must, of necessity, adopt an environmentally friendly attitude. Consider a proponent of materialism, someone (let us suppose) who subscribes to the notion that everything, she included, is made of matter. Such an individual clearly believes that we are one with nature (for her, the material universe), but there is no good reason to think that she must be moved by a positive moral regard for the natural world. She *might* be. But she might be a terrible scourge of the environment.

Or consider Spinoza's conviction that humans, and indeed all things, are parts of a single reality, 'God or Nature' (*Deus sive*

Natura). Despite believing that humans are in this special sense 'one' with nature, Spinoza himself was an inveterate anthropocentrist. Here he is:

> . . . Not that I deny that the lower [i.e., nonhuman] animals have sensations. But I do deny that we are therefore not permitted to consider our own advantage, use them at our pleasure, and treat them as is most convenient for us. (1996: 135)[3]

Despite his conviction that humans are 'one' with nature, Spinoza maintains that we are justified in doing whatever we like with our cousins in the animal world.

The salient point here is that general claims about humanity's continuity or identity with the rest of nature can, in different hands, generate diametrically opposed prescriptions for how one ought to treat the natural world.[4] And the upshot of this is that *even if* it turned out that Buddhist references to the emptiness of all things signaled a holistic view of the world, according to which humans are 'one' with nature, that in itself would not suffice to demonstrate that Buddhism is environmentally friendly.

5.

There are therefore grounds for denying that the teaching of empti- ness, even if it did entail the oneness of humans and nature, would necessarily engender any kind of positive regard for the natural world. There are good reasons, that is, for thinking that Premise 1 is false.

What, though, of Premise 2, the claim that the teaching of empti- ness indicates an 'ecological' variety of holism? One thing to note, in judging the veracity of this claim, is that, for many ecological holists, to say that humans are 'one' with the world that surrounds them is to say that they are subject to the same ecological laws, of energy transfer and the like, as everything else. This, for instance, is part of Aldo Leopold's point in claiming that we ought to regard ourselves as 'plain member[s] and citizen[s]' of the 'land-community' (1949: 204).

The Buddhist account is, however, quite different. For one thing, to say that all things are empty of self-existence is not to say, in the manner of the ecological scientist, that all things are caus- ally connected, for such talk would imply precisely that degree of distinctness among things that the teaching of *śūnyatā* is meant to undermine (Cooper, 2003: 48). For according to that teaching, the relations between things (again, using the term in its widest sense) are internal, which is to say that any particular thing would not be the thing it is in the absence of certain relations between it and other things. As David E. Cooper explains, 'Just as the relatives in a family require one another in order to be the cousins, brothers or whatever which they are, so [according to the emptiness teaching] things . . . in general require one another in order to be what they are' (2003: 49).

This observation does not, in itself, fatally undermine all attempts to ground some conception of the unity of humans and nature on the emptiness teaching. Indeed, that teaching *does* entail that, in one quite particular sense, humans and the world (if not, perhaps, nature) are inseparable. For it is said that to fully appreciate the teaching of emptiness is to realize, not just that things 'out there' in the world, are bound together by internal relations, but that what we take to be the world is internally related to *us*, to those human concerns, perspectives and 'conceptual proliferations' that are brought into play in its presenting itself to us as a world in the first place (Burton, 2001: 179). Hence, picking up, presumably, from such scriptural remarks as 'it is in . . . perceptions and thoughts that there is the world, the origin of the world' Nyanaponika Thera and Bhikkhu Bodhi, 1999: 90), *The Diamond Sūtra* maintains that material objects are 'a convention of language' (Iyer, 1983: 27) and the Sixth Patriarch of Ch'an (Zen) that 'all things were originally given rise to by man' (Yampolsky, 1967: 151). This anti-realist tendency certainly furnishes a sense to the proposition that the world is not separate from human existence, but this is evidently not the sense intended by ecological holists such as Leopold.

And there are still other differences between ecological holism and the teaching of emptiness. Consider, for example, what the world of emptiness must actually be like. There is, of course, a limit to how far reflection can get you here: emptiness, recall, is something to be experienced, rather than merely pondered. Indeed, the world of emptiness, the world as it appears in awakening, is said to be ineffable. The upshot of this is that any world that can, as it were, be 'effed' cannot, on the Buddhist account, be the world of awakening but must instead (in line with the anti-realist conclusions canvassed above) reflect certain unawakened concerns, perspectives, and so forth. This, in turn, means that the world of ecological science, precisely because it is *not* ineffable, must to a certain extent reflect our state of unawakened ignorance (*avidya*). Indeed, on the Buddhist view, any world we can capture in words, whether natural or urban, is considered to belong to *samsāra*, the realm of craving and delusion. And this, for its part, is said to be a realm from which the wise will seek *liberation*. Hence the liberated person, far from celebrating his or her oneness with the realm of nature, is one who is said to have 'overcome the world', to have overcome nature (Mascaró 1986: 72).[5]

The views of the ecological holist and the Buddhist are in this respect quite different. It is certainly not the aim of Buddhist practice to realize that we are one with nature in anything like the sense identified by ecological scientists. But although the arguments developed above may suffice to demonstrate this, they do not, in themselves, refute Premise 2. For, after all, not all ecological holists seek to ground their ideas in science. While, as we have noted, many follow Leopold in appealing to the findings of ecology, many others follow Naess in looking to holistic metaphysical systems of the kind articulated by thinkers such as Spinoza and Whitehead. 'We have seen that references to emptiness bear scant resemblance to the holistic views espoused by scientifically-minded ecological holists such as Leopold. Might they have more in common with these metaphysical conceptions of ecological holism? Indeed, might the ultimate aim of Buddhist practice be to realize, not one's continuity with the natural world as described by ecological science, but one's unity or even identity with Nature, conceived as reality as a whole?

Suggestions of this kind certainly have a popular appeal. It is often supposed that to awaken to Nirvana is to realize one's unity with the universe. (The notion is there, for example, in the joke about the Zen master and the hot-dog seller. 'What can I get you?' asks the latter. 'Make me one with everything,' the Master replies.) Popular they may be, but claims to this effect are false. For talk of becoming one with everything encourages the idea that the 'everything' referred to is some kind of self-existent metaphysical whole, one that exists 'through itself', like Spinoza's *Deus sive Natura*. But for Buddhism any such talk of self-existent Absolutes evinces a failure fully to appreciate the universality of the teaching of emptiness. For to say that all things are empty is not to say that they are what they are in relation to some self-existent abso-lute, Emptiness. On the contrary, the emptiness teaching holds true of all 'things', so that even *śūnyatā* is said to be devoid of self-existence.[6]

So Buddhists do not aspire to realize their 'oneness' with the nature described by ecological science nor, indeed, with the Nature referred to by holistically-inclined metaphysicians such as Spinoza. But there are yet more reasons for doubting the veracity of Premise 2. For consider, once again, the ecological holist's position. The crucial thing to note here is that it is precisely that, a position: the ecological holist is clearly committed to a particular view (that the world is a network of interrelated elements, and so on). Buddhist references to the emptiness of things, however, must be interpreted differently. To be sure, one might be suspicious of claims, voiced by Zen Buddhists in particular, to the effect that such talk has *no* philosophical connotations; yet it must be admitted that its primary aim is not to articulate a position that could, as it were, be set down on paper and subjected to critical evaluation. Although talk of emptiness 'does work' in the teachings of Buddhism, its function is essentially practical. Its work, in the context of intellectual debate, is not to articulate a position but to expose the emptiness of, and thus to loosen one's attachment to, any particular position—not, one might say, to paint a picture of the world, but to loosen the grip any such pictures have on us. (Indeed, this was essentially the aim of the founding text of the Madhyamaka tradition, Nāgārjuna's *Mūlamadhyamakakārikā* (Fundamentals of the Middle Way).)[7]

6.

Premises 1 and 2 of The Unity Thesis are therefore both false. Buddhist talk of emptiness does not imply a conception of holism of the kind espoused by modern-day ecological holists. Moreover, even if it *did* imply such a conception, that would not necessarily engender any kind of positive moral regard for the natural environment. What is more, even if the teaching of emptiness entailed ecological holism and ecological holism entailed some form of environmental concern, that would not justify the conclusion that Buddhism as a whole is environmentally friendly. For as I noted earlier, we have been considering the teaching of emptiness as it has been developed in one specific (yet influential) Buddhist tradition, the Madhyamaka, and the general conclusion would not therefore be warranted.[8]

Admittedly, other writers have criticized 'ecological' readings of Buddhism. Ian Harris, for one, has questioned whether the religion ought to be regarded as offering a form of ecological holism. ('[M]uch that masquerades under the label of ecoBuddhism . . .' he concludes, 'turns out to be an uneasy partnership between Spinozism, New Age religiosity and highly selective Buddhism'(2000: 132).) Yet for Harris these reflections cast doubt on the conclusion of The Unity Thesis, as well. He suggests, in other words, that because Buddhism is not presenting an environmentally friendly form of holism it should not be thought of as environmentally friendly at all (or at least, that it shouldn't be thought of as being as environmentally friendly as it is often supposed to be).

But this conclusion is unjustified. For one thing, Buddhists do have some interesting things to say about holism, and indeed some things that are relevant to environmental issues.⁹ Furthermore, leaving aside the issue of holism, there is no need to conclude that because the premises of The Unity Thesis are false, Buddhism can have nothing to offer environmental thinkers. For perhaps Buddhism is, in some sense, environmentally friendly—just not for the reasons set out in The Unity Thesis.

7.

But if not to The Unity Thesis, where is one to turn? What other basis could there be for environmental concern in Buddhism?

Here it may be helpful to recall the question with which we began:

Q1. What do Buddhists believe nature is?
   In trying to answer this question, and in trying to relate that answer to environmental matters, we have been led to what looks on the face of it to be a dead-end.

In view of this, it may be best to begin anew with a different question:

Q2. How do Buddhists think one should live?
   This is a more promising beginning. After all, the Buddhist teachings do not focus on the nature per se. It is true that ancient sources provide an elaborate cosmology; however, nowhere in the scriptures can one find a 'theory of nature' in anything like the modern sense, one on a par with those offered by Neo-Darwinism or, earlier, by Aristotelian teleology. The focus is elsewhere, on the question of how one should live in order to attain freedom from *duhkha*. Speculations on nature are regarded as being worthwhile only to the extent that they bear upon this, more pressing issue.

So, how do Buddhists think one should live? This question can be approached from several angles; however, one especially illuminating response focuses on those traits of character that, according to Buddhism, one would do well to develop. Thus one answer to Q2 runs roughly as follows. For Buddhists, one should be generous, compassionate, mindful, and so on—one would do well to live a life exemplifying these 'virtuous' character traits. Furthermore, one should develop these particular traits because of their relation to the ultimate goal of awakening from *samsāra*. So one should be generous, compassionate, etc., because these are the virtues by which an awakened life is marked.

The general claim here, then, is that Buddhism provides a conception of the good life (or what is equivalent, human well-being) as well as an account of the virtues by which such a life may be defined. The claim, in short, is that Buddhism can be framed as a (eudaimonist) virtue ethic, one similar, in certain formal respects, to Aristotle's ethics or that of the Stoics. Now this is a bold proposal, and one that would not be endorsed by all writers on the topic. But it is not my aim here to provide a thorough defense of it.[10] In the remainder of this paper, I will turn instead to the task of examining the 'environmental' implications of some candidate Buddhist virtues. My suggestions in this regard can therefore be regarded as contributions to the wider project of demonstrating that Buddhism can yield an 'environmental virtue ethic'.[11] I will not be able, in the few pages remaining, to provide an adequate defense of this larger claim. (I will not be able, for instance, to do justice to the differences between Buddhist traditions on these matters.) Nonetheless, I hope that I may be able to give some indication as to how such a virtue ethical treatment of Buddhist environmental ethics might proceed.[12]

8.

Let's begin with compassion (*karunā*). Translated into the idiom of virtue ethics, the Buddhist view is that a disposition to feel and act compassionately is an integral part of a good (i.e., awakened) life.[13] At first sight, this might seem a banal observation. After all, who, apart from Nietzscheans and sergeant majors, doesn't think compassion a good thing? Yet *karunā* is different from compassion of the common or garden variety, not least because it is said to be an occasion for bliss, rather than sorrow (Buddhaghosa, 1991: 310). This might seem surprising, given the Buddha's assessment of the amount of suffering in the world. Yet on the Buddhist account, the awakened individual is not depressed by the sufferings of others because his sympathy is always tempered by non-attachment. So although he feels for 'samsaric' beings, he does not, so to speak, feel their feelings in the same way they feel them. For the kinds of feelings we are here discussing are classified as *duhkha*, and this means that they are bound up with a host of self-centered delusions, Now an awakened individual must be able to recognize, in a comparatively detached and objective sense, that the feelings of whatever being he is faced with are deluded in this way; however, in empathizing with 'samsaric' beings he does not find himself party to their delusions. Hence he does not suffer in the same way as those he aims to help (Gowans, 2003: 142).

But here is, perhaps, not the place for a detailed analysis of the concept of *karuṇā*. The important point for the present discussion is that if compassion is a virtue, then it is, on the Buddhist account, one that extends naturally to all sentient beings, not just to humans, so that someone who is compassionate in his dealings with other humans but not in his relations with nonhuman sentient beings would not be considered genuinely compassionate at all. Hence, assuming what seems obvious, that some non-human animals are sentient, *karuṇā* counts as an 'environmental' virtue, one, that is, that may be associated with a positive moral regard for the natural (roughly, non-artefactual) world.

As well as being compassionate, a good Buddhist is said to exemplify a certain gentleness of disposition—not timidity (think, for example, of the fearsome figures portrayed in some of the literature of Zen), but an unwillingness to stamp one's mark upon the world. This is partly a result of the great emphasis placed on abiding by the 'First Precept' of Buddhist practice, the injunction against intentionally killing—or more broadly, harming or injuring—sentient beings. The good Buddhist takes care not to harm her fellow travelers in *saṃsāra*, human or non-human. But this is not to say that she is gentle *only* in her relations with sentient beings. True, one would not expect her to spend her leisure time hunting foxes or shooting pigeons, but neither would one expect to find her tramping through the temple gardens, kicking up the carefully raked sand or carving her initials into the ornamental rocks. On the contrary, the woman who is non-violent in her relations with sentient beings would also be gentle in her dealings with non-sentient beings, with plants, even rocks, and not just with humans and foxes. She would, in the words of one commentator, have developed a 'delicacy' towards her surroundings (Herrigel, 1999: 79).

This gentleness, for its part, is intimately related to a third Buddhist virtue, the humility that, in the *sutrās*, is said to correspond to the 'destruction' of pride (*māna*) (e.g., Walshe 1995: 469). As with *karuṇā*, this differs from what one might ordinarily think of as humility. To be sure, the humble man does not regard himself as being superior to his fellows, but neither does he rank himself 'worse than, or equal to anyone' (Saddhatissa 1994: 107; cf. 110). To say that he is humble is, rather, to say that he has freed himself from the self-centeredness evident, amongst other things, in a preoccupation with such self-estimation. Indeed, no longer obsessed with the relation of things or people to himself, the humble man finds himself able to 'see other things as they really are' (Murdoch, 1997: 385), in their 'thusness' (*tathatā*). It seems reasonable to suppose that such humility would counteract, not just egoism, but also that variety of anthropocentric conceit, epitomized in Spinoza's attitude towards animals, that reckons things only in relation to human satisfaction. Thus, in one Buddhist *sutrā*, we are encouraged to think of cows, not only as producers of milk and 'medicinal drugs', but as 'our great friends' and as beings endowed with their own 'beauty' and 'health'. A few verses later, those who kill and sacrifice cows are rebuked for regarding them as nothing more than 'appendage[s]' to our lives (Saddhatissa, 1994: 33–4).

A fourth Buddhist virtue is, perhaps, that of mindfulness (*smrti*)— an alert awareness of, amongst other things, feelings, thoughts and bodily sensations (the rise and fall of the breath, for instance). In the context of Buddhist practice, a dispassionate awareness of these factors is thought to foster a sense of their transience and, accordingly, freedom from attachment (see further, Gowans, 2003: 189–91). But as ever in Buddhism, the ability to do this is not regarded as being of benefit only to the practitioner. Mindfulness is thought to go hand in hand with a caring and attentive attitude towards others. And, indeed, the virtue would seem to bear upon one's comportment towards the natural world, as well. After all, many of us behave poorly in relation to the environment, not because we are uninformed about environmental issues, nor even because we don't care about them, but because we do not pay sufficient attention to how we are acting at any particular moment. I, for one, tend unthinkingly to leave lights on in my house, to throw beer cans in the trash, to leave the TV on 'standby', and so on. In doing these things I am like the novice who, in one Zen story, is scolded by his teacher for thoughtlessly pouring bathwater on the bare ground, rather than giving it to the plants (Senzaki and Reps, 1971: 83–4). Like compassion, gentleness and humility, the virtue lacking in such behavior clearly has implications for our moral relations to the natural world, even if more work would be needed to identify what precisely those implications are.

9.

As I have conceded, this is merely a thumbnail sketch of a Buddhist environmental virtue ethic.

Nonetheless, I hope that the general thesis I have defended in this paper is clear. To recap: I have suggested that Buddhism is, in certain respects, an environmentally friendly religion. But I have argued that this is not on account of the fact that Buddhists believe we are 'one' with nature in anything like the ecological holist's sense (which they don't) and because such a belief necessarily engenders environmental concern (which it doesn't). Instead, I have made the tentative suggestion that Buddhism is environmentally friendly, not because of what it says about nature per se, but on account of its view of human life, and, in particular, because of what it says about the virtues an ideal such life would exemplify. The good Buddhist treats nature well, I have argued, not because she believes she is 'one' with the natural world, but because she has, through practice, come to develop certain virtues of character. She treats nature well, that is, because she is compassionate, gentle, humble, mindful, and so on, not just in relation to her fellow humans, but in her dealings with all things.

REFERENCES

Abe, Masao. 1989. *Zen and Western Thought*, edited by William LaFleur. Honolulu: University of Hawaii Press.

Badiner, A.H., ed. 1990. *Dharma Gaia*. Berkeley, CA: Parallax Press.

Buddhaghosa. 1991. *The Path of Purification (Visuddhimagga)*, Bhikkhu Ñānamoli (trans.). Kandy: Buddhist Publication Society.

Burton, David. 2001. 'Is Madhyamaka Buddhism really the Middle Way? Emptiness and the problem of nihilism', *Contemporary Buddhism* 2, No.2: 177–90.

Cooper, David F. and James, Simon P. 2005. *Buddhism, Virtue and Environment*. Aldershot: Ashgate.

Cooper, David E. 2003. *World Philosophies: An Historical Introduction*. Oxford: Blackwell.

Devall, Bill. 1990. 'Ecocentric Sangha', in A.H. Badiner (ed.) *Dharma Gaia* (Berkeley, CA: Parallax Press), pp. 155–164.

Eckel, Malcolm David. 1997. 'Is there a Buddhist philosophy of nature?', in M. E. Tucker and D. R. Williams (eds.), *Buddhism and Ecology: The Interconnection of Dharma and Deeds* (Cambridge, MA: Harvard University Press), pp. 327–349.

Flood, Gavin, 1996. *An Introduction to Hinduism*. Cambridge: Cambridge University Press.

Fox, Warwick. 1999. 'Deep ecology: A new philosophy of our time?', in N. Witoszek and A. Brennan (eds.), *Philosophical Dialogues: Arne Naess and the Progress of Ecophilosophy* (Lanham, MD: Rowan & Littlefield), pp. 153–165.

Ganeri, Jonardon. 2001. *Philosophy in Classical India: The Proper Work of Reason*. London: Routledge.

Gowans, Christopher W. 2003. *Philosophy of the Buddha*. London: Routledge.

Harris, Ian. 2000. 'Buddhism and ecology', in D. Keown (ed), *Contemporary Buddhist Ethics* (Richmond: Curzon), pp. 113–136.

Harvey, Peter. 2000. *An Introduction to Buddhist Ethics*. Cambridge: Cambridge University Press.

Harvey, Peter. 1990. *An Introduction to Buddhism: Teaching, History and Practices*. Cambridge. Cambridge University Press.

Herrigel, G. 1999. *Zen in the Art of Flower Arranging*, translated by R. F. C. Hull. London: Souvenir.

Iyer, Raghavan, ed. 1983. *The Diamond Sutrā, with Supplementary Texts*. Santa Barbara: Concord Grove Press.

James. Simon P. 2006. 'Human virtues and natural values', *Environmental Ethics* 28 (4): 339–353.

James, Simon P. 2004. *Zen Buddhism and Environmental Ethics*. Aldershot: Ashgate.

Kapleau, Philip. 1985. *The Three Pillars of Zen: Teaching Practice, and Enlightenment*. London: Rider.

Keown, Damien. 2001. *The Nature of Buddhist Ethics*. Basingstoke: Palgrave.

Leopold, Aldo. 1949. *A Sand County Almanac*. New York: Oxford University Press.

Mascaró, Juan. *The Dhammapada: The Path of Perfection*. Middlesex: Penguin.

Murdoch, Iris. 1997. *Existentialists and Mystics: Writings on Philosophy and Literature*. Harmondsworth: Penguin.

Musashi, Tachikawa. 1993. 'The Madhyamika Tradition', in T. Yoshinori (ed.), *Buddhist Spirituality: Indian, Southeast Asian, Tibetan, Early Chinese* (London: SCM Press), pp. 188–202.

Naess, Arne. 1999. 'The shallow and the deep, long-range ecology movements: A summary', in N. Witoszek and A. Brennan (eds.), *Philosophical Dialogues: Arne Naess and the Progress of Ecophilosophy* (Lanham, MD: Rowman & Littlefield), pp. 3–7.

Nyanaponika Thera and Bhikkhu Bodhi, trans. 1999. *Numerical Discourses of the Buddha: An Anthology of Suttas from the Anguttara Nikāya*. New Delhi: Vistaar Publications.

Ryōen, Minamoto. 1999. 'Three Zen Thinkers', in T. Yoshinori (ed), *Buddhist Spirituality: Later China, Korea, Japan and the Modern World* (London: SCM Press), pp. 291–306.

Saddhatissa, H., trans. 1994, *The Sutta Nipāta*. Richmond: Curzon.

Sandler, Ronald and Cafaro, Phillip, eds. 2005. *Environmental Virtue Ethics*. (Lanham, MD: Rowman & Littlefield).

Schmithausen, Lambert. 1991. *Buddhism and Nature: The Lecture delivered on the Occasion of the EXPO 1990, An Enlarged Version with Notes*. (Tokyo: The International Institute for Buddhist Studies).

Senzaki, Nyogen and Reps, Paul. 1971. *Zen Flesh, Zen Bones*. (Middlesex: Penguin).

Smart, Ninian. 1989. *The World's Religions*. (Cambridge: Cambridge University Press).

Spinoza, Baruch. 1996. *Ethics*, trans. E. Curley. (London: Penguin).

Walshe, Maurice, trans. 1995. *The Long Discourses of the Buddha: A Translation of the Dīgha Nikāya*. (Boston: Wisdom Publications).

Witoszek, N. and Brennan, A., eds. 1999. *Philosophical Dialogues: Arne Naess and the Progress of Ecophilosophy*. (Lanham, MD: Rowman & Littlefield).

Yampolsky, P., trans. 1967. *The Platform Scripture of the Sixth Patriarch*. (New York: Columbia University Press).

Notes

1. The view that a religion must be defined in terms of the beliefs it embodies is culturally specific. Compare Ninian Smart's assessment of the importance of belief in Christianity (1989: 247) with Gavin Flood's account of the difficulties faced by any attempt to define Hinduism in terms of a set of beliefs (1996: 12).

2. Or more precisely, our tendency to crave what we take things to be. See Section 5 below. Furthermore, I am using the term 'things' here in a very broad sense to denote, not just material objects, but any object of craving.

3. Note 1 to Proposition 37 of Part 4. On the environmental implications of Spinoza's thought, see chapters 11—13 of Witoszek and Brennan, 1999.

4. It could be contended that environmental concern is engendered not merely by a commitment to the view that humans and nature are 'one', but by the feeling of being 'at one' with nature. This possibility is worth exploring: there are, no doubt, all manner of ways in which one might feel atone with nature, some of which might foster certain kinds of environmental concern. Whether any such experiences *necessarily* foster environmental concern is, however, another matter. After all, though talk of being 'at one' with nature tends to conjure up images of benign harmony, it is possible to conceive of someone who acts poorly with his dealings with nature but who nonetheless feels 'at one' with it. Think, for instance, of the trophy-seeking hunter's feeling that he is 'at one' with a nature red in tooth and claw.

5. Verse 254, See further, Harris. 2000: 122–123 and Schmithausen, 1991: 12–13. Such statements must be balanced against the view, embodied in traditions such as Zen, that the world of awakening is in some sense identical to the world as it appears to the unawakened. On the roots of such views in Madhyamaka thought, see Harvey, 1990: 103–104. On their implications for our relations with the natural world, see Eckel, 1997.

6. See further, Abe, 1989: 128–129 and Ryōen, 1999: 294. This is not to deny that some Buddhist traditions (notably, Yogācāra and Tathāgatagarbha) have been more amenable to 'metaphysical' readings of *śūnyatā*, according to which it is not simply an adjectival quality of things, but 'something' existing in its own right.

7. As Jonardon Ganeri notes, a metaphysical holism, according to which the world is 'like a net, where entities are merely the knots in interlocking ropes . . . acquiring whatever capacities they have by virtue of their relative position in the whole network and not in virtue of having intrinsic properties' 'sits ill' with Nāgārjuna's 'scepticism' (2001: 67).

8. Some ecological holists maintain that the Buddhist teaching of conditioned arising (*pratīya-samutpāda*), rather than that of emptiness, indicates a form of ecological holism. (The teachings are in fact intimately related—see further, Musashi (1993: 192–195).) On the differences between the teaching of conditioned arising and ecological holism, see Cooper and James, 2005: 111.

9. For a discussion of Buddhist holism and its implications for environmental ethics, see James, 2004: Chapter 4.

10. For a detailed defense of this claim, see Keown, 2001; Cooper and James, 2005: Chapter 4.

11. On environmental virtue ethics, see Sandler and Cafaro, 2005.

12. For a more detailed account, see Cooper and James, 2005.

13. Which is not to say, of course, that the genuinely compassionate person will be moved to develop such dispositions by a self-interested wish to better herself. On the relation between virtue ethics, environmental concern and self-interest, see James, 2006.

CHAPTER 6

Causation and 'Telos': The Problem of Buddhist Environmental Ethics

IAN HARRIS

Published material relating to Buddhism and environmental ethics has increased in a moderate fashion over the last few years and may be divided into four broad categories:

1. Forthright endorsement of Buddhist environmental ethics by traditional guardians of doxic truth, of whom HH Dalai Lama[1] is perhaps the most important representative.
2. Equally positive treatments by predominantly Japanese and North American scholar/activists premised on an assumption that Buddhism is blessed with the resources necessary to address current environmental issues. Generally this material limits itself to identifying the most appropriate Buddhist doctrinal bases from which an environmental ethic could proceed, e.g., the doctrines of interpenetration, *tathāgatagarbha*, etc. (e.g., Aramaki,[2] Macy,[3] and Brown[4]).
3. Critical treatments which, while fully acknowledging the difficulties involved in reconciling traditional Asian modes of thought with those employed by scientific ecology, are optimistic about the possibility of establishing an authentic Buddhist response to environmental problems (e.g., Schmithausen[5]).
4. Outright rejection of the possibility of Buddhist environmental ethics on the grounds that the otherworldliness of "canonical" Buddhism implies a negation of the natural realm for all practical purposes (e.g., Hakamaya[6]).

In this paper I shall move backwards and forwards between positions 3 and 4—my heart telling me that 3 makes sense with my mind more in tune with position 4. Category 1 material mainly relates to dialogue with other religions and aims to paint Buddhism in a favorable light. I shall have nothing further to say on this. I hope to show that work belonging to the second category, while super-ficially attractive, falls some way short of providing an adequate and rigorous basis for the erection of a thoroughgoing Buddhist environmental ethic. The minimum qualification for an authentic Buddhist ethics is that it is able to construe causation in such a way that goal-oriented activity makes sense. In other words, Buddhist causation must be shown to be teleologically meaningful. In our context a positive moral stance towards the environment is premised on the idea that one state of affairs can be shown to be preferable to another; for instance, that the world will be demonstrably worse if the black rhino becomes extinct. Now, I would not wish to argue against this in general terms, but I shall contend that it is difficult to ground such a view on a sound Buddhist footing, most importantly because any activity of this kind presupposes a certain teleology and an accompanying belief in the predictability of cause/effect relations.

Let us now examine the idea of causation in more detail. Yamada, in an article that draws on a very substantial body of prior Japanese scholarship, shows that the *pratītyasamutpāda* formula can be read in two significantly differing ways—the so-called "reversal" and "natural" sequences. The first he believes to be a characteristic of the *Abhidharma*, with the second more closely associated with the Buddha himself.[7] The reversal sequence, beginning with ignorance (*avijjā*) and ending with becoming-old and dying (*jarāmaraṇa*), is said to describe elements causally related in temporal succession. In this manner the time-bound and soteriologically meaningful, concepts of *karma*, *bhava*, *bhāvanā*, etc., so crucial to the whole idea of Buddhist *praxis* are made comprehensible. The natural sequence, by contrast, beginning with *jarāmaraṇa* and ending in *avijjā*, stresses non-temporal relations of interdependence, simultaneity, or mutuality. In this way:

> The twelve *angas* are not so much causal chains, in which the cause precedes the effect in rigid succession, but the factors of human exis-tence which are interdependent upon each other simultaneously in a structural cross-section of human life.[8]

This typically *Mahāyānist* rendering, then, associates chronological causation with the *Abhidharma* of the old canon, while simultaneous relations (*akālika*) represent a complementary position implicit in the teachings of the Buddha yet only made explicit in the *Mahāyāna*. The implication here seems to be that the natural sequence, while obviously present in the writings of the old canon, was either consciously or unconsciously neglected.

For Yamada, *Abhidharmic* scholiasts deviated, for some inexplicable reason, from an atemporal understanding of causation to the extent that they came to adopt a theory of strict one-to-one cause-effect relations "along the flow of time"[9] known in Japanese as *gookan engi setsu* (karma activated dependent origination theory). I shall now suggest that the Abhidharmic adherence to asymmetry, i.e., to a strict temporal sequencing of *dharmas*, is not quite as strong as may have been expected from Yamada's treatment of the subject.

The *Sarvāstivāda* accepts six basic kinds of relation (*hetu*) between entities. Of these six, two—the simultaneous relation (*sahabhūhetu*) and the associated relation (*samprayuktahetu*)—suggest a roughly similar character of mutuality. In fact, the *Sarvāstivāda* came under attack from a variety of other Buddhist schools[10] under the suspicion that these two interrelated *hetu* undermined the basis of temporal causation understood as essential to the efficacy of ethical and soteriologically meaningful activity. It is clear, for instance, that Sanghabhadra was perfectly happy with the notion of mutuality in relations to the extent that he derives his simultaneously produced relation (*sahotpannahetu*) from the ancient "when this . . . that" formula.[11]

Some scholars[12] have attempted to show that simultaneous and temporal theories of causation are complementary. While the latter represents a unidirectional flow of causes and effects, the former points to the spatial relations that must also hold between co-existent entities. *Sahabhūhetu*, then, concerns relations in space, not in time. It indicates a principle of spatial unity or aggregation. Of the twenty-four modes of conditionality (*paccaya*) recognized by the Pali *Paṭṭhāna*, the sixth and seventh, in their traditional order, are closely related. These are, respectively, the co-nascence condition (*sahajātapaccaya*) and the mutuality condition (*aññamaññapaccaya*). The former condition occurs in four basic kinds of relation, i.e., those between mentals and mentals, mentals and physicals, physicals and physicals and physicals and mentals. So exhaustive is this list that we could be forgiven for thinking that the vast majority of the possible relations between the entities envisaged by *Theravāda* Buddhism may be found under this heading. In fact, relations of the first type, i.e., mentals to mentals, are acknowledged, by a range of *Theravāda* thinkers, to be:

> . . . symmetrical. That is, the relation between the two terms A and B holds good as between B and A.[13]

Karunadasa accepts that, under certain circumstances, a relationship of pure reciprocity can apply, specifically in what he regards to be a special case of *sahajāta* defined in the traditional list of *paccayas* as no. 7—the mutuality condition (*aññamañña*). Indeed, Ledi Sayadaw happily conflates these two *paccayas* and there is a widely held view, endorsed by Karunadasa, among others, that the *aññamañña* condition is "the same as the *sahabhūhetu* of the *Sarvāstivādins*."[14]

Buddhaghosa in his *Vibhaṅga* commentary, *Sammohavinodanī*, distinguishes between a strictly *sutta*-based, temporal form of causation extending over many thought-moments (*nānācittakkhaṇika*) on the one hand, and an abhidhammic, non-temporal version said to occur in a single thought-moment (*ekacittakkhaṇika*), i.e., to all intents and purposes, instantaneously.[15] According to Buddhaghosa then, the *suttas* favor asymmetry with the *abhidhamma* plumping for a spatio-symmetric view of relations. This categorization differs sharply from Yamada's understanding of an *Abhidhamma* unequivocally promoting uni-directional causation, and, in my opinion, his less than enthusiastic support for non-*Mahāyānist* positions tends to make him uncritically conflate a great range of sources. In fact, the true situation on *sutta* and *abhidhamma* readings is probably somewhere between the positions of Buddhaghosa and Yamada. It seems that the Pali commentarial traditional never successfully managed to reconcile these two radically divergent readings and in the final analysis, elegant solutions to complex textual traditions are impossible to achieve. Nevertheless, it is obvious that *akālika* relations i.e. those not bound by time were not entirely overlooked by the *Theravāda* even though some modern apologists have been reluctant to admit this fact.[16]

The *Sautrāntika* school seems to have offered four basic objections to the *Sarvāstivādin* position on mutual relations not least because it seemed thoroughly imbued with a spirit of symmetry. The *Sautrāntika* also advanced a more radical theory of momentariness (*kṣaṇavāda*) by denying any element of stasis. For the *Sautrāntikas*, *dharmas* disappear as soon as they arise though this response to the problem of true causal efficiency is no more satisfactory than the position it sought to replace. Nagao's rather flimsy defense of *kṣaṇavāda* fails to come to terms with this fact. He argues that the doctrine:

> does not mean the total extinction of the world; on the contrary, it is the way by which the world establishes itself as *full of life and spirit* (my emphasis).[17]

Now, though irresolvable differences remain, all three early schools of Buddhism exhibited a tendency to view causation in spatial/horizontal terms, even though this tendency was often obscured behind the lush vegetation of temporal/vertical thinking.

It looks likely that, as Buddhism developed, a gradual radicalization of the concept of impermanence occurred with rather more emphasis placed on symmetric relations between entities. The common sense view, perhaps related to the introspective/empirical observations of an early meditator's tradition that set a radically impermanent mental flux against the relative permanence of non-mental entities, was in time reformulated and rationalized by an emerging scholastic tradition.[18] These scholastic traditions, then, begin a process that results in the severing of links with common sense asymmetric causation to the extent that the temporal flow of a single chain of causes and effects was eclipsed by the space-like aspect of symmetry. In my view, the increasing dominance of symmetry in Buddhist thought provides a fertile breeding ground for the development of the *Avataṃsakasūtra* doctrine of the radical interpenetration of all things and this, in a circuitous manner, undoubtedly has come to influence the writings of many contemporary environmental thinkers.

Mahāyānists in general wish to preserve a time-like asymmetry of causation in its common-sense form, while negating it from the ultimate perspective. Nāgārjuna holds that four alternative positions, the tetralemma or *catuṣkoṭi*, logically exhaust the possible connections between causally related entities. Now, the dominant view within the *Mahāyānist* exegetical tradition is that Nāgārjuna's negation of the four alternatives is absolute. In other words, relations between entities can never be meaningfully articulated in terms of any of the four positions of the *catuṣkoṭi*. Indeed, no other position is possible. Absolute negation (*prasajyapratiṣedha*) in this case results in the total denial of causal relations between substantial entities. Using this as a starting point, Nāgārjuna moves on swiftly to propose that entities engaged in causal relations must be empty (*śūnya*). Of course, he has already underlined the centrality of *pratītyasamutpāda* as the bedrock, the central authority from which all Buddhist thought must flow. This being so, the affirmation of causal relations leads inexorably to a negation of substantiality. Now, an empty entity has no distinguishing mark, its value is zero (*śūnya*). Furthermore, all conditioned entities must share this same null value and in this sense they are equivalent. If this is accepted Charles Hartshorne's intuition[19] that Nāgārjuna exhibits a prejudice in favor of symmetry is confirmed and we shall expect Nāgārjuna to experience some difficulty in accounting for any purposeful directionality of change, or "emergence into novelty" to use the jargon of process theology.

The earliest extant commentary on the *Mūlamadhyamakakārikā*, the *Akutobhayā*[20], is traditionally ascribed to Nāgārjuna, though this attribution tends to be rejected by modern scholarship. Interestingly, the use of absolute negation (*prasajyapratiṣedha*) of the four positions of the *catuṣkoṭi* is not one of the obvious features of this early text. In its treatment of *MMK*.XVI I I.8, the four *koṭis* are said to represent a series of graded steps related to the spiritual propensities of those engaged on the Buddhist path. This reading, in part confirmed by the later commentaries of Buddhapālita and Bhāvaviveka[21], singles out the fourth and final *koṭi* as the closest approximation, given the constraints of language, to the true nature of things. If we relate this to our earlier discussion of the four possible modes of production, it is apparent that the "neither different nor non-different" position, if is legitimate to invoke the law of the excluded middle here, reflects a rejection of both symmetric and asymmetric accounts of causation—a deeply puzzling notion. We might have expected a more satisfactory resolution of the problem, assuming of course that anyone in the early *Madhyamaka* was aware of, or indeed interested, in the matter. If so, we shall be disappointed, for the early *Madhyamaka* transcends, rather than resolves the tension. By retaining his strong adherence to the Buddha's teaching on *pratītyasamutpāda*, i.e. by insisting on the objectivity of the causal process, Nāgārjuna and his followers adopt a view of reality that, in so far as it can be articulated, is constituted by causally related and empty entities that are neither different nor non-different one from another. Elsewhere I have termed this outlook "ontological indeterminacy."[22] Naturally Ruegg is reluctant to accept that the *Madhyamaka* would have countenanced such an irrational depiction of reality as *coincidentia oppositorum* but what strikes one forcibly here is the parallel with the doctrine of symmetric interpenetration characteristic of some of the later phases of Buddhism, such as the Chinese Hua-Yen school.[23] In the *Yogācāra* again we find some evidence of a distinction between *akālika* and unidirectional relations, even though the precise form of the distinction does not fully harmonize with that observed in other strands of the Buddhist tradition. As we would expect of a philosophical tradition with a specific interest in the mechanics of consciousness (*vijñāna*), the *Yogācāra* treatment of causation gives priority to the nontemporal factors that, as we have already seen in the Pali literature, apply to relations between mental entities.

Nagao goes on to suggest that the term *pratītyasamutpāda* is not intended to define causal relationships as customarily understood for it represents " . . . the realm of mutual relatedness, of absolute relativity [which] constitutes an absolute otherness over against selfhood and essence."[24] Chronological proliferation operates only from the perspective of conventional understanding, for, in reality, *pratītyasamutpāda* denotes "unity in a transhistorical realm."[25]

Returning now to Nāgārjuna's picture of causation and reality at *MMK*. XVI I I.9, we hear:

> Independent of another (*aparapratyaya*) (Ruegg's[26] rendering of this difficult term), at peace (*śānta*) not discursively developed through discursive developments, without dichotomizing conceptualisation, and free from multiplicity (*anānārtha*): this is the characteristic of reality (*tattva*)."[27]

This verse occurs in the context of a discussion of causal factors so we may, without doing violence to the text, conclude that *tattva* is inextricably related to *pratītyasamutpāda*. Comparison with the *maṅgalaśloka* reveals a number of parallels. *Tattva*, for instance, is said to be at peace, or still (*śānta*). The term *anānārtham* also occurs in *MMK*.XVI I I.9, although significantly *tattva* is not related to the usual binegation of positive and negative positions, i.e., neither without differentiation nor devoid of unity (the fourth *koṭi*), as one would expect by reference to the *maṅgalaśloka*. A consistent reading suggests that the quiescence and non-multiplicity of causally related entities is a function of their entirely symmetrical relations and one might be inclined to term this kind of relation "interpenetration". Ruegg, of course, rejects this interpretation. However, his treatment of the passages is ambiguous for he upholds Candrakīrti's view that a reality devoid of differentiation has the value of emptiness while, elsewhere in the same important article, he also wants to maintain that the *Madhyamaka* understanding of causal relations is "in a certain sense indeterminate and irrational."[28] In the less equivocal opinion of la Vallee Poussin, Nāgārjuna holds only to the conventional expression of temporal causation, for: "There is, in absolute truth, no cause and effect."[29]

To summarize, the centrality of the notion of causation is non-negotiable, located, as it were, at the heart of the tradition. This seems to have led some early Buddhist schools to emphasize spatiality as against temporality, perhaps because this was perceived as entailing fewer intractable philosophical problems. The early *Madhyamaka* does not follow this lead preferring instead a transcendent approach to the problem of causation.

Conclusion

The gulf between spatial and temporal interpretations of causation was never satisfactorily reconciled in early Buddhism. An obvious starting point in any theoretical construction of an authentic Buddhist environmentalist ethic must be the doctrine of causation understood in its temporal sense yet, though the doctrine allows for a highly coherent account of the arising and cessation of suffering, and in particular of the interaction of mental factors, it has rarely been invoked as the basis of a "scientific" explanation of the natural world. This is, in good measure, because Buddhism has regularly embraced chrono-logical causation at one moment only to reject it in the next. Here is an excellent example of the corrosive character of the "rhetoric of immediacy".

From the cosmological perspective Buddhism recognizes an *ad nauseam* unfolding and dissolution of worlds that act as receptacles for countless beings yet this picture is essentially anti-evolutionary or dysteleologic. All is in a state of flux yet all is quiescent for all forward movement lacks a sense of purpose. As Faure has made clear, the gulf between these two levels is not always easy to negotiate, even given the "teleological tendencies of controlled narrative"[30] that Buddhism has generally employed to minimize the incongruence of its various building blocks.

The theory of *karma* is clearly crucial to any Buddhist explanation of the world. On this account the "natural realm" is, at any point in time, regarded as a direct result of Stcherbatsky's "mysterious efficiency of past elements or deeds."[31] There is, then, no magnet at the end of history drawing events inexorably towards their ultimate goal, no supra-temporal *telos* directing events either directly or indirectly. The narrative and soteriological structure of Buddhism appears, despite some recent attempts to indicate otherwise, essentially dysteleologic.[32]

Now, this need not preclude the possibility of purposiveness altogether, yet, when other available teleologies are considered, prospects are not especially encouraging. Woodfield, in an important study, shows that only two further positions remain for the Buddhist and one of these, the animistic alternative premised on the notion that entities are directed by the souls or minds that inhere within them, cannot possibly be appropriate. We are left then with the Aristotelian idea of immanent teleology in which objects behave teleologically because it is in their nature to do so. In other words the "source of a thing's end-directedness is to be found within the nature of the thing itself, not in some external agency."[33]

It is clear that, from the *Madhyamaka* perspective, no entity exists that could possibly possess a nature of this kind. The fact of *niḥsvabhāvatā* then precludes the possibility of immanent *tele*. The *Abhidharma* position, bearing in mind our earlier discussion, is perhaps more difficult to characterize. *Dharmas* are the ultimately unanalyzable constituents of nature but can *dharmas*, which are at least regarded as possessing own-natures (*svabhāva*), also be said to act as the source of their own end-directed movement? There is general agreement of all of the early schools of Buddhism that *dharmas* are simple and discrete entities. As such their capacity for internal relations with other *dharmas* makes no sense. Relationships must be of a purely formal kind. If this is accepted two things follow:

1. *dharmas* cannot mutually cooperate to bring about events on the macro scale—we may wish to compare this with process theology's[34] comparatively successful attempt to account for change, and even novelty, as the result of the prehension [i.e., serial co-operation] of internally related simples within an overarching Christian teleological structure.

2. *dharmas* do not possess *tele* though, on the level of convention, societies of such entities may be said to possess ends, though only in the most highly provisional sense.

The theory of *dharmas* represents a pseudo-explanation, a reformulation of the original insight of the Buddha into the fact that all things change. It gives no information on how this may occur. The theories of causation and of *karma* hover above all mechanical explanations and are never successfully earthed within them. In this sense we can talk about an "ontological indeterminacy" at the heart of Buddhist thought. At best all we can say is that Buddhism accepts *de facto* change. It cannot account for it!

If we now root our discussion in the more concrete situation of environmental ethics we begin to see the difficulty in determining a coherent Buddhist approach. There are difficulties in determining how best to act with regard to the natural world, unless that response has been specifically authorized by the Buddha. The problem here is twofold. In the first place, few of the Buddha's injunctions can be used unambiguously to support environmentalist ends[35] and in the second, the dysteleological character of Buddhist thought militates against anything that could be construed as injecting the concept of an "end" or "purpose" into the world. It is, for example, very hard to see how a specifically Buddhist position on global warming or on the decrease in diversity of species can be made, unless of course one can appeal to the supranormal intelligence of a handful of contemporary Buddhist sages. In this connection, the Far-Eastern appeal to the Buddhist notion of the "interpenetration of all entities" will not do, for I hope that I have shown that the symmetric bias of this approach cannot even satisfactorily account for the raw fact of change itself, let alone for those aspects of change deemed harmful to the natural environment.

Schmithausen has observed that Buddhist spiritual and everyday practice may contribute to a sort of *de facto* environmentalism, though he's careful to point out that this does not, in itself "establish . . . nature . . . as a value in itself"[36]. It is worth pointing out that even in the realm of interpersonal relations, and in relations between humans and the higher animals, "commitment to extrapersonal welfare" is found only in a "highly qualified and rather paradoxical sense."[37] In this light Schmithausen's program for a reformation of Buddhism through de-dogmatization of the inconvenient Buddhist teachings on animals, etc. is little more than a bit of tinkering around on the margins. I hope that I have been able to show that it is the dysteleology deeply rooted within Buddhism that is the essential problem for any future Buddhist environmental ethic, not a bit of local difficulty with animals. It is not so much that Buddhism has a difficulty in deriving an ought from an is, it is that it faces the more fundamental difficulty of defining an "is" in the first place. On the theoretical level, then, the best Buddhism can offer at the moment is an endorsement of those aspects of the contemporary environmentalist agenda that do not conflict with its philosophic core. The future development of a coherent and specifically Buddhist environmentalism, assuming that this is indeed possible, will be fraught with many difficulties.

NOTES

1. For example, Tenzin Gyatso, His Holiness the 14th Dalai Lama "A Tibetan Buddhist Perspective on Spirit in Nature" in Rochefeller, Steven C. and John C. Elder (eds.) *Spirit and Nature: Why the Environment is a Religious Issue* (Boston: Beacon Press, 1992), pp. 109–123.

2. Noritoshi Aramaki, "*Shizen-hakai kara Shizen-sasei e—Rekishi no Tenkai ni tsuite*" (From destruction of Nature to Revival of Nature: On a Historical Conversion) *Deai*, 11.1 (1992), pp. 3–22.

3. Joanna Macy, "The Greening of the Self" in A. Hunt-Badiner (ed.) *Dharma Gaia: A Harvest of Essays in Buddhism and Ecology* (Berkeley: Parallax, 1990), pp. 53–63. Also, *Mutual Causality in Buddhism and General Systems Theory: The Dharma of Natural Systems* (Albany: State University of New York Press, 1991).

4. Brian Brown, "Toward a Buddhist Ecological Cosmology" *Bucknell Review*, 37.2 (1993), pp. 124–137.

5. Lambert Schmithausen, *Buddhism and Nature. The Lecture Delivered on the Occasion of the EXPO 1990 (An Enlarged Version with Notes)* (Tokyo: The International Institute for Buddhist Studies, 1991 [Studia Philologica Buddhica, Occasional Paper Series VI I]). Also, The Problem of the Sentience of Plants (Tokyo: The International Institute for Buddhist Studies, 1991 [Studia Philologica Buddhica, Occasional Paper Series VI]).

6. Noriaki Hakamaya, "*Shizen-hihan to-shite no Bukkyoo*" (Buddhism as a Criticism of *Physis/Natura*) *Komazawa-daiguku Bukkyoogakubu Ronshū*, 21 (1990), pp. 380–403. Also, "*Nihon-jin to animizmu*" *Komazawa-daiguku Bukkyoogakubu Ronshū*, 23 (1992), pp. 351–378.

7. I. Yamada, "Premises and Implications of Interdependence" in S. Balasooriya, et al (eds.) *Buddhist Studies in Honour of Walpola Rahula* (London: Gordon Fraser, 1980), p. 279f.

8. Ibid., p. 271.

9. Ibid., pp. 272–273.

10. The main opponents to this apparent notion of simultaneous causation were the *Dārṣṭāntikas* (cf. *Mahāvibhāṣā* [*Taishoo* 27, p.79c7–8]) and the *Sautrāntikas* (Vasubandhu *Abhidharmakośa* 83.18-84.24). The *Sautrāntika* objections to the notion of mutual causality were fourfold.

11. See *Nyāyānusāra* [*Taishoo* 29.419b7–8] quoted in K.K. Tanaka, "Simultaneous Relation (*Sahabhū-hetu*): A Study in Buddhist Theory of Causation," *Journal of the International Association of Buddhist Studies*, 8, 1 (1985), pp. 91–111; p.95.

12. Ibid.

13. Ledi Sayadaw "On the Philosophy of Relations II," Journal of the Pali Text Society, (1915–16), pp. 21–53; p.40. This reading is confirmed by W. M. McGovern's discussion of this matter in *A Manual of Buddhist Philosophy* Vol. 1—Cosmology (London: Kegan Paul, Trench, Trubner & Co., 1923), pp. 194–195.

14. Y. Karunadasa, *Buddhist Analysis of Matter* (Colombo: Dept. of Cultural Affairs, 1967), p. 131. Funnily enough Kalupahana takes a rather different line. For him, *sahajātapaccaya*, not *aññamaññapaccaya* is the correlate of *sahabhūhetu* while, on the authority of Haribhadra, *aññamañña* is said to be the correlate of the *Sarvāstivāda sabhāgahetu*. See David J. Kalupahana, *Causality: The Central Philosophy of Buddhism* (Honolulu: University Press of Hawai'i, 1975), pp. 167–168.

15. *Sammohavinodanī* pp. 199–209.

16. It is certainly curious that Ledi Sayadaw (op cit) fails to make any specific reference to *aññamañña* in his treatment of the *paccayas*. Again, Nyanatiloka is extremely cautious in treatment of simultaneity in causal relations; see Nyanatiloka Mahāthera, *Guide Through the Abhidhamma-Pitaka: Being a Synopsis of the Philosophical Collection Belonging to the Buddhist Pali Canon* (Kandy: Buddhist Publication Society, 1971), p. 156.

17. Gadjin Nagao, "The Logic of Convertibility" in *Madhyamaka and Yogācāra: A Study of Mahāyāna Philosophies: Collected Papers of G.M. Nagao* [Edited, collated and translated by L.S. Kawamura in collaboration with G.M. Nagao] (Albany: State University of New York Press, 1991), p. 130 [first appeared as "*Tenkan no Ronri*" in *Tetsugaku Kenkyu* (Journal of Philosophical Studies), 35.7 (1952), p. 405ff.

18. This distinction between cadres of spiritual praxis and philosophical reflection builds on the distinction first made by Lambert Schmithausen in "Spirituelle Praxis und Philosophical Theorie im Buddhismus," *Zeitschrift fur Missionswissenschaft und Religionswissenschaft*, 57.3 (1973), pp. 161–186 [Republished & translated into English as "On the Problem of the Relation of Spiritual Practice and Philosophical Theory in Buddhism" in German Scholars on India, Vol. II (New Delhi: Cultural Department of the Embassy of the Federal Republic of Germany, 1976. pp. 235–250].

19. Charles Hartshorne, *Creative Synthesis and Philosophic Method* (London: SCM Press, 1970 [The Library of Philosophy and Theology]), pp. 205–226.

20. On the authorship, etc., of *Akutobhayā*, see C.W. Huntingdon, Jr., *The Akutobhayā and Early Indian Madhyamaka,* unpublished dissertation, University of Michigan, 1986.

21. See David S. Ruegg, "The Uses of the Four Positions of the *Catuṣkoṭi* and the Problem of the Description of Reality in *Mahāyāna* Buddhism", *Journal of Indian Philosophy*, 5 (1977–8), pp. 37ff.

22. Ian Charles Harris, *The Continuity of Madhyamaka and Yogācāra in Indian Mahāyāna Buddhism* (Leiden: E.J.Brill, 1991); especially see chapter 7.

23. See my "An American Appropriation of Buddhism" in T. Skorupski (ed.), *Buddhist Forum*, Vol. 3 (Tring: Institute of Buddhist Studies, 1994), forthcoming.

24. Gadjin M. Nagao, *The Foundational Standpoint of Madhyamika Philosophy* [translated by John P. Keenan] (Albany: State University of New York Press, 1989), p. 8.

25. Ibid., p. 17.

26. Ruegg, "The Uses of the Four Positions of the *Catuṣkoṭi* and the Problem of the Description of Reality in *Mahāyāna* Buddhism," p. 10.

27. *aparapratyayaṃ śāntam prapañcair aprapañcitaṃ. Nirvikalpam anānārtham etat tattvasya lakṣaṇaṃ.*

28. Ruegg, "The Uses of the Four Positions of the *Catuṣkoṭi* and the Problem of the Description of Reality in *Mahāyāna* Buddhism," p. 11 n. 44.

29. Louis de la Vallee Poussin, "Identity (Buddhist)" in J. Hastings (ed.), *Encyclopaedia of Religion and Ethics* (Edinburgh: T. & T. Clark, 1914), Vol. VI I, p. 100.

30. Bernard Faure, *The Rhetoric of Immediacy: A Cultural Critique of Chan/Zen Buddhism* (Princeton: Princeton University Press, 1991), p. 4.

31. Th. Stcherbatsky, *The Central Conception of Buddhism* (Delhi: Motilal Banarsidass, 1974), p. 31.

32. The term "dysteleology" seems to have been coined by the Protestant theologian E. Heckel to denote the "purposelessness of nature".

33. Andrew Woodfield, *Teleology* (Cambridge: Cambridge University Press, 1976), p. 6.

34. For example, David Ray Griffin, "Whitehead's Deeply Ecological Worldview," *Bucknell Review* 37.2 (1993), pp. 190–206.

35. See my "How Environmentalist is Buddhism?" *Religion*, 21 (1991), pp. 101–114.

36. Lambert Schmithausen, "How can Ecological Ethics be Established in Early Buddhism", p. 15 (forthcoming).

37. David Little and Sumner B. Twiss, *Comparative Religious Ethics: A New Method* (San Francisco: Harper and Row, 1978), p. 240.

Section II

Environmental Philosophy in Chinese Traditions of Thought

CHAPTER 7

The Relevance of Chinese Neo-Confucianism for the Reverence of Nature

MARY EVELYN TUCKER

The continuing assault on the natural world by industrial processes has awakened in many concerned persons the awareness that corrective action is needed to begin to halt the desecration of our planet. But if such action is to be truly effective, it must arise from sources as deep as life itself, namely from a new or renewed understanding of cosmological and ecological processes that sustain all forms of life. Without such a comprehensive context in which to rethink sustainable development we may be unable to counter the powerful pragmatic logic of present technological and industrial growth. We cannot minimize the complexity of the problem at hand nor can we simply condemn all industrial processes. Nonetheless, the emerging conflict of economic demands for growth versus environmental concerns for protection will continue to be a major challenge of our times.

How to balance these areas of economic growth and environmental protection is a critical question in both the domestic and the international arenas. It is abundantly clear that we are involved with complex interrelated global problems regarding the pollution and the depletion of our air, our water, our soil, and other life forms. The growing hole in the ozone layer, the diminishment of the aquifers, the loss of topsoil, the destruction of the forests, and the disappearance of species are occurring on a magnitude never before witnessed in human history. We cannot underestimate the scale of human energy and ingenuity that will be necessary to reverse these alarming trends. An essential challenge, then, is how to foster sustainable life, growth, and development for all species while not undermining the very sources of our common existence, now and in the future.

The term "sustainable development" has emerged as a key concept in relation to the problem of encouraging an economic growth that is balanced by environmental integrity. The concept has been used widely since 1987 when the World Commission on Environment and Development (also known as the Brundtland Commission) issued a report entitled *Our Common Future*. It was formulated around the principle that economic growth must "be based upon policies that sustain and expand the environmental resource base."[1] It emphasized a fact that had heretofore been largely overlooked, namely that economic development must begin to use a cost accounting that includes the effect of development on the environment and on the depletion of resources.

The importance of this formulation is highlighted by Lester Brown and the World Watch Institute in a report also released in 1987 on the *State of the World*. The report notes that progress has come with an enormous price. Indeed, the radical changes brought about by humans in altering atmospheric chemistry, global temperatures, and the abundance of living species "reflect the crossings that may impair the earth's capacity to sustain an ever-growing human population. A frustrating paradox is emerging. Efforts to improve living standards are themselves beginning to threaten the health of the global economy. The very notion of progress begs for redefinition in light of the intolerable consequences unfolding as a result of its pursuit."[2]

In calling for a rethinking of the meaning of progress and reformulating the notion of a sustainable society the study observes: "A sustainable society satisfies its needs without diminishing the prospects of the next generation. By many measures, contemporary society fails to meet this criterion. Questions of ecological sustainability are arising on every continent. The scale of human activities has begun to threaten the habitability of the earth itself. Nothing short of fundamental adjustments in population and energy policies will stave off the host of costly changes now unfolding, changes that could overwhelm our longstanding efforts to improve the human condition."[3] Thus, there is a growing movement to encourage sustainable development that will incorporate environmental concerns.

Attitudinal Changes Toward Nature

In addition to new economic approaches to our environmental problems there is a growing realization that attitudinal changes toward nature will also be essential for creating sustainable societies. Humans will not be apt to preserve what they do not respect. What is currently lacking, however, is a broad moral basis for changing our exploitative attitudes toward nature. In other words, we are still without a sufficiently comprehensive environmental ethic for altering our consciousness about the earth and our life on it.

This has been changing during the last ten years as the issues have been fiercely argued and a new journal of *Environmental Ethics* has been published. Seminal work is being done in this area by philosophers such as Ian Barbour, J. Baird Callicott, Kristen Shrader-Frechette, Eugene Hargrove, Arne Naess, Tom Regan, Holmes Rolston, and George Sessions. In addition, there have been the contributions of theologians such as John Cobb and Jay McDaniel, biologists such as Charles Birch and E. O. Wilson and historians such as Roderick Nash. Issues of animal rights as well as the rights of trees, plants, and other forms of life have been vigorously debated. Important philosophical distinctions have been drawn between utilitarian rights of nature versus intrinsic rights and strong disagreements have emerged between conservationists and deep ecologists. A major point of contention concerns the anthropocentric view versus the ecocentric or biocentric view. In other words, how does humanity fit into the natural world without domination or exploitation, but with a deepened sense of reverence in being one species among many?

Part of the confusion arises from our own Western vision of reality focusing almost exclusively on the primacy of humans as the crowning point of evolution over against other species and natural entities, animal, vegetable, and mineral. In the philosophical tradition humans have been seen as the rational, reflective center of creation while in the religious traditions the relationship of humans with the divine has dominated all else. The earth and its myriad species were secondary to the significance of human beings.

Various philosophers have struggled with this problem of anthropocentrism for the last decade. With a few notable exceptions, theologians and historians of religion have been slower to reflect on this issue. Only recently has the critique of anthropocentrism in relation to environmental problems been raised with renewed force in the field of religion. It is to this development that the comments here are directed.

The question we might pose is this: to what extent can the religious traditions of the world provide us with cosmological and ethical perspectives that supersede anthropocentrism and offer theoretical positions to confront the growing environmental crisis? Can the insights of some of the world's religions be brought to bear on the question of the role of the human in relation to the natural world? While very few of the world's religions have traditionally espoused an ecological morality, their attitudes toward the natural world may well have some light to shed on our own current crisis of values. I would suggest that this can be done from a variety of different traditions including indigenous, monotheistic, and Asian religions.

The Chinese in particular have a significant contribution to make in this regard because from their earliest recorded history, the earth has been an integral part of their religious discourse.[4] The great triad of Chinese thought is heaven, earth, and humans. This is quite a different perspective from the Western religious traditions, which are almost exclusively concerned with salvation in terms of divine-human interaction. God as Creator, as transcendent, and as One are the shared characteristics of Western monotheism in its Jewish, Christian, and Islamic forms. It has been suggested that concomitant with the understanding that God is transcendent to the natural world there is frequently a devaluation of the sacredness of nature. This point was forcefully made nearly twenty-five years ago by Lynn White in his landmark article on "The Historical Roots of Our Ecologic Crisis."[5] White blamed the Western biblical traditions in part for the ecological crisis by suggesting that with the idea of the divine being removed from nature and with the biblical injunction for human dominion over the other species there was no obvious moral basis for revering nature. This has subsequently been vigorously debated by biblical scholars, theologians, philosophers and historians.[6] While the controversy probably will never be settled completely, the argument that monotheism tends to preserve the separation of God from nature is a compelling one.

Furthermore, the locus of the meeting of divine and human in Western religions has been largely in the human soul, and concern for personal salvation has often overridden all other issues. Western theology tends to concentrate on discussions of the characteristics of God, the problem of evil in the world, the fallen nature of humans, and the means of overcoming this fallen nature through grace or actions leading to redemption. Morality, then, has been largely a matter of humans in relation to other humans and of humans in relation to God. Thus, our religious concerns in the West have been almost exclusively anthropocentric. Questions of sin, morality, guilt, redemption, and salvation supersede all others. Over the centuries of human history Western religions have developed ethical responses to suicide, homicide, and more recently genocide. However, we have yet to hear adequate responses to "biocide" or "geocide" from the institutional religions.[7]

Where has this anthropocentric vision left us? With regard to nature, our religious legacy has been largely one of hubris, self-obsession, and disconnection from the natural world. Indeed, as the late historian of religions, Mircea Eliade, has pointed out, we have lost sight of the fact that many of our religious rituals have their origin in the cycles of the season and in the symbolic patterns of the natural world.[8] Lacking, therefore, a sense of the sacrality of the earth on which we live, we have little moral basis for countering the assault on the earth that we have launched in the name of progress.

In our search for profit we have lost sight of the fact that we are undercutting the very sources of life by toxifying the water we drink, contaminating the land we cultivate, spraying the food we grow, and polluting the air we breathe. In the name of progress we are consciously or unconsciously undermining our very survival as a species.[9] The gloomy picture is all too easy to draw. Without enumerating these problems further, it may be useful to turn to various religious traditions for a different perspective. Several of the world's religions may be able to offer some important insights for approaching these environmental issues and for resituating the discussion in a context larger than only divine-human relations.[10] Here the cosmological and ethical worldview of the Chinese may be instructive.

THE CHINESE TRADITION: NATURE IN NEO-CONFUCIAN THOUGHT

We will be speaking largely out of the Confucian context, which in its Neo-Confucian form has a clear commitment to the importance of harmonizing with the dynamics of change in the natural world. It is evident that Taoism also has a great deal to offer in the discussion of developing an environmental ethic; however, that would require a separate paper in itself. We will therefore confine our comments to that Neo-Confucian thought which represents the flourishing of the Confucian tradition in the eleventh and twelfth centuries, especially with the metaphysical synthesis of Chu Hsi (1130–1200). There are at least two ways in which Neo-Confucian thought has something to contribute to our present ecological concerns. The first is in terms of its naturalistic cosmology, the second is in relation to its understanding of the ethics of self-cultivation. The two are intimately connected. Before discussing the cosmology and ethics of Neo-Confucianism it may be helpful to provide some background on the development of Confucian thought in China.

The Development of the Confucian Tradition

The acknowledged founder of the Confucian tradition was the sage-teacher K'ung Fu-tzu (551–479 B.C.E.) whose name was Latinized by the Jesuit missionaries as Confucius. Born into a time of rapid social change, Confucius devoted his life to reestablishing order through rectification of the individual and the state. This involved a program embracing moral, political, and religious components. As a creative transmitter of earlier Chinese traditions, Confucius, according to legend, compiled the Five Classics, namely, the *Book of History*, *Poetry*, *Changes*, *Rites*, and the *Spring and Autumn Annals*.

The principal sayings and teachings of Confucius are contained in the *Analects*. He emphasized the practice of moral virtues, especially humaneness or love (*jen*) and filiality (*hsiao*). These were exemplified by the "noble person" (*chun tzu*) particularly within the five relations, namely, between parent and child, ruler and minister, husband and wife, older and younger siblings, and friend and friend. The essence of Confucian thinking was that to establish order in the society one had to begin with harmony in the family. Then, like concentric circles, the effect of virtue would reach outward to the society. Likewise, if the ruler was moral, it would have a "rippling down" effect on the rest of the society.

Confucian thought was further developed in the writings of Mencius (372–289 BCE) and Hsun Tzu (298–238 BCE) who debated whether human nature was intrinsically good or evil. Mencius' argument on the inherent goodness of human nature gained dominance among Confucian thinkers and gave an optimistic flavor to Confucian educational philosophy and political theory.

Confucianism culminated in a Neo-Confucian revival in the eleventh and twelfth centuries, which resulted in a new synthesis of the earlier teachings. The major Neo-Confucian thinker, Chu Hsi (1130–1200), designated four texts as containing the central ideas of Confucian thought. These were two chapters from the *Book of Rites*, namely, the *Great Learning* and the *Doctrine of the Mean*, as well as the *Analects* and *Mencius*. He elevated these Four Books to a position of prime importance over the Five Classics mentioned earlier. These texts and Chu Hsi's commentaries on them became, in 1315, the basis of the Chinese civil service examination system, which endured for nearly six hundred years until 1905. Every prospective government official had to take the civil service exams based on Chu Hsi's commentaries on the Four Books. The idea was to provide educated, moral officials for the large government bureaucracy that ruled China. The influence, then, of Neo-Confucian thought on government, on education, and on social values was enormous.

Chu Hsi's synthesis of Neo-Confucianism was recorded in his classic anthology, *Reflections on Things at Hand*. In this work, Chu provided, for the first time, a comprehensive metaphysical basis for Confucian thought and practice. In response to the Buddhists' metaphysics of emptiness and their perceived tendency towards withdrawal from the world in meditative practices, Chu formulated a this-worldly spirituality based on a balance of religious reverence, ethical practice, scholarly investigation, and political participation.

Unlike the Buddhists who saw the world of change as the source of suffering, Chu Hsi, and the Confucians after him, affirmed change as the source of transformation in both the cosmos and the person. Thus Confucian spiritual discipline involved cultivating one's moral nature so as to bring it into harmony with the larger pattern of change in the cosmos. Each moral virtue had its cosmological component. For example, the central virtue of humaneness was seen as that which was the source of fecundity and growth in both the individual and the cosmos. By practicing humaneness, one could effect the "transformation of things" in oneself, in society, and in the cosmos. In so doing, one's deeper identity with reality was recognized as "forming one body with all things."

To realize this identification, a rigorous spiritual practice was needed. This involved a development of poles present in earlier Confucian thought, namely, a balancing of religious reverence with an ethical integrity manifested in daily life. For Chu Hsi and later Neo-Confucians such spiritual practices were a central concern. Thus interior meditation became known as "quiet sitting," "abiding in reverence," or "rectifying the mind." Moral self-discipline was known as "making the will sincere," "controlling the desires," and "investigating principle." Through conscientious spiritual effort and study one could become a "noble person" who was thus able to participate in society and politics most effectively. While in the earlier Confucian view the ruler was the prime moral leader of the society, in Neo-Confucian thought this duty was extended to all people, with a particular responsibility placed on teachers and government officials. While ritual was primary in the earlier view, spiritual discipline became more significant in Neo-Confucian practice. In both, major emphasis was placed on mutual respect in basic human relations.

Neo-Confucian thought and practice spread to Korea, Japan, and Vietnam where it had a profound effect on their respective cultures. It continues to have a major influence in many aspects of East Asian society, including the importance placed on education, on social mores, and on dedication to working for the group rather than for the individual alone. Indeed, some studies have suggested that part of the success of the Japanese in achieving rapid development is due to the Confucian values that bind the society. The same argument has been made for the achievement of the other "four tigers" which have also been influenced by Confucianism, namely South Korea, Taiwan, Hong Kong, and Singapore. Since 1949, the government of the People's Republic of China has ostensibly repudiated the Confucian heritage; however, the Confucian tradition is currently being reexamined in China, often relying on new publications of European and American scholars. Several conferences have been held in recent years in China on the thought of Confucius and Chu Hsi. Let us turn now to examine the cosmology and ethics of Neo-Confucianism.

Naturalistic Cosmology of Neo-Confucianism

Chinese naturalism as a primary ingredient of Neo-Confucianism is characterized by an organic holism and by a dynamic vitalism.[11] It is a cosmological sensibility that undergirds Neo-Confucianism and gives rise to a distinctive understanding of ethics and self-cultivation. Clearly, how one views the universe affects our understanding of our interaction with nature, with ourselves, and with other human beings. It is this understanding that I hope to clarify, namely the Neo-Confucian view of nature and of cultivating virtue in human nature.[12]

Chinese Neo-Confucianism is characterized by organic holism because the universe is viewed as an integrated unit not as discrete mechanistic parts.[13] The universe (nature) is seen as unified, interconnected, and interpenetrating. Everything interacts and affects everything else, which is why the notion of microcosm and macrocosm is so essential to Neo-Confucian cosmology. The elaboration of the interconnectedness of reality can be seen in the correspondence of the elements with seasons, directions, colors, and even virtues.[14]

This type of classification began in the third millennium BCE and resulted in texts such as the *I Ching* (*The Book of Changes*). It was further elaborated two thousand years ago in the Han dynasty by such thinkers as Tung Chung-shu and remains an important aspect of Neo-Confucian thinking down to the modern period. Within the context of correspondences the relation of oneself as microcosm to the universe as macrocosm is a central theme arising directly from the underlying idea of organic wholeness.

This sense of holism is characterized by the view that there is no Creator God behind the universe. As Frederick Mote has written: "The Chinese . . . have regarded the world and man as uncreated, as constituting the central features of a spontaneously self-generating cosmos having no creator, god, ultimate cause, or will external to itself."[15] He goes on to say that, "the genuine cosmogony is that of organismic process, meaning that all of the parts of the entire cosmos belong to one organic whole and that they all interact as participants in one spontaneously self-generating life process."[16]

While the issue of the absence of a creator god may seem strange to those born within a Judeo-Christian framework, the Neo-Confucians would probably be quite comfortable with the notion of a primordial cosmic explosion. It is clear, in any case, that the Chinese Neo-Confucians are traditionally concerned less with theories of origin or with concepts of a personal God than with what they perceive to be the ongoing reality of a self-generating, interconnected universe. This interconnected quality has been described by Tu Wei-ming as a "continuity of being."[17] This implies a kind of great chain of being, which is in continual process and transformation linking inorganic, organic, and human life forms. For the Neo-Confucians this linkage is a reality because of the fact that all life is constituted of *ch'i*, the material force or psycho-physical element of the universe. This is the unifying element of the cosmos and creates the basis for a profound reciprocity between humans and the natural world.

This brings us to a second important characteristic of Neo-Confucian cosmology and that is its quality of dynamic vitalism inherent in *ch'i* (material force). The seventeenth century scholar, Wang Fu-chih, has described material force in the following manner:

> The fact that the things of the world, whether rivers or mountains, plants or animals, those with or without intelligence, and those yielding blossoms or bearing fruits, provide beneficial support for all things is the result of natural influence of the moving power of

material force. It fills the universe. And as it completely provides for the flourish and transformation of all things, it is all the more spatially unrestricted. As it is not spatially restricted, it operates in time and proceeds with time. From morning to evening, from spring to summer, and from the present tracing back to the past, there is no time at which it does not operate, and there is no time at which it does not produce.[18]

In Neo-Confucian thought, then, it is the material force as the substance of life that is the basis for the continuing process of change and transformation in the universe. The term, *sheng sheng*, namely, "production and reproduction" is repeatedly used in Neo-Confucian texts to illustrate the ongoing creativity and renewal of nature. This recognition of the ceaseless movement of the cosmos arises from a profound meditation on the fecundity of nature in continually giving birth to new life. Furthermore, it constitutes a sophisticated awareness that change is the basis for the interaction and continuation of the web of life systems—mineral, vegetable, animal, and human. And finally, it celebrates transformation as the clearest expression of the creative processes of life with which humans should harmonize their own actions. In essence, human beings are urged to, "model themselves on the ceaseless vitality of the cosmic processes."[19] This approach is an important key to Neo-Confucian thought, for a sense of holism, vitalism, and harmonizing with change provide the metaphysical basis on which an integrated morality can be developed.

The Ethics of Self-Cultivation

This brings us to our final major point with regard to nature and virtue in Neo-Confucianism, namely its doctrine of self-cultivation. For the Neo-Confucians of the eleventh and twelfth centuries the idea of self-cultivation implied, as Tu Wei-ming writes, a "creative transformation."[20] Such a transformation can be elaborated only within the context of an understanding of Neo-Confucian views of nature as already outlined. The fact that the universe is seen as organic, whole, dynamic, and vital has a direct bearing on the moral and spiritual formation of human beings and on their action in the world.

In trying to understand self-cultivation as creative transformation we should begin by noting that the essential metaphor for the human in relation to the cosmos is expressed in the idea of the human as forming one body with heaven and earth. This dynamic triad underlies the assumption of our interconnectedness to all reality and acts as an overriding goal of self-cultivation. Thus through the deepening of this sense of basic identity the human may participate fully in the transformative aspects of the universe. In doing so they are participating in an *anthropocosmic* worldview rather than in an anthropocentric one.

The implications of such an understanding have a direct connection to views of nature and to the cultivation of virtue. They need not be seen as two distinct processes. Tu Wei-ming has suggested how this is different from a purely anthropocentric viewpoint. He writes, "Confucian humanism is fundamentally different from anthropocentrism because it professes the unity of man and Heaven rather than the imposition of the human will on nature. In fact the anthropocentric assumption that man is put on earth to pursue knowledge and, as knowledge expands, so does man's dominion over earth is quite different from the Confucian perception of the pursuit of knowledge as an integral part of one's self-cultivation."[21] He continues, "The human transformation of nature, therefore, means as much an integrative effort to learn to live harmoniously in one's natural environment as a modest attempt to use the environment to sustain basic livelihood. The idea of exploiting nature is rejected because it is incompatible with the Confucian concern for moral self-development."[22]

In developing their moral nature, then, human beings are entering into the cosmological processes of change and transformation. Just as the universe manifests this complex pattern of flux and fecundity, so do human beings nurture the seeds of virtue within themselves and participate in the human order in this process of ongoing transformation. This is elaborated by the Neo-Confucians through a specific understanding of a correspondence between virtues practiced by humans as having their natural counterpart in cosmic processes. For example, the virtue of *jen* or humaneness is seen as a counterpart in humans of the principle of origination or fecundity in the universe. Accordingly, the great Neo-Confucian synthesizer, Chu Hsi, for example, speaks of humaneness as similar to the spirit of life and growth. He writes, "Humaneness as the principle of love is comparable to a tree and the spring of water."[23] Elsewhere he notes, "It is like the will to grow, like the seeds of peaches and apricots."[24] Thus, humaneness is like "the vital force of spring"[25] which blossoms in humans, linking them to heaven, earth, and all things. "For humaneness as constituting the Way, consists of the fact that the mind of Heaven and Earth to produce things is present in everything."[26]

In his "Treatise on Humaneness" Chu Hsi speaks of the moral qualities of the mind of Heaven and Earth as four, namely origination, flourish, advantage, and firmness. These have also been translated as sublime beginnings, pushing through to success, usefulness that furthers, firm perseverance. Similarly in the mind of humans there are four moral qualities, namely humaneness, righteousness, propriety and wisdom. The cosmological and the human virtues are seen as part of one dynamic process of transformation in the universe.

The *anthropocosmic* view of the human as forming a triad with heaven and earth and, indeed, affecting the growth and transformation of things through their self-cultivation and their institutions is very old in Chinese thought. As the Confucian thinker Hsun Tzu wrote in the third century, B.C.E., "Heaven has its seasons, earth its resources, and man his government. This is how man is able to form a triad with Heaven and Earth. If man should neglect his own part in this triad and put all his hope in Heaven and Earth with which he forms the triad, he is making a grave mistake."[27] In the following century another Confucian scholar, Tung Chung-shu, wrote, "Heaven, Earth, and man are the basis of all creatures. Heaven gives them birth, Earth nourishes them, and man brings them to completion. Heaven provides them at birth with a sense of filial and brotherly love, Earth nourishes them with clothing and food, and man completes them with rites and music. The three act together as hands and feet join to complete the body and none can be dispensed with."[28]

This relationship of heaven, earth, and human becomes expressed as a parental one and central to this metaphor is the notion of humans as being children of the universe. Perhaps the most well-known statement of this idea is the Neo-Confucian Chang Tsai's *Western Inscription* written in the eleventh century:

> Heaven is my father and Earth is my mother and even such a small
> creature as I finds an intimate place in their midst.
> Therefore, that which extends throughout the universe I regard as my
> body and that which directs the universe I consider as my nature.
> All people are my brothers and sisters and all things are my compan-
> ions.[29]

He goes on to say:

> Respect the aged . . . Show affection toward the orphaned and the
> weak. The sage identifies his character with that of Heaven and

Earth, and the virtuous man is the best [among the children of Heaven and Earth]. Even those who are tired and infirm, crippled or sick, those who have no brothers or children, wives or husbands, are all my brothers who are in distress and who have no one to turn to.[30]

The larger cosmological implications of this important statement have been clearly articulated by Tu Wei-ming:

> Chang Tsai reminds us that no matter how small a being we find ourselves to be in the vastness of the cosmos, there is not only a locus but also an intimate place for each of us. For we are all potentially guardians and indeed co-creators of the universe. In this holistic vision of man, an ontological gap between Creator and creature would seem to be almost inconceivable. It appears that there is no post-lapsarian state to encounter and that alienation as a deep-rooted feeling of estrangement from one's primordial origin is nonexistent. Furthermore, the idea of man as a manipulator and conqueror of nature would also seem to be ruled out.[31]

CONCLUSION

To summarize, then, it is clear that Neo-Confucianism may be a rich source of rethinking our own relationship between nature and virtue or between cosmology and ethics in light of present ecological concerns. Its organic holism and dynamic vitalism give us a special appreciation for the interconnectedness of all life forms and renews our sense of the sacredness of this intricate web of life.

Moreover, the Neo-Confucian understanding of the dynamic vitalism underlying cosmic processes gives us a new basis for reverencing nature. From this perspective, it is evident that nature cannot be thought of as being composed of inert, dead matter. Rather, all life forms share the element of *ch'i* or material force. This shared psychophysical entity becomes the basis for establishing a reciprocity between the human and non-human worlds.

In this same vein, in terms of the ethics of self-cultivation and the nurturing of virtue, the Neo-Confucian tradition provides a broad framework for harmonizing with the natural world in its doctrine of the human as a child of heaven and earth, as well as in its understanding of virtues as having both a cosmological and a personal component. Thus nature and virtue, cosmology and ethics, and knowledge and action are intimately linked for the Neo-Confucians in both China and Japan.

Finally, just as Neo-Confucianism has passed to the other countries of East Asia and Southeast Asia, it may be that in our own time we are witnessing its further transmission to the West. It was two hundred years ago when the European Enlightenment thinkers, impressed by the rational and humane aspects of Chinese Confucian and Neo-Confucian thought, utilized the insights of this tradition as a stimulus to their own thinking.[32]

How appropriate it is, then, that we are beginning to call on the Chinese Neo-Confucian tradition, as well as others from Asia, to resituate ourselves in relation to the cosmos, to each other, and to the deepest sources of our own humanity. It is this *anthropocosmic* vision of the interconnected Way of heaven, earth, and human that has engaged the Confucians for more than two millennia. It is a perspective that may stimulate us in our search to articulate new modes of interrelationship among all life forms on the planet.

NOTES

1. Gro Brundtland, ed., *Our Common Future* (Oxford: Oxford University Press, 1987).
2. Lester Brown, *State of the World* (Boston: Norton and Co., 1987), p. 4.
3. *Ibid.* pp. 4–5.
4. It should be noted that the Chinese, like many other "higher civilizations" have not had a strong record of ecological conservation in the modern period as the book *The Bad Earth* has convincingly documented. See Vaclay Smil, *The Bad Earth* (Armonk, NY: M E. Sharpe, 1984) and Lester Ross, *Environmental Policy in China* (Bloomington: Indiana University Press, 1988). Although moral theories and practices have had a more personal focus in Chinese thought in the past, its broad cosmological basis merits further investigation and adaptation to the present.
5. *Science* 155 (1967): 1203–1207.
6. See David & Eileen Springer, ed., *Religion and Ecology in History* (New York: Harper and Row, 1974).
7. This point has been forcefully made by Thomas Berry in his book *The Dream of the Earth* (San Francisco: Sierra Club, 1988). I am indebted to Berry's analysis of current environmental concerns as well as to his articulation of the organic holism of Chinese thought. With regard to an understanding of the richness and variety of Chinese thought I would also like to acknowledge my appreciation of the teaching and writing of Wm. Theodore deBary under whose direction I studied at Columbia University.
8. See Mircea Eliade, *The Sacred and the Profane* (New York: Harcourt Brace, 1959) or his *Images and Symbols* (New York: Sheed and Ward, 1969).

9. For an analysis of contemporary environmental problems and their potential solutions see *Gaia: An Atlas of Planet Management* edited by Norman Myers (Garden City, NY: Anchor Press, Doubleday & Co, 1984) and Lester Brown, ed., *State of the World* (New York: Norton, 1991).

10. Books which point in this direction are: Eugene Hargrove, ed., *Religion and Environmental Crisis* (Athens: University of Georgia Press, 1986),). J. B. Callicott & R. Ames, eds., *Nature in Asian Traditions of Thought: Essays in Environmental Philosophy* (Albany: State University of New York Press, 1989), and Allan Hunt Badiner, ed., *Dharma Gaia* (Berkeley: Parallax Press, 1990).

11. The full articulation of naturalism in the Chinese context has yet to be accomplished although scholars such as Tu Wei-ming at Harvard are working in this direction. When Chinese naturalism is more fully articulated in philosophical terms or through the methods of history of religions we will have another pattern in the mosaic of world religions that will be quite distinct. See especially Tu Wei-ming's collection of essays *Confucian Thought: Selfhood as Creative Transformation* (Albany: State University of New York Press, 1985) and his book entitled *Centrality and Commonality: An Essay in the Chung-yung* (Honolulu: University Press of Hawaii, 1976).

12. I have attempted to do this for Japanese Neo-Confucianism in my book, *Moral and Spiritual Cultivation in Japanese Neo-Confucianism* (Albany: State University of New York Press, 1989).

13. This sense of holism is so evident in Chinese thought that a conference volume has been published with the title *Individualism and Holism: Studies in Confucian and Taoist Thought*, ed. by Donald Munro (Ann Arbor: University of Michigan, 1985).

14. For an elaboration of the importance of correspondences in Han thought see chapter VIII in *Sources of Chinese Tradition* vol. 1, ed. by Wm. Theodore deBary, et al. (New York: Columbia University Press, 1960).

15. Frederick F, Mote, *Intellectual Foundations of China* (New York: Alfred A. Knopf, 1971), pp. 17–18.

16. *Ibid.* p.19.

17. See chapter two entitled "The Continuity of Being: Chinese Visions of Nature" in Tu Wei-ming's *Confucian Thought: Selfhood as Creative Transformation.*

18. Wing-tsit Chan, A Source Book in Chinese Philosophy (Princeton: Princeton University Press, (1963), pp. 698–699.

19. Tu Wei-ming, *Confucian Thought: Selfhood as Creative Transformation*, p. 39. Professor Tu notes, "For this reference in the *Chou I*, see *A Concordance to Yi-Ching*, Harvard Yenching Institute Sinological Index Series Supplement no. 10 (reprint; Taipei: Chinese Materials and Research Aids Service Center, Inc., 1966), 1/1."

20. See Tu Wei-ming's essays in *Confucian Thought: Selfhood as Creative Transformation*.

21. *Ibid.*, p. 75.

22. *Ibid.*, p. 75.

23. *Chu-tzu ch'uan shu* 47:37a. Translated by Wing-tsit Chan in "The Concept of Man in Chinese Thought" in *Neo-Confucianism, Etc.* (Hanover, NH: Oriental Society, 1969), p. 115.

24. *Chu-tzu ch'uan shu* 47:3a. Translated by Wing-tsit Chan in *Neo-Confucianism, Etc.*, p. 155.

25. *Chu-tzu wen-chi* CTTC, 67: 20a. Translated by Wing-tsit Chan in *Source Book*, p. 594.

26. *Ibid.*, p. 594.

27. *Sources of Chinese Tradition*, p. 101.

28. *Ibid.*, p. 162.

29. *Ibid.*, p. 469.

30. *Ibid.*, p. 469.

31. *Confucian Thought: Selfhood as Creative Transformation*, p. 158.

32. It would not be incorrect to say, however, that their view of Confucianism overemphasized the rational and ethical aspects at the expense of the cosmic and spiritual dimensions which we are appreciating more in our own time as translations are gradually being made available.

CHAPTER 8

Beyond Naturalism: A Reconstruction of Daoist Environmental Ethics

R. P. PEERENBOOM

Zhuang Zi was obsessed by thoughts on nature . . . and did not understand the importance of man.

—Xun Zi[1]

Lao Tzu's philosophy is fundamentally a simple naturalism.

—Chen Ku-ying[2]

I.

From Xun Zi at the end of the Warring States Period to Chen Ku-ying in the present, sinologists, both Chinese and foreign alike, have interpreted Daoism as naturalism.[3] This widespread view has recently caught the attention of environmental philosophers in the West.[4] Confronted as we are with a vast array of environmental problems, one might hope to discover in Daoism conceptual resources for redressing inadequacies in our understanding of the relationship between humans and nature.

For this cross-cultural conceptual mining to be successful, however, one needs to dig more deeply into the metaphysical foundations underlying naturalist interpretations of Daoism than we have up to this point. Once we penetrate the surface and begin to strip away layer by layer the rhetorical sediment concealing the bedrock—"organicism," "holism," "harmony of humans and nature"—we discover that prevailing naturalist interpretations of the philosophy of Lao Zi and Zhuang Zi, despite their popularity, are of little assistance to the would-be comparative environmental ethicist. Indeed, it is only when one abandons the standard reading of Daoism as naturalism and *wu wei* as "acting naturally" that one can begin to reconstruct a philosophically interesting Daoist environmental ethics which, while perhaps not a cure for all that ails us, does merit serious attention.

Although the many naturalist interpretations of Daoism differ in significant ways, with few exceptions they share a concern with the issue of whether humans are a part of nature or apart from nature.[5] Joseph Needhanl is a leading spokesperson for the former position:

> For the Taoists the Tao or Way was not the right way of life within human society, but the way in which the universe worked; in other words the Order of Nature. . . . The Tao as the Order of Nature, which brought all things into existence and governs their very action, not so much by force as by a kind of natural curvature in space and time, reminds us of the *logos* of Heracleitus of Ephesus, controlling the orderly process of change. . . . the Tao was thought of not only as vaguely informing all things, but as being the naturalness, the very structure, of particular and individual things.[6]

On this reading, *dao* is what Feng Yu-Lan calls "the all-embracing first principle of things."[7] It is the *logos* of the universe; it determines the cosmos and all that is in it.[8] The universe is an a priori organic whole in that all the myriad things that collectively comprise the totality, including humans, are part of the natural order. As such, they are all subject to *dao* as the governing principle/the natural laws: "Tao as the Order of Nature . . . governs their very action."

A corollary of this and indeed all naturalist interpretations is that humans realize the *Way/dao* by being "natural." Expressed in Daoist terms, one is to *wu wei:* "Lao Tzu's concept of *wu wei* . . . implies doing only those things which are in accordance with nature."[9]

Advocates of the alternative position that humans are apart from nature, while agreeing with Needham that to realize *dao* one must *wu wei,*[10] take issue with the notion that the cosmos is a priori an organic whole. Rather this is something that humans must achieve:

> It is not an exaggeration to say that Tao operates according to certain laws which are constant and regular. One may even say there is an element of necessity in these laws, for Tao by its very nature behaves

in this way and all things in order to achieve their full realization, have to obey them. Tao, after all, is *the* Way. . . . When things obey its laws, all parts of the universe will form a harmonious whole and the universe will become an integrated organism.[11]

In contending that humans need not inevitably comply with the natural Way, Wing-tsit Chan denies that *dao* is the all-encompassing metaphysical principle of the universe. *Dao,* strictly speaking, determines only the nonhuman, natural realm. Nature is a distinct and normatively prior order to which humans must conform if they are to realize the ideal of "forming a harmonious whole," an "integrated organism." By objectifying *dao* as the laws of nature, Chan sets the human subject apart from nature. If one is to find in either type of naturalist interpretation of Daoism the conceptual resources for an environmental ethic, one must resolve a dilemma according to which acting "naturally" is either inevitable or analytically false. If humans are part of nature—as is the case for Needham and all naturalists who attribute all-inclusiveness to *dao*—the exhortation to comply with *dao* (to obey the laws of nature, to act naturally) is unnecessary. What else can one do? *Dao* is the logos of the natural order, the laws of nature governing the universe and everything in it. Humans are part of the universe. Therefore, *dao* governs humans. Humans must inevitably conform to laws of nature; they cannot *not* obey them. It is just as impossible for humans to avoid undergoing the physical, chemical, and biological processes governed by natural laws as it is for any nonhuman thing in the universe. To instruct one that he or she "has to" obey in a normative sense is therefore useless advice: one need not tell a person jumping off the Empire State Building to obey the law of gravity.

Further, because *wu wei* for the naturalist means to do what is natural, which in turn means to comply with *dao,* one must inevitably *wu wei.* Because one cannot possibly *you wei* (act contrary to nature), the term is meaningless: it has no possible referent and the distinction between the *you wei* and *wu wei* collapses.

However, this distinction is widely acknowledged to be a cornerstone of Lao Zi's philosophy. As Chen Ku-ying declares, "the concept of 'complying with nature through non-action (*wu wei*)' must be taken as the very essence of the *Tao Te Ching.*"[12] That this interpretation vitiates the crucial *wu wei/you wei* distinction casts doubt on its viability as a reading of Daoist philosophy. Of course, the larger philosophical issue at stake here is not peculiar to Daoism, for in any theory which treats humans as part of nature the term *natural* loses its normative value: eating white sugar, dumping nuclear waste into the river, and so forth all become "natural." Proponents of this interpretation must redefine natural if they are to salvage their theory.

At this point, one might be tempted to test the other horn of the dilemma and deny along with Chan that humans are part of the natural order. Doing so, however, is exegetically problematic, which may explain why most naturalists not only shy away from this route but join Needham in actively promoting the holistic, organic interpretation.[13] While one can appreciate Chan's motives, it seems peculiar, to say the least, that although *dao* "is *the* Way," it is not the way of humans. At any rate, to avoid begging the hermeneutical question, it will repay us to bracket the above objection, and assume for the moment that to separate humans from the rest of nature is consistent with Lao-Zhuang thought.

Given that assumption, the statement "humans should act naturally" (i.e., *wu wei*) is, to begin with, prima facie contradictory. If humans are not be part of nature, they can only act humanly. Suppose someone were to say, "I am acting naturally" ("this action of mine is natural"). The statement would be analytically false in the same way that "a bachelor is married" is. It is necessarily false because *natural* by *their* definition excludes the human, just as *married* by definition excludes bachelorhood.

To tell one to follow nature is, as on the other view, rather curious and unhelpful advice. As the cardinal normative rule of an (environmental) ethical system, it is a non-starter. Again, for the naturalist's suggestion that "one should do what is natural" to be meaningful, *natural* must be redefined.

Thus, it appears that an environmental philosopher seeking to build an ethic on the foundations of Daoist metaphysics is sure to be skewered whether he opts for the part-of-nature horn or the apart-from-nature horn. Yet this is not his only cause for concern. Zhuang Zi, reflecting on the human/nature relationship and the ancillary normative claim that one is to follow nature, raises an epistemological objection as well:

> ["Knowing that which nature does and that which man does is the utmost in knowledge. Whoever knows what nature does lives the life generated by nature. . . ."] Still, there's a difficulty. Knowing depends on something with which it is later matched; however, [in this case] what it depends on is never fixed. How do I know that which I deem "nature" is not "man?" How do I know that which I deem "man" is not "nature?"[14]

With this Rortian critique of epistemological foundationalism, Zhuang Zi undermines the whole metaphysical debate: how can one know what is natural and what is human? How can one possibly justify the claim that humans are part of nature or the contrary claim that they are not? One cannot escape from one's human perspective to some "objective" Archimedean point to verify one's metaphysical hypothesis—to access, so to speak, nature's own vocabulary. This epistemic objection, coupled with the aforementioned dilemma, appears to constitute an insurmountable roadblock to those who have turned to the Way in hopes of finding an alternative metaphysical basis for their environmental philosophy.

II.

Yet, there is still hope for a philosophically sophisticated Daoist-inspired environmental ethics. One can overcome the epistemic objection and avoid impaling oneself on either horn of the dilemma by resisting the temptation to construct one's ethical system on meta-physical foundations. Rather than taking as one's departure point a dogmatic stance on whether humans are part of nature or apart from nature, a potentially more fruitful approach is to abandon metaphysics and tackle the interpretive problem of redefining the human/nature relationship in a way which allows humans to be both apart of nature and yet in some sense apart from nature.[15]

As one might expect, the literature abounds with the Herculean efforts of many a sinologist to accomplish this feat. Some argue that to act naturally, to *wu wei,* means to avoid artificiality; others contend that one is to act nonpurposively, or to act so as to be in accord with the laws of nature, or to follow one's inherent nature. Before tallying the specific merits and demerits of these individual theories, it is worth considering one general difficulty, which plagues them all alike. Zhuang Zi's epistemological critique of foundationalism, while perhaps helpful in undercutting an appeal to metaphysics, also entails the idea that there can be no final solution to the interpretive question. In departing from the foundational realm of absolutist metaphysics and venturing into the hermeneutical realm of value-relative human interpretation, one leaves behind the quest for certainty, for infallible judgments as to what is natural and what is human. In the absence of epistemological foundations, where one draws the line—how one defines *natural*—*will* necessarily be relative to one's values, goals, and beliefs about the world. Hence, what it is natural to do may differ from case to case as interests, aims, and scientific theories differ. As Zhuang Zi puts it, "what it depends on is never fixed."

As a result, attempts to construct Daoist environmental ethics on the basis of a redefinition of *natural* often fail because there is no way to adjudicate between conflicting claims as to what is natural. If there is no way to determine what is natural in a given situation, then the *wu wei/you wei* distinction collapses and the advice to *wu wei* (follow nature, be natural) becomes moot.

This objection must not be overstated. That there is no apodictic, foundational way of verifying or justifying one's interpretation of what is natural does not mean that one must bite the bullet of absolute relativism and allow that any candidate is as good as any other. Most likely there are instances where unanimous, or near unanimous, agreement can be reached. For instance, inasmuch as life forms need clean air to survive, to pollute the air to the point where life can no longer be sustained seems to fall safely within the range of action contrary to nature, of *you wei* behavior. Apart from those whose metaphysical views of humans as part of an organic natural cosmos circumvent *any* attempt to characterize human action as unnatural, few would deny this point.

Yet, while there may be extreme cases in which a consensus can be attained, Zhuang Zi's criticism retains its force for all practical purposes. There is, for openers, a slippery-slope problem. Although we might all agree about acts which cause the air to be polluted to the point where no life can be sustained, what about acts which pollute only to a level at which not all people die, just senior citizens with bronchial disorders, or only birds and other animals die, or no death is involved, just medical problems, either serious, debilitating ones or minor ones, for example, eye and nose irritations?

Slippery-slope problems are, of course, commonplace: judges, doctors, and legislators draw reasoned, but "arbitrary at the margin" lines every day. While troublesome to a philosopher in search of absolute, univocal ethical judgments, they need not compromise all attempts on the part of a pragmatic environmentalist to differentiate between natural and unnatural behavior. A potentially more serious drawback is that although all or most may agree in an extreme case, it is not clear that they do so on the basis of a shared rule or standard. In the above case, in which polluting the air to the point where life forms cannot survive is agreed to be unnatural, is the rule that "unnatural" is "what runs contrary to our fundamental needs as human beings?" Obviously, this formulation is still much too vague: do we mean biological needs, psychological needs, or social needs? On the other hand, it may be too specific: are only human needs to be considered? Although people might agree that a given action is "unnatural," what they mean by that differs, indicating that the problem of redefining *natural* in an acceptable way may be more of an obstacle than it appears at first glance. Even granting that we might agree on a basic definition of *natural* which might allow for a consensus in cases like the one above, it does not follow that this general standard or definition is sufficiently robust to enable reasonable people to reach agreement in less extreme cases. Simply put, the rule may underdetermine the choices.

Let us assume that some degree of clean air is needed for our biological survival and that it is unnatural to act contrary to our fundamental biological needs.[16] There are, obviously, many possible ways to realize this end. To focus on measures dealing with automobiles alone, one could ban them outright, tax their owners, require devices to decrease the amount of harmful gasses expelled, and so on. Our role is of no use in choosing between these various acts. One must come up with a standard which is broad enough to appeal to most reasonable people and yet robust enough to be of some use as a normative guide for real-life choices. While this cannot be ruled out a priori, an examination of the leading Daoist contenders up to this point reveals the difficulties inherent in this approach.[17]

First, however, let us take stock. Attempts to understand Daoism as naturalism and *wu wei* as "doing what is natural" face the following dilemma: (A) if humans are part of the natural order and governed by the laws of nature, then doing what is "natural" is inevitable—and hence, the advice to "follow nature" is meaningless; or (B) if humans are not part of nature, statements of the form "X is natural" where X refers to humans, human acts, feelings, etc. are analytically false. In either case, *natural* must be redefined in terms of standards applicable to humans that permit humans to be both part of, and at the same time, apart from nature.[18] Maintaining this distinction, however, is easier said than done. As the product of human interpretation, these standards do not lend themselves to apodictic justification, they often place one on a slippery slope, and they are in many instances, perhaps nearly always, inadequate for arbitrating between conflicting interpretations of what is natural.

III.

Natural can be interpreted in terms of a number of conflicting positions: the natural law theory, the "human as artificial", school, the inherent nature theory, and the nonpurposive interpretation. Let's consider each of these in turn.

A. The Natural Law Theory

Chan attempts to address the hermeneutical question of what it is natural, and hence normatively correct, for humans to do by appealing to the laws of nature. *Dao* operates according to regular and constant laws. Humans must obey these laws if they are to achieve full realization and form a harmonious whole, an integrated organism.

But what are these laws? Are they the laws of nature in terms of natural science? If so, one cannot help but obey them. Thus, Chan seems to be saying that one should look to the laws of nature as *normative guidelines* for human behavior. Asserting that "man is to follow Nature," he adds that "the ideal life for the individual, the ideal order for society, and the ideal type of government are all based on [*dao*] and *guided* by it.[19]

Nevertheless, to be guided by the laws of nature one must first know what they are; one cannot follow the laws of nature if one does not know them. We need not at this point get into a debate over the philosophical merits of scientific realism. Lao Zi and Zhuang Zi were not staunch advocates of scientific investigation of nature. If anything, Lao Zi seems opposed to technological advances, which often go hand in hand with such scientific inquiry.[20]

Assuming one knew the laws, Chan's project would still require interpretation to determine their application to the human realm. But many of our actions are not readily understood in terms of natural laws: what color suit should one wear to a funeral? Is it more natural to eat at McDonald's or Pizza Hut? Should the rangers in Yellowstone put out fires not started by humans or let them burn? We are, in short, confronted with underdetermination: the laws of nature do not speak with a single voice to every choice of human behavior. In some cases the laws of nature offer conflicting advice, in others no apparent advice at all.

Were these problems not worrisome enough, Chan must also explain why we should accept the laws of nature as a normative guide for human conduct in the first place. First, from a Humean standpoint, there is the problem of moving from *is* to *ought*:[21] must we opt for so-called social Darwinism simply because nature seems to be governed by a law of survival of the fittest? Second, from the standpoint of the postmodern epistemological view that all facts are theory- and value-laden, it is not clear that he has a warrant for privileging this particular standard as *the* normative criterion. Either way, Chan's position does not appear very promising as a starting point for reconstructing Daoist environmental ethics.

B. The "Human as Artificial" School

According to a second common interpretation, one must follow *dao* by doing what is natural rather than what is "artificial."[22] Advocates of this ubiquitous view point to the many delightful passages in which Lao Zi and Zhuang Zi attack their Confucian counterparts for their emphasis on "man-made" rules of etiquette and pedantic social mores.[23]

Lao Zi and Zhuang Zi's censure of Confucianism is taken by the naturalists to be a rejection of anthropocentricism, *and* conversely an endorsement of naturalism. It is thought to be a condemnation of the human realm in deference to the supremacy of the natural. According to Chen:

> We can see a major difference between the Taoist and Confucian schools. Whereas Confucius lays great stress on 'ornamentation' in the form of rites, ceremonies, and moral standards, Lao Tzu condemns them as an obstruction to the expression of man's natural spontaneity.[24]

Yet while Lao Zi and Zhuang Zi attack Confucian morality, they are not necessarily attacking anthropocentricism. That is, it is possible that one might take exception to the Confucian moral code specifically and not to the general humanistic bias of Confucius.

Even if Lao Zi and Zhuang Zi do object to the primacy of the human realm in the Confucian tradition, as I would argue, this does not mean that they subscribe to naturalism. On the contrary, they are against the excessive limitations of Confucian humanism. They favor, not the *exclusion* of humans in a radical dualism with nature, but the *inclusion* of nonhumans with humans in an organic whole. The ideal, as Zhuang Zi states, is a balance between the two, a harmony in which neither is subjugated to the other.[25] Furthermore, there are two interpretations of what *artificial* means here. First, *artificial* may refer to human artifacts, anything "man-made."[26] Thus, boats and chariots, not to mention computers and cars, are artificial and should not be used because they are man-made.

These arguments, however, are circular. To see this, recall that the initial motivation for redefining *natural* arises from the assumption that humans are distinct from nature. This assumption makes it necessary to redefine *natural* in a way applicable to humans. Yet the argument of the anti-artificiality school is that there is a distinction between the human and the natural such that what is natural is nonhuman (the metaphysical assumption). What is unnatural is artificial (the redefinition) and what is artificial is anything man-made, any human artifact. Thus, anything human is unnatural and anything natural is nonhuman, and so on and so on. In failing to redefine *natural* in terms of a standard applicable to humans, this approach simply begs the question as to what is natural for humans by introducing an intermediary term, *artificial,* in such a way that natural is still simply nonhuman. Hence, we are again left without a standard for judging which human actions are natural.

One might be able to rescue *artificial* as a normatively useful term by conceiving of *artificial* and *natural* as polar ends of a continuum, rather than as a dualistically opposed dichotomy according to which something is either absolutely one or the other. However, this move requires that one forgo the metaphysical claim that necessitated this reinterpretation in the first place: namely, that humans are apart from nature. In return, one secures the benefit of being in step with common usage in that what is natural and artificial becomes a matter of degree. For example, many consider it "more natural" to eat whole grain bread than processed white flour bread even though both are "man-made."

Nevertheless, giving up the cut and dried, metaphysically motivated criterion of anything man-made reinstates the original hermeneutical problem: what is natural or artificial depends on the judgment of the concerned person(s). Consequently, one faces the same problems— slippery slopes, underdetermination, and the like—as I have already pointed out.

Although there is a second possible reading of *natural* as "not artificial," the situation is not significantly improved. According to the primitivist interpretation of the *Dao De Jing,* Lao Zi espouses a return to the rustic "good old days."[27] In this way, artificiality is juxtaposed with the simple, unadorned (and thus natural) way of life. This approach has the merit of partially responding to our earlier criticism in that it redefines *natural* in terms of a criterion—(primitive) simplicity—applicable to humans. Nevertheless, this interpretation also has its own problems. First, there are difficulties with the practical application of such a standard. Is mourning in white (as in China) more simple and genuine than mourning in black (as in the West)? Would it be more natural—more simple, less artificial—for people in twentieth-century America to live in caves rather than in houses or to use Lao Zi's knotted ropes for keeping records instead of pen and paper or computers? Once we allow for any change, it becomes difficult to determine where the line ought to be drawn to demarcate what is sufficiently simple to be considered natural. Once again, we find ourselves sliding down a slippery slope.

We also confront anew the more serious problem of the warrant for one's chosen standard. As Zhuang Zi has argued, one's choice is relative to one's values. While this does not preclude the possibility of agreement, in this case it seems unlikely. Many Americans today would find living in a cave without cable television a most unnatural way of living and computer users might very well take issue with the primitivist's claim that tying knots to keep track of information is more natural than storing it on hard disks.

Even were a consensus attainable as to what constitutes natural behavior in these specific cases, it hardly follows that one need adopt primitivist naturalism as *the* normative criterion for all of one's behavioral choices. While it may be an acceptable standard in some cases, perhaps even as a guide for one's general life plan, it may at times be reasonably overridden by other normative considerations. For instance, the *locus classicus* of the primitivist view is chapter 80 of the *Dao De Jing*: "Although neighboring villages are within sight of each other, and the sounds of dogs barking and cocks crowing can be heard across the way, the people of one village will grow old and die without having any dealings with the people of another." To set into motion the complex machinery of international relief for victims of a disaster on the other side of the world seems to run counter to the simple, primitivist lifestyle being promoted; yet, surely one would not wish to deny that it is a morally legitimate thing to do.

C. The Inherent Nature Theory

Feng Yu-Lan suggests that to act naturally is to act in accordance with one's inherent self-nature (*de*):

> *Wu Wei* can be translated literally as 'having-no-activity' or 'non-action'. According to the theory of 'having-no-activity,' a man should restrict his activities to what is necessary and what is natural. 'Necessary' means necessary for a certain purpose, and never over-doing. 'Natural' means following one' s [*de*] with no arbitrary effort.[28]

Feng's initial attempt to define *wu wei* as that which is "necessary" for a "certain purpose" as long as one does not "overdo" it is of little help as the same questions can be asked about these criteria: how does one determine what is necessary?

What is a valid purpose? What is overdoing?

Feng's second criterion is of little use as well. First, *natural* means to "follow one's *de* with no arbitrary effort." One's *de* for Feng is "what individual objects obtain from Tao and thereby become what they are." But in redefining nature in terms of self-nature, Feng has co-opted humans back into the natural realm, and hence criticism A of the basic dilemma applies: humans, inevitably conforming to natural laws, this time internal ones, necessarily do what is natural.

Second, each person has a unique *de*. If one's self-nature is the standard for what is natural, then what is natural is relative to each individual. As a result, one is left without a way to adjudicate between conflicting claims.[29] Zhuang Zi, in challenging the view that one's heart-mind is a functional normative standard, makes this very criticism:

> If you go by the heart-mind and take it as your authority, who is without such an authority? . . . The fool has one just as [the sage] has.[30]

Everybody, including the fool, has a heart-mind—and a unique *de*.[31] If either is to serve as the sole guide to behavior, then everybody is equally an authority. Hence, neither can be used as a standard for judging between conflicting interpretations of what is *wu wei/natural*.

D. The Nonpurposive Interpretation

Nonpurposiveness is another often-championed criterion for determining what is natural:

> The Taoist Saint . . . keeps to the weak and lowly, and refrains from any conspicuous effort, any striving after a set purpose. In a sense therefore he may be said to have a purpose. His *wu wei* is practiced with a conscious design; he chooses this attitude in the conviction that only by so doing the 'natural' development of things will favor him.[32]

Duyvendak himself points out the inherent inconsistency of this position: the sage acts nonpurposively because he has the purpose of according with nature. Further, what gives rise to the nonpurposive interpretation is the need for a standard to determine what is *wu wei*/natural in a given situation. One requires such a standard when confronted with a decision between conflicting courses of action in the realm of praxis. However, such a situation occasions precisely the kind of activity—reflection, analysis, calculation—which is considered purposive. Telling one to act nonpurposively is thus contradictory and of little practical value: it is like telling an anxious job applicant before a big interview to stop looking so nervous and just relax.

Let us assume for the sake of the argument that the apparent difficulties in life are actually illusory and one is able to wander along without any purpose: that presumably such concerns as food, shelter, warmth, and the like will take care of themselves. In theory, one would then be in "accord with the natural development of all things." This conclusion, however, rests on the underlying assumption that humans are part of nature. If they were not, there would be no reason to believe that one's nonpurposive actions necessarily accord with the "natural development of things."

The claim seems to be that humans, as part of nature, inevitably do what is natural unless they foul up the process by acting purposively. Nevertheless, if humans are part of nature, then whatever one does is natural, including one's purposive as well as nonpurposive actions. Humans, in acting purposively when confronted with certain situations in life, inevitably conform to what is natural for them in such circumstances.

Furthermore, what does "acting nonpurposively" mean? Animals surely act purposively. A beaver has a definite purpose in swimming around collecting wood, building a dam, storing food, and so on. Yet animals are part of nature and their purposive actions are natural. Like *artificial, purposive* is merely a nonexplanatory intermediary term inserted into a circular argument which begs the question: unnatural actions are purposive; *purposive* means a kind of action but only when done by humans; therefore, *unnatural* is something only applicable to humans. *Purposiveness* still needs to be redefined to distinguish between that of humans and that of other animals.

Consider one typical example: man is rational and animals are not. Thus, *purposive,* (and *a fortiori unnatural*), means rational action. However, one could very well argue that rational behavior is just as natural for humans as hibernating is for bears. All animals use whatever capabilities they possess to survive. Some animals, such as the monkey, rely heavily on their intelligence. Similarly, man uses what powers he has available to him—one of which is rational thinking.

This interpretation has, in addition, the following curious consequence. If one were to join with Duyvendak in arguing that humans should act nonpurposively, one would be advocating that humans *should not* act rationally. This is not to say one ought to act irrationally, but merely nonrationally—that is, that one must not engage in reasoning. Even so, it still seems like a peculiar bit of normative advice to tell one *not* to let *any reasons* influence one's decisions.

Of course, one could argue that to act purposively means to act willfully, rather than rationally.[33] That is, we are constrained by laws of nature, even if we may not know (in an epistemologically rigorous sense) exactly what they are. To act willfully is to go against these laws of nature. For instance, one could try to defy gravity and jump off a building in hopes of flying. This action would be, it is suggested, willful *you wei* behavior. But could it be an example of what we mean by acting unnaturally? When this foolish fellow takes his leap, he in no way violates the laws of nature. Quite the contrary. He hits the ground with a splat just as the laws predict. His acting willfully is not unnatural; it is just stupid.[34] There is no question that one should not act stupidly. Thus, if one is going to claim that to *wu wei* is to act naturally, which in turn means to act intelligently, one might as well state directly that to *wu wei* is, at a minimum, to act intelligently.

The argument over what is natural turns out to be a red herring. The real question facing the environmental philosopher becomes not what is natural, but what is the intelligent thing to do. When people, all things considered, act intelligently, whether they act willfully, artificially, in accordance with their natures or against them, they do what is normatively best in the given situation.

IV.

To reconstruct Daoist (environmental) philosophy, one must free oneself from the conceptual fetters of metaphysical and naturalist interpretations of Daoism, and reconsider what is meant by such key terms as *dao, de, wu wei, wu zhi, wu yu,* and *zi ran.* Only then is it possible to understand how Daoist ethics requires pragmatic, intelligent action.[35]

Chapter 42 of the *Dao De Jing* tells us that "the Way models *zi ran.*" *Zi ran* has usually been understood, as in modern Chinese, to refer to *nature* in the natural science sense. As we have seen, the phrase is taken metaphysically to mean that *dao* or the Way is subject to, or is itself an expression of, predetermined first principles or natural laws that somehow inform or become the model for human behavior.

David Hall and Roger T. Ames suggest that *ziran* is better understood as what is "so-of-itself," and that *dao* be looked on not as a predetermined order disciplined by first principles but as an emergent order.[36] *Dao*—both normatively, as the sanctioned way, and descriptively, as the order of the universe, the environment, the society, the person[37]—emerges out of our contextual choices rather than as an instantiation of a predetermined blueprint. It is the result of a creative, active, participatory process. The kind of world we live in, in terms of our ethical as well as natural environment, depends in part on the choices we humans make.

While reason has a role in our choices, it is not the reason of pure Kantian rational principles. In the seemingly paradoxical language of Daoism, one relies on *wu zhi,* literally translated as "non-knowledge," but insightfully interpreted by Hall as "unprincipled knowing.[38] In the Daoist world, each particular, human and nonhuman, has a unique value or virtue (*de*). The sage is the one who has the power (*de*)[39] to unite the many individual particulars with their unique interests and abilities into a harmonious whole. There are no fixed patterns, no categorical imperatives or ethical absolutes to guide him. Rather he proceeds in an unprincipled *wu zhi* fashion, sensitive to the spontaneously generated and continually changing patterns of interrelationships formed by the particulars in the given context. Such a pragmatic case-by-case approach to problems produces "ad hoc" solutions that cannot be subsumed under or reduced to a single or foundational set of principles. This leaves the sage, at least in the eyes of his Platonic counterpart, the systematic philosopher, seemingly *wu zhi*—without knowledge.

Yet to be successful, the sage must act in a manner appropriate for the given situation (*wu wei*). Attuned to his environment, his actions, though perhaps quite strenuous, have an air of effortlessness about them, like those of a great athlete at the top of his or her form. Firm and decisive, the Daoist sage, nevertheless, comes off as non-assertive and non-threatening. He does not seek to force or compel others to obey, but rather hopes to induce them to participate willingly. He is a facilitator. He relies on persuasion and the intrinsic appeal of his vision to bring about a voluntary and active involvement in the creation of the emerging harmony. In this sense, he is well-depicted as *wu yu*—literally "without desire," but more appropriately "without selfish desire."

Hall, in characterizing *wu yu* as "objectless desire," has captured one of the Daoist's distinctive features.[40] Rather than viewing others in his environment as mere objects for the exercise of his will and power, as means to his ends, the Daoist takes each person and every thing as complementary notes for the realization of a beautiful score. There is no one "correct" way to combine the notes; many beautiful scores are possible. The Daoist, as composer and composed, as player and played, seeks to be part of a never-ending symphony.

Applying this approach to our more specific concerns, the Daoist environmental philosopher does not attempt to deduce what is correct from ethical or metaphysical first principles, which in their universality are abstractions divorced from a particular context. The issue is not which action corresponds to nature's own choice, but what, from our inescapably human perspective, is best, most intelligent, for us to do.[41] By weighing the available options in light of our best-confirmed theories about nature, one hopes to balance the often conflicting values, interests, and goals to achieve a consensual equilibrium.

This method is similar in many respects to John Rawls' reflective equilibrium, and the coherence model of Joel Feinberg.[42] The objective of the ethical reasoning process is to bring one's judgments into equilibrium with one's moral intuitions, with one's personally and communally held moral beliefs. As Feinberg observes, foundational philosophers may object to this approach:

> They will find no semblance of a complete moral system, no reduction of moral derivatives to moral primitives, no grounding of ultimate principles in self-evident truths, or in 'the nature of man,' the commandments of God, or the dialectic of history. . . . [One may] appeal . . . to all kinds of reasons normally produced in practical discourse, from efficiency and utility to fairness, coherence, and human rights. But I make no effort to derive some of these reasons from others, or to rank them in terms of their degree of basicness.[43]

Noting that this method cannot be reduced to utilitarianism, Kantianism, or any single-criterion ethical system, Feinberg goes on to point out that we can through this kind of practical reasoning make progress on the immediate problems confronting us while waiting, perhaps in vain, for eternal solutions to the ultimate value questions.

This pragmatic, postmodern approach to environmental ethics seems promising on several fronts. As we have seen, it allows us to sidestep the metaphysical dilemma. By refusing to countenance epistemic claims about the way nature is in and of itself, one is able to avoid the metaphysical bifurcation of the cosmos into humans and nature.

Perhaps most importantly, by abandoning metaphysics and giving up the quest for certainty, Daoism cuts the legs out from under dogmatism on environmental issues. Nonhuman nature, no longer subjugated to the "little lord," need not simply serve the interests of humankind. When balancing the scales, one is certainly permitted to consider the effects on nonhumans as well as humans.

On the other hand, no individual species or specimen is a priori entitled to protection either. This militates against the knee-jerk "keep it the way it is" attitude associated with the classical preservation of John Muir and the reverence-for-life ethic of Albert Schweitzer. On this view, nothing is sacrosanct. The value of everything, even human life, is, at least in theory, open to question. No single criterion is privileged a priori as *the* criterion. When conflicts arise, the focus turns not to adjudicating according to a fixed rule who is right and who is wrong, but to achieving a harmonization of the disparate interests that will benefit all.[44]

While this interpretation may be philosophically promising, it is not without its shortcomings. One wonders of how much assistance it will be to the environmental philosopher faced with real-life problems. Not every situation can be resolved in a way that benefits all parties. In fact, resolution of many, if not most, conflicts requires a compromise of the interests of at least one party. Faced as we often are with a zero-sum game, is it realistic to assume that those concerned will be able to come to an agreement as to which balance of interests, which harmony, is best? After all, one person's harmony may be another's cacophony: what sounds to one like a melodious blending of the interests of humans with those of the rest of an ecosystem may strike another as grossly out of tune. The hopes of reaching a consensus on environmental issues, even if one is willing to set aside dogmatic metaphysical assertions, may seem, given the historical record, dim at best.

In actual practice, this process of balancing interests to attain an equilibrium is susceptible to the politics of power.[45] *In theory,* the Daoist notion of a harmony of the many disparate interests of all concerned parties does entail what Roger Ames has called the "doctrine of the parity of things." That is, each particular member of the Daoist environmental orchestra has a kind of aesthetic parity with every other in that without that member's unique participation, the harmony achieved would be different. Each particular is in this sense necessary for there to be that whole. But despite this thin sense of parity, there is still a real disparity as some members exercise a greater influence over the end result than others: some are conductors, composers, and maestros; others are bit players.

It would seem that in the absence of any fixed standard(s) for adjudicating conflicting claims, the process of balancing and harmonizing interests could degenerate into, at least in cases where consensus as to a positive-sum solution cannot be reached, a contest of power. While this may be so, one must hasten to point out that since no ethical theory has ever received universal acceptance, this problem plagues every other system as well. Whenever reasoning fails, might wins. In defense of the Daoist method, recognizing that one initially aims to achieve a harmony agreeable to everybody (*wu yu*), and that no standard is privileged a priori (*wu zhi*), may lead to a more tolerant atmosphere in which the concerned parties will be willing to compromise (*wu wei*).

Although this conciliatory atmosphere may be nothing to scoff at, it is clear that Daoism is no panacea for the environmental ills facing the modern world, Eastern or Western. From a philosophical standpoint, Daoist environmentalists are in much the same position as their Western counterparts. While they might lean more toward an organic, holistic world view than do some in the West, they cannot justify an ecological environmental ethic on those grounds any more than one can justify exploitation of the natural resources on the basis of a Judeo-Christian world view. They too must tackle the thorny environmental issues, drawing the line between the interests of humans and the rest of the ecosystem on the basis of their own fallible reasons. As Yi-fu Tuan and others have argued, Daoists, and Easterners in general, have been no more successful than Westerners.[46]

At best, in undermining dogmatism and focusing on an achievement of harmony, Daoism tests human creativity, placing the responsibility for creating a quality living environment on our shoulders. While the current state of environmental affairs might not leave one overly optimistic, whether we will rise to the challenge remains to be seen. In principle, Daoism holds out the possibility—and the hope—that some day the cosmos will become a harmonious, organic whole. As Zhuang Zi counsels, "there can be no genuine knowledge until there are Realized Persons. . . . That is, those in whom neither nature nor man is victor over the other."[47]

NOTES

1. Xun Zi, *Xun Zi Yin De* (A Concordance to Xun Zi), no. I, (Taibei: Nanyu Publishing, n.d.), 79/21/22. See Burton Watson, trans., *Hsun Tzu* (New York: Columbia University Press, 1963), p. 125.

2. Chen Ku-ying, *Lao Tzu: Texts, Notes and Comments,* trans. Rhett Y. W. Young and Roger T. Ames (Taibei: Chinese Materials Center, 1981), p. 34.

3. In this paper alone, I cite in addition to Xun Zi and Chen, Feng Yu-Lan, Burton Watson, Joseph Needham, Wing-tsit Chan, J. J. L. Duyvendak and Roger T. Ames.

4. J. Baird Callicott provides a review of the literature which has grown out of this attention to Eastern philosophies in general and Daoism in particular. See his "Conceptual Resources for Environmental Ethics in Asian Traditions of Thought: a Propaedeutic," *Philosophy East and West* 37 (1987): 115–31. See also Ip Po-keung, "Taoism and the Foundations of Environmental Ethics," *Environmental Ethics* 5 (1983): 335; Russell Goodman, "Taoism and Ecology," *Environmental Ethics* 2 (1980): 73–80. Some have questioned the need and the utility of turning to Daoism and Asian traditions: cf. Yi-fu Tuan, "Discrepancies Between Environmental Attitude and Behavior," *Canadian Geographer* 12 (1968): 176–83; Holmes Rolston, III, "Can the East Help the West to Value Nature?" *Philosophy East and West* 37 (1987): 172–90.

5. Peter Fritzell develops this distinction and the resulting dilemma in "The Conflicts of Ecological Conscience," in J. Baird Callicott, ed., *Companion to a Sand County Almanac* (Madison: University of Wisconsin Press, 1987). The *locus classicus* in the West for the view that humans are apart from nature is the Judeo-Christian paradigm presented in Genesis which sets humans above nature, leading some to conclude that nature is there to be exploited as humans see fit; cf. Lynn White, Jr. "The Historical Roots of Our Ecological Crisis," *Science* 155 (1967): 1203–07. David Hall and Roger T. Ames attempt to move away from metaphysics as a starting point for a Daoist naturalist world view. They suggest that environmental ethics can be based on an "aesthetic cosmology." See Hall, "On Seeking a Change of Environment-A Quasi-Taoist Proposal," *Philosophy East and West* 37 (1987): 160–71; Ames, "Taoism and the Nature of Nature," *Environmental Ethics* 8 (1986): 317–50.

6. Joseph Needham, *Science and Civilisation in China,* vol. 2 (Cambridge: Cambridge University Press, 1956), pp. 36–37.

7. Feng Yu-Lan, *A Short History of Chinese Philosophy,* trans. Derk Bodde (New York: Macmillan, 1984), p. 177.

8. It is not clear that advocates of this position actually want to equate *dao* with the laws of nature in the natural science sense. Needham, for one, does not believe that early Chinese conceived of nature in such terms. Nevertheless, as the *logos,* the order of nature, the naturalness that controls the orderly process of change, *dao* does seem

to be some kind of natural law. Regardless of exactly how we cash out the "naturalness" of *dao* and the means by which it informs all things, the basic problem remains: if *dao* is all-inclusive and governs all things, then one cannot help but conform to *dao.* For a debate of Needham's position on the laws of nature, see Derk Bodde, "Evidence for the 'Laws of Nature' in Chinese Thought," *Harvard Journal of Asiatic Studies* 20 (1957): 709–27.

9. Chen, *Lao Tzu,* p. 23. See also Needham, *Science,* pp. 68-69; Feng, *Short History,* pp. 100–01; Burton Watson, *The Complete Works of Chuang Tzu* (New York: Columbia University Press, 1968), p. 6.

10. Wing-tsit Chan contends that *wu wei* entails "taking no action that is contrary to nature . . . man is to follow nature." *A Source Book in Chinese Philosophy* (Princeton: Princeton University Press, 1963), pp. 136–37.

11. Ibid., p. 9.

12. Chen, *Lao Tzu,* p. 15. See also Herrlee Creel, *What is Taoism* (Chicago: Chicago University Press, 1970); Holmes Welch, *Taoism: The Parting of the Way* (Boston: Beacon Press, 1967).

13. Cf. Lao Zi, *Dao De Jing* (Taibei: Nanyu Publishing, n.d.), chap. 42. For an English translation, see Chen, *Lao Tzu,* p. 207. See also Zhuang Zi, *A Concordance to Zhuang Zi,* no. 2, (Taibei: Nanyu Publishing, n.d.), 16/6/20, 19/7/1–4. For an English translation, see Watson, *Chuang Tzu,* pp. 77, 92.

14. Zhuang Zi, *A Concordance,* 15/6/1–4; Watson, *Chuang Tzu,* p. 77.

15. Rolston, in an article brought to my attention by J. Baird Callicott, addresses the question "Can and ought we to follow nature?" In considering what one might mean by "to follow nature," he discusses the dilemma that I have suggested confronts the would-be Daoist naturalist. He too notes that one must interpret "to follow nature" in a relative sense which permits human conduct to be more or less natural. While I argue below that we do well to abandon the problematic of determining what it means for humans to follow nature, Rolston finds it both meaningful and useful to think of following nature in an axiological and tutorial sense; see Holmes Rolston, III, "Can and Ought We to Follow Nature?" *Environmental Ethics* 1 (1979): 7–30.

16. Attempts to define *natural* teleologically, as that which conforms to the principal purpose or function of X, are common but problematic. This method is plagued by disagreements as to which of the many purposes is principal. If one were to suggest that human purposes need not be reduced to a single end, but could be conceived of as a relatively small set—even allowing that one could determine which ends properly belong to this set-the plurality of ends would in many cases conflict and in those cases underdetermine the choices.

17. Rolston is keenly aware that the central ideas of Eastern thought which are most commonly put forth as potential conceptual resources for

Western environmental ethics often underdetermine real-life decisions. He illustrates this most clearly in connection with the Buddhist notion of the interpenetrating relationality of Indra's net; Rolston, "Can the East Help the West?" pp. 185–86.

18. The school of Huang-Lao—an offshoot of Daoism—attempts to circumvent the dilemma by capitalizing on the ambiguity in the concept of nature (understood in terms of *dao, tian, tian zhi dao)*. Nature may refer to either the cosmic order which embraces both the human and nonhuman realm (as on an organic model) or it may refer to the nonhuman realm alone. As the cosmic realm, nature *(dao, tian, tian zhi dao)* is normatively privileged and predetermined: both humans and nonhumans have a preassigned place in the cosmic harmony. Zhuang Zi's anti-foundationalist attack, however, cuts oneoff from all such transcendent orders: humans are not discovering a normatively predetermined Way, but are and must be creating their own way in light of their best judgments as to the appropriate relation between humans and nonhuman nature.

19. Chan, *Source Book,* pp. 136–37.

20. See, for instance, Lao Zi, *Dao De Jing,* chap. 80.

21. Cf. Rolston, "Can the East Help the West?" p. 177.

22. For instance, Watson states, "Nature . . . pertains to the natural as opposed to the artificial"; Watson, *Chuang Tzu,* p. 12.

23. See Lao Zi, *Dao De Jing,* chaps. 18, 38, 48; Zhuang Zi, *A Concordance,* 18–19/6/82–84; Watson, *Chuang Tzu,* p. 89.

24. Chen, *Lao Tzu,* p. 122.

25. Zhuang Zi, *A Concordance,* 15–16/6/4–20; Watson, *Chuang Tzu,* p. 77.

26. For a discussion of troublesome consequences of the "human artifact" view, see Rolston, "Can and Ought We to Follow Nature?" p. 10.

27. Angus Graham uses the label "primitivist" to describe a group of passages from the "Outer Chapters" of the *Zhuang Zi.* As he points out, the primitivist interpretation is characteristic of Lao Zi, but not Zhuang Zi. The existence of such writings in *Zhuang Zi* reflects the eclecticism of the "Outer Chapters." See Graham, *Chuang Tzu: The Inner Chapters* (London: George Allen and Unwin, 1981).

28. Feng, *Short History,* pp. 100–01.

29. The appeal to self-nature as the determinant of what is natural is characteristic of the *Qing Tang* and *Xuan Xue* schools of the Wei and Jin dynasties. The term for *self-nature* is not *de,* however, but *xing.* *Xing* does not occur in either the *Dao De Jing* or the "Inner Chapters" of *Zhuang Zi,* perhaps because *de* is its functional equivalent as a principle of individuation. Nevertheless, it becomes an important philosophical concept soon after as evidenced by its occurrence in the "Outer Chapters." The relativity inherent in the notion that what is natural for humans depends on their self-nature led in practice to

hedonistic excesses and indulgence in the natural proclivities. Some of the most famous and popular characters in Chinese history, the Seven Sages of the Bamboo Grove, were exponents of this position. They were known to spend their time lounging around naked, drinking wine, and composing poems in the woods.

30. Zhuang Zi, *A Concordance,* 4/2/20–21; Watson, *Chuang Tzu,* pp. 28–29.

31. Zhuang Zi's attack on a "completed heart-mind" is a criticism of Mencius' alleged innatism. Mencius argues that each person is born with a disposition toward moral goodness. This disposition will be realized as the Confucian virtues of *ren* and *yi* (conventionally translated as "benevolence" and "righteousness" respectively) unless hampered by external factors such as a bad environment, an evil ruler, and so forth. Zhuang Zi attacks the validity of an innate guide as a standard for behavior in arguing that (a) everybody has an internal guide and is therefore equally an authority, (b) responses of the heart-mind are not actually innate but learned from past experiences based on conventions and (c) even if there is an innate guide that does not mean one ought to follow its advice: one could just as easily follow the advice of the eyes or stomach as that of the heart-mind. For further elaboration, see Chad Hansen, "A Tao of Tao in Chuang Tzu," *Experimental Essays on Chuang Tzu,* ed. Victor Mair (Honolulu: University of Hawaii Press, 1983), p. 41.

32. J. J. L. Duyvendak. *Tao Te Ching* (London, n.p., 1954). p. 12.

33. J. Baird Callicott suggested this interpretation to me in private communication.

34. Indeed, that this interpretation is at all plausible rests on our understanding *willful* not in the sense of "deliberate," "purposive," but as "stubborn," "without reason"—in other words, "stupid."

35. Intelligent action is, of course, a key component of the pragmatism of John Dewey. One difference, however, between Dewey and his Daoist counterparts is that Dewey placed a greater emphasis on, and had a greater faith in, the ability of science and technology to solve social problems. As we have seen, Lao Zi and Zhuang Zi are skeptical about such a solution. Nevertheless, Dewey's notion of experience as an aesthetic event is promising as the basis for the development of a Daoist version of pragmatic, "intelligent" action. In this paper, I can only sketch in the broadest strokes what such a position would be like. See also in this regard, William Chaloupka, "John Dewey's Social Aesthetics as a Precedent for Environmental Thought," *Environmental Ethics* 9 (1987): 243–60.

36. David Hall and Roger T. Ames, *Thinking Through Confucius* (Albany: SUNY Press, 1987), pp. 223–49.

37. Indeed, one of the problems facing an advocate of a metaphysical or naturalist interpretation of *dao* is what to make of the many different

daos found in Daoist writings: there is the *dao* of *tian* (heaven/nature), of humans, of butchering an ox, of swimming, etc.

38. David Hall, "On Seeking a Change of Environment," in *Nature in Asian Traditions of Thought: Essays in Environmental Philosophy,* ed. J. Baird Callicott and Roger T. Ames (Albany: SUNY Press, 1989), p. 108.

39. Interestingly, the Latin *virtus* also has the sense of "power," "manliness," and "strength." Note also the English expression "by virtue of."

40. Hall, "Change of Environment," p. 109.

41. That the judgment is made according to our (human) lights does not mean that our domain of concern must be limited to narrowly defined self-interest. One's decision may, and one hopes would, reflect not only one's best confirmed scientific theories about the ecosystem and the environment, but one's feelings and attitudes about the value of animals and the nonhuman part of this world we all communally inhabit.

42. One difference between the Daoist method and that of reflective equilibrium or the coherence model is that the former does not privilege rational coherence as an overriding value. Of course, a consistency with past decisions and previously accepted principles would be *a* factor in favor of a proposed solution. However, while coherence is something to be desired, the main emphasis is on reaching consensus in the particular case. The Daoist is interested in what might be referred to as synchronic as opposed to diachronic coherence. That is, the Daoist is more willing to accept what would be an unpalatable ad hoc solution than would those endowed with a more robust "sentiment of rationality," as William James has called it. It is not clear whether Feinberg is in disagreement with the Daoists on this point. After mentioning coherence as one of the relevant considerations, he adds that he would not like to rank them or say which is most basic. Cf. Joel Feinberg, *Harm to Others* (New York: Oxford University Press, 1984), p. 18. Reflective equilibrium is only one component of Rawls' methodology. His attempt to secure universality for his principles of justice through a thought experiment by "rational agents" who make life-plan choices from behind a "veil of ignorance" runs counter to the context-specific character of Daoist ethics. See Rawls, *A Theory of Social Justice* (Cambridge: Harvard University Press, 1971).

43. Feinberg, *Harm,* p. 18.

44. Ames, "Taoism and the Nature of Nature," develops the notion of a harmony of interests in his reading of Daoism as an "aesthetic cosmology."

45. Gerald James Larson is critical of the politics of the very enterprise of looking for philosophical solutions to environmental problems. Philosophy, no longer ceded a privileged position among academic disciplines, has become "marginalized" such that one cannot turn to it in hopes of finding in the cognitive life a solution to our environmental problems.

See his " 'Conceptual Resources' in South Asia for 'Environmental Ethics,' " in *Nature in Asian Traditions,* pp. 267–77. While I agree that the environmental crisis is more than a philosophical/ethical problem, and that philosophy can claim no privileged status among the various disciplines by virtue of somehow having a better grip on "truth," it does not follow that one need abandon philosophy or the hope that we can come to reasonable decisions. Philosophy, like botany, zoology, anthropology, economics, may offer some guidance—fallible and incomplete though it may be.

46. Cf. Tuan, "Environmental Attitude and Behavior."

47. Zhuang Zi, *A Concordance,* 15–16/6/4–20; Watson, *Chuang Tzu,* pp. 78, 81.

CHAPTER 9

Conceptual Foundations for Environmental Ethics: A Daoist Perspective

KARYN L. LAI

I. INTRODUCTION

The Daoist classic, the *Daodejing*, has often been cited for its complex, metaphysical insights regarding the nature of reality and the theory of relations between individual things and beings. There is a growing body of literature on the application of Daoist thought to contemporary debates about the environment.[1] The literature ranges from basic proposals, such as a reexamination of the human relationship to nature,[2] to more complex arguments which utilize certain Daoist ideas in order to provoke a reassessment of assumptions and categories in contemporary thought.[3] Some include suggestions that the aesthetic order which underlies Daoist thought provides important conceptual frameworks for environmental philosophy.[4]

Such explorations into the relevance and effectiveness of Daoist philosophy as applied to contemporary environmental problems should be taken seriously, albeit with care. For instance, there are chapters in the *Daodejing* that appear to advocate primordial simplicity (19, 25, 32, 37, 62, 80),[5] which some thinkers have sought to appropriate in the service of their own naturalistic outlooks:

In the Far east the man-nature relationship was marked by respect, bordering on love, absent in the West . . . Chinese Taoists postulated an infinite and benign force in the natural world . . . . Taoism fostered love of wilderness rather than hatred.[6]

The first clear expression of ecological thinking appears in ancient China from about the sixth century B.C . . . . The Taoists resented [the] meddling [of the Confucianists] and believed all could live in spontaneous harmony with nature. They offered the most profound and eloquent philosophy of nature ever elaborated and the first stirrings of an ecological sensibility.[7]

These assertions need to be carefully investigated, however. One needs to ask whether the dictum to "live in spontaneous harmony with nature" provides sufficient justification, conceptual resources and motivational force for an effective environmental ethic.

In this essay, I attempt to avoid simplistic applications of Daoist philosophy and aim to demonstrate that it provides critical conceptual tools for addressing certain debates in environmental philosophy. I argue that, both in its key concepts and in its anti-anthropocentric tenor, the *Daodejing* provides a justification for an environmental ethic that reaches beyond humans, individuals, or species. This project draws upon both the metaphysical and ethical resources that are available in the *Daodejing* to justify an environmental ethic which espouses a holistic perspective but which nevertheless recognizes the integrity of individuals.

The second section of the essay explores the Daoist concept, *de*, both in secondary commentaries and in the *Daodejing* itself. The third section investigates two sets of related concepts in the *Daodejing*. The first is the concepts *dao* and *de*, focusing primarily on their interdependence, and the second is the notions of *wuwei* and *ziran*. I argue, with reference to these four concepts, that the Daoist notion of interdependence may be invoked to support a pluralistic account of value in the context of holism. The final section reviews various significant themes such as anthropocentricism, human-nature dualism, and holism, in the light of Daoist philosophy. I also establish that Daoist philosophy provides important philosophical and ethical resources for dealing with contemporary environmental issues.

II. Interpretations of *De*

De, often translated as "virtue," is one of two cardinal concepts in the *Daodejing*, the treatise on *dao* and *de*.[8] However, some scholars have noted with concern that analyses of Daoist philosophy have too frequently failed to accord the concept *de* the significance it is due.[9]

There is a range of possible meanings of the concept *de* deriving from its usage in the chapters of the *Daodejing*. The term is commonly translated to mean moral principle or virtue in the conventional sense, indicating one's moral cultivation. This approach has been taken in various ways by Chinese philosophy scholars such as Lionel Giles,[10] Wing-tsit Chan,[11] and D.C. Lau.[12]

However, the interpretation of *de* to denote moral goodness is unsatisfactory because it overlooks the vagueness of the text regarding questions of ethics or axiology. Additionally, the interpretation of *de* as "virtue" or "moral principle" neglects the Daoist criticism of existing norms and values. The *Daodejing* is incisive in its criticism of contemporary values and virtues in the ancient Chinese context.[13] This criticism was, at its most fundamental level, a universal rejection of the all-too-human activity of promoting values, which are superficial and unnecessarily dichotomous, divisive and hence, which tend to mislead:

When the people of the world all know beauty as beauty,
There arises the recognition of ugliness.
When they all know the good as good,
There arises the recognition of evil . . . . (2)

The five colors cause one's eyes to be blind.
The five tones cause one's ears to be deaf.
The five flavors cause one's palate to be spoiled . . . . (12)[14]

Against this background of skepticism regarding conventional values, the interpretation of *de* to denote a conventional sense of moral goodness would sit uneasily with Daoist philosophy. The problem with this interpretation is compounded by the fact that there is another term in the *Daodejing*, *shan*, which does refer to moral goodness, and which at times occurs in the same passage with *de*.[15]

It needs to be noted, however, that Wing-tsit Chan's and Lau's analyses of *de* are not confined to human ethical action. Both scholars recognize multiple interpretations of *de*. Chan argues that *dao* is the ontological source from which all things derive their existence, and *de* refers to the particular instantiation (the essence, so to speak), of each existing thing:

> . . . *te* is Tao endowed in the individual things. While Tao is common to all, it is what each thing has obtained from Tao, or its *te*, that makes it different from others. *Te* is then the individualizing factor, the

embodiment of definite principles which give things their determinate features or characters.[16]

According to Chan's analysis, *de* may be understood within an overarching framework, *dao*, within which individual beings manifest their distinctiveness. In this way, an emphasis on *de* is an emphasis on the particularity or distinctiveness of individual beings. Additionally, the theme of relationality is also important: each thing embodies its particular *de within* the contextual environment of *dao*.

Similarly, Lau's analysis highlights the connection between *de* and *dao*, explicitly drawing out the interdependent nature of all existence. On his definition, *de* refers to the *integrity* of being a particular thing, rather than to its ability or willingness to conform to predetermined standards. The ontology is particularly interesting because all things are seen to embody their distinctive natures *in and through their common origin, dao*. It is unfortunate, though, that Lau's analysis stops short of fleshing out this ontology.[17]

Chan's and Lau's claim that *de* signifies individuality within the context of the whole is articulated in the *Daodejing*:

> When one cultivates [*de*] in his person, it becomes genuine [*de*]
> When one cultivates [*de*] in his family, it becomes overflowing [*de*]
> When one cultivates [*de*] in his community, it becomes lasting [*de*]
> When one cultivates [*de*] in the world, it becomes universal . . . (54)

Here, there is a strong suggestion that the respective function of each individual thing is context-specific rather than normative, and also that *de* generates different ends in each of these contexts.

Other Daoist scholars such as J. J. L. Duyvendak,[18] Arthur Waley,[19] and Max Kaltenmark[20] provide interpretations of *de* which are multidimensional. Duyvendak contends that the archaic sense of the term is actually a morally neutral one, signifying some kind of magic power rather than moral goodness: "good conduct," in a naturalistic sense and spontaneous manner, is the older sense of the term; "good conduct" in a human and ethical sense only came into use later, due partly to Confucian influence.

In a similar tone, Waley contends that the term *power* is a more appropriate translation of *de* because the earlier usage of *de* allows for *de* to be understood as bad as well as good, not unlike the Indian karma in the following respects:

> *Te* is anything that happens to one or that one does of a kind indicating that, as a consequence, one is going to meet with good or bad luck.

It means, so to speak, the stock of credit (or the deficit) that at any given moment a man has at the bank of fortune.[21]

Kaltenmark offers a compelling analysis of *de*. His study is particularly insightful because it is multifaceted and accommodates different conceptions of *de*. Quoting Marcel Granet's study of Chinese thought, Kaltenmark states that *de* is "the ideal efficacy that becomes particular as it becomes real."[22] He also notes that *de* is generally used with positive connotations, though his analysis strives to retain the original sense of potency, which may be good or bad. He suggests that

> . . . [*te*] always implies a notion of efficacy and specificity. Every creature possessing a power of any kind, natural or acquired, is said to have *Te* . . . . [*Te*] has varied meanings ranging from magical potency to moral virtue. But the latter is a derived meaning, for originally *Te* was not necessarily good . . . . Nevertheless, *Te* is generally used in the good sense: it is an inner potency that favorably influences those close to its possessor, a virtue that is beneficent and life-giving.[23]

Kaltenmark's articulation of the concept *de* has the advantage of recognizing and allowing for a range of understandings of the concept that are necessitated by the cryptic and piecemeal nature of the text.

Based on the discussion of *de* in this section, two important features of *de* may be detected: (a) there is a strong suggestion of an intrinsic relatedness between individuals within the framework of the *dao*. Relations are intrinsic rather than extrinsic in that individuals are determined in part by their respective places in the *dao*. Here, the remarks of Chung-ying Cheng, who contrasts a superficial notion of the term *environment* with its deeper (Daoist) sense, are pertinent:

> [According to a superficial sense of the term, environment means] simply "the surroundings," the physical periphery, the material conditions and the transient circumstances . . . . [However, environment] cannot be treated as an object, the material conditions, a machine tool, or a transient feature. Environment is more than the visible, more than the tangible, more than the external, more than a matter of quantified period or time or spread of space. It has a deep structure as well as a deep process, as the concept of Tao indicates.[24]

A corollary to the theme of intrinsic relatedness is that of *interdependence* of individuals. The interdependent relation between the self and others within the context of the whole engenders a relational and contextual concept of the self. Within such a structure, individuals can only achieve full realization *in the context of* their interdependence with others.

(b) Associated with the deeper notion of environment articulated in (a), *de* seems to provide the specifications for an individual's *integrity* in the context of its relations with other individuals. Within an environment where interdependence is emphasized, the integrity of individuals is important as it is necessary to prevent the obliteration of individual distinctiveness, interests and needs, which might too easily be subsumed under the rubric of the whole.

These two features—interdependence and integrity—are held in a finely tuned balance. The individual seeks and attains meaning *within* contextual and relational boundaries and affiliations. However, if these are overly restrictive, the integrity of the individual will be diminished or eradicated. Hence, *de* is important in setting the extent of self-determination. *De* refers to (a development or cultivation of) the distinctive characteristics of individuals. Yet, the sense of integrity is far removed from any suggestion of independent, separate existence. In the view of the *Daodejing*, severe fragmentation of the different forms of life is brought about partly by the imposition of a rigid axiological framework upon all aspects of existence; this cuts up the uncarved block, so to speak (see *Daodejing* 28).

III. INTERDEPENDENCE AND INTEGRITY: *DAO* AND *DE* ALLOWING FOR SPONTANEITY: *WUWEI* AND *ZIRAN*

The paradigmatic *dao* of Heaven is inclusive (73), standing in contrast to the tendencies of the human world to create inequalities (77). The method of *dao* is to treat all equally: ". . . Heaven and earth unite to drip sweet dew. Without the command of men, it drips evenly over all" (32).

Additionally, the interdependence of things within the whole is implicit in the idea that all draw benefit from *dao* (34, 81). This theme of *dao* benefiting all things is effectively epitomized by the action of water:

> The best [man][25] is like water,
> Water is good; it benefits [*li*] all things and does not compete with them.
> It dwells in (lowly) places that all disdain.
> This is why it is so near to Tao (8)

From an ontological point of view, the concept *dao* signifies the shared context within which all things exist. In the case of the natural environment, this assertion is, at one level, undeniably true: all species and beings that live within the natural environment are ontologically connected; beings encroach on others, they contribute to and extract from their natural environments and, most importantly, they share the same biosphere.

However, an understanding of *dao* from a purely ontological point of view can be limiting. At points in the *Daodejing*, the concept is referred to not as an ontological reality but as a metaphysical ideal. In this latter sense, *dao* is an abstraction, not an actual existence. In other words, it also functions as a conceptual tool or a psychological device to assist in the visualization of an ideal state of affairs whereby particulars come together in fulfillment of their particular *de*, in a way that is maximally possible within an environment that includes multiple others. This vision draws from an integration of the concepts *dao* and *de*.

The metaphors that the *Daodejing* is renowned for also illustrate the inclusivity of *dao*. Collectively, the images of the infant, water, rivers and seas, the female, and the valley exemplify the qualities of softness [*rou*],[26] weakness [*ruo*],[27] quietude [*jing*],[28] and non-assertiveness [*buzhen*].[29]

It may appear that these characteristics make a virtue of submissiveness in order to facilitate a realization of a harmonious whole. On such a view, the integrated whole is achieved at a cost to some individuals: they are required to be non-assertive, still, or weak. On this interpretation, Daoism would collapse into a trivial and implausible holism, one that calls for the unconditional denial of the integrity of individuals. However, it is clear that some key passages in the *Daodejing* challenge such a trivial holism:

> Tao produces them.
> Te fosters them.
> . . . They always come spontaneously.
> . . . (Tao) produces them but does not take possession of them.
> . . . It leads them but does not master them.
> This is called profound and secret te. (51)[30]

There are two key phrases here which recognize the importance of integrity. That "tao produces them but does not take possession of them" (*sheng er buyou*) could be translated to mean "to produce or to assist in (their) growth *but* not to possess (them)." Similarly, that *dao* "leads them but does not master them" (*chang er buzai*) expresses the view of leading without dominating. Within the context of the passage, there is a strong suggestion that the holistic perspective does not entail the negation of individual or distinctive features or concerns.

Furthermore, it is striking that *dao* and *de* are mentioned together, highlighting the themes of interdependence and integrity. *De* is that distinctiveness, integrity, or excellence of each individual thing that can be realized only in the context of the whole, the ideal *dao*. A Chinese philosophy scholar, Roger Ames, expresses a similar view of the *dao-de* polarity:

> . . . [*te*] denotes the arising of the particular in a process vision of existence. The particular is the unfolding of a *sui generis* focus of potency that embraces and determines conditions within the range and parameters of its particularity . . . . Just as any one ingredient in the stewpot must be blended with all of the others in order to express most fully its own flavor, so harmonization with other environing particulars is a necessary precondition for the fullest self-disclosure of any given particular.[31]

Ames' conceptualization of *dao* and *de* is not unlike the account expressed in this paper in that it stresses the maintenance of integrity of individual beings while simultaneously emphasizing the importance of context and environment. Ames also makes the important point that the individual-environment nexus should not be seen as dichotomous. In other words, while the individual may be restricted by various aspects of its environment and by its relations with others, this restriction is not necessarily a negative condition.[32]

The maintenance of the integrity of each individual entity is also espoused in two integral Daoist concepts, non-action (*wuwei*) and spontaneity (*ziran*):

> He who takes action fails.
> He who grasps things loses them.
> For this reason the sage takes no action (*wuwei*) and therefore does not fail.
> He grasps nothing and therefore he does not lose anything.
> . . . He learns to be unlearned, and returns to what the multitude has missed (Tao).
> Thus he supports all things in their natural state (*ziran*) but does not take any action. (64)

Scholars have often puzzled over of both these concepts, notorious for their ambiguity. The first, *wuwei*, is most frequently though somewhat misleadingly translated as "non-action." This translation evokes a sense of passivity and inaction, rendering any suggestions for activity or change incoherent. Some scholars have argued that the interpretation of *wuwei* as "non-intrusive action" or "non-interfering action" is more philosophically profound and interesting.[33]

These latter translations support a meaningful rendition of the concept *wuwei* both at the sociopolitical level (arguing against the imposition of artificial, conformist and universally binding norms) and at the metaphysical level (acknowledging the inappropriateness and fatality of imposing egocentric or anthropocentric norms upon other individuals or species).[34]

The term *ziran* has often been translated as "nature" or "natural." It functions both as a noun, corresponding with the notion of the natural environment, or as an adjective which means "spontaneous." Chapter twenty-five illuminates this concept:

> There was something undifferentiated and yet complete,
> Which existed before heaven and earth.
> . . . I do not know its name; I call it Tao.
> . . . Tao models itself after Nature (*ziran*).

It needs to be noted that the commonly used translation of *ziran* as "nature" is misleading, locating in the concept *ziran* an inherent concern for the natural environment. However, the unquestioning ease with which Daoist thought has been adopted to address certain issues in environmental philosophy has recently been brought under scrutiny by scholars such as Ramachandra Guha:

> The detection of a "love of wilderness" and of the "first stirrings of an ecological sensibility" in Daoist thought reflect a selective reading of the Daoist texts as well as conjecture regarding the intention and attitudes of the early Daoists toward environmental concerns . . . . such utopic renditions of Daoist thought need further to be justified in the face of ecological disasters in Chinese history.[35]

The interpretation of the message of the *Daodejing* as supporting naturalistic primitivism also leads to triviality. Either human beings belong to the realm of the natural—in which case the dictum to be natural, like *dao*, is superfluous— or they do not—in which case the dictum to be natural is a misdirected aim.[36]

The alternative translation of *ziran* as a principle or as a *modus operandi* is both more plausible and fruitful.[37] On this interpretation, *wuwei* and *ziran*, understood in combination, provide a coherent picture of Daoist non-assertiveness: *allowing* for the spontaneity of any one individual requires the other, or others, not to impose unnecessary constraints on this individual.[38] In other words, *wuwei* expresses the methodology of *dao,* which, in respecting the integrity of individuals, allows room for their *spontaneous* development.

Cheng alludes to this latter interpretation of *ziran* in his views on environmental ethics inspired by Daoist philosophy:

> . . . tzu-jan (*ziran*) is not something beyond and above the Tao. It is the movement of the Tao as the Tao, namely as the underlying unity of all things as well as the underlying source of the life of all things. One important aspect of tzu-jan is that the movement of things must come from the internal life of things and never results from engineering or conditioning by an external power.[39]

Cheng identifies *ziran* not merely in ontological terms, but also as a process, a "movement." His analysis also links *ziran* with the notions of *de* (the "internal life of things") with *wuwei* (not being conditioned by an external power).

In the application of *wuwei* and *ziran* to environmental thought, it may be argued that those who share in the Daoist insight will refrain from imposing a human-centered perspective on all things and will not expect the myriad creatures (*wanwu*) to conform to human norms.[40] Kirill Thompson, who argues for an aesthetic organization inherent in Daoist philosophy, suggests that

> . . . in a Taoist world characterized by aesthetic order, each particular from flea to red giant emerges as a center of things, a bona fide point of reference . . . . Significantly, none is intrinsically better than any other; our preferences among them simply reflect our own perspectives and cannot be given any ultimate justification.[41]

The organizational picture presented by Thomson is supported by *Daodejing* 5, which opens with

> Heaven and Earth are not humane *(ren)*,
> They regard all things as straw dogs.
> The sage is not humane.
> He regards all people as straw dogs.

D. C. Lau, a scholar of Chinese thought notes in his translation that "[i]n the *T'ien yun* chapter in the *Chuang Tzu* it is said that straw dogs were treated with the greatest deference before they were used as an offering, only to be discarded and trampled upon as soon as they had served their purpose."[42]

Apart from its anti-anthropocentric tone, the notion of straw dogs is philosophically interesting, its significance reaching beyond issues of instrumentality. While the straw dog serves a certain function within the sacrifice, it is also *central* to it; without the straw dog, the sacrifice loses its fuller, broader and richer significance, and perhaps cannot proceed at all. In this way, the issue of the straw dogs—a symbol for "all things" (*wanwu*)—transcends debates on intrinsic and instrumental value. The tone of *Daodejing* 5 impels us to see everything as holding its distinctive significance *within the context of the dao*.

From this analysis, the two sets of concepts, *dao* and *de*, and *wuwei* and *ziran*, are seen in their fullest cooperation: the recognition and valuing of individual distinctiveness (*de*) entails an appreciation of its spontaneous expression (*ziran*); allowing for (*wuwei*) spontaneity, on the other hand, is not simply idiosyncratic and uncoordinated self-fulfillment. The realization of each individual is meaningful only within the context of its relatedness and responsivity to others within the whole (*dao*). The affirmation of the value of individual beings *within the environmental context* feeds into a complex holism that emphasizes both the integrity and interdependence of individuals.

IV. A Daoist Proposal for an Environmental Ethic

Anti-Anthropocentrism

A major theme that cuts across many debates in environmental philosophy is that of anthropocentricism. At its most general level, anthropocentricism, construed as the inability or unwillingness of human beings to accord moral standing or moral consideration to other species, has been held responsible for the degraded state of the natural environment and for the extinction of species. The issue of anthropocentricism has been at the center of debates about the nature and scope of environmental ethics. A number of environmental ethicists see anthropocentricism as the basic problem in environmental ethics. They argue that to construct an environmental ethic based on human concerns is to beg the question about the need for environmental ethics to address the issue of human-centeredness in environmental thought.

For instance, Val Plumwood, articulating an ecofeminist philosophy, argues against integrating "nature" into an essentially anthropocentric model. Plumwood sets up five features that a viable, non-hierarchical and non-anthropocentric environmental ethic should include. These are

(a) the acknowledgment of dependency between human beings and other beings (the well-being of other species is not merely accidentally or externally related to that of human beings and vice versa);

(b) the avoidance of radical exclusion of human beings from other beings (radical exclusion denies the possibility of continuity and community between the human and the nonhuman; a proper resolution requires not just a recognition of similarities and differences but also a recognition of a complex, interacting pattern both of continuity and difference);

(c) the avoidance of merely incorporating other beings within the notion of humanity (Plumwood calls this an "assimilating" strategy which may result in other species being seen as inferior humans);

(d) the avoidance of instrumentalism at all costs (a viable environmental ethic should consider other beings and species, and the natural environment, not merely as means to human ends); and

(e) the avoidance of homogenization or stereotyping (involving a recognition that the beings within the natural environment are not homogenous; other species have some different needs from those of human beings and different individuals and species have their distinctive characteristics and interests).[43]

The view in the *Daodejing* described in this essay incorporates the points articulated by Plumwood. In response to Plumwood's concerns, the philosophy of the *Daodejing* as outlined in this essay may be presented as follows:

(a$_1$) The perspective of the *dao* presents an ideal inclusive whole that does not permit the mere assertion of human priority. The flourishing of *dao* is predicated upon the well-being of individuals within the *dao*. Hence, the assertion of independence on the part of human beings, or any other being or species, will be ultimately futile because it severs essential interdependencies between beings.

(b$_1$) The Daoist criticism of the Confucian project of creating a human cultural identity, distinct and separate from all other species and the natural environment, addresses this concern of radical exclusion. Daoism deems human institutions, ranks and hierarchies as "unnatural" because they remove continuities and similarities between humans and their natural environment.

(c₁) Daoist axiology is irreducible to one group, kind or species, or even to the whole. Daoist thought strongly urges a transcendence of the merely human. It is also skeptical regarding the values that are upheld by humankind, and imposed on all aspects of human and nonhuman existence. In particular, the concepts *wuwei* and *ziran* support a conceptual system that recognizes the integrity of each individual and allows for their spontaneous development, within the parameters of its environment.

(d₁) The rejection of conventional values involves an overturning of dualism through a shattering of dualistic pairs, embodied in the *dao-de* polarity. This rejection of dualism entails a rejection of the unconditional valuing of all that is human as deserving absolute priority. Additionally, it is not the case that only human beings possess noninstrumental value. The theme of intrinsic relatedness of beings and species is one that casts doubt on the whole debate regarding which beings have intrinsic value and which others have only instrumental value. First, it blurs the clear individuation and separation of particulars. Second, it endorses a multitiered value system where relationships, in addition to individuals, are valued.

(e₁) The *Daodejing* recognizes the integrity of individuals within the whole and seeks to promote their well-being within the context of the whole. The valuing of individuals also prompts a recognition of a multiplicity of needs, interests and values.

The depth of the philosophy of the *Daodejing* lies not merely in the fact that it is able to respond to the requirements of a non-anthropocentric environmental ethic as proposed by Plumwood. It could also provide a more thorough evaluation of the issue of anthropocentricism itself, which has been intensely debated. Some philosophers reject the methodology of merely extending existing normative ethical theories to include nonhuman species, individuals and entities in our moral consideration.[44] Others argue against anthropocentricism inherent in existing normative theories, contending that the only viable environmental ethic is one with a non-anthropocentric, ecological focus.[45]

In response, there are arguments against the viability or plausibility of a nonanthropocentric ethical system, instigating some to make a distinction between *weak* anthropocentricism and *strong* anthropocentricism.[46] While anthropocentric environmental ethics may fall anywhere within this range—and, indeed, the credibility of the distinction has been questioned—the key difference between weak and strong anthropocentricism is not that the latter lacks any tangible concern for the natural environment. Rather, strong anthropocentrists in general perceive the appreciation of value, and the act of valuing, as essentially human enterprises. In that connection, they normally move on to posit that the concerns of nonhumans or the natural environment are only instrumental or secondary to human concerns and hence are only worth pursuing or preserving within that framework. In contrast, the range of weak anthropocentric theories uphold that at least some nonhuman interests are morally considerable, although they may be overridden by human ones. Here, again, the distinctness of such positions from non-anthropocentric views has been challenged.[47]

The *Daodejing* circumvents debates about whether environmental ethics should seek to be anthropocentric or non-anthropocentric. It bypasses debates on whether individuals, entities, or species possess intrinsic or instrumental value, proposing instead to understand value in terms of the individual's place within the whole. The value of the straw dog within the context of the whole is neither *only instrumental* nor *only intrinsic*. When applied to environmental issues, the analogy is clear: individuals, species, or entities are *situated in*, and *connected to others within*, the natural environment. In this context, they seldom, if ever, possess only intrinsic value or only instrumental value. It is perhaps through this method of moving beyond both debates on anthropocentrism, and intrinsic versus instrumental value, that environmental ethics can begin properly to consider the ethical development of human attitudes and behavior within the natural environment.

Against Human Separateness and Other Dualisms

It has been asserted that anthropocentric attitudes are based partly in a commitment to the view that humans are separate and independent of other species and the environment. Such a perspective is, in turn, often linked to a dualistic framework set up between humans and other species, such as that between man-nature, subject-object, master-slave, or dominant-dominated. This fundamental dualism is problematic as it is associated with the viewing of humans as discontinuous with, independent of, superior to, and perhaps even antithetical to, the natural environment. Such a perspective is damaging not only for the natural environment but for humans as well. It legitimizes a false dichotomy between humans and the environment, and it warrants, specifically, the mastery, domination and exploitation of the natural environment by human beings.[48] Additionally, such assumptions of the human-nature dichotomy tend to oversimplify aspects of connectedness between humans, other species, and the environment, and thus restrict a full and proper evaluation of ethical issues, often presenting these as simplistic trade-offs.

The *Daodejing* questions the human tendency to assert independence from all other existing beings.[49] It upholds a concept of the related self as basic. All beings are determined in part by others in their environment. There is not one being that successfully maintains independence from all others in its environment. Each being seeks fulfillment within the boundaries and parameters in its environment. In this context, the curtailment of the immediate needs and interests of particular individuals and groups is not seen as necessarily, or always, negative. Ideally, individuals in that context are able to pursue their interests in a maximal way *within their environment.*

In a fundamental way, the rejection of dualism and its corresponding assertions of separateness of the human species from others touches on issues of human identity. The *Daodejing* urges a reevaluation of the conceptual framework that asserts *independent* human existence. It is perhaps paradoxical that such an attempt to cast doubt upon the significance of human independence actually creates the conditions for the development of a far richer and more substantial meaning of human identity.

Holism and Integrity

Within environmental philosophy, holism is articulated in a variety of ways. It operates in many ecocentric accounts, with a variety of meanings.[50] However, holism has not received universal acceptance amongst environmental philosophers. Some philosophers are rightly critical of certain versions of environmental holism because they may neglect the needs of individuals.[51]

R. P. Peerenboom, in his attempt to apply Daoist views to environmental ethics, relies on a holism with some consideration of outcomes:

> . . . no individual or species or specimen is a priori entitled to protection . . . . No single criterion is privileged as *the* criterion. When conflicts arise, the focus turns not to adjudicating according to a fixed rule who is right and who is wrong, but to achieving a harmonization of the disparate interests that will benefit all.[52]

Peerenboom is cautious, however, that such harmony may be merely conceptual. He writes:

> While this interpretation may be philosophically promising . . . [o]ne wonders of how much assistance it will be to the environmental philosopher faced with real life problems . . . . In actual practice, this process of balancing interests to attain an equilibrium is susceptible to the politics of power . . . [because of] real *dis*parity as some members exercise a greater influence over the end result than others: some are conductors, composers, and maestros; others are bit players.[53]

Peerenboom is a little pessimistic regarding the applicability of Daoist philosophy to contemporary environmental debates. It is clear that the "process of balancing interests is susceptible to the politics of power." However, this is not a problem specific to a Daoist environmental ethic. Peerenboom himself makes this point later in the same essay, that these problems surface in every ethical system.

Indeed, the fact that there are power differentials should be engaged with directly, instead of avoided, in environmental debates and negotiations. The contention here is that Daoist philosophy can provide more to environmental ethics than Peerenboom allows it to. As argued previously, holism in Daoist philosophy maintains a sense of individual integrity. The balance between the interdependence of all things and the maintenance of their *de*, their individual excellences, allows for the realization of a whole that is not merely the sum of its parts. Rather, the integrity and the stability of the larger whole is valued not because the whole is valued as an end-in-itself, but because these conditions combine to assist in the preservation of the well-being of its constituent parts. Furthermore, the principles of *wuwei* and *ziran* highlight the importance of acknowledging the distinctive identities of the many. The endorsement of nondominating or non-intrusive action is a corollary of the imperative to recognize and allow for the spontaneous development of (the many) others. The legitimacy of individuals in their distinctiveness should be adopted as a fundamental feature of any environmental ethic.

This view of the self-in-relation and self-in-context necessitates a fundamental change in conceptual frameworks, particularly in philosophies where identity is construed in essentially individualistic and atomistic terms. On this view, impartiality or detachment, for example—or more generally the requirement to treat all like cases alike, irrespective of the individuals or factors involved—would not be accorded priority. Rather, decision making would involve taking into account the particulars involved and the relationships that obtain between them, in the context of the whole.

It is also obvious that a viable holistic theory must account for conflict of the sort Peerenboom refers to, where there are power imbalances. The issue of conflict is not simplified within a Daoist axiology proposed in this paper. Indeed, it should be expected that a Daoist assessment of values would culminate in a multitiered account that resists unitary evaluations that reduce or assimilate a wide variety of particulars to the standard. Such an assessment *should* yield a more complex entanglement of issues: a proper resolution will take into account the interests of individuals, species and of the whole, together with the relevant relations that obtain between individuals within the whole. Clearly, in certain situations, conflict may facilitate development or precipitate positive change.

The view articulated in this paper transcends a simplistic view of the whole as a mere sum of its parts. In this more complex view, the whole is not more important than, or independent of its parts; rather, an adequate understanding of individuals comes only when we view them relative to the system of interdependencies in which they exist. Daoist philosophy provides the basis for valuing human *and* nonhuman individuals and species, and for a proper acknowledgment that individuals may also possess value by virtue of the relations in which they stand, with other beings in the context of the whole.

From a holistic perspective, it is clear that not all individuals or groups may achieve their desired outcomes on any one issue and that, at times, compromise is essential. Within the framework of the *Daodejing*, negotiation and compromise are to be understood in the context of the whole. If this view is accepted, then, like conflict, compromise is not necessarily or always negative. That compromise may have positive effects or outcomes is predicated on a related and contextualized self. Both individuals, and the relations that hold between them, are morally significant. Hence, decisions could be made, for example, that entail a loss for the individual, but which enrich a particular other or others. In this way, the loss suffered by that individual is not a complete or absolute loss. Holism in the *Daodejing* refers to a comprehensive harmony between the realization of individual excellence (*de*) within a context of interdependent, mutual enrichment (*dao*).

In a Daoist environmental ethic, what is ultimately sought is not the satisfaction of all parties concerned but rather a *maximally* coherent and superlative state of affairs. How this ideal condition might be attained is best demonstrated through analogy. Here, an analogy from philosophy of religion is helpful.

Philosophers of religion and theologians have been concerned with the issue of god's attributes, noting that the set of them taken together—omnipotence, omniscience, and maximal goodness—may appear to be internally inconsistent. For instance, doubts have been articulated regarding the traditional understanding of omnipotence, that god is able to do *everything*; such questions include god's powers to overturn logical necessities, to change god's own past, or to conduct evil acts.

A traditional response is that god is capable of evil acts, but will not bring them about because god is good. However, this response is unsatisfactory for two reasons. First, this approach could lapse into a circularity regarding the definition of good and evil. Second, and more significantly, it does not deal with the root of these problems regarding god's different attributes. The traditional methodology of assessing god's attributes has been to take each of these characteristics in turn, and to discuss them independently of god's other attributes. Such a strategy isolates the different attributes and fails to conceive of them as properties embodied by the one being; the result is a fragmented picture of the one being who embodies these attributes.

A solution that has come up in response to this difficulty is one that emphasizes the need to see god as the embodiment of these different characteristics, and appropriately to construe the latter in interplay. On this view, one should see the different characteristics of god not in isolation, but as embodied by the one being. God, in his exercise of abilities, consistently achieves a maximally satisfactory state of affairs. In other words, ". . . the rationale behind ascribing great-making qualities to God is to make explicit the emphatic, central belief that God is perfect or maximally excellent."[54] On this view, god possesses, in the best way possible, his great-making properties: god has the *"greatest compossible* [co-possible] *set of properties."*[55] In practical terms, this would mean that "[i]f God's being perfectly good in any way limits God's being all-powerful, it does so only in a fashion that, overall, contributes to the excellence of God."[56]

This approach to the issue of god's attributes in the philosophy of religion could benefit discussion on environmental holism. In particular, the notion of compossibility calls for a recognition and acceptance that, from the point of view of the whole, a maximally fruitful outcome is not necessarily one that attempts to ensure the full satisfaction of all parties involved. The application of this idea to debates about environmental holism yields significant results: decisions are made *neither* exclusively for the whole and against the individual, *nor* for the individual and against the whole. Indeed, from the point of view of compossibility, it would appear that such characterizations of holism are naïve and simplistic. An example of this unhelpful oversimplification of issues is in the presentation of issues regarding the northern spotted owl in the Pacific Northwest ancient forests as a simplistic trade-off between those owls and loggers ("Owl versus Man"),[57] ignoring significant factors such as aspects of the shared environment, other interdependent species which share that habitat, and biodiversity.

In order to achieve a maximally compossible state of affairs in an environmental context, the diversity of beings, species, and habitats needs to be taken in to account. It may strike some that the notion of compossibility evoked here, and applied to environmental ethics, is too hazy to be useful. However, a holistic environmental ethic which seeks to recognize all involved, including the relations between beings, their respective places within the environment and both the short-term and long-term effects of particular decisions, will necessarily be wide-ranging and multifaceted.[58]

That the measure of what is maximally compossible in the case of environmental ethics is not a mere sum of individual happinesses, forces human beings to examine the bases of anthropocentric thinking. Such a holistic environmental ethic, when applied to real-life situations in the contemporary setting, does not necessarily seek a return to the primitive, antitechnological and anti-developmental way of life: a rejection of anthropocentrism is not necessarily anti-humanitarian. The insights of the *Daodejing* apply both to the *process* and *attitudes* according to which decisions are made about the natural environment. *Wuwei* is a *methodology* that allows for spontaneity (*ziran*), recognizing variety and complexity in value, rather than simplicity and unitariness. Additionally, the *Daodejing* prompts a critical awareness of the self-in-environment and of interdependence between individuals, species and habitats within the earth environment. This perspective, coupled with an *attitude* prepared to negotiate and to accept compromise in some situations, would lead to some very significant changes in existing behavioral and consumptive patterns.

The Daoist model proposed here is a potent one in challenging the selfishness and shortsightedness of anthropocentrism by arguing that there are no empirical or moral grounds for asserting human superiority and independence. Additionally, the holistic framework provided by Daoist thought provides a stimulus for reassessing human identity beyond the isolated and insulated immediate environments. These elements will provide the bases for a rich and fruitful environmental ethic.

Notes

1. Prominent collections include *Environmental Ethics* 8, no. 3 (Winter 1986); *Philosophy East and West* 37, no. 2 (April 1987); and J. Baird Callicott and Roger T. Ames, eds., *Nature in Asian Traditions of Thought: Essays in Environmental Philosophy* (Albany: State University of New York Press, 1989).

2. Po-Keung Ip, "Taoism and the Foundations of Environmental Ethics," *Environmental Ethics* 5 (1983): 335–43.

3. See, for example, Chung-ying Cheng's "On the Environmental Ethics of the Tao and the Ch'i," *Environmental Ethics* 8 (1986): 351–70.

4. See Roger Ames, "Taoism and the Nature of Nature," *Environmental Ethics* 8 (1986): 317–50; R. P. Peerenboom, "Beyond Naturalism: A Reconstruction of Daoist Environmental Ethics" in *Environmental Ethics* 13 (1991): 3–22; Chung-yuan Chang, *Creativity and Taoism: A Study of Chinese Philosophy, Art, and Poetry* (New York: Julian Press, 1963); Chung-yuan Chang, *Tao: A New Way of Thinking* (New York: Harper and Row, 1975); and Kirill Thompson, "Taoist Cultural Reality: The Harmony of Aesthetic Order," *Journal of Chinese Philosophy* 17 (1990): 175–86.

5. The numbers here refer to chapter numbers in the *Daodejing*; this system of referencing (bracketed numbers) will be used throughout this essay unless otherwise indicated.

6. Roderick Nash, *Wilderness and the American Mind* (New Haven: Yale University Press, 1967), pp. 192–93.

7. Peter Marshall, *Nature's Web: Rethinking Our Place on Earth* (New York: Paragon House, 1992), p. 9.

8. The terms *dao* and *de* (Pinyin transliteration system) correspond to *tao* and *te* (Wade-Giles system commonly used in earlier literature) respectively. The Pinyin system is used in this essay because it is more up-to-date and widely used.

9. With the oldest existing versions of the *Daodejing* excavated from the Han tombs at Mawangdui in China in 1973, the bamboo strips on which the texts are inscribed are arranged in such a way that the final forty-four chapters of the received text, the *De Jing*, are placed first. Hence, a translator of the Mawangdui *Daodejing* has labelled his translation the "*Dedaojing.*" See Robert Henricks, *Lao-tze Te-tao Ching: A New Translation Based on the Recently Discovered Ma-Wang-Tui Texts* (New York: Ballantine Books, 1989). See also Ames, "Taoism and the Nature of Nature," esp. sec. 4: "Taoism Misnamed."

10. Lionel Giles, *The Sayings of Lao Tzu* (London: John Murray. 1907).

11. Wing-tsit Chan, *The Way of Lao Tzu* (New York: Library of Liberal Arts, Bobbs-Merrill, 1963). Chan writes, "[t]he main objective of [the *Daodejing*] is the cultivation of virtue or *te*" (pp. 10–11).

12. D. C. Lau, *Lao Tzu: Tao Te Ching* (Harmondsworth: Penguin, 1963). Although Lau contemplates a richer interpretation of *de*, he proceeds very quickly to dismiss the significance of that interpretation, together with the role of *de* within the *Daodejing*. He writes: "In its Taoist usage, *te* refers to the virtue of a thing (which is what it 'gets' from the tao). In other words, *te* is the nature of a thing, because it is in virtue of its *te* that a thing is what it is. But in the *Lao tzu* the term is not a particularly important one and is often used in its more conventional senses" (p. 42).

13. See *Daodejing* 5, 18, 19, 20, 38.

14. Chan's translation from *The Way of Lao Tzu*. This translation is used throughout this essay, unless otherwise specified.

15. See *Daodejing* 8, 27, 30, 49, 54, 61, and 81.

16. Chan, *The Way of Lao Tzu*. Chan's interpretation of *de* is based partly on a traditional definition of the term which draws from its homophone, *de* (to obtain). See Chan's comments on p. 11.

17. Lau, *Lao Tzu*, p. 42.

18. J. J. L. Duyvendak, *Tao Te Ching: The Book of the Way and Its Virtue* (London: John Murray, 1954).

19. Arthur Waley, *The Way and Its Power: A Study of the Tao Te Ching and Its Place in Chinese Thought* (New York: Grove Press, 1958).

20. Max Kaltenmark, *Lao Tzu and Taoism*, trans. Roger Greaves (Stanford: Stanford University Press, 1969).

21. Waley, *The Way and Its Power*, p. 31. Waley's view of *de* is predicated on correlative thought. The theme of correlative thinking assumes an intrinsic relatedness between all things and beings, covering a wide sweep of all existence including cosmic forces, all species and natural objects, and even aspects of human life such as government. Chinese philosophy scholar A. C. Graham provides a comprehensive account of correlative thinking in "Yin-Yang and the Nature of Correlative Thinking," Singapore: Institute of East Asian Philosophies, Occasional Paper and Monograph Series, no. 6, 1986.

22. Marcel Granet, *La Pensee Chinoise* (Paris, 1934), p. 303; cited in Kaltenmark, *Lao Tzu and Taoism*, p. 27.

23. Kaltenmark, *Lao Tzu and Taoism* pp. 27–28.

24. Cheng, "On the Environmental Ethics of the Tao and the Ch'i," p. 353.

25. Chan (*The Way of Lao Tzu*) adds the word *man* at this point in the statement. Chan states that some interpreters have taken the phrase to mean the best man, while others take it to mean the "highest good." In Chan's view, both interpretations are possible (see pp. 113–14). However, I prefer to ellipt the word because the addition narrows the applicability of these ideas to humankind.

26. *Daodejing* 10, 36, 43, 76, 78.
27. Ibid., 36, 52, 55, 76, 78.
28. Ibid., 15, 16, 26, 37, 39, 45, 57, 64.
29. Ibid., 8, 22, 66, 68, 73, 81.
30. The sentiments in this passage are echoed in *Daodejing* 2 and 10.
31. Ames, "Taoism and the Nature of Nature," p. 331.
32. Ames takes issue with the fact that reasoning in Chinese philosophy is not reducible to, or cannot be subsumed under existing categories in Western philosophies. However, where the ideas in this paper might differ from Ames' is in the latter's suggestion that an aesthetic rather than logical order is fundamental in Chinese thought (as contrasted with Western science) in ibid, pp. 320–26. While the distinction between aesthetic and logical order is meaningful and useful, Ames' assertion that the aesthetic order is the ground of Chinese cosmology may neglect or omit other integrated modes of operation such as the moral or the rational (or reasonable).
33. See the comprehensive discussions of *wuwei* by Benjamin Schwartz, "The Ways of Taoism," in *The World of Thought in Ancient China* (Cambridge: Belknap Press of Harvard University Press, 1985), and Angus C. Graham, "Heaven and Man Go Their Own Ways" in *Disputers of the Tao* (La Salle, Ill.: Open Court Publishing, 1989).
34. See *Daodejing* 5, discussed later in this section.
35. "Radical American Environmentalism and Wilderness Preservation: A Third World Critique," in Andrew Brennan, ed., *The Ethics of the Environment* (Brookfield, Vt.: Dartmouth, 1995), pp. 239–52.
36. Peerenboom, "Beyond Naturalism."
37. This understanding of *ziran* as spontaneity, when applied to the final sentence in chapter sixty-four, would read, "[the Daoist sage] supports all things in their spontaneous development by not taking any action that interferes with their spontaneity." The translation of *ziran* as "spontaneity" instead of "nature" in chaps. 23, 51, and 54 is also particularly effective.
38. See *Daodejing* 12, 18, 19, 20, 37, and 53.
39. Cheng, "On the Environmental Ethics of the Tao and the Ch'i," p. 356.
40. *Daodejing* 4, 5, 25, and 64.
41. Thompson, "Taoist Cultural Reality: The Harmony of Aesthetic Order," p. 177.
42. Lau, *Lao Tzu*, p. 61.
43. Val Plumwood, *Feminism and the Mastery of Nature* (London: Routledge Publishing. 1993), pp. 48–55.
44. See, for example, John Rodman, "Review Discussions: The Liberation of Nature?" *Inquiry* 20 (1977): 83–145; Richard and Val Routley, "Human Chauvinism and Environmental Ethics," in Don Mannison, Michael McRobbie, and Richard Routley, eds., *Environmental Philosophy*

(Canberra: Australian National University, Research School of the Social Sciences, 1980), pp. 96–99.

45. See, for example, Arne Naess, "The Shallow and the Deep, Long-Range Ecological Movement," *Inquiry* 16 (1973): 95–100, and Plumwood, *Feminism and the Mastery of Nature.*

46. Defenders of weak anthropocentricism include Eugene Hargrove, "Weak Anthropocentric Intrinsic Value," in Max Oelschlaeger, ed., *After Earth Day: Continuing the Conservation Effort* (Denton, Tex.: University of North Texas Press, 1992). Those who propose versions of strong anthropocentricism include William Baxter, *People or Penguins: The Case for Optimal Pollution* (New York: Columbia University Press, 1974). See also Bryan Norton, "Environmental Ethics and Weak Anthropocentricism," *Environmental Ethics* 6 (1984): 131–48.

47. See Norton, "Environmental Ethics and Weak Anthropocentricism."

48. See Plumwood (1993) *Feminism and the Mastery of Nature,* chap. 2: "Dualism: The Logic of Colonisation."

49. *Daodejing* 2, 5, 7, 19, 32.

50. There are fine distinctions made between some versions: *metaphysical holism* (that wholes exist apart from their part and may be more real than their parts), *methodological holism* (which asserts that in order to understand the constituent parts, we need to understand various phenomena associated with the whole), and *ethical holism* (that moral consideration should be extended to wholes). See the discussion in Joseph DesJardins, *Environmental Ethics,* 3rd ed. (Belmont, Calif.: Wadsworth Thomson Learning, 2001), pp. 176–77.

51. For example, Eric Katz, "Organiscism, Community and the 'Substitution Problem,'" *Environmental Ethics* 7 (1985): 241–56; Tom Regan, *The Case for Animal Rights* (Berkeley: University of California Press, 1983); and Don Marietta, Jr., "Environmental Holism and Individuals," *Environmental Ethics* 10 (1988): 251–58.

52. Peerenboom, "Beyond Naturalism," pp. 20–21.

53. Ibid., p. 21.

54. See Charles Taliaferro, *Contemporary Philosophy of Religion* (Oxford: Blackwell Publishers, 1999), p. 74.

55. Ibid.

56. Ibid.

57. Cover story, "Owl versus Man," *Time Magazine,* 25 June 1990. The report article itself is not as polarized as the cover suggests, but the point here is how such issues are commonly distorted and misrepresented.

58. A Chinese philosophy scholar, Chung-yuan Chang, trans., *Tao: A New Way of Thinking* (New York: Harper and Row, 1975), suggests that Daoist philosophy upholds a holism that strives to achieve the best "unity of multiplicities." Chang's idea resembles the notion of compossibility discussed here.

Chapter 10

Process Ecology and the 'Ideal' Dao

Alan Fox

"One who wants to grasp the world and change it—I anticipate such a one will not be successful. The world is a sacred vessel, and one cannot change it. To change it is to spoil it; to grasp it is to lose it."

—*Dao De Jing* 29[1]

Introduction

This article takes as its starting point the process-oriented understanding of Daoism as championed by the work of Ames/Hall.[2] First, a brief introduction to the basics of process thinking will be provided, and on this basis, we can deduce normative practices related to minimally interfering processes. These normative attitudes are essentially ecological and have a lot to contribute to current discussions of ecology and environmental issues.

Historically, we see a problem with grounding the Daoist tension between intention and submission. That is, there is an apparent contradiction between the willingness to submit to the natural course of events, and the idea that if one does so, one is able to accomplish one's ends more effectively. This situation is similar to what Edward Slingerland describes as the "paradox of wuwei," the fact that one needs to make an effort to overcome effort.[3] Another way of describing the problem that arises by equivocation is found in the *Zhongyong*, which says "as for *dao*, it is not possible to depart from it for even one moment" (*dao ye zhe bu ke shun yu li ye*), even though the preceding sentence says "cultivating *dao* is called education" (*xiu dao zhi wei jiao*).[4] If one cannot depart from *dao*, then why must one cultivate it?

One historical impediment to reaching such a grounding is a certain equivocation concerning the term *dao*. On the one hand, *dao* has an abstract, hypothetical reference, and on the other hand, it has a totally concrete reference. Chung-ying Cheng notes this in a recent paper when he observes that "The word *dao* in some sense is used as a rigid designator. Yet it must be pointed out that it is also at the same time used as a non-rigid designator, a term, which refers to anything in the world without [being] identified with anything. It is both transcendent and immanent."[5] However, unlike Cheng and many who understand *dao* metaphysically,[6] I am suggesting that the transcendent or "ideal" sense of *dao* is merely heuristic and hypothetical. Once we clear up the equivocation by distinguishing between two senses of *dao*, namely, the ideal and the actual, we will be in a position to better articulate the normative implications of a Daoistic process ecology.

This article will proceed by briefly describing the process understanding of *dao*, and then articulating the difference between "ideal" and "actual" *daos*. Ideal *daos* will also be correlated with the idea of destiny, as the optimal trajectory of any given process. This will lead into the normative, ecological implications, which emphasize the importance of approximating ideal *daos* to the greatest possible extent. This will be described as one way of understanding the practical principle of *wei wu wei*.

Dao as Process

The process conception of *dao* differs dramatically from the various metaphysical conceptions that understand *dao* as an abstract, metaphysical term, referring to some fundamental, ontological entity. In this metaphysical sense, *dao* is often capitalized and translated in the singular, noun form, i.e., as "The Dao." The problems with this reading have been described elsewhere by myself and others, so the focus of this article will not be on the problems with the metaphysical view.

Instead, we will focus on the meaning and normative implications of the process understanding. In order to articulate the process sense of *dao*, it is first necessary to emphasize the gerundical nature of the Chinese language and the absence of clearly defined grammatical distinctions between parts of speech such as nouns and verbs. In both classical and modern Chinese, most words function gerundically. A gerund is a noun form of a verb, such as "running" or "playing." Furthermore, not only can verbs function as nouns, but also nouns can function as verbs, though, as Calvin and Hobbes point out: "Verbing weirds language."[7] Classical Chinese, consistent with the ways of thinking found in the classical traditions, treats objects as events. Things occur; they proceed through time. Whereas in English we might say "there is a table there," seeing the word "table" as a noun and invoking the verb "to be," the Chinese equivalent would be something like "tabling is going on there." The table "tables," that is, it functions as a table, it does what tables do. This means that most nouns are what might be called "static" or "stative" verbs. In fact, both the classical and the modern Chinese languages lack a distinct verb, such as "to be," which describes the "act of being" in the abstract. Instead of saying, as we would in English, that "the book *is* on the table," the Chinese expression suggests that "the table *has* the book," or that the book "resides" on the table. There is no need to invoke the concept of static existence or the verb "to be," which would seem to reflect, for example, a classical Greek, Platonic concern with ontological essence.

So "things" are seen as events, which proceed through time, and are constantly changing. This leads to the process understanding with which we are here concerned. Everything is in fact a process, and therefore all nominal terms are gerundical, describing what things do rather than what they are. It is in this sense that *daos* can be described as processes. If "tabling" describes specifically the process undergone by a table, and if "chairing" describes specifically the process undergone by a chair, then daoing is a more general term for all processes, such that the chair which is chairing and the table which is tabling are both daoing.

There are several immediate implications of this. One is that there is not only one *dao*—there are a virtually infinite number of *daos*. This is because there are a virtually infinite number of entities, and each entity is itself infinitely fractal both macro- and microcosmically. That is, every process is made up of other processes, and every process is embedded in other processes. For instance, as a human being, I am composed of a variety of microcosmic processes, each of which is composed of a variety of microcosmic processes. I am composed of muscular, skeletal, digestive, metabolic, respiratory, and other types of processes. Further, each of these processes is composed of cellular processes. Each cellular process is composed of molecular processes. Each molecule is composed of atomic processes, and so on. On the other hand, I am embedded in a series of macrocosmic processes as well. I am, for instance, part of the process of the class

I am currently teaching; this class is part of a course, this course is part of a semester, this semester is part of a career, which is part of a life, which is part of a historical epoch, and so on. Given this variety of micro- and macrocosmic processes (or *daos*), there can be said to be a virtually infinite number of *daos*.

Since there are arguably an infinite number of *daos*, it must be the case that these *daos* overlap and, to a certain extent, interfere with each other. For instance, I find it difficult to think clearly after a big meal, because my digestive processes draw energy from my mental processes. By breathing, I am interfering with the air. By being visible, I am interfering with light. This is important, because it leads to the distinction between hypothetical, "ideal" *daos* and "actual" *daos*.

Ideal vs. Actual Daoing

If *daos* are processes, then they follow trajectories of a sort. That is, we can track their movement over time. If we could establish the ideal trajectory, then we could determine the extent to which any particular trajectory matches up to its ideal potentiality. As an example, imagine an archer. The archer contemplates the target and tries to determine the exact trajectory an arrow would take from the bow to the bull's-eye. If he is a totally competent archer, he is able to determine the angle at which the arrow must be launched and the force with which it must leave the bow in order to hit the mark. Under ideal circumstances, a skilled archer would be capable of launching the arrow with the proper force and at the proper angle, and thus he would be successful in hitting the target. Nevertheless, there are many reasons why the arrow might still fail to hit the bull's-eye, even for such a skilled archer, because circumstances are rarely, arguably never, ideal. Thus, the "ideal" *dao* is ideal in two specific senses: on the one hand, it is perfect, unblemished, and unimpeded; on the other hand, it is unattainable, asymptotic, and intellectual.

This is because all *daos* experience interference from other *daos*. There is no way to avoid this. Since, as has been suggested, the world is composed of a virtually infinite number of *daos*, no *daos dao* in isolation, but encounter the daoing of other *daos*. *Daos* operate in characteristic ways: tables table, books book, and so on. But also built into the character of each *dao* is a characteristic way of responding to interference from other *daos*. When water encounters an obstacle, it responds in characteristic ways. For instance, water flowing down a mountain will encounter the ground under it and will respond by washing away a gully in the dirt. This becomes a stream. A tree starts to grow on the side of the stream, stimulated by the presence of water and continuously refreshed nutrients in the soil. Eventually, though, the erosion caused by the flow of the water washes away the soil supporting the tree. The water is interfering with the daoing of the tree, and eventually the tree responds by falling down into the stream, where it now interferes with the flowing of the stream. So then the water responds in a characteristic way by flowing around or under the tree, or by rotting the tree and dissolving it. This admittedly simplistic example is intended to demonstrate that the natural world, so to speak, is basically a delicately negotiated balance among a virtually infinitely complex web of overlapping *daos*, each of which is interfering with, and being interfered with by, all other *daos*. This balance is maintained because each *dao* has a certain amount of tolerance built into it.

Tolerance and Integrity

Tolerance, in the technical sense, refers to the ability of any structure to withstand stress—that is, it is the capacity to experience stress without losing structural integrity. Architecturally speaking, the Empire State Building is constructed so that it sways several feet in each direction in high winds. This amount of tolerance to the stress provided by the wind pressure allows it to withstand that pressure—without such tolerance, it would fall down. This sentiment is expressed clearly in the *Dao De Jing*, which suggests, for instance, that "the hard and rigid is associated with death, while the soft and supple is associated with life" (*jian qiang zhe si zhi tu; rou ruo zhe sheng zhi tu*).[8] In some translations of the *Dao De Jing*, this flexibility (*ruo*) is translated as "weakness,"[9] but in fact it is clear that such flexibility or pliancy is not a weakness, but a strength, since it permits stability and survival under stress conditions.

This means that *daos* with sufficient tolerance will be more likely to persist than rigid *daos* with limited tolerance. Here again, the *Dao De Jing* confirms this: "[daoing] wears down sharp edges, untangles knots, softens glare, and reduces to dust."[10] As a concrete example, a potter who works with clay must first wedge the clay before making a vessel out of it. Wedging the clay means rolling it and kneading it in a particular fashion and direction. This is necessary because clay particles are longitudinal, that is, they are longer than they are wide. Wedging the clay forces it to flow in a certain direction, and this lines up the particles, since the particles line up in the direction of flow. When the particles are lined up, they are more structurally sound, and the resulting vessel will be sturdier, more durable, and more water-resistant. The natural processing of things forces the particles to line up in the way that best minimizes resistance. This is also evidenced by the effects of friction—when one thing rubs up against another, both are bound to be somewhat eroded and worn down. There is therefore a very good reason why a bobsledder doesn't stick out his elbows or drag his heels. At the speeds at which the bobsled is traveling, one is bound to cause serious damage to oneself by doing this, and certainly it will slow one down so that one will not travel as far or as fast as one who keeps all body parts tucked in tightly against the body at all times.

It is clear that stress is the problem here, expressed in the *Dao De Jing* as *zheng* or "conflict, friction, resistance." At numerous places in the text, it is made clear that *zheng* is what impedes the natural flow of *daos*, and one is encouraged to limit or eliminate *zheng* in order to maximize one's effectiveness and well-being. As the text says, "If one does not contend, there will be no blame" (*fu wei bu zheng, gu wu you*)[11] Of course, given our current argument, it is impossible to entirely eliminate *zheng*, since all *daos* interfere with all other *daos*, and this interference or conflict is what constitutes stress.

At this point, it is possible to define our terms more precisely. "Ideal *daos*" are a way of referring to those *daos* or processes that would hypothetically encounter absolutely no interference, resistance, or friction. They would be those that follow their perfect trajectory, from beginning to end, without any variance from the ideal. The problem, as described, is that no *daos* operate in this fashion, since all *daos* encounter interference from other *daos*. So the idea of an ideal *dao* must remain hypothetical, heuristic, asymptotic, and in fact, "ideal." Actually, all *daos* encounter resistance, and so the idea of "actual *dao*" refers to how *daos* actually do operate in the face of resistance and interference. Furthermore, interference is not unilateral. If *dao* "A" interferes with *dao* "B," *dao* "B" is also interfering with *dao* "A." But even though actual *daos* always cause and experience interference with other *daos*, some *daos* can be described as more or less ideal than others, depending on the amount of interference they experience. So the goal is optimize non-interference, to *dao* optimally, which means to interfere as little as possible with other *daos*, so as not to violate their own tolerance limits or those of other *daos*.

Another example of this comes from the science of electricity. Electrical current consists of electrons flowing along a medium of some kind. Some media conduct electrons more efficiently than others, because they manifest less resistance. A particularly bad conductor, for instance, would be wood. Because wood offers significant resistance to electron flow, it damages the signal integrity of the electrical signal and the electrons quickly disperse in the wood. This interference also results in harm to the wood, since the current will heat and eventually burn the wood. On the other hand, some media are reasonably effective conductors, such as copper. Using copper wire, an electrical signal can be sent further, with less energy input, and with greater preservation of signal integrity. But until recently all such media exhibited some significant amount of resistance, so that historically it has been difficult to establish electrical circuits that maintain signal integrity over long distances. The discovery of what are called "superconductors," however, has changed all this. Superconductors are media that exhibit negligible amounts of resistance and therefore are capable of sustaining electrical signals with minimal loss of integrity, and without massive inputs of energy. Still, it is important to point out, even though superconductors exhibit minimal resistance, they still do provide *some* resistance, and this supports our suggestion that all we can hope to do is to minimize interference between *daos*, though we cannot hope to eliminate it entirely.

It is important to point out that in this case, "ideal *dao*" does not refer to some ontological or metaphysical entity, which exists in some isolated perfection, but serves rather as a heuristic device, enabling us to establish an asymptotic ideal against which we can measure the effectiveness of actual *daos*. As in our initial example, we can tell how far the arrow falls from its mark only because we have established where it would have fallen if all conditions had been perfect. Of course, what interferes with the arrow is air pressure, wind, humidity, and so on. But the most ideal *dao* would be the one that that encounters optimal conditions and comes as close as possible to the ideal. When Bob Beamon long jumped 29 feet 2½ inches in the 1968 Olympics in Mexico City, which was almost two feet longer than anyone had ever jumped before, he described it as the virtually perfect jump under virtually perfect conditions—the high altitude, the fact that there was a wind behind him that measured just below the allowable limit, the fact that he hit the takeoff mark perfectly, and so on. If any of these conditions had not been so conducive, he might not have jumped so far. Because this jump was so close to the ideal, it took almost thirty years for someone to jump farther, and to this day only two people have ever done it, or even come close.

So the ideal condition is one of ease and lack of stress.[12] I will suggest that in the *Dao De Jing*, this ideal condition is described as *de*, often translated as "virtue," but more properly understood here as "virtuosity." In the context of the current discussion, this virtuosity can be understood as an effortless gracefulness, or the gracefulness that accompanies effortlessness. We tend to regard virtuosos as those who are not only good at what they do, but who make it look easy. Examples of virtuosity of that type include, for instance, Michael Jordan, Fred Astaire, or Jimi Hendrix. They are so good at what they do, that it doesn't even look like they are trying at all. It looks as easy as falling off a log. Because there is minimal resistance, there is an ease and fluidity to the process. When *daos* minimally interfere with other *daos*, then, we can say that they "are" or "possess" *de*. That is, processes that are most ideally daoing can be described as *de*, and are thus likely to most optimally follow their ideal trajectory.

The ideal trajectory for a given process can be understood as a kind of destiny, especially if we distinguish between destiny and fate. Fate implies determinism, an inevitable outcome that is established beforehand and cannot be changed or interfered with. But destiny, in the sense I am using it here, refers to the set of possibilities that represent the optimal outcome for a given process. When applied to humans, this set of possibilities is determined by a number of factors, and that is why there are a number of possibilities that constitute one's destiny. For instance, the optimal outcome for a human life might be the one that maximizes pleasure or satisfaction; it might be the one that makes best use of one's talents and abilities; or it might be the one that makes the best contribution to society. Since there are more than one single determinant of destiny, there are likely to be a number of possibilities that maximize the equation. What prevents this from being deterministic is the fact that there are many reasons why this optimal outcome might not come to pass. One might never have the opportunity to develop one's talent; one might choose some alternative path out of fear or insecurity, or because of pressure from others; one might be disabled or have a piano fall on one's head. Therefore, destiny represents not what must happen, but what it would be best to have happened, that is, not the necessary, but the optimal trajectory of a life.

When it comes to non-human processes, or processes other than a human life, destiny represents the optimal trajectory, such as the calculated path of the arrow or a rocket. Or, in the case of a plant, we might say that under ideal conditions, the plant might grow to a certain height, or produce a certain amount of flowers or fruit, or last for a certain amount of time. But if conditions are less than ideal, that is, without proper rainfall or protection from elements, the plant is likely not to accomplish its optimal outcomes, that is, its growth and productivity might be stunted or it might not last as long as it could.

Ecological and Normative Implications

Since all actual *daos* actually interfere, reality is a delicately negotiated ecology of actual *daos* (daoings). The world is the sum of all *daos* that coexist with other *daos*, interfering within allowable tolerance limits. Nature has a way of balancing things out—that which does not bend will break, so everything that survives without breaking must be capable of adjusting to the interference of other *daos* without losing its integrity. The optimal situation is for each *dao* to interfere as little as possible with other *daos*. This condition of minimal interference with other *daos* is what is described in Chinese thought as *weiwuwei*, or "action without action." This kind of effortless activity is that which is non-confrontational and cooperative with other *daos*.

This is a typical normative implication of any ecological insight, and it is not so much a moral norm as it is a practical one. Once one realizes that one is part of a balanced ecology, then one understands one's obligation to maintain that balance to the greatest possible extent. Since to interfere with is to be interfered with, it is in the self-interest of each *dao* to minimize interference, so that it might fulfill itself as optimally as possible. In other words, for any *dao* to maximally accomplish its destiny it must minimize interference with other *daos*. As the *Dao De Jing* says, for instance: "act without interference, and nothing will be out of order" (*wei wu wei ce wu bu zhi*),[13] "If one does not contend, there will be no blame" (*fu wei bu zheng, gu wu you*),[14] and "Whatever is contrary to dao will soon end" (*bu dao zao yi*).[15]

We can apply this ecological insight across the board. It pertains to every interaction and every activity of every *dao*. Of course, nonhuman *daos* naturally find their balance or are wiped out; that is, they tend not to excessively interfere with other *daos*. Humans have the unique capacity to interfere gratuitously, more than is necessary to accomplish our ends. When we build houses, we don't just cut down a few trees, we tend to level forests, and ironically, give the housing development an oxymoronic title like "The Woods." Given our characteristic capacity for gratuitous interference, it becomes even more incumbent upon us to reign in our over-indulgence. We are normatively obligated to consider the broader web of ecological relations, since the harder we push against the flow of the world, the harder the world will push back, and it is clear that the world has greater weight and momentum than we do, and in any such confrontation, we are likely to find ourselves on the losing end. In order to thrive, or even to survive, not only must we extend our own tolerance limits to the best of our ability, but we must also be careful to remain within the tolerance limits of other *daos*, since to interfere is to be interfered with.

So we are courting our own extinction by ignoring the greater good. Even though it may seem in the short run that we are serving our interests, we are doing ourselves a disservice in the long run. This is not a novel insight in environmental or ecological discourse. But the process understanding of Daoism helps us to articulate the logic behind this insight from a Daoist perspective.

Finally, articulating the distinction between the heuristic ideal of complete non-interference on the one hand and the actual situation of an infinite number of *daos* all mutually interfering within a delicate balance of tolerance levels helps us to make sense of the equivocation we find in treatments of the concept of "*dao*." We are able on this basis to reconcile the concept of the so-called "eternal" or "metaphysical" *dao*, on the one hand, with the need to cooperate or operate in accordance with the *dao* that actually consists in the actual world. Indeed, even though *dao* is sometimes described as eternal, and even though some texts suggest that we can never stray from *dao*, nevertheless we are encouraged to act in accordance with it, as though it were possible for us to not remain "in" *dao*. The metaphysical or eternal senses are the heuristic, ideal sense of *dao*. This sense of *dao* does not really exist, except as an asymptotic ideal that can be approximated but never accomplished. As the asymptotic ideal, it never changes, but actual practices can come closer to or further from that ideal. So what is variable is *dao* in the actual sense, but whether or not we live up to the ideal, the ideal is not diminished by our inability to achieve it. "Ideal" here then sustains two common senses of the term: "perfect," in the sense of operating completely without any kind of interference; and "unachievable," because, given the infinitude of *daos*, all *daos* necessarily interfere with other *daos*. But it is important to emphasize that the ideal *dao* here is heuristic and not ontological or metaphysical.

It doesn't necessarily exist except as a theoretical entity, as what would be the case if things were different than they actually are.

Notes

1. *Jiang yu qu tian xia er wei zhi, wu jian qi bu de yi. Tianxia shen qi, bu ke wei ye. Wei zhe bai zhi, zhi zhe shi zhi. Dao De Jing*, chapter 29.

2. For example, see Roger Ames and David Hall, *Daodejing "Making Life Significant": A Philosophical Translation* (New York: Ballantine Books, 2003).

3. Slingerland describes the paradox as the "tension [which] arises from the fact that the state of effortless, perfected action represented by wu-wei is portrayed as a state that needs to he achieved... . How is it possible to *try* not to try?" Edward Slingerland, *Effortless Action* (Oxford: Oxford University Press, 2003), p. 6.

4. Zhongyong, chapter 1, verses 1 and 2.

5. Chung-ying Cheng, "Dimensions of the *Dao* and Onto-Ethics in Light of the *DDJ*," *Journal of Chinese Philosophy* 31:2 (June 2004): 145–146.

6. Cheng seems to suggest that the *Dao* is the "root source" of everything, going to the extent of adding the word "source" to his paraphrase of chapter 1 of the *Dao De Jing*: "Laozi further points out that *you* and *wu* are rooted in the same *source* and assumes two different names." Ibid., p. 147.

7. Bill Watterson, *Calvin and Hobbes*, newspaper cartoon, *Wilmington News Journal*, January 25, 1993.

8. *Dao De Jing*, chapter 76. All translations are mine unless otherwise indicated.

9. For example, see John Wu, trans. *Tao Teh Ching* (Boston: Shambhala Publications, 1989). p. 155, p. 159, etc.

10. *Dao De Jing*, chapter 4.

11. *Dao De Jing*, chapter 8.

12. It is important to note that there is good stress (eustress) and bad stress (distress), the difference between the extent to which such stress is helpful or harmful in the long run. For instance, exercise produces stress on the physiology, but such stress is conducive to developing a healthy organism. This is because, in terms of the current argument, such stress remains within, and in fact increases, one's tolerance level. If you work out too strenuously, on the other hand, you will tear or pull a muscle and set yourself back, so it is important not to overdo it, at which point eustress becomes distress. So when I discuss the harmful effects of stress, I am referring mainly to distress and not eustress.

13. *Dao De Jing*, chapter 3.

14. *Dao De Jing*, chapter 8.

15. *Dao De Jing*, chapter 30.

CHAPTER 11

The Viability (*Dao*) and Virtuosity (*De*) of Daoist Ecology: Reversion (*Fu*) as Renewal

SANDRA A. WAWRYTKO

In 1793, at the age of 69, Immanuel Kant published a brief but philosophically profound article entitled "Über den Gemeinspruch: Das mag in der Theorie richtig sein, taugt aber nicht für die Praxis" (On the Old Saw: That May Be Right in Theory But It Won't Work in Practice). In it he responded to critics who argued that his idealist speculations were tempting, but ultimately impractical.

> When an ignorant individual calls theory unnecessary and dispensable in his supposed practice, this is not as unbearable as when a know-it-all admits its academic value (as a mere mental exercise, perhaps) while asserting that in practice things look altogether different, that with one's emergence from school into the world comes an awareness of having pursued empty ideals and philosophical dreams—in a word, that what sounds good in theory is invalid in practice.[1]

Anyone who has expounded on Daoist ecological philosophy is likely to react sympathetically to Kant's obvious outrage, for Daoism struggles under a similar burden. While many are quick to admire its principles, they also tend, with much regret, to deny the practicality of their implementation. I should like to challenge this assumption by presenting a case for Daoist philosophy as the most efficient and most effective philosophy ecologists can adopt. In sharp contrast to stereotypical views of Daoism as mindless mysticism, its concepts will be matched with concrete ecological examples of how those concepts apply in practice.

Daoist philosopher Lao Zi clearly considers the human strategies and plans endorsed by "common sense" as the truly unworkable theories, commenting: "Certainly, humankind has been astray for a long time" (DDJ, 58).[2] Since misery loves company, we can derive some comfort from Lao Zi's observation. It demonstrates that humans were misguided and misdirected even in his own time, some 2,500 years ago, and in a distinctly different cultural setting than our own. Ecological devastation is not the invention of the twentieth century, but a constant companion of civilization (in the Daoist sense of a society dominated by "cunning intellect"; DDJ 3, 57, 58, 65). Our ecological problems are symptoms of a deeper disease, that is, a dysfunctional mindset grounded in a philosophy that is not in harmony with Dao.

Lao Zi's *Dao De Jing* will be the primary source for the theoretical principles of a Daoist ecology set forth here. In keeping with my focus on a theory-practice continuum within Daoist philosophy, I suggest that we modify the popular English rendering of the title from *The Classic (Jing) of the Way (Dao) and its Virtue/Power (De)* to the *Viability (Dao) and Virtuosity (De) Classic (Jing).*[3] Viability (from the Latin *via* or way) highlights the do-ability of Dao as the way things are. Virtuosity broadens the scope beyond virtue/power to include the nuances of artistry, excellence (as in the Greek *arete*), fluency, and even finesse encompassed by Daoist *De*.

Lao Zi believes a cure for our disease does exist, but it requires us to change our attitudes toward the relationship between self and "Nature."[4] By readjusting our priorities to resonate with reality, we can "get real," reverting or returning (*fu*) to our original state of harmony with Dao. All vestiges of our estrangement from Dao, as engendered by civilization, must be removed, which involves three successive realignments:

- It's not what you *think* that matters—but what you *unthink.*
- It's not what you *do* that matters—but what you *undo.*
- We can't *work against* the natural flow (*zi-ran*), or even *with* that flow; rather we must *participate in, play within* the natural flow.

This approach resonates with the seeming negativity of much Daoist terminology, such as no-thingness (*wu-wu*) and *wei-wu-wei.* These formulas indicate the means to deconstruct the deadly constructs that threaten all life by artificial interference (*wei*) in the natural process. Contemporary author Rebecca Walker voices a similar view:

> if you let the culture happen to you, you end up fat and broke, in a house full of junk, with no time. If you just sit in front of a television and let it carry you along, without making an effort to resist it or deconstruct it, you really suffer.[5]

Before we can return to spontaneity, we must confront the existing obstacles to natural harmony in the guise of common sense and *wei*. We then can engage the functional elements of *hui* and *wei-wu-wei* to revert to *zi-ran*. In what follows, four stages in the process of securing ecological sustainability will be examined:

(I)   Deconstructing "Common Sense"
(II) Unthinking—What's Wrong with *Wei*, and the Antidote of *Hui*
(III) Undoing—The Viability of *Wei-wu-wei*
(IV) Playful Participation in the Dao of Heaven—The Virtuosity of *Zi-ran*

I. Deconstructing "Common Sense"

Who can clarify murky water to make it gradually clean?
Who can overcome stagnation to become gradually invigorated? (DDJ, 15)

Deeply imbedded, and deeply delusional, human values undermine ecological sustainability now as much as in the time of Lao Zi. Unexamined assumptions must be challenged in light of Daoist values. Consider the following examples of "common sense":

It is better to light one candle than to curse the darkness[6]
Something is better than nothing[7]

The erroneous nature of these assumptions can be illustrated by reference to a recent ecological crisis. In 1996 scientists and engineers reached an impasse in their ongoing efforts to revitalize the environmental damage done to the Colorado River. Previously they had acted on the "commonsensical" notions that they needed to continually improve on the natural situation, that humans had to *do* something, all to no avail. In desperation, a drastic plan was proposed to undo the damage wrought by the artificial dam: releasing the pent up waters of the Glen Canyon Dam. Despite the opposition of naysayers, a "controlled flood" was unleashed—45,000 cubic feet per second—between March 26 and April 2.[8] The resulting revitalization of the natural habitat exceeded the expectations of the most enthusiastic proponents of the plan.

In October 2003 a similar decision was made by the PPL Corporation and an environmental coalition. After years of failed attempts to revitalize the salmon population, two dams on the Penobscot River in Maine were removed. This unprecedented agreement demonstrated that the usual adversarial relationship between business and environmental interests could be avoided in the interests of promoting effective results.[9]

Another example of "common sense" resides in a famous quotation from Lord Acton (1834–1902), which has achieved such status as a truism that few in our society would dare to question it: "Power tends to corrupt, and absolute power corrupts absolutely."[10] This claim is predicated on the notion of power as it relates to human beings, particularly in the sense of political power. However, viewing power in the Daoist sense of *De* (virtue/power), the absolute power of Dao does not occasion absolute corruption. On the contrary, it is the source of empowerment for all the Ten Thousand Things, evoked by the image of a nurturing mother, "the suckling mother" (DDJ, 20) and her children. Drawing upon "profoundly dark virtue" (*xuan*), Dao is non-possessive, harboring no expectations of gratitude or intentions to "claim mastery" over its charges (DDJ, 2, 10).

II. Unthinking—What's Wrong with *Wei*, and the Antidote of *Hui*

To know the enduring is called "enlightenment";
Not to know the enduring is to blindly invite disaster. (DDJ, 16)

Lao Zi points to the "cunning intellect" as a prime contributor to our deluded mindset. The use of this narrow calculating approach by a ruler amounts to pillaging the state (DDJ, 65). Such a person "stands on tiptoe . . . takes long steps . . . is self-pretentious . . . self-affirming . . . self-boastful . . . self-important," and hence constitutes "leftovers and cancerous growths" (DDJ, 24). These maladies are precisely what need to be unthought, peeled away by means of "daily diminution" (DDJ, 48), being derived from the dysfunctional way of *wei*.

Wei is represented by a very provocative character—the image of a hand on an elephant. Usually rendered as "to do" or "to act," the image qualifies the action as involving an interfering imposition on another. Hence the affirmative action of *wei* is proactive, assertive, and calculating, escalating to manipulation and exploitation. Significantly, the other indicated by the elephant is large, powerful—and ultimately beyond human control.

This same obsession with control is all too evident in human schemes to "improve" the natural environment. Catastrophic results follow in the wake of *wei* "control freaks." For example, two engineers in nineteenth-century America, James Buchanan Eads and Andrew Atkinson Humphreys, sought to harness the Mississippi River for human purposes. Their plan was essentially to control the flow of the river by means of levees and jetties, thereby placing their hands on the watery elephant. All seemed to go well until 1927, when the elephant shook off the would-be tamers. Massive floods inundated the levees, leaving previously inhabited areas under thirty feet of water and displacing nearly one million people.[11]

More recently, in 2002, following the onslaught of Hurricane Isabel, the Outer Banks of North Carolina became a battleground between *wei*-ridden humans and the recalcitrant forces of Nature. It was a task worthy of Sisyphus, as a news headline from that time succinctly states: "Nature Tries to Shift Outer Banks, But Man Keeps Shoveling Back."[12] Engineers continue to argue about what plan will restore the beloved beaches and a washed-out highway. No one seems to be suggesting anything other than a *wei* approach.

In a more subtle assault, scientists have sought to "improve on" Nature by means of biocontrol. Despite the superficial resemblance to Daoist approaches, this too falls into the *wei* category due to the homocentric bias. Species and their evolution are manipulated for the presumed good of human beings. For example, insects have been released into new habitats with the intent to control other populations that threaten crops. The long-term consequences of such an introduction are often both unforeseen and equally devastating, including the extinction of native species. Entomologist George H. Boettner has studied this phenomenon and observes: "The advantage to biocontrol is that when you do it right, it's a permanent fix. The problem is that when you make a mistake, it's permanent too. There's no way to get them back."[13] Lao Zi warns against just such self-righteous arrogance:

> Whoever attempts to do the killing for the Executioner,
> Is One Who Chops Wood for the Great Carver.
> Whoever chops wood for the Great Carver,
> Rarely does not harm his own hands. (DDJ, 74)

When *wei* advocates are criticized for pushing the envelope, they tend to assume that the only alternative is to literally do nothing. *Wei* has as its polar opposite *bu-wei*, the negation (*bu*) of action (*wei*). Characterized by passivity, reaction, powerlessness, *bu-wei* leaves one open to *wei* manipulation and exploitation. The Daoist position is often confused with this stance, a confusion bolstered by the misleading translation of *wei-wu-wei* as non-action. However, the Daoist is not proposing a simple conflict between competing values, but a radical transcendence of human values. More precisely, the Daoist invites us to dig deeper than the superficial veneer of human values and human fixes, which are exposed as relativistic (see DDJ 2, 20).

To unthink human errors in the Dao of Humanity requires the wisdom of *hui*. The character for *hui* graphically illustrates the unthinking process, as a hand clutching a pair of brooms sweeps the heart/mind clean. The work of contemporary cognitive scientists corroborates this Daoist insight. When Dr. Patricia Kuhl, Department of Speech and Hearing Sciences at the University of Washington, describes the astounding capacity of infants as "the greatest learning machines in the universe," a distinctly Daoist note is sounded:

> Babies revise their views about people and things in the world based on new information, just as scientists do. A difference is that babies do it more quickly and more profoundly than adults, because their brains are less committed—literally less cluttered—than ours are.[14]

Consider a dry sponge, which is capable of absorbing much more than a wet one. What sponge could be drier than "an infant who has yet to smile" (DDJ, 20)?[15] The Daoist Sage has been able to wring that saturated sponge dry again or, using the imagery of *hui*, has swept it clean of the accumulated dust and debris of imposed conditioning. Hence, the Sage is able to respond to reality co-creatively. Dr. John Bruer marshals scientific data in support of the flexible nature of the brain in his work, *The Myth of the First Three Years: A New Understanding of Early Brain Development and Lifelong Learning* (New York: Free Press, 1999), although the Daoist would prefer mention of unlearning. The Sage's brain emulates Yin receptivity through *wei-wu-wei*, in contrast to the calculating mind's unyielding Yang addicted to *wei*.

Accordingly, researchers are finding that the anti-thesis of *hui*, multi-tasking, is both counterproductive and hazardous to your health: "If you try to do more than one thing at a time you will most likely suffer a very substantial loss of efficiency" (Professor David Meyer, University of Michigan); "People who are doing multitasking often aren't able to take in new information fully . . . it's not available for retrieval later on" (Winfred Sachs, Harvard Medical School).[16] Lao Zi specifically warns against sensory overload:

> Five colors[17] blind the human eyes;
> Five sounds[18] deafen the human ears;
> Five flavors[19] dull the human mouth.
>   . . .
> Therefore, discard that [*wei*] and pursue this [*wei-wu-wei*] (DDJ, 12)

III. Undoing—the Viability of *Wei-Wu-Wei*

> If one desires to rule[20] the world by means of artifice,
> I see no way one will succeed.
> The world is a sacred vessel,[21]
> It may not be mis-handled,
> [Nor may it be coveted.]
> Whoever mis-handles it will ruin it.
> Whoever covets it will lose it. (DDJ, 29)

Neither *wei* nor *bu-wei* is a viable option for Daoists. The antidote to this dualistic dilemma is found in the "teaching of no words" (DDJ, 42) embedded in *wei-wu-wei*, action (*wei*) without (*wu*) artificial action. "Discard human artifice, abandon profit—/Thieves and bandits will cease to exist" (DDJ, 19). Or, in an updated version: "Discard human artifice, abandon profit—/corrupt CEOs, polluters, and toxic dumps will cease to exist."

To undo the damage of dualism, the Daoist Sage neither acts upon (manipulates/exploits), nor is acted upon (is manipulated/exploited) by the environment, but rather *inter*acts with it, doing the dance of Dao. This third option is "the middle" which we must "hold onto" (DDJ, 5). Both extremes of *wei* and *bu-wei* are equally dangerous because each engenders its polar opposite. That "Excessive frugality necessitates great waste" (DDJ, 44) is verified by garbologists, who have found that people waste more food when they try to economize by buying cheaper foods or hoarding food during shortages.[22] The same chapter also notes: "Excessive accumulation necessitates heavy losses," as can be attested to by all the dot-com millionaires who saw their paper fortunes obliterated in a nano-second during the abrupt economic downturn of the late 1990s.

> ... better to stop [at the right time] ....
> Withdraw when your task is accomplished. (DDJ, 9)
> Thus, to know that enough is enough is always to have enough. (DDJ, 46)

Our "common sense" notions of efficiency must be redefined to reflect the viability of the Daoist message. The Daoist Sage does indeed accomplish the task, when the Dao of Heaven is followed rather than the self-circumscribed Dao of Humanity. Thus, "In everyday dealings, [the Sage] loves efficiency" (DDJ, 8). The first step toward efficient action (spontaneity) is the recognition of the sickness of dysfunctional dualism: "Only because one recognizes sickness as sickness, / That is why one is free from sickness."

However, an additional step is required: letting go of the sickness: "The Sage is free from sickness, / Is sick of sickness, / And accordingly is free from sickness" (DDJ, 71). If sickness and its resulting suffering are perceived as "normal," people will cling to them. Spinoza concludes his discussion of blessedness in the *Ethics* by contrasting the wise (who is sick of sickness) and the ignorant (who clings to sickness):

> ... how potent [*De*] is the wise man, and how much he surpasses the ignorant man, who is driven only by his lusts. For the ignorant man is not only distracted in various ways by externals causes without ever gaining the true acquiescence of his spirit, but more-over lives, as it were unwitting of himself, and of God, and of things, and as soon as he ceases to suffer, ceases also to be.[23]

Friedrich Nietzsche seems to have the same deluded individuals in mind when he talks about the "camel waiting to be well loaded . . . for the sake of truth, suffering hunger in one's soul."[24]

Ecological solutions offered by those sick, and hence free, of sickness can readily be cited in support of Daoist philosophy. Three areas of ecological activity will be surveyed to demonstrate the broad applicability of *wei-wu-wei*, including hydraulic engineering, resource management, and ecological design.

HYDRAULIC ENGINEERING

An ancient engineering marvel in China's Sichuan Province, the still-functioning Dujiangyan Irrigation System is a model of design-with-Nature efficiency. In sharp contrast to the ill-advised attempts to control the Mississippi River cited above, this project adopts a more Daoist approach. Li Bing, governor of what was then the Shu Prefecture of the Qin State in the third century BCE, carefully observed natural processes to arrive at a means of preventing devastating cycles of flooding across the Chengdu Plain due to the exuberant Minjiang River. His philosophy is succinctly summarized in a six-character directive inscribed at the site: "Dredge the sand deeper, build the dam lower." The *wei* strategy of artificial impositions such as dams to counter the natural flow of the water, which had long proved futile, is downplayed. Instead Li Bing relied on preventive measures to facilitate the natural flow by dredging. This was combined with monitoring of and practical responses to such conditions as seasonal water levels and silt deposits, *wei-wu-wei*.

As a result of this innovative co-creativity with the natural process, agriculture prospered in the region. Originally encompassing 126,000 hectares, the project gradually has been expanded to cover 600,000 hectares servicing 36 urban centers. In 2000 the Dujiangyan Irrigation System was listed as a World Heritage Site by UNESCO and hailed as "a major landmark in the development of water management and technology . . . still discharging its functions perfectly."[25]

Unfortunately the Chinese government has not learned from its own past. Officials have staunchly resisted attempts to stop the extreme *wei* approach undertaken with respect to the Three Gorges Dam Project in Hubei Province, which environmentalists decry as a disaster waiting to happen.[26]

RESOURCE MANAGEMENT

Wildfires increasingly wreak havoc for both the natural environment and adjacent human communities. As they burn out of control, besieged firefighters are forced into a *bu-wei* stance, at the mercy of changing weather conditions. Prevention is the only recourse. The most effective form of wildfire prevention has proven to be distinctly low tech, and in fact no tech. The solution arrives on four hoofed feet, or more precisely herds of goats and sheep. As one scientist explains: "We can't change the topography, and we can't do anything about the weather. The only variable to reduce is the fuel load. That's what goats do for us."[27] In other words, where chemicals and helicopters fear to tread, sheep and goats can get the job done.

Similarly, the Freecycling movement has undertaken preventive measures, a dissolution, with regard to overflowing trash heaps and incipient landfills.[28] Computer technology is used to match donors with seekers of a variety of goods that would otherwise be discarded. This approach echoes Zhuang Zi's championing of the usefulness of the useless: the salve once used to soothe the hands of silk washers earns a more imaginative man a fief, while "useless" oversized gourds inspire Zhuang Zi to creative reveries on true usefulness (*Zhuang Zi*, chapter 1). Thanks to the Freecycling movement, even socks with holes have found a new home, recycled into hand puppets.

One delighted participant seems to have experienced a Daoist glimmer of enlightenment concerning our dysfunctional values: "We get it drilled into us on television ads: 'Consume, consume, consume. You want more, you need more,' and do we really? I think what's coming out with freecycling is, 'Gee, it's kind of fun not to be into all of this.'"[29] Daoist devotee Tao Qian (365–427) expresses the same sentiment much more poetically:

> Door and yard devoid of worldly confusion,
> empty rooms overflowing with ease/tranquillity
> So long caged/confused within,
> [now] returned back to *zi-ran*.[30]

ECOLOGICAL DESIGN

In search of ultimate efficiency, "science imitates life." The very engineers who once assumed they could improve on Nature are now looking to it for innovative solutions. The lotus flower serves as model for a self-cleaning house paint based on its self-cleaning leaf. The gecko's ability to walk upside down is providing inspiration for developing interactive connections in industry. This co-creativity with Nature allows us to think outside of the *wei/bu-wei* box. Commercial designer David Oakley explains: "The question we ask is, How would nature solve this problem? When you ask that question, you move in directions you would never have thought about."[31] Similarly, plants are being pressed into service to remove toxic pollution, although scientists admit they do not understand precisely how the process works: "We know what goes in, we know what comes out; but we're not sure what's going on inside."[32] Such is the "mysteriously mysterious mystery" (*xuan*) of Lao Zi's opening chapter, as quaintly rendered by Professor Thomé H. Fang!

One of the most thorough and well thought-out applications of values that resonate with Daoist ecology can be found in the Ecological Life Systems Institute (ELSI).[33] Founder Jim Bell, an architect by training, promotes sane development through his many projects, lectures, publications, social activism, and weekly radio show ("Common Sense"). Bell's seminal work, *Achieving Eco-nomic Security On Spaceship Earth*, shares a focus on viability and virtuosity with Daoist philosophy:

> How can we, as individuals and as a species, do the things that we need and want to do, on all levels, in ways that are economically viable and ecologically sustainable? . . . if we are doing things in ways that damage our planet's life support system, how can we do them differently to avoid these problems? . . . The human species is endowed with unbounded cleverness. Unfortunately, this cleverness is poorly balanced with wisdom.[34]

Like Lao Zi, Bell even resorts to poetry to convey his message. The following lines highlight harmony and co-creativity:

> We are part of the process
> Of the universe knowing itself.
> We are the light of stars looking back at ourselves
> As we ponder the future it is our destiny to Create.[35]

IV. Playful Participation in the Dao of Heaven— The Virtuosity of *Zi-ran*

> [My] words have a ground [Dao];
> [My] deeds have a guide [Dao].
> Only, due to the lack of knowledge [of Dao],
> None ever understand me. (DDJ, 70)

The end result of unthinking and undoing the dysfunctional Dao of Humanity is the bubbling up of spontaneity, *zi-ran*. Dao itself is said to emulate *zi-ran* (DDJ, 25). Flow and play are the way of *wei-wu-wei*. Hence, fluid images abound in the *Dao De Jing*: flowing water, a pliant infant, resilient grass. The supple and the soft are aligned with life, while the stiff and the hard foreshadow death (DDJ, 76). We must become partners with the natural process, not competitors.

How does one dance with, or within, Dao? Let us conclude with some concrete examples of life virtuosos. Buck Brannaman, the "Horse Whisperer," has become renowned for his ability to work with difficult equines. In attempting to explain what he does, Brannaman resists the label of spirituality in the sense of the supernatural, and invokes *zi-ran*:

> ... it's something perfectly natural, something that the horse has to offer us, that some of us have to offer the horse. I think it's there for anybody who wants it. . . . There's no secret to this. I just know what we need to do in order for both of us to speak the same language and dance the same dance.[36]

Brannaman rejects the *wei* approach as counterproductive: "I've got the horse to focus on me mentally, without being physically pulled. I want him to feel he'd rather be with me than anywhere else . . . If it's a fight, you've already lost ground." Another horse expert, Stanford Addison, demonstrates much insight into the futility of *wei/bu-wei* dualism, even though he is wheelchair-bound (having severed his spinal cord more than twenty years ago). Addison sees his work with horses as inextricably linked to self-understanding: "If you're selfish, you disconnect [*wei*], and if you give too much, you disconnect [*bu-wei*]. If you're good to yourself and the horse, that's communication [*wei-wu-wei*]."[37]

Communication and communion are sorely needed in the face of mounting ecological crises. To reverse our estrangement, both egotistical *wei* and passive *bu-wei* must be supplanted by *wei-wu-wei*. Thus we can be good to both ourselves and our surroundings, in harmony with Dao and flowing with *zi-ran*.

> The Dao of Heaven reduces what is excessive,
> Supplements what is deficient;
> The Dao of Humanity functions contrariwise:
> It further reduces what is already deficient,
> Thereby offering it to the excessive.
> Who can have excess to offer to the world?
> Only those who follow Dao. (DDJ, 77)

One who follows Dao has grasped its viability, and thus is the consummate virtuoso of life. This is Zhuang Zi's True Person of Dao, who manifests when "man and Heaven do not defeat each other."[38]

By returning to Dao we can renew both ourselves and the ecosystem of which we are a functioning (rather than dysfunctional) part. Even Confuian Meng Zi realized the amazing capacity for renewal and self-healing inherent in the natural process, as symbolized by Bull Mountain (*Mencius*, 6A.8). A recent example of this involves Monarch butterflies in Mexico. A year after a massive die-off of more than 200 million butterflies, due to a winter storm in 2002, population levels returned to normal without any human aid or interference.[39] Such is the infinite capacity for renewal/reversion found in Dao as well as in ourselves as children of Dao.

Paralleling the Daoist concept of returning/reversion (*fu*) as renewal, ecologist and philosopher David Abram speaks of our need to remember our oneness with the sensuous world. In so doing, he echoes the wisdom of an ancient philosophy recast for a time of contemporary ecological crisis. His words are a fitting finale to this discussion (italics added).

> We may acknowledge, intellectually, our body's reliance upon those plants and animals that we consume as nourishment, yet the *civilized mind* still feels itself somehow *separate, autonomous, independent of the body and of bodily nature* in general. Only as we begin to notice and to experience, *once again*, our immersion in the invisible air do we start to *recall* what it is to be *fully a part of this world* . . . the inwardness or interiority that we have come to associate with the personal psyche begins to be encountered in the world at large . . . a *potentized* [*De*] *field* of intelligence in which our actions *participate . . . we awaken . . .* the shapes around us seem to awaken, to come alive. . . . [40]

NOTES

1. Immanuel Kant, *On the Old Saw: That May Be Right in Theory But It Won't Work in Practice*, trans. E. B. Ashton (Philadelphia: University of Pennsylvania Press, 1974), p. 42. Published in the *Berlinische Monatsschrift*, this is considered to be one of Kant's popular works. Nonetheless, John R. Silber, in his foreword to Ashton's translation, refers to it as "one of the most neglected, though most important documents of the Enlightenment"; p. 7.

2. All quotations from the *Dao De Jing* have been translated by Charles Wei-hsun Fu and Sandra A. Wawrytko, indicated by DDJ and the appropriate chapter number.

3. I cannot claim sole credit for the hermeneutical recasting of Dao as viability and *De* as virtuosity, since other scholars have applied one or the other translation. However, it is possible that I am the first to pair these terms with reference to the title of Lao Zi's text. Multiple Internet searches yielded only one match for "Lao Zi Viability and Virtuosity Classic," namely my own webpage; Google, Yahoo, AltaVista, accessed June 24, 2004.

4. The common translation of *zi-ran* as "Nature" implies an objectification of reality separable from human nature that is inconsistent with

the sense of harmony and oneness permeating Daoist metaphysics. A more precise rendering is "natural flow" or "natural process," paralleling Benedict de Spinoza's term *Natura Naturans* (Nature naturing) applied to Substance as dynamic rather than the static *Natura Naturata* (Nature natured). With this clarifying caveat, all three renderings will be used here interchangeably.

5. Rebecca Walker, as quoted by Deorah Solomon in "Reimagining Boyhood," *New York Times Sunday Magazine*, June 13, 2004, p. 19.

6. For an intriguing rebuttal to this sentiment, see Jun'ichiro Tanizaki, *In Praise of Shadows* (*In'ei raisan*), trans. Thomas J. Harper and Edward G. Seidensticker (New Haven, Conn.: Leet's Island Books, 1977).

7. For more on this topic, see Sandra A. Wawrytko, "Why Nothing Is Better Than Something: Lessons from the Diamond and the Heart Sutras," presented at the seventh conference of the International Society for Philosophy & Psychotherapy, Appalachian State University, Boone, North Carolina, July 20–23, 2000, whose overall theme was "Nothing."

8. For detailed analyzes of this project, see the Department of Interior U. S. Geological Survey, www.usgs.gov. Environmental groups are now intent on having the dam removed permanently, referring to it as "an ecological death sentence for the river." See Living Rivers: Canyons of the Colorado Campaign, http://www.livingrivers.net/ campaigns/ fdrainit/colorado.cfm; accessed March 31, 2004.

9. Pam Belluck, "Agreement in Maine Will Remove Dams for Salmon's Sake," *New York Times*, October 7, 2003, A1, A25.

10. Lord Acton, in a letter to Bishop Mandell Creighton, 3 April 1897, included in *Life and Letters of Mandall Creighton* (1904), as cited by *The Oxford Dictionary of Quotations*, third ed. (Oxford: Oxford University Press, 1979), p. 1.

11. For a full account of the theory and politics involved in this national and ecological disaster, see John M. Barry, *Rising Tide: The Great Mississippi Flood of 1927 and How It Changed America* (New York: Simon & Schuster, 1997).

12. Cornelia Dean, "Nature Tries to Shift Outer Banks, But Man Keeps Shoveling Back," *New York Times*, September 22, 2003, A1, A14.

13. Carol Kaesuk Yoon, "When Biological Control Gets Out of Control," *New York Times*, March 6, 2001, F3.

14. Erica Goode, "Mozart for Baby? Some Say Maybe Not," *New York Times*, August 3, 1999, F1.

15. The process of learning how to smile has been discussed by such groups as the National Network for Child Care: "At about 6 weeks . . . [infants] smile in response to someone else. By four months, they smile broadly and laugh when pleased"; http://www.nncc.org/; accessed June 25, 2004.

16. "The Multitasking Conundrum," *Healthwise* (Illinois Wesleyan University), December 2003, 1–2. This topic is entering the mainstream media,

as represented by Nina Martin's, "Multitasking Makes You Sick," *Organic Style*, November/December, 2003, 55–60.

17. The five colors—black, green, red, white, and yellow—represent the Five Elements (*wu xing*).

18. The five tones of the ancient Chinese pentatonic scale (FGACD) are *gong, shang, jiao, zhi*, and *yu,* respectively.

19. The five tastes are salty, bitter, sour, sweet, and hot/spicy.

20. *Ju* literally means "to capture"; however, in this context it should be read as "to rule."

21. Bronze vessels were commonly used in ancient China for ritual purposes. Demonstrating technological expertise as well as artistry, such vessels represented the wealth and prestige of a ruler.

22. See William Rathje and Cullen Murphy, *Rubbish: The Archeology of Garbage* (Tucson: University of Arizona Press, 2001). The book discusses cases of increased waste during times of first meat and then sugar shortages between 1973 and 1975, as documented by the Garbage Project.

23. Benedict de Spinoza, *Ethics* part V, Note to Proposition XLII, translated by R. H. M. Elwes and included in *The Chief Works of Benedict de Spinoza* Volume II (New York: Dover Publications, Inc., 1951), p. 270. For an extended comparison of the philosophies of Lao Zi and Spinoza, see Sandra A. Wawrytko, *The Undercurrent of Feminine Philosophy in Eastern and Western Thought* (Washington D.C.: University Press of America, 1981).

24. Friedrich Nietzsche, "On the Three Metamorphoses," *Thus Spoke Zarathustra* in *The Portable Nietzsche*, trans. Walter Kaufmann (New York: Viking Press, 1968), p. 139.

25. Visit http://whc.unesco.org/sites/1001.htm; accessed June 23, 2004.

26. See the work of activist Dai Qing, *Yangtze! Yangtze!* (Mass Market Paperback, 1994) and *The River Dragon Has Come! The Three Gorges Dam and the Fate of China's Yangtze River and Its People* (Armonk, New York: M. E. Sharpe Inc., 1997). For more books on this topic, see http://www.threegorgesprobe.org/tgp/books.html#yangtze

27. Edwin Kiester, Jr., "Getting Their Goats: Communities worried about the ravages of wildfire are embracing a four-legged solution," *Smithsonian Magazine,* October 2001, pp. 24–25.

28. Visit http://www.freecycle.org/; when accessed on June 23, 2004 the homepage reported that the program is active in 844 cities and has attracted 177,506 participants.

29. Tina Kelley, "Socks? With Holes? I'll Take It: Freecycling Brings Castoff Goods Back from the Bin," *New York Times*, March 16, 2004, A21.

30. Tao Qian, "Going Back to the Farm (*Gui Yuan Tian Ju*)," my translation.

31. Jim Robbins, "Engineers Ask Nature for Design Advice," *New York Times*, December 11, 2001, D1, D2. These same issues are explored by Janine M. Benyus in *Biomimicry: Innovation Inspired by Nature*

(New York: William Morrow & Company, 1997) and Stephen R. Kellert in *Kinship to Mastery: Biophilia in Human Evolution and Development* (Washington D.C.: Shearwater Book/Island Press, 1997).

32. Andrew C. Revkin, "New Pollution Tool: Toxic Avengers with Leaves," *New York Times*, March 6, 2001, D1, D7.

33. Visit http://www.elsi.org/; accessed June 23, 2004.

34. Jim Bell, *Achieving Eco-nomic Security on Spaceship Earth* (San Diego: ELSI, 1994), http://www.jimbell.com/bkintro.htm, http://www.jimbell. com/Book/book_ch1.html; accessed June 24, 2004.

35. Concluding lines of "We Are Everything," http://www.jimbell.com/ bkintro.htm; accessed June 24, 2004.

36. Paul Trachtman, "The Horse Whisperer: Legendary Trainer Buck Brannaman Relies on Trust, Not Terror," *Smithsonian Magazine*, May 1998, vol. 29, no. 2, pp. 56–66.

37. Lisa Jones, "Talking to Horses: Stanford Addison Uses Intuition, Compassion and Persistence to 'Break' Wild Horses," *Smithsonian Magazine*, September 2003, p. 36.

38. Chuang Tzu (Zhuang Zi), Chapter 6, *The Complete Works of Chuang Tzu*, trans. Burton Watson (New York: Columbia University Press, 1968), p. 80.

39. Carol Kaesuk Yoon, "Monarch Butterflies Alive and Well in Mexico," *New York Times*, February 14, 2003, A6.

40. David Abram, *The Spell of the Sensuous: Perception and Language in a More-Than-Human World* (New York: Pantheon Books, 1996), p. 260.

CHAPTER 12

Ecology, Aesthetics and Daoist Body Cultivation

JAMES MILLER

INTRODUCTION

Despite the best efforts of Habermas and others, the project of modernity, grounded in the values of the European Enlightenment has been undergoing severe internal and external challenges. The source of those criticisms lies in the way that the project of modernity grasped the disembodied concept of autonomous reason formulated in the Enlightenment period in such a way that it became the sole source of authority and value in the social and cultural sphere. The Korean-American philosopher Hwa Jol Jung wrote:

> European modernity is set to prejudge truth-claims by the criterion of Enlightenment. While privileging and valorizing the authority and autonomy of reason for allegedly human (material) progress and emancipation, it marginalizes, disenfranchises, and denigrates the (reason's) Other whether it be (1) body, (2) woman, (3) nature, or (4) non-West which happen to be four central postmodern landmarks and subversive possibilities. While its protagonists insist on modernity as an unfinished project, its postmodern antagonists consider it as a failure and are determined to unpack and audit it.[1]

The most interesting and useful approach of late modern intellectuals to this problem has been the attempt to rethink the foundational dualism which underpins this whole project, namely the Cartesian dualism between the disembodied mind, the *res cogitans*, and the *res extensa,* the body that occupies space and time and houses our mental functioning. In my view, the most profound problem engendered by this way of thinking about thinking is that it divorces reasoning from the biological and evolutionary matrix that has made it possible. If reason can be reinscribed within the body and, ultimately, within the 15 billion years of cosmic evolution, then this will go a long way to bridging the divide between humanity and nature. The body, then, should be the site *par excellence* for environmentalism as a social movement. In fact, I would go so far as to say that the failure of the environmental movement can be attributed largely to the way it perpetuates the type of dichotomous reasoning that precipitated humankind's divorce from nature in the first place. So long as environmentalists urge others to respect, heal, or value nature as an object beyond the hermetically-sealed walls of their bodies, they subtly and unconsciously reinforce the absolute separation of the mind from the world.

To rewrite environmentalism thus requires rewriting the discourse so as no longer to perpetuate the false reification of nature as a thing outside the body, and the false reification of the mind as a wholly abstract and non-material central processing unit within human bodies. This is by no means unheard of in the West. The French philosopher of science, Gaston Bachelard, developed a theoretical understanding of the way that the human imagination is implicated in the materiality of human experience. Merleau-Ponty's concept of "limbed experience" also drew attention to the somatic character of experience. Contemporary neuroscience is also beginning to understand the mind as a function of the whole body, not just the brain. Despite this, the Western tradition is not particularly known for its deep insight into the notion of "bodily experience" and in many ways lags behind the insights generated in Indian and Chinese cultures and religions. Hindu, Buddhist, and Daoist traditions, for instance, have focused for centuries on systematically cultivating an experience of the inner body and on understanding this experience in terms of broader cosmological concepts. In so doing they connect the lived experience of the body with the broader contexts of space, time and the fabric of the natural world. While contemporary environmentalists may not live in the same metaphysical world as these religious practitioners, they do inhabit the same bodies. The premise of this essay derives from this principle: rather than focusing on worldview and cosmology as a point of contact between religion and ecology, it would be better to focus on somatic experiences as a way to overcome the dichotomy between body and world. What follows thus focuses on Chinese somatic traditions, specifically Daoist body cultivation, as non-discursive techniques for reinscribing the body within the world and the world within the body.

BACHELARD

The French philosopher of science, Gaston Bachelard (1884–1962), developed a theory of the "material imagination," which drew on the earliest foundations of Western science, namely, the four elements known to Greek natural philosophy: earth, air, fire, and water. According to Bachelard the human imagination invests these elements with a poetic quality that elicits a "passionate liaison" between humans and their objects.[2] These affective bonds evoke what he termed the "intimate beauty of materials; their mass of hidden attraction, all that affective space concentrated inside things."[3] Bachelard's concept of the "material imagination" thus signifies the way in which human imagination is grounded in the very materiality of nature: the imagination engages the material character of the world; and it does so not in intellectual or disembodied way but through the affective, poetic character. He writes:

> It is not knowledge of the real which makes us passionately love it. It is rather feeling which is the fundamental value. One starts by loving nature without knowing it, by seeing it well, while actualizing in things a love which is grounded elsewhere. Then, one seeks in it detail because one loves it on the whole, without knowing why.[4]

For Bachelard, then, the foundation for the connection between the mind and the world lies in the affect, the feelings and sensations that the natural world evokes in us. This affective bond precedes epistemology and ontology, and it has the power to shape our imagination and our creativity. It is because humans do not simply perceive nature but imbue it with value (even "over-rating" it) that we have the capacity to engage in the creative transformation of the world.[5]

The seductive power of the material imagination was viewed by Bachelard as the initial foundation for the human understanding of nature, a phenomenon that could give rise to science, but which science in its objectivity had to overcome. In fact science, to Bachelard, seemed increasingly incapable of understanding the natural phenomena that were most evocative for the human imagination. Take for example his discussion of fire:

> Contemporary science has almost completely neglected the truly primordial problem that the phenomena of fire pose for the untutored

mind. In the course of time the chapters on fire in chemistry textbooks have become shorter and shorter. There are, indeed, a good many modern books on chemistry in which it is impossible to find any mention of flame or fire. *Fire is no longer a reality for science.*[6]

Bachelard's analysis suggests to me that science's objectivity impels it to overlook the psychic affect of natural processes with the result that societies become increasingly blind to affective dimension of material experience. The process of modernization, therefore, entails a loss of the "affective space" that mediates between human subjects and their lived environments. Though firmly committed to the principles of materialism and science, Bachelard was one of the first modern scientists to recognize and understand the precise nature of this loss. He laments, for instance, the loss of phenomenological depth that occurred in the transition from oil lamps to electric lighting turned on with the flick of a switch.[7] Electric light does not have nearly as much capacity to evoke the material imagination as a flickering flame. The "administrative light" of an electric bulb, bound up in processes of bureaucracy and mechanization was typical of the modern condition. The spaces inhabited by humans thus become increasingly abstracted spaces, homogenized, geometrized, and quantified.

This theme is picked up by later French thinkers. Baudrillard, for instance, noted how bodily engagement with labor and tools in traditional societies became replaced by mere "gestures of control."[8] Heating houses becomes no longer an effort of collecting wood and lighting fires but regulating the thermostat in the hallway.[9] The post-modern condition, moreover, is characterized by technological forms that aim to simulate (and stimulate) the affective bonds that were lost in the transition to modernity. Thus, we have electric fires that look like real log fires, and online social networks that compensate for the loss of community in the abstract space of modernity. Such simulations and virtualizations are testament to the deep-seated poetic power of the material imagination, rooted in millennia of physical engagement of human bodies in their physical contexts. The psychological power of such phenomena cannot be underestimated.

If we are to take Bachelard seriously, then poetry is as important as physics for understanding the human experience of the world. Indeed, this is the reason why in his *Psychoanalysis of Fire*, Bachelard undertakes a survey of the poetic rather than the physical ways in which fire has sparked the human imagination. The consequence of this way thinking about experience and imagination is of particular importance for environmentalists. It suggests that human imagination is driven at a fundamental level by aesthetics. Those who are concerned about the human relationship with the natural world should be concerned with discourse about the aesthetic experience of nature, as much as moral and legal issues, or indeed scientific issues. If Bachelard is right, then *aesthesis*, or feelings about nature underlie, our imagination and perception of the world. So long as the enlightenment mentality and the processes of modernization overlook the aesthetic realm as foundational for the human engagement with the natural world, then they will be incapable of addressing the ecological crisis in any seriously meaningful way.

MERLEAU-PONTY

If Bachelard is right about the primordial psychic power of material phenomena, then this should lead us to develop a philosophical account of the nature of lived experience as a psychosomatic unity rather than the Cartesian account of a *res cogitans* and a *res extensa*. Indeed this has been the major project of Merleau-Ponty and other philosophers who were convinced that the Heideggerian emphasis on lived experience should point us in the direction of the body not simply as the container for experience but as the generative matrix of those experiences. Indeed, it is not simply that the body functionally generates an "experience" of an external "world" but rather that the body provides the spatial location that is necessary for the perception of a phenomenological world. Without a body there could be no experience of the world as it is given to us, and without a world there could be no body. He writes:

> My body is not an object, but a means, an organization. In perception I organize with my body an association with the world. With my body and through my body, I inhabit the world. The body is the field in which perceptions localize themselves.[10]

The emphasis here on the carnal unity of the body and the world is particularly significant for ecological discourse. Of particular note is the famous statement that the body as

> flesh is not matter, is not mind, is not substance. To designate it, we should need the old term 'element,' in the sense it was used to speak of water, air, earth, and fire, that is, in the sense of a general thing, midway between the spatio-temporal individual and the idea, a sort of incarnate

principle that brings a style of being wherever there is a fragment of being. The flesh is in this sense an element of Being.[11]

Merleau-Ponty regards the body akin to Bachelard's elements, that is to say, as the fundamental building block of our lived experience of the world.

In *The Visible and the Invisible*, Merleau-Ponty develops his understanding of perception with the notion of reversibility, that when perception is understood as being constituted in the flesh, then to perceive the world is also to be perceived by the world: one cannot touch without being touched; one cannot see without simultaneously presenting oneself to be seen by the world. In contrast to Descartes's *cogito,* we can say *tango et tangor* (I touch and I am touched). Whatever we touch, perceive and even think, we do so from within a world, not from outside it.

This approach to phenomenology has been instrumental in generating what has been termed the "enactive approach" of embodied cognitive science.[12] According to Colombetti and Thompson, this "dynamical systems approach has challenged the idea that cognition is the manipulation of abstract representations according to syntactic rules, and has proposed instead that cognition emerges from the coupled interactions of the brain, body, and environment."[13] This approach is, moreover, challenging the dominant tradition of cognitive science that draws on Cartesian understandings of the mind/body dualism. Colombetti and Thompson summarize this field as follows:

> In summary, according to the enactive approach, the human mind is embodied in our entire organism and embedded in the world, and hence is not reducible to structures inside the head. Meaning and experience are created by, or enacted through, the continuous reciprocal interaction of the brain, the body, and the world.[14]

But Merleau-Ponty's work has been significant not simply for rethinking the process of embodied cognition, but also on the other side of the coin, for thinking about the lived world that is generated through the process of cognition. Indeed his work has been instrumental for a new line of ecological phenomenology that seeks to explore the value of phenomenology for contributing to a holistic, ecological, systemic view of the relationship between the body and the world. One of chief protagonists of this movement is David Abram. In an early essay, published in 1988, Abram first alludes to the ecological possibilities of Merleau-Ponty's phenomenology. He writes:

His work suggests a rigorous way to approach and to speak of the myriad ecosystems without positing our immediate selves outside of them. Unlike the language of information processing and cybernetics, Merleau-Ponty's phenomenology of the flesh provides a way to describe and disclose the living fields of integration from our experienced place within them. The convergence of Merleau-Ponty's aims with those of a genuine philosophical ecology cannot be too greatly stressed.[15]

Despite the work that has been undertaken in Western philosophy to recuperate the body as the foundation for the human experience of the world, such work remains remarkably abstract given that its focus is on the body. Two criticisms are readily apparent. The first is that made by the American pragmatist philosopher Richard Shusterman who criticizes Merleau-Ponty for emphasizing the way in which somatic perception operates spontaneously. Most of us most of the time do not need to think about or reflect upon how precisely we are constructing our bodily experiences of the lived world. The great marvel of perception is that we do not have to consciously think about how to navigate a crowded party without bumping into a waiter carrying a trayful of cocktails: we just do it. But Shusterman wants more than simply being able to be successful in ordinary pursuits. He advocates what he calls "somaesthetics" that is training the body's perceptual engagement with the world so as to achieve greater pragmatic benefits. He writes:

> While I share Merleau-Ponty's appreciation of our inexplicit, unreflective somatic perception, I think we should also recognize that it is often painfully inaccurate and dysfunctional. I may think I am keeping my head down when swinging a golf club, though an observer will easily see I do not. Disciplines of somatic education deploy exercises of representational awareness to treat such problems of mis-perception and misuse of our bodies in the spontaneous and habitual behavior that Merleau-Ponty identifies as primal and celebrates as miraculously flawless in normal performance.[16]

The problem, as Shusterman sees it, is that if perception is somatic, then it can and should be trained somatically so as to create pragmatically better representations of our place in the world. The value of such representations, however, may extend beyond purely physical activities such as tennis and golf. Theoretically at least it should be possible to engage in training so as to overcome the false reification of self and world so as to arrive at a perception of the self within the world and not outside of it. In short why not use somaesthetic disciplines—the training of the habits of bodily perceptions—so as to bring about an ecological sensitivity?

I mentioned earlier that two major criticisms have emerged of Merleau-Ponty's abstract discussion of the phenomenology of the body. The first was Shusterman's criticism that Merleau-Ponty emphasized the spontaneous nature of perception and neglected to consider the way perception and experiences can be shaped through somatic disciplines. The second criticism focuses on Merleau-Ponty's reluctance to speak about the depth of the inner body. While his philosophy makes it perfectly clear that perception depends upon a depth of field for experience, he does not consider that this depth, or experience of dimensionality, can also be applied to the perception of the inner body. The Indian philosopher Sundar Sarukkai commented on this in a 2002 essay published in *Philosophy East & West*. Discussing Merleau-Ponty and his interpreters he writes:

> But nowhere in these discussions do we find any detailed attempt to explicate the idea of the 'inner' body. The lack of such a discussion suggests that these writers view the body as a homogeneous entity, because of which there is little possibility of articulating a phenomenology of the inner body. I believe that the most important reason for this continued ambiguity regarding the notion of inner with respect to the body is to be found in the absence of a tradition of lived experience of the inner body in the West, one that could have been used by Merleau-Ponty in a manner similar to the case histories of Schneider.[17] In contrast, the phenomenological experiences of yoga strongly suggest the possibility of a lived experience of the inner body.[18]

Before discussing yoga, Sarukkai gives the example of eating in order to argue for the phenomenological experience of dimensionality or depth within the inner body. He writes:

> The body experience of eating is equivalent to the phenomenological experience of dimensionality and thus is intertwined with the notion of 'inside.' The process of eating is never visible to us. Further actions related to eating, such as mashing the food, swallowing, and so on, are all events in the 'dark side' of the body. We can never 'see' ourselves eating, but we experience it all the time. We experience swallowing the food; we experience its passage through the food pipe into the region of the stomach. These experiences all constitute an experience of dimensionality, an expression of the 'inside' of the body. We are usually unaware of these processes except

in times of pain and distress of the inner body. But practices like yoga allow us a continuous, conscious grasp of the inner body.[19]

Sarukkai's approach is instructive in that it opens up a new dimension to the question of embodied experience, one that embodied traditions such as Yoga, Tantra, or Daoist body cultivation can function as interlocutors, and not mere as data to be studied. In the second half of this paper I analyze the depiction of the inner body that emerges in Daoist body cultivation, and I suggest that this depiction can be instructive not simply for Shusterman's project of understanding somaesthetic disciplines, but also for Abram's project of eco-phenomenology.

SOMATIC DISCIPLINES

The argument, put briefly, is that the traditions of Daoist body cultivation can be understood as non-discursive somatic disciplines that inscribe the body within the world and the world within the body. As such they may be fruitfully illuminated by Merleau-Ponty's analysis of the reversibility of phenomenal perception. Secondly, I wish to advance the hypothesis that training in these somatic disciplines can overcome the experience of the world as other, and can provide the aesthetic or sensory foundation for ecologically responsible patterns of behavior. In short, the visual and sensual experience of the body inside the world and the world inside the body can constitute the proper aesthetic grounds for ecologically sensitive praxis.

To those who are familiar with early Daoist philosophy, such a project might seem rather surprising. In comparison to the deep attention paid to the body's inner workings in Yoga, early Daoist texts emphasize spontaneity and unreflective skill when it comes to the body's engagement with the world.[20] In describing the meditation technique known as "sitting and forgetting" *(zuowang),* the *Zhuangzi* ch. 6 puts the following words in the mouth of Confucius's favorite student Yan Hui:

墮肢體, 黜聰明, 離形去知, 同於大通, 此謂坐忘
I smash up my limbs and body, drive out perception and intellect, cast off form, do away with understanding, and make myself identical with the Great Thoroughfare. This is what I mean by sitting down and forgetting everything.[21]

At first glance it might seem that this passage advocates an understanding of perception that goes against Merleau-Ponty's limbed and lived experience of the world. "Do away with limbs and body" says

Yan Hui. The key to understanding such a passage, however, is to recognize that *zuo wang* or "sitting and forgetting" is actually somatic discipline the aim of which is to "forget" or discard conventional phenomenal perception in order to arrive at a state of equivalence (*tong*) with the Way. The foundation of this method of somatic discipline lies in paying attention to the limbed experience of reality, even if the ultimate goal is somehow to move beyond such an experience. But as Merleau-Ponty would surely agree, the only way to there is from here. The foundation for many Daoist practices lies first of all in becoming sensitive to the way that our body conditions our experience of the world, that is to say, paying attention first of all to the "here" rather than the "there." If the Daoist is to attain some kind of all-pervading unity with the Way, this cannot be done except from within the bodily experience of the world.

It would be a mistake, therefore, to spiritualize one's interpretation of the *Zhuangzi* in the manner of perennial philosophy. Making oneself identical with the "Great Thoroughfare" should not be interpreted as a kind of neo-Platonic mystical intellection of Being-Itself. At least, that is not how the Daoist tradition came to understand unity with the Way. We know this because the Daoist tradition developed an extraordinary repertoire of physical cultivation practices that focus, like Yoga, upon the inner body. Daoists, however, tend to express the goal of cultivation slightly differently from Yoga: the aim is not so much liberation from the world, that is, the realm of phenomenal experience; but rather dissolving the boundaries between the lived body and its lived environment. To put it more bluntly, the goal is not transcendence, but translucence, that is to say the body thoroughly pervading and being pervaded by the world. Before I go on to explain this idea of pervasion 通 more fully, it is worth while focusing briefly on some of the methods by which Daoists have cultivated their bodies.

The Way of Highest Clarity

The Way of Highest Clarity (上情道) existed as a distinct tradition for about 1,000 years from the fourth century onwards. This tradition advocated and refined a tradition of internal visual meditation, in which the body was perceived as a rich and splendid cosmos inhabited by gods. This meditative practice was generally known as *cun* 存, which is normally translated in textbooks as "visualization" since the goal of such a practice was to bring about a vision of a god inside the body. The term 存 however has a rich web of meanings that deserves careful explication. In modern Chinese it is combined with 在 to form the binome 存在, commonly translated as "existence." More accurately, however, this binome might be translated as "to persist in a particular location" for it refers not to an abstract concept—existence as such—but to the haecceity or "this-ness" of some discrete particular. The metaphysical presupposition is that to exist means to assume a particular temporal and spatial condition. To exist temporally means to have the quality of persistence that occupies a temporal duration that has a beginning and an end. To exist spatially means to occupy a particular finite space. Such a view coheres with the Heideggerian insight into the givenness of *Dasein:* existence is irreducibly locative.

In his analysis of the term *cun* the Sinologist Edward Schafer notes:

> Here *ts'un* is used as a transitive verb, taking the divine being whose appearance is desired as its object. It would be inadequate to translate this word as 'visualize': the adept's efforts produce more than a mental picture. The word means 'to make sensibly present,' 'to give existence to'—almost 'to materialize.'[22]

In Highest Clarity cultivation, therefore, adepts are seeking to materialize the perception of cosmic powers within the inner space of their bodies.

A typical example is as follows:

> 以正月本命日甲子甲戌日平旦帝, 君太一五神壹共混 合, 變為一大神, 在心之內。號曰天 精君, 字飛生上 英, 貌如嬰兒始生 之狀。是其日平 旦, 當入室接手於兩膝上, 閉氣冥目, 內視存天精君 坐在心中, 號曰大 神, 使大神口出紫氣, 鬱然以繞我心外九重氣, 上衛泥丸中, 內外如一。

> In the first month, on your fate day, the jiazi day, and the jiaxu day at dawn the Five Spirits, the Imperial Lord and Supreme Unity merge together into one great spirit which rests in your heart. His title is the Lord of Celestial Essence, his courtesy title Highest Hero of Soaring Birth, and his appearance is like an infant immediately after birth. On this day at dawn, enter your chamber, clasp your hands together on your knees, keep your breath enclosed and shut your eyes. Look inside and visualize the Lord of Celestial Essence sitting in your heart. He is called a great spirit. Make him spew forth purple qi to coil thickly around one's heart in nine layers, and let it rush up into the niwan. Inner and outer [dimensions] are as one.[23]

As this brief but highly typical passage makes clear, Highest Clarity meditation is characterized by generating rich perceptual experiences in the inner body, described in terms of gods spewing forth energy which floods the various organs of the adept. The cryptic statement at the end indicates the overall goal: 內外如一 the inside and the outside are the same. I interpret this statement as an experience of the translucence of the body. Whereas Merleau-Ponty focused on the way the phenomenon of depth constructs an experience of the world as existing as a horizon surrounding the body of the individual, the goal of Daoist cultivation seems to be to attempt to dissolve the boundary between the body and its environment so that the inner and outer dimensions are perceptively and sensually experienced as a unity.

The metaphor of translucence is even thematized in certain Daoist hagiographies as a quality that applies to the body of the adept. In the Esoteric Biography of Perfected Purple Yang 紫陽真人內傳 the protagonist, Zhou Ziyang 周紫陽 concocts a recipe for conquering the three death-bringing worms that were thought to inhabit the mortal body. The result of ingesting the herbal concoction for five years was that Zhou's body "produced a glossy sheen so that it was possible to see right through to his five organs 身生光澤, 徹視內見五臟".[24] In this case the theme of translucence is even applied to the materiality of the Daoist's body.

Adepts who attained this level of translucence were also thought to be able to travel great distances in an instant, hear what was taking place far away, and make themselves visible and invisible at will.[25] It is intriguing that these "magical" powers are all concerned at some level with perception. They suggest that the perceptual world of the successful Daoist practitioner is bounded by a much further horizon than that of the ordinary human. Whereas ordinary people have limited vision and hearing, the empirical sensitivity of the Daoist adept is much greater.

I am not arguing here that such Daoist practices were undertaken for purposes that could be considered remotely akin to today's environmentalism. What I am saying is that Daoist tradition exhibits a range of practices that depend upon what we can anachronistically refer to as an ecological sense of self, a sense of the body and its environing context being inextricably embedded in each other. Such practices are of interest to the project of rewriting environmentalism because they suggest that non-discursive modes of somatic discipline can bring about an experiential awareness of the body in the world and the world in the body.

The Daoist tradition contains various famous images of the body as a landscape, the most widely known of which is the 內經圖 or Diagram of the Internal Pathways, a late nineteenth-century stone stele housed at the White Cloud Monastery in Beijing. The stele depicts the human body as a landscape of streams, mountains, stars, human figures and deities. Broadly speaking these represent the energetic pathways, the meridians of qi which flow through the body, and also specific energy points within the body. As Louis Komjathy writes:

> The Neijing tu is an illustration not only of the meridians of qi running through the body, but also of the Daoist body as terrestrial and cosmo-logical landscape and as the dwelling-place of inner luminosities or effulgences. From a Daoist perspective, the human body corresponds to, embodies, various "external" presences—mountains, altars, colors, rivers, constellations, temples, spirits, forests, and so forth. The Neijing tu maps the landscape which is the human self. . . . The Neijing tu may be understood as the "Internal Landscape Map."[26]

In his analysis of the *Neijing tu*, Komjathy is clear that its purpose is to depict the internal landscape of the body as revealed through the tradi-tions of body cultivation practiced within the Dragon Gate (*Longmen* 龍門) lineage of the Way of Complete Perfection (*Quanzhen dao* 全真道), the major sect of monastic Daoism that exists in present-day China. The map in fact draws on a long tradition of representing the "internal" body using images from the "external" world. Such imagery at its heart transgresses the intuitive psychology that is based on strict categories of inside and outside. As we saw earlier, the Daoist tradi-tion has an interest in breaking this default conception of the way the body is related to the world, and in positing a psychosomatic unity of the "internal body" and the "external world."

It is my contention that the transgressive emphasis on the unity of inner and outer experience can be used as the basis for developing an aesthetic sensitivity to environmental concerns. Consider for instance, the problem of moral proximity, that moral reasoning does not easily extend to situations that are beyond the perceptual horizon of the moral agent. For instance, it is easier to kill an enemy soldier by pressing a button on a computer and launching a missile across the world than it is to walk up to someone and strangle them to death. Similarly it is easy to be offended by someone dumping litter on the street in your hometown than by the environmental and social effects of waste being transported across the world to be dumped into land-fills or picked over by child laborers in desperate poverty. Equally, it is difficult for some people to be concerned by the rapid extinction of species in distant places. The issue here is that because of the limits to our senses, and the limited range of our aesthetic powers, we are unable to formulate the necessary moral vigor to bring about a change in behavior. What we put beyond the horizon of our perception, we condemn to aesthetic and moral irrelevance.

If we are serious about cultivating an environmental ethic that can pay attention to the globalized nature of environmental issues, then we also need a method of cultivating the aesthetic sensitivity to ecological devastation that seems to be beyond the horizon of our ordinary experience. Paradoxically, the Daoist tradition seems to work on expanding the horizon of experience not by encouraging people to travel across the world or by "expanding their minds" but by developing disciplines for experiencing the depth of the lived world within the depth of the living body. This is an extremely valuable insight for developing an eco-aesthetic sensitivity. I am not suggesting that this is what Daoists have historically done, but I am suggesting that this is what the tradition is capable of.

Qi Cultivation

The Neo-Confucian tradition of course pursued such insights with a great deal of philosophical force, focused on understanding the relationship between vital force (*qi* 氣) and principle (*li* 理) in shaping the dynamics of the cosmos. While I have a great deal of respect for the metaphysical speculations of Confucian philosophy, I would contend that eco-aesthetic sensitivity is generated in the realm of practice rather than theory. I would like to conclude by giving one example of how this can take place. This example is found in an autoethnographic study written by Denver Nixon of the effects of practicing Qigong, a type of moving meditation, under the instruction of a Daoist master in China. In his account of this practice, Nixon compares his own experience of practicing Qigong with accounts of how those suffering from chronic illnesses can develop an internal dialogue with their own bodies. He writes:

> Kathy Charmaz (1991) describes the manner in which those suffering from chronic illness tend to develop a dialectic self, comprised of the physical self and the monitoring self. By going through the ordeal of illness, people develop a heightened sense of awareness of their own bodies, and can thus respond to their body's needs. This monitoring self, once created, usually remains after the illness has subsided. Regarding her ill body, Sara Shaw explained, "I got to know it; I got to understand it. . . . I got to respect it. . . . [I got to know] how my body was doing, how my body was feeling" (Charmaz 1991: 70–72). In the case of illness, the process of sensitive self-monitoring typically requires

a level of self-objectification or personification; "dialogue" with one's sick kidney, for example, may demonstrate this type of "split".[27]

Nixon goes on to use this as a comparison for explaining how the practice of qigong affected his own perceptual sensitivity:

> During my research, it seemed that qigong also cultivated sensitivity and awareness, but in a way that did not objectify and thereby bifurcate experience along an inward/outward fracture. That is, the awareness generated through the practice of qigong does not stop at the skin, but rather "knows" the body as whole and part of its environment.[28]

Nixon seems to be suggesting, therefore, that even basic Qi movement practices can have the effect of reshaping the mode of awareness of our bodies within their lived environments. He concludes that this practice may even be considered an alternative epistemology, one that complements normative approaches that privilege discursive knowing over practical knowing. Nixon's interest in this approach is similar to my own, that is to say, attempting to assess the extent to which somatic disciplines cannot merely improve your golf swing, but contribute to your ecological sensitivity. According to Nixon:

> Substituting or complementing normative epistemic approaches with those less privileged may facilitate different, if not more comprehensive, environmental understandings. It appears that *qigong*, by breaking the discursive mediation and bifurcation of reality and improving present, perceptive depth, sensitizes the practitioner to the emerging context within which they are increasingly undifferentiated, and thus allows them to engage with it "harmoniously."[29]

In Nixon's experience, therefore, Qigong led to an increased sensitivity to the emerging context of his lived world, and overcame the conventional bifurcation of reality into subject and object. It did so by improving "perceptive depth," which we may interpret as reshaping the mode of bodily perception and engagement with the lived environment. This sense of the unity of the body with the emergent phenomena of the world is termed "pervasion" 通 in the Daoist tradition.

PERVASION (*tong* 通) AND ECO-AESTHETICS

Pervasion may be understood as the somatic experience of the mutual constitution of the lived body and its lived environment. The term appears in the quotation from Zhuangzi, cited above, in which the Yan

Hui wishes to make himself "identical with the Great Thoroughfare" or Great Pervasiveness (*tong yu da tong* 同於大通). This experience is thematized in the Daoist with the metaphor of "translucence," with depictions of the inner landscape of the body, and through the experience of qi as the psychophysical stuff that constitutes the vitality of the lived body and the lived world. While Confucian philosophy reflected deeply on the harmonious unity of nature and humanity (*tian ren he yi* 天人合一), it was the Daoist tradition that sought to enact such a unity through non-discursive somatic practices.

If the approach of embodied cognition is correct, then it would seem that the unity of the world and the lived body is predicated on the body as the system that enacts experience. The problem faced by environmentalists, however, is that this process of cognition takes place unconsciously so that our minds generate a perception of a world that is external to our bodies and a perception of our bodies as an invisible interior, fundamentally disconnected from the world that envelops them. Though embodied cognitive science and embodied religious traditions may perceive that this dualism is constructed as part of the process of cognition and not intrinsic to the reality of things, this does not accord with the ordinary experience of ordinary people. Only theoreticians in laboratories, philosophers in libraries, and monks in monasteries come close to understanding the ways that our bodies enact the world that we experience. Overcoming this fundamental dualism of self and other, body and world, is simply counterintuitive to conventional perceptions. And yet it is necessary for generating an aesthetic awareness that can be the foundation for ecologically responsible action.

I would like to conclude this essay by repeating the point that I made at the beginning of this: So long as people urge others to respect, heal, or value nature as an object beyond the hermetically-sealed walls of their bodies, they subtly and unconsciously reinforce the absolute separation of the mind from the world. Such an approach to environmentalism is doomed to failure. Embodied traditions such as Daoist cultivation could play an important role in teaching people how to overcome this dualism, and how to create alternative experiences of the world not as external to body, but within the body. The Daoist experience of pervasion is predicated on the possibility of the world flooding into the body and the body flooding into the world. Such transgressive experiences may serve to break down the ordinary perception of a world disconnected from the body of the individual. In their place such experiences could generate an ecological aesthesis, a psychosomatic sensitivity to the mutual implication of the lived body and the lived world. Such a sensitivity could serve as a much-needed complement to discursive modes of environmental action, such as earth charters, policies, ethics, and legislation.

REFERENCES

Abram, David. "Merleau Ponty and the Voice of the Earth." *Environmental Ethics* 10.2 (1988).

Bachelard, Gaston. *L'Eau et les rêves. Essai sur l'imagination de la matière.* Paris: Corti, 1942.

_____. *The Psychoanalysis of Fire.* Trans. Alan C. M. Ross. Boston, MA: Beacon Press, 1962.

Baudrillard, Jean. *Le Système des objets.* Paris: Gallimard, 1968.

Charmaz, Kathy. *Good Days, Bad Days: The Self In Chronic Illness and Time.* New Brunswick, NJ: Rutgers University Press, 1991.

Colombetti, Giovanna and Evan Thompson. 2007. "The feeling body: Towards an enactive approach to emotion." In *Developmental Perspectives on Embodiment and Consciousness* edited by Willis F. Overton, Ulrich Müller, and Judith Newman, 45–68. New York: Lawrence Erlbaum Associates.

Jung, Hwa Jol. "Enlightenment and the Question of the Other: A Postmodern Audition." *Human Studies* 25 (2002): 297–306.

_____. 2007. "Merleau-Ponty's Transversal Geophilosophy." In *Merleau-Ponty and environmental philosophy: dwelling on the landscapes of thought* edited by Sue Cataldi and William Hamrick, 235–258. Albany: SUNY Press.

Kaplan, Edward K. "Gaston Bachelard's Philosophy of Imagination: An Introduction." *Philosophy and Phenomenological Research* 33.1 (1972): 1–24.

Komjathy, Louis. "Mapping the Daoist Body Part One: The *Neijing tu* in History." *Journal of Daoist Studies* 1 (2008): 67–92.

Lane, Jeremy F. "Towards a Poetics of Consumerism: Gaston Bachelard's 'Material Imagination' and Narratives of Post-War Modernisation." *French Cultural Studies* 17.1 (2006): 19–34.

Miller, James. *The Way of Highest Clarity: Nature, Vision and Revelation in Medieval China.* Magdalena, NM: Three Pines Press, 2008.

Nixon, Denver Vale. "The Environmental Resonance of Daoist Moving Meditations." *Worldviews: Environment, Culture, Religion* 10.3 (2006): 380–403.

Sarukkai, Sundar. "Inside/Outside: Merleau-Ponty/Yoga." *Philosophy East and West* 52.4 (2002): 459–478.

Schafer, Edward. "The Jade Woman of Greatest Mystery," History of Religions 17:3/4 (1978): 387–398.

Shusterman, Richard. "Body Consciousness and Performance: Somaesthetics East and West." *The Journal of Aesthetics and Art Criticism* 67.2 (2009):133–145.

Varela, Francis. J., Evan Thompson, Evan, and E. Rosch, *The Embodied Mind: Cognitive Science and Human Experience*. Cambridge, MA: MIT Press, 1991.

Watson, Burton, trans. 1968. *The Complete Works of Chuang Tzu*. New York: Columbia University Press.

Notes

1. Hwa-Jol Jung, "Enlightenment and the Question of the Other: A Post-modern Audition" *Human Studies* 25 (2002): 298.

2. Gaston Bachelard, *La Poétique de l'espace,* (Paris: PUF/Collection 'Quadrige', 7e édition, 1998 [1957]), 33; quoted in Jeremy F. Lane, "Towards a Poetics of Consumerism: Gaston Bachelard's 'Material Imagination' and Narratives of Post-War Modernisation" *French Cultural Studies* 17.1 (2006): 21.

3. Gaston Bachelard, *La Terre et les rêveries de la volonté* (Paris: José Corti, 1948), 9; quoted in Lane, "Poetics," 20.

4. Gaston Bachelard, *L'Eau et les rêves. Essai sur l'imagination de la matière,* (Paris: Corti 1942), 155; quoted in Edward K. Kaplan, "Gaston Bachelard's Philosophy of Imagination: An Introduction," *Philosophy and Phenomenological Research* 33.1 (1972), 4.

5. Kaplan, "Gaston Bachelard," 5.

6. Gaston Bachelard, *The Psychoanalysis of Fire,* trans. Alan C. M. Ross, (Boston, MA: Beacon Press, 1964), 2.

7. Lane, "Poetics," 23.

8. Jean Baudrillard, *Le Système des objets,* (Paris: Gallimard, 1968), 77.

9. Lane, "Poetics," 28.

10. Maurice Merleau-Ponty, "Husserl et la Notion de Nature (Notes Prises au Cours de Maurice Merleau-Ponty)" *Revue de Metaphysique et de Morale* 70 (1965): 261; quoted in Hwa-Jol Jung, "Merleau-Ponty's Transversal Geophilosophy," in *Merleau-Ponty and Environmental Philosophy: Dwelling on the Landscapes of Thought,* ed. Sue Cataldi and William Hamrick, (Albany: SUNY Press, 2007), 241.

11. Maurice Merleau-Ponty, *Le Visible et L'Invisible* (Paris: Gallimard, 1964), 139–140; quoted in Jung, "Transversal," 242–243.

12. See Varela et al., *The Embodied Mind: Cognitive Science and Human Experience,* (Cambridge, MA: MIT Press, 1997).

13. Giovanna Colombetti and Evan Thompson, "The feeling body: Towards an enactive approach to emotion," in *Developmental Perspectives on Embodiment and Consciousness* ed. Willis F. Overton, et al., (New York: Lawrence Erlbaum Associates: 2007), 46.

14. Colombetti and Thompson, "Feeling body," 56.

15. David Abram, "Merleau Ponty and the Voice of the Earth," *Environmental Ethics* 10.2 (1988), 119.

16. Richard Shusterman, "Body Consciousness and Performance: Somaesthetics East and West," *The Journal of Aesthetics and Art Criticism* 67.2 (2009): 139.

17. Schneider suffered head injuries and consequently many mental disorders. Merleau-Ponty used his case notes as evidence to refute empiricist and intellectualist theories of perception.

18. Sundar Sarrukai, "Inside/Outside: Merleau-Ponty/Yoga," *Philosophy East and West* 52.4 (2002): 462.

19. Sarukkai, "Inside/Outside," 466.

20. Shusterman, "Body," 136.

21. Burton Watson, trans., *Chuang Tzu: Basic Writings*, (New York: Columbia, 1964), 87.

22. Edward Schafer, "The Jade Woman of Greatest Mystery," *History of Religions* 17:3/4 (1978): 387–398.

23. Central Scripture of the Nine Perfected (*Jiu zhen zhong jing* 九真中經) trans. adapted from James Miller, *The Way of Highest Clarity: Nature, Vision and Revelation in Medieval China* (Magdalena, NM: Three Pines Press, 2008), 173.

24. Miller, *The Way of Highest Clarity*, 123.

25. Miller, *The Way of Highest Clarity*, 65.

26. Louis Komjathy, "Mapping the Daoist Body Part One: The *Neijing tu* in History," *Journal of Daoist Studies* 1 (2008): 82–83.

27. Denver Vale Nixon, "The Environmental Resonance of Daoist Moving Meditations," *Worldviews: Environment, Culture, Religion* 10.3 (2006): 389–90.

28. Nixon, "Environmental," 390.

29. Nixon, "Environmental," 395.

SECTION III

Environmental Philosophy in Japanese Traditions of Thought

CHAPTER 13

The Japanese Concept of Nature in Relation to the Environmental Ethics and Conservation Aesthetics of Aldo Leopold

STEVE ODIN

INTRODUCTION

Taoism, with its metaphysics of nature as creative and aesthetic transformation, and East Asian Buddhism, with its view of nature as an aesthetic continuum of organismic interrelationships, have been sources of inspiration for environmental philosophy, recently consolidated in an anthology edited by J. Baird Callicott and Roger T. Ames, entitled *Nature in Asian Traditions of Thought: Essays in Environmental Philosophy.*[1] Here I focus especially on the concept of nature in Japanese Buddhism as a valuable complement to the environmental philosophy of Aldo Leopold. In this context I clarify the hierarchy of normative values whereby a land ethic is itself grounded in a land aesthetic in the ecological worldviews of both Japanese Buddhism in the East and Aldo Leopold in the West.

The Environmental Philosophy of Aldo Leopold

The Land Ethic

One can point to various sources for the newly emerging field of "environmental ethics," for instance, the Romantic movement, beginning with Rousseau and running through Goethe and the Romantic poets (Blake, Wordsworth, Coleridge, Shelly), continuing in America through the Transcendentalism of Whitman, Emerson, and Thoreau as well as later conservationists such as John Muir and Gary Snyder. However, the *locus classicus* for environmental ethics as a distinctive branch of philosophy is widely regarded by those in the discipline as a volume by Aldo Leopold entitled *A Sand County Almanac,* first published in 1949, and in particular the capstone essay of this work called "The Land Ethic".[2] According to Leopold's threefold division of ethics, "The first ethics dealt with the relation between individuals. . . . Later accretions dealt with the relation between the individual and society."[3] It is here that he makes a significant leap by enlarging the field of ethics to include a third element: namely, man's relation to the land. In Leopold's words:

> There is as yet no ethic dealing with man's relation to land and to the animals and plants which grow upon it. . . . The land-relation is still strictly economic, entailing privileges but not obligations. The extension of ethics to this third element in human environment is, if I read the evidence correctly, an evolutionary possibility and an ecological necessity.[4]

Leopold defines ethics in terms of his key notion of "community." An individual is always contextually located in a social environment, or as Leopold puts it, in communities of interdependent parts that evolve "modes of cooperation," called *symbioses* by ecologists. However, while in the past ethical discourse has been confined to the human community so as to pertain solely to the relation between individuals and society, environmental ethics extends this over into the realm of the "biotic community" of soil, plants, and animals so as to include the symbiotic relation between humans and the land. He writes:

> All ethics so far evolved rest upon a single premise: that the individual is a member of a community of interdependent parts. . . . The land ethic simply enlarges the boundaries of the community to include soils, waters, plants, and animals, or collectively: the land.[5]

Leopold goes on to argue that "a land ethic changes the role of *Homo sapiens* from conqueror of the land-community to plain member and citizen of it."[6] Further, his land ethic redefines conservation from maximizing the utility of natural resources to "a state of harmony between men and land."[7] For Leopold, the principles of a land ethic not only impose obligations in the legalistic sense, but entail the evolution of what he calls an "ecological conscience,"[8] understood as an "extension of the social conscience from people to land."[9] According to Leopold, then, a land ethic reflects the existence of an ecological conscience, and this in turn reflects an inner conviction of individual responsibility for the health of the land.[10]

THE CONSERVATION AESTHETIC

In Aldo Leopold's ecological worldview, his "land ethic" is inseparable from what he calls a "land aesthetic."[11] As Leopold writes in the original 1947 foreword to his work: "These essays deal with the ethics and esthetics of land."[12] It is significant that Leopold's *A Sand County Almanac* ends with an essay entitled "Conservation Esthetic."[13] For Leopold, it is the beauty or aesthetic value intrinsic to nature that places a requirement upon us to enlarge ethics to include the symbiotic relation between humans and land, to extend the social conscience from the human community to the biotic community, and thereby to establish an ecological harmony between people and their natural environment of soil, plants, and animals. The importance of this land esthetic as the ground for a land ethic is further indicated by Leopold in his 1948 foreword to *A Sand County Almanac,* where he asserts that the essays contained in his work "attempt to weld three concepts": (i) "That land is a community the basic concept of ecology:" (ii) "that land is to be loved and respected an extension of ethics"; and (iii) "that land yields a cultural harvest" or, as he alternatively puts it, an "esthetic harvest."[14] According to Leopold, the norm for behavior in relation to land use is whether or not our conduct is aesthetically as well as ethically right. The beauty of the land is, therefore, one of the fundamental criteria for determining the rightness of our relationship to it: "A thing is right when it tends to preserve the integrity, stability, and beauty of the biotic community."[15] Hence, the architectonic structure of *A Sand County Almanac* suggests a kind of Peircean hierarchy of normative values whereby environmental ethics is itself grounded in the axiology of a conservation aesthetics.[16] In other words, our moral love and respect for nature is based on an aesthetic appreciation of the beauty and value of the land. Along these lines, it should be noted that Eugene C. Hargrove has pursued a similar line of reasoning, arguing that not only the land ethic, but the historical foundation of all broad Western environmental sentiments is ultimately aesthetic.[17] Indeed, this aesthetic foundation for a land ethic is one of the deepest insights into the human/nature relation developed in the ecological world views both East and West.

JAPANESE BUDDHISM—AN ASIAN RESOURCE FOR ENVIRONMENTAL ETHICS

The principles of environmental ethics articulated by Aldo Leopold find a powerful source of support in the concept of living nature formulated by traditional Japanese Buddhism. A profound current of ecological thought runs throughout the Kegon, Tendai, Shingon, Zen, Pure Land, and Nichiren Buddhist traditions as well as modern Japanese philosophy. In what follows I briefly present the Japanese concept of nature as an aesthetic continuum of interdependent events based on a field paradigm of reality. In this context I show how the Japanese concept of nature entails an extension of ethics to include the relation between humans and the land. Moreover, I argue that the land ethic is itself grounded in a land aesthetic in the Japanese Buddhist concept of nature as well as for Aldo Leopold. I further seek to clarify the soteric concept of nature in Japanese Buddhism wherein the natural environment becomes the ultimate locus of salvation for all sentient beings. Finally, I argue that the Japanese Buddhist concept of nature represents a fundamental shift from the egocentric to an ecocentric position, i.e., a non-anthropocentric standpoint which is nature-centered as opposed to human-centered.

THE FIELD MODEL OF NATURE IN ECOLOGY AND JAPANESE BUDDHISM

The environmental ethics of Aldo Leopold arises from a metaphysical presupposition that things in nature are not separate, independent, or substantial objects, but relational fields existing in mutual dependence upon each other, thus constituting a synergistic ecosystem of organisms interacting with their environment. According to Leopold's field concept of nature, the land is a single living organism wherein each part affects every other part, and it is this simple fact that imposes certain moral obligations upon us in relation to our environment. As J. Baird Callicott argues in "The Metaphysical Implications of

Ecology," at the metaphysical level of discourse, ecology implies a paradigm shift from atomism to field theory.[18] In this context he underscores various metaphysical overtones in the "field theory of living nature adumbrated by Leopold."[19] Callicott, following the insights of Leopold, argues that "object-ontology is inappropriate to an ecological description of the natural environment," and adds, "Living natural objects should be regarded as ontologically subordinate to 'events' . . . or 'field patterns.'"[20] According to Callicott, in the worldview of ecology, as in the New Physics, organisms in nature are a "local perturbation, in an energy flux or 'field'" so that the "subatomic microcosm" is analogous to the "ecosystemic macrocosm," "moments in [a] network" or "knots in [a] web of life."[21] He further points out that for the Norwegian environmental philosopher Arne Naess, ecology suggests "a relational total field image [in which] organisms [are] knots in the biospherical net of intrinsic relations."[22] It should be noted that in the Western philosophical tradition, the field concept of nature implied by ecology has received its fullest systematic expression in the process metaphysics and philosophy of organism developed by A. N. Whitehead, which elaborates a panpsychic vision of nature as a creative and aesthetic continuum of living field events arising through their causal relations to every other event in the continuum.[23]

The primacy accorded to "relational fields" over that of the "substantial objects" implicit in the ecological world view is also at the very heart of the organismic paradigm of nature in East Asian philosophy, especially Taoism and Buddhism. In his article "Putting the *Te* back into Taoism," Roger T. Ames interprets the key ideas of *te* and *tao* in the Taoist aesthetic view of nature as representing a "focus/ field" model of reality with clear implications for an environmental ethic.[24] Likewise, Izutsu Toshihiko in *Toward a Philosophy of Zen Buddhism* has clearly explicated what he refers to as "the field structure of Ultimate Reality" in traditional Japanese Zen as well as Kegon (Hua-yen) Buddhism, in which each event in nature is understood as a concentrated focus point for the whole field of emptiness *(kū)* or nothingness *(mu)*, comprehended in Buddhist philosophy as a dynamic network of causal relationships, in other words, the process termed "dependent coorigination" *(engi)*.[25] Moreover, this traditional Zen and Kegon Buddhist field model of reality has been reformulated in terms of the concept of *basho* or "field" (locus, matrix, place) in the modern Japanese syncretic philosophy of Nishida Kitarō (1870–1945) and the Kyoto School: namely, what Nishida calls *mu no Basho,* the field of Nothingness.[26] Nishida's concept of *basho* or field was itself profoundly influenced by Lask's scientific *Feldtheorie* (field theory). As Matao Noda has observed: "In this connection the modern physical concept of field of force, taken by Einstein as a cosmic field, seems to have suggested much to Nishida."[27]

The primacy of *basho* or relational fields in modern Japanese philosophy has been developed specifically with regard to the human/nature relationship in the ethics of Watsuji Tetsurō (1889–1960), Nishida's younger colleague in the philosophy department at Kyoto University. In his work *Ethics as Anthropology (Ningen no gaku toshite no rinrigaku)* Watsuji calls his "ethics" *(rinrigaku)* the science of the person, based upon the Japanese concept of human nature as *ningen*, whose two *kanji* characters express the double structure of selfhood as being both "individual" and "social."[28] Accordingly, the "person" as *ningen* does not mean simply the individual *(hito)*, but the "relatedness" or "betweenness" *(aidagara)* in which people are located. In his book entitled *The Body*, the Japanese comparative philosopher Yuasa Yasuo clearly expresses the relation of Watsuji's concept of person *(ningen)* as the life-space of "betweenness" in which people are situated to the general idea of *basho* as a relational field or spatial locus. He writes: "But what does it mean to exist in betweenness *(aidagara)*? . . . Our betweenness implies that we exist in a definite, spatial *basho* (place, topos, field)."[29] However, Watsuji's ethics based on the double structure of personhood as *ningen* does not emphasize the spatial locus of relationships between individual and individual or between the individual and the social only; rather, he further extends his moral considerations to the relationship between the individual and nature. In his work entitled *Climate, an Anthropological Consideration (Fūdo ningengakuteki kosatsu)*, Watsuji develops as his main philosophical theme the embodied spatiality of human existence in various social environments, so that the individual both influences and is influenced by the family, the community, and ultimately the natural environment of a *fūdo* or "climate."[30] As Yuasa puts it, "Watsuji wrote a book called *Climates* in which he said that to live in nature as the space of the life-world—in other words, to live in a 'climate'—is the most fundamental mode of being human."[31] Hence, Watsuji clearly formulates an ethics in which the individual must be conceived as being situated in a spatial field of relatedness or betweenness not only to human society, but also to a surrounding climate *(fūdo)* of living nature as the ultimate extension of embodied subjective space in which man dwells. Watsuji's ethical philosophy is, therefore, one of the most suggestive Asian resources for environmental ethics as outlined by Aldo Leopold, in which morality is enlarged so as to include not simply individual/individual and individual/social relations, but also the encompassing human/nature relation as a major extension of practical ethics.

THE JAPANESE CONCEPT OF NATURE—A UNITY OF ONOZUKARA/MIZUKARA

The extension of ethics to include the human/nature relationship in the philosophy of Watsuji Tetsurō itself reflects a traditional Japanese concept of living nature as a unity of *onozukara* (nature) and *mizukara* (self). The Japanese term for *nature, shi-zen* (also pronounced *ji-nen*), originally derived from the Chinese word *tsu-jan,* corresponds to the English word *nature,* which comes from the Latin *natura*, which was used by the Romans to translate the Greek term *physis.* As various scholars have pointed out, the Japanese concept of *shizen/jinen* can be compared to the ancient Greek concept of nature through Heidegger's uncovering of the original Greek understanding of *physis* as that which presences or unfolds of itself into primordial appearance as openness, unhiddenness, and nonconcealment. In ancient Japanese, a common expression for *shizen/jinen* was *onozukara,* which like Greek *physis* indicates "what-is-so-of-itself." *Onozukara,* written with the first of the two characters for *shi-zen,* also stands for another original Japanese term, *mizukara* or "self." The implications of this connection have been clarified by Hubertus Tellenbach and Kimura Bin in their article on "The Japanese Concept of Nature":

> As of itself *Onozukara* expresses an objective state. . . . *Mizukara* as self expresses, on the other hand, a subjective state. . . . That the Japanese believe they can express these seemingly autonomous terms by means of a single character points towards a deeper insight by which they apprehend *Onozukara* and *Mizukara,* nature and self, as originating from the same common ground.[32]

Consequently, in the Japanese concept of nature as a unity of *onozukara/mizukara,* both self and nature are grounded in a common field of reality as the subjective and objective aspects of a single continuum or relational matrix.

One of the most interesting expressions of this traditional Japanese view of nature as a unity of *onozukara/mizukara* is to be found in the concept of *eshō funi* or "oneness of life and its environment" formulated by Nichiren Daishonin (1222–1282) and his followers in the Nichiren Shoshu sect of Buddhism. Nichiren is most famous for his apocalyptic teaching that enlightenment can be attained in the Latter Day of the Law (*mappō*) only by reciting the *daimoku* or title of the Lotus Sutra, *Myōhō renge kyō,* which he inscribed in a mandala called the *Daigohonzon* for the purpose of awakening Buddhahood in all sentient beings. In his eschatological and apocalyptic teaching about *mappō* or the Latter Day of the Law, Nichiren prophesized that not only human social disasters like civil wars and foreign invasions, but also such natural catastrophes as floods, fires, earthquakes, droughts, plagues, and other calamities would all result from a failure of people to follow the Mystic Law of cause/effect which he called *Myōhō renge kyō.* For Nichiren, *Myōhō renge kyō* is the Mystic Law of life itself, which embodies the supreme principle of Tendai (Ch. T'ien-t'ai) Buddhism known as *ichinen sanzen,* "three thousand worlds in one life-moment." Moreover, as the embodiment of *ichinen sanzen,* the Mystic Law of *Myōhō renge kyō* contains the principle of *eshō funi,* the "oneness of life and its environment." In his text, "The True Entity of Life," Nichiren writes: "Where there is an environment, there is life within it. Miao-Io states, 'Both life (*shohō*) and its environment (*ehō*) always manifest *Myōhō-renge-kyō.*'"[33] By this view, both the subjective human being and its objective environment are two aspects of a single reality, the true entity of life, in other words, the Mystic Law of *Myōhō renge kyō.* In his exegesis of the above passage by Nichiren, Ikeda Daisaku concludes: "People (*shohō*) and their environments (*ehō*) are inseparable. . . . Both are aspects of the Law of *Myōhō-renge-kyō* . . . . Thus we can see the powerful principle in Buddhism that a revolution within life (*shoho*) always leads to one in the environment (*ehō*)."[34] From this insight it follows that at the level of practice, the inseparability of life and its environment is discovered by fusing with the Mystic Law, which in Nichiren Buddhism is caused by reciting the mantric formula "*Namu myōhō renge kyō.*" Furthermore, chanting "*Namu Myōhō renge kyō*" is thought to produce a "human revolution," that is to say, a transformation of subjective selfhood which in turn effects a corresponding change in the objective environment, thereby resulting in the metamorphosis of nature into a Buddha land of peace and harmony. Hence, according to Nichiren Buddhism, the principle of *eshō funi* constitutes the doctrinal foundation for an ecological worldview based on the inseparability of life and its environment.

The Kegon Infrastructure of Nature in Zen Buddhisim

In the case of Nichiren Buddhism, the concept of nature as a cosmic field in which life and its environment are integrated is explained by invoking the master concept of Tendai Buddhism, namely, *ichinen sanzen*, "three thousand worlds in one life-moment." However, in Zen Buddhism, this kind of field theory of nature is elaborated in terms of an analogous Kegon (Ch. Hua-yen) Buddhist doctrinal formula known as *riji muge* (Ch. *shih-shih wu-ai*), the "interpenetration of part and whole." Like the *ichinen sanzen* principle of Tendai, the Kegon principle of *riji muge* articulates a microcosmic/macrocosmic paradigm of reality that depicts nature as a sacred matrix of inter-relationships. This Kegon infrastructure underlies not only traditional Zen Buddhist teachings but also the modern Japanese philosophy of Nishida and the Kyoto School.[35] The profound ecological worldview implicit in the Kegon or Hua-yen vision of organismic interrelatedness is discussed by Francis H. Cook in his essay "The Jewel Net of Indra." At the outset he writes:

> Only very recently has the word "ecology" begun to appear in our discussion, reflecting the arising of a remarkable new consciousness of how all things live in inter-dependence. . . . The ecological approach . . . views existence as a vast web of interdependencies in which if one strand is disturbed, the whole web is shaken.[36]

Cook goes on to situate the ecological model of organismic inter-dependence in a wider context by discussing the relationship between humans and nature in the "cosmic ecology" of Hua-yen Buddhism.[37] He presents the Chinese Hua-yen vision of nature in terms of the microcosmic/macrocosmic paradigm expressed by the famous metaphor of "Indra's Net," which depicts a cosmic web of dynamic causal interrelationships wherein at every intersection in the lattice work there is a glittering jewel reflecting all the other jewels in the net, infinite in number.[38] In the pattern of interconnectivity depicted by Indra's Net, each and every event in nature arises through an interfusion of the many and the one, thus being likened to a shining jewel that both contains and pervades the whole universe as a micro-cosm of the macrocosm. By this view, all events arise through their functional relationships to all the other events and to the whole so that each thing is interconnected to everything else in the aesthetic continuum of nature. This relational cosmology is codified by the famous doctrinal formulas of Kegon Buddhism, named *riji muge*

(Ch. *li-shih wu-ai*) or "interpenetration of part and whole" and *jiji muge* (Ch. *shih-shih wu-ai*) or "interpenetration of part and part." In such a manner Hua-yen Buddhism has established a compelling axiological cosmology, according to which, given that everything functions as a causal condition for everything else, there is nothing which is not of value in the great harmony of nature. This view further entails a morality of unconditional compassion and loving kindness for all sentient beings in nature. Hence, it can be argued that Hua-yen Buddhism has provided an explicit, comprehensive, and systematic relational cosmology which fully supports the fundamental principles of ecological ethics propounded by Aldo Leopold and other environmental philosophers, whereby the atomistic paradigm of nature is wholly abandoned in favor of a model of organismic interdependence.

The Aesthetic Concept of Nature in Japanese Buddhism

Scholars of Asian civilization have often pointed to the primacy of aesthetic value as the distinguishing feature of traditional Japanese Buddhist culture. During the medieval period of Japanese history (ca. 950–1400), art and religion were fused to the extent that spiritual and aesthetic values became virtually identified in what was called *geidō*—the "*tao* (or Way) of art." In the concept of nature developing out of Japanese *geidō,* the natural environment is seen as not only laden with aesthetic but also religious values so that it becomes the ultimate ground and source of salvation itself. This Japanese aesthetic concept of nature has long been articulated by a lexicon of technical terms based on the canons of art and literature, including *aware, yūgen, wabi, sabi,* and *yojō.* In Japanese Buddhism nature is not conceived in eternalist or substantialist terms as static being, but through process categories as a dynamic becoming, i.e., *mujō* or "impermanence." Yet, as opposed to a nihilistic view of becoming, Japanese Heian poetics affirms the positivity of nature as a flux of impermanence with the aesthetic value notion of *aware,* the sorrow-tinged appreciation of transitory beauty. In this way the Japanese value-centric concept of nature as creative and aesthetic process is a worldview based on the Middle Way between eternalism on the one side and nihilism on the other. Moreover, in the *waka* poetry of Fujiwara Teika, the *sumie* monochrome inkwash paintings of Sesshu, and the *Noh* drama of Zeami, the beauty of *yūgen* or "mysterious depths" was evoked by visions of nonsubstantial phenomena in nature fading into the background field of *mu* or nothingness. In *chanoyu* or the tea ceremony of Sen no Rikyū, nature is described in terms of *wabi,* the beauty of simplicity and poverty, while the *haiku* poetry of Bashō conjures the feeling of *sabi,* the beauty of the solitude and tranquility of events in nature. All of these aesthetic value categories are regarded as aspects of *yojō* or "overtones of feeling," reflecting a deeply emotional and artistic sensitivity to the sublime beauty of nature as a continuum of organismic relationships and dynamic processes.

In the final chapter of his book *Zen and Japanese Culture,* "Love of Nature," D. T. Suzuki underscores the Kegon or Hua-yen (Skt. Avatamsaka) infrastructure underlying the traditional aesthetic concept of nature in Japanese Zen Buddhism. Suzuki writes: "The balancing of unity and multiplicity or, better, the merging of self with others in the philosophy of Avatamsaka (Kegon) is absolutely necessary to the aesthetic understanding of Nature."[39] According to the organismic paradigm of Zen and Kegon Buddhism, nature is to be comprehended as an undivided aesthetic continuum wherein each momentary and unsubstantial event arises through the harmonic interfusion of oneness and multiplicity, unity and plurality, or subjectivity and objectivity, thus emerging as a cosmic field of relationships which both contains and pervades the universe as a microcosm-qua-macrocosm. Because for Zen there is a mutual containment or reciprocal penetration of subject and object, there is said to be a continuity or interfusion between humans and nature. In Suzuki's words:

> Zen proposes to respect Nature, to love Nature, to live its own life; Zen recognizes that our Nature is one with objective Nature . . . in the sense that Nature lives in us and we in Nature. For this reason, Zen asceticism advocates simplicity, frugality, straightforwardness, virility, making no attempt to utilize Nature for selfish purposes.[40]

I would like to make two observations about this passage concerning the relation of Zen to Aldo Leopold's environmental ethics. First, as Suzuki points out, the insight that humans and nature are interdependent has led to Zen ideals of simplicity, frugality, and poverty in relation to land use so that nature is not exploited out of selfish motivations. Hence, in his famous work *Small is Beautiful: Economics as if People Mattered,* E. F. Schumacher synthesizes the environmental ethics of Leopold with the Zen ecology of nature to develop what he calls a "Buddhist economics" oriented toward attaining given ends with minimal consumption.[41] Second, the Zen Buddhist love and respect for nature described by Suzuki in this passage directly accords with a major theme in the environmental philosophy of Leopold, namely, "that land is to be loved and respected

[a]s an extension of ethics."[42] This love and respect for the natural world, viewed as an extension of ethics, is itself directly related to the aesthetic and religious concept of nature. From a comparative standpoint, these connections can be helpful in illuminating the axiological foundations underlying the ecological worldview of Aldo Leopold, in which the land ethic is grounded in a conservation aesthetic.

The Salvific Function of Nature in Japanese Buddhism

The religio-aesthetic concept of nature as a continuum funded with value and beauty is a correlate to what can be referred to as the "salvific function" of nature in traditional Japanese Buddhism. A paradigm of one who endeavors to find salvation through nature is provided by a novel entitled *Kusamakura (Grass Pillow)* by Sōseki Natsume.[43] This novel describes the *haiku* journey of a twentieth-century artist-poet from Tokyo who ventures into the solitude of a mountain wilderness for the sole purpose of attaining Zen *satori* or enlightenment through the tranquil beauty of nature. By exercising aesthetic detachment the poet hero of *Kusamakura* attempts to envision all things in the landscape as displaying the religio-aesthetic value of *yūgen,* "mystery and depth," such that everything in nature is transformed into a scene from a monochrome *sumie* inkwash painting, a *Noh* drama, or a *haiku* poem. In this way, living nature is prized not only for its beauty, but also for its salvific function as the ultimate locus for spiritual awakening.

Sōseki's artist hero is a modern literary prototype for a long and profound tradition of Japanese figures seeking salvation through nature by means of the religio-aesthetic path of *geidō* or the *"tao* of art," including Teika, Saigyō, Bashō, Sesshu, and Sen no Rikyū. In his article, "Probing the Japanese Experience of Nature," Omine Akira traces this soteric concept of nature in the Japanese literary tradition beginning with the earliest eighth-century anthology called the *Man'yo-shu* (Collection of Myriad Leaves), and running through Saigyō (1118–1190), Ippen (1239–1289), and Bashō (1644–1694) as set in the context of the Japanese Buddhist world view formulated by Zen master Dōgen (1200–1253) as well as the founder of True Pure Land Buddhism (*Jōdō Shinshū*), Shinran (1173–1263). Omine emphasizes the religio-aesthetic concept of nature in this tradition as having two aspects: "nature as companion and nature as Buddha."[44] When viewed as friend or companion, nature holds the significance of the Buddhist terms "sentient being" or "living things" (*shujo*), such that mountains and rivers, stones and trees, flowers and birds, all have the potential for enlightenment and tread the path to Buddhahood together. The other aspect is nature, just as it is, as sacred Buddha.[45] In this context, he quotes directly from Dōgen's "Sutra of Mountains and Waters" (*Sansui-kyō*), the twenty-ninth chapter of *Shōbōgenzō:* "Mountains and rivers right now are the emerging presence of the ancient Buddhas."[46] As implied by Dōgen's theories of *hōsshin seppō*, "the Dharmakaya expounds the dharma," and *genjōkōan,* "presencing things as they are," mountains, rivers, and all phenomena in nature are presencing forth in their suchness so as to disclose the Buddha-nature inherent in all things, understood in Dōgen's Buddhist philosophy of *uji* or "being-time" as *mujō-busshō,* "impermanence-Buddha-nature." Omine further makes reference to Shinran's Pure Land theory of salvation by the grace of "Other-power" (*tariki*), reformulated in later writings through his famous doctrine *jinen honi,* "naturalness." To be saved by Buddha, to be born in the Pure Land, is simply a function of *jinen* (*shizen*), "nature," defined by Shinran as "from the very beginning made to become so."[47] Omine concludes with his assessment that Shinran's Pure Land Buddhist notion of *jinen honi* reflects an ancient Japanese concept of living nature as the ground and source of human salvation.

The soteriological function of nature in the poetics of Saigyō and the Japanese literary heritage as understood against the background of traditional Buddhist philosophy has also been developed in a fine scholarly essay by William R. LeFleur, "Saigyō and the Buddhist Value of Nature."[48] LaFleur demonstrates that Saigyō must be interpreted in the historical context of a Buddhist tradition including both Saichō (766–822) and Kūkai (774–835) that regards "nature as a locus of soteriological value."[49] This tradition emphasizes the capacity of nature to provide solace and some type of "salvation" for individuals looking for a locus of value other than that provided by city life.[50] Buddhist philosophers in this tradition such as Saichō and Kūkai underscore the potential Buddhahood of all things in nature so as to dissolve the older distinction between sentient (*yūjō*) and insentient (*mujō*) beings.[51] LaFleur argues that Buddhism in Japan developed arguments on behalf of the Buddhahood potentialities of the natural world, because it was compelled to accommodate itself to the long-standing and pre-Buddhist (Shinto) attribution of high religious value to nature as the locus of salvation.[52] He summarizes the soteric function of nature depicted in the poetry of Saigyō as follows:

> The natural "images" in Saigyō's poetry are not something which must themselves be transcended. . . . For Kūkai and for Saigyō, there is no beyond. The concrete phenomenon . . . is both the

symbol and the symbolized. It is the absolute which theorists might call "Emptiness," but which is, in fact, nothing other than the phenomenon itself.[53]

Hence, as LaFleur emphasizes here, the understanding of the religio-aesthetic function of poetic symbols in Saigyō and the Japanese tradition of nature poetry is derived from the Mikkyō (Tantric) tradition of Saichō and Kūkai wherein Buddhahood can be revealed only through "expressive symbols" (*monji*). In accord with Japanese Mikkyō Buddhism, the aesthetic and spiritual symbols of Saigyō's nature poetry do not point beyond themselves to a transcendent or supra-sensible reality over and above the natural world, but fully contain the reality that they symbolize.

In the final analysis, this traditional soteric concept of nature in Japan is itself grounded in a Mahayana Buddhist metaphysic of Emptiness (J. *kū*; Skt. *Śūnyatā*), wherein the mountains and rivers of the natural world, just as they are here and now, are the revelation of impermanence-Buddha-nature in the dynamic and nonsubstantial flux of being-time. According to the Japanese Buddhist doctrine of Emptiness, there is nothing which is "more real" beyond the interdependence of everything in nature. The Buddhist metaphysics of Emptiness with its explicit identification of *samsāra* and *nirvāna* therefore results in the complete dialectical interfusion of transcendence and immanence, absolute and relative, or sacred and profane. In this way, Japanese Buddhism overturns all models of transcendence and dualism so as to effect a radical paradigm-shift from "otherworldliness" to "this-worldliness." For Japanese Buddhism, ultimate reality is not to be found in a transcendent beyond as in the conventional Judeo-Christian paradigm, but in fields of interrelationships that confer to each event a boundless depth of aesthetic and religious value. It is in this philosophical context that nature becomes the "locus of salvation" in traditional Japanese Buddhism as reflected by poet seers following the religio-aesthetic path of *geidō* in Japan.

Conclusion: An East-West Gaia Theory of Nature

In East Asia the delicate harmony between humans and nature has long been maintained through geomancy, what is known in China as *feng shui*. In his book, *Feng Shui: The Chinese Art of Designing A Harmonious Environment*, Derek Walters defines *feng shui* as follows: "A complex blend of sound commonsense, fine aesthetics, and mystical philosophy, *Feng Shui* is a traditional Chinese technique which aims to ensure that all things are in harmony with their environment."[54] Walters further explains that the geomantic philosophy of *feng shui* came to permeate every aspect of traditional Japanese culture, including city planning, temple construction, inkwash painting, flower arranging, and gardening. He adds: "Indeed, there are few areas of Japanese thought which are not in some way affected by the influence of *Feng Shui*."[55] Long before the discovery of the Earth's magnetic field and the modern physics theory of lines of force, nature was conceived as an energy pattern comprised of flowing *ch'i* (J. *ki*) or vital-power, a grid network of intersecting *yin/yang* forces, known as *lung-mei* or "dragon and tiger" currents in the study *of feng shui*.[56] As Tu Wei-Ming puts it in "The Continuity of Being: Chinese Visions of Nature," according to the Chinese "philosophy of *ch'i*," which later spread to Japan, the Earth forms one body as a single living organism created out of the interfusion and convergence of numerous streams of vital force which together establish the wholeness and continuity of nature.

Throughout *A Sand County Almanac* Aldo Leopold also describes the land as "a single living organism," understood as an "energy circuit," a "fountain of energy," a "flow of energy," and a "circuit of life." He thus writes:

> Land, then, is not merely soil; it is a fountain of energy flowing through a circuit of soils, plants, and animals. . . . This interdependence between the complex structure of the land and its smooth functioning as an energy unit is one of its basic attributes.[57]

In this way, the ecological worldview of Aldo Leopold, along with the geomantic philosophy of East Asia based on Taoism and Buddhism, can be seen as providing theoretical support for what is known in environmental philosophy as the Gaia hypothesis. According to Gaia theory, the Earth is a single living organism forming a vast biotic community in which a complex grid network of energy currents or lines of force constitute nature as a synergistic ecosystem of symbiotic relationships in an interconnected web of life.[58] It is precisely such an East-West Gaia theory of living nature that might point a way toward healing our plundered planet, overcoming today's environmental crisis, and establishing a harmony between man and the land.

NOTES

1. J. Baird Callicott and Roger T. Ames, eds., *Nature in Asian Traditions of Thought: Essays in Environmental Philosophy,* (Albany: SUNY Press, 1989).

2. Aldo Leopold, *A Sand County Almanac: With Essays on Conservation from Round River* (New York: Ballantine Books, 1966). See especially "The Land Ethic," pp. 237–64. All citations refer to this edition unless otherwise noted.

3. Ibid., p. 238.

4. Ibid., pp. 238–39.

5. Ibid., p. 239.

6. Ibid., p. 240.

7. Ibid., p. 243.

8. Ibid.

9. Ibid., p. 246.

10. Ibid., p. 258.

11. For a careful scholarly analysis of Aldo Leopold's land ethic in relation to his land aesthetic as formulated in *A Sand County Almanac,* see J. B. Callicott, "The Land Aesthetic" in J. B. Callicott, ed., *Companion to A Sand County Almanac* (Madison: University of Wisconsin Press, 1987), chap. 7, pp. 157–71.

12. Aldo Leopold, "Foreword," in Callicott, *Companion,* p. 281. This statement is the opening sentence in Aldo Leopold's original foreword to *Great Possessions* (the author's own title of what later became *A Sand County Almanac*), dated 31 July 1947. However, the revised foreword dated 4 March 1948 is the one with which readers are now familiar.

13. "Conservation Esthetic" is the final essay in the enlarged edition of *A Sand County Almanac,* subtitled *"With Essays on Conservation from Round River,* "edited by Luna B. Leopold, the author's son, and first published by Ballantine Books in 1966. "The Land Ethic" is the final essay in the original edition, subtitled, "And Sketches Here and There," published posthumously by Oxford University Press in 1949. However, Leopold's manuscript of the book, *Great Possessions,* conformed to the arrangement of the enlarged edition of 1966. According to Dennis Ribbens, "The Making of *A Sand County Almanac,"* in J. Baird Callicott, ed., *Companion to A Sand County Almanac,* "possibly the most important change to the manuscript after Leopold's death was the decision to shift 'The Land Ethic' from its original first position in Part III to its present final position" (p. 107). Confirming Ribbens' information, Curt Meine, *Aldo Leopold: His Life and Work,* says that in the process of preparing Leopold's manuscript for publication, "'The Land Ethic' was moved to the end of Part III, 'The Upshot'" (p. 524). Thus, it appears that the author himself

intended for "Conservation Esthetic" to be the final essay of the book that became *A Sand County Almanac.*

14. Leopold, *A Sand County Almanac,* p. xix.

15. Ibid., p. 262.

16. In the context of developing his "architectonic" of theories, the American process philosopher Charles Sanders Peirce suggested a "hierarchy of the normative sciences" in which logic depends on ethics and ethics depends on aesthetics. See *Philosophical Writings of Peirce: Selected and Edited with an Introduction by Justus Buchler* (New York: Dover Publishing, 1955), p. 62.

17. Eugene C. Hargrove, *Foundations of Environmental Ethics* (Englewood Cliffs: Prentice Hall, 1989). See especially chap. 3 on "Aesthetic and Scientific Attitudes" (pp. 77–103), and a section entitled "The Aesthetics of Wildlife Preservation" (pp. 122–23) from chap. 4 on "Wildlife Protection Attitudes."

18. J. Baird Callicott, "The Metaphysical Implications of Ecology," in Callicott and Ames, *Nature in Asian Traditions Thought,* pp. 51–64.

19. Ibid., p. 57.

20. Ibid., p. 58.

21. Ibid., p. 59.

22. Arne Naess, "The Shallow and the Deep, Long-Range Ecology Movement: A Summary" *Inquiry* 16 (1973): 98.

23. For examples of Alfred North Whitehead's concept of nature as aesthetic and creative process in relation to his general philosophy of organism, see *Concept of Nature* (Cambridge: Cambridge University Press, 1971); "The Romantic Reaction," in *Science and the Modern World* (New York: Collier Macmillan, 1925): "The Order of Nature" and "Organisms and Environment," in *Process and Reality* (New York: Collier Macmillan, 1978); and "Nature and Life," in *Modes of Thought* (New York: Macmillan, 1968).

24. Roger T. Ames, "Putting the *Te* Back into Taoism," in Callicott and Ames, *Nature in Asian Traditions of Thought,* pp. 113–44.

25. Toshihiko Izutsu, *Toward a Philosophy of Zen Buddhism* (Boulder: Prajna Press, 1982), especially "The Field Structure of Ultimate Reality," pp. 45–49.

26. Nishida first developed his notion of *basho* or field as the fundamental concept in his philosophy of Nothingness in *Hataraku mono kara miru mono e* (From the Acting to the Seeing), published in 1927, included in *Nishida Kitarō Zenshū* (Tokyo: Iwanami Shoten, 1947–53), Vol. 4, pp. 207–89.

27. Matao Noda, "East-West Synthesis in Kitarō Nishida," in *Philosophy East and West* 4 (1955): 350.

28. Watsuji Tetsurō, *Ningen no gaku toshite no rinrigaku* (Tokyo: Iwanami Shoten, 1936).

29. Yuasa Yasuo, *The Body: Toward an Eastern Mind-Body Theory,* ed. T. P. Kasulis, trans. Nagatomo Shigenori and T. P. Kasulis (New York: SUNY Press, 1987), p. 38.

30. Watsuji Tetsurō, *Fūdo ningengakuteki kosatsu,* 2nd ed. (Tokyo: Iwanami Shoten, 1951). For an English translation, see *A Climate: A Philosophical Study,* trans. Geoffrey Bownas (Tokyo: Japanese National Commission for UNESCO, 1961); now reprinted as a volume in the new series, Classics of Modern Japanese Thought and Culture (Westport, Conn.: Greenwood Press, 1989).

31. Ibid., p. 38.

32. Hubertus Tellenbach and Bin Kimura, "The Japanese Concept of Nature," in Callicott and Ames, *Nature in Asian Traditions of Thought,* pp. 154–55.

33. Daisaku Ikeda, *Selected Lectures on the Gosho* (Tokyo: Nichiren Shoshu International Center, 1979), p. 22.

34. Ibid., p. 23.

35. For an account of Hua-yen (J. Kegon; Skt. Avatamsaka) Buddhism developed from the standpoint of Alfred North Whitehead's philosophy of organism, see Steve Odin, *Process Metaphysics and Hua-yen Buddhism* (Albany: SUNY Press, 1982).

36. Francis H. Cook, "The Jewel Net of Indra," in Callicott and Ames, *Nature in Asian Traditions of Thought,* p. 213.

37. Ibid., p. 214.

38. Ibid., p. 226.

39. D. T. Suzuki, *Zen and Japanese Culture* (Princeton: Princeton University Press, 1959), p. 354.

40. Ibid., pp. 351–52.

41. E. F. Schumacher, *Small is Beautiful: Economics as if People Mattered* (New York: Harper & Row, 1973). See especially pt. 1, chap. 4, "Buddhist Economics," pp. 53–62.

42. Leopold, *A Sand County Almanac,* p. xix.

43. Sōseki Natsume, *Kusamakura* (Tokyo: Kodansha, 1972). For an English translation, see *The Three-Cornered World,* trans. Alan Tumey (Tokyo: Charles E. Tuttle, 1968).

44. Omine Akira, "Probing the Japanese Experience of Nature," translated from *Nihon-teki Shizen no Keifu* by Dennis Hirota in *Chanoyu Quarterly: Tea and the Arts of Japan,* no. 51 (1987).

45. Ibid., p. 7.

46. Ibid., p. 19.

47. Ibid., p. 28.

48. William R. LaFleur, "Saigyō and the Buddhist Value of Nature," in Callicott and Ames, *Nature in Asian Traditans of Thaught,* pp. 183–209.

49. Ibid., p. 196.

50. Ibid.

51. Ibid., pp. 186–87.
52. Ibid., p. 195.
53. Ibid., p. 203.
54. Derek Walters, *Feng Shui: The Chinese Art of Designing A Harmonious Environment* (New York: Simon & Schuster, 1988), p. 8.
55. Ibid., p. 14.
56. Ibid., p. 10.
57. Leopold, *A Sand County Almanac,* pp. 253–54.
58. See J. E. Lovelock, *Gaia: A New Look at Life on Earth* (New York: Oxford University Press, 1979).

CHAPTER 14

Dōgen, Deep Ecology, and the Ecological Self

DEANE CURTIN

> . . . to see mountains and rivers is to see Buddha-nature.
> To see Buddha-nature is to see a donkey's jaw or a
> horse's mouth.
>
> 'This' is Buddha-nature. . . . We can find this in everyday
> life, eating a meal or drinking green tea.
>
> —Dōgen[1]

INTRODUCTION

Following the lead of Arne Naess,[2] deep ecologists contend that the most urgent task of ecophilosophy is the articulation of a new understanding of the self. The autonomous mental substance of Descartes, which still permeates Western thinking, is alienated from nature. This conception encourages environmental degradation since damage to nature does not directly affect an immaterial self. Naess therefore advocates that the narrow, Cartesian self must be expanded to include identification with the whole of nature—nature as Self—thus, eliminating alienation, and with it the deep causes of our mistreatment of the environment.

In exploring a range of possibilities for a new ecological self, I draw heavily on the Japanese philosopher Dōgen (1200–1253).[3] Dōgen is often cited by deep ecologists, along with the philosopher Spinoza and the poet Robinson Jeffers, as one of the progenitors of deep ecology. In Devall and Sessions' *Deep Ecology*, the distinguished Sōtō Zen roshi,

Robert Aitken, writes about "Gandhi, Dōgen, and Deep Ecology." Devall and Sessions themselves quote liberally from Dōgen in explaining deep ecology. Naess has argued for the unity, though not the identity, of Spinoza's philosophy, Mahāyāna Buddhism, and deep ecology. Warwick Fox quotes Dōgen approvingly at the conclusion of his recent book *Toward a Transpersonal Ecology*. Indeed, many deep ecologists have been influenced by Buddhist philosophy, often by Dōgen in particular, including Devall, Naess, Aitken, Fox, Carla Deicke, Joan Halifax, Dolores LaChapelle, Gary Snyder, John Seed, Jeremy Hayward, and Andrew McLaughlin.[4]

I do not focus on Dōgen, however, because I think environmental philosophers should turn East for enlightenment. If anything, the constant references to Eastern philosophy as a whole in the deep ecology literature have obscured what is unique and individual in Dōgen. Rather, my purpose in examining his thought is to show that deep ecologists have neglected an important conception of a transformed sense of self. Starting from nondualist, nonanthropocentric premises that are consistent with the theoretical framework of deep ecology, Dōgen turns out to be saying something fundamentally different about the ecological self than Spinoza, Jeffers, or Naess. Although I do not develop the point fully here, I believe Dōgen's characterization of the self is even more sympathetic to a possible version of ecofeminism than to deep ecology.

I confine my interest in Dōgen's philosophy to two areas.[5] The first is his idea of Buddha-nature as the impermanence of *all* beings, not just sentient beings. Dōgen thus lays a nondualistic, nonanthropocentric grounding common to all beings (sentient and nonsentient) that reveals their interconnectedness. The second is Dōgen's understanding of the relational self as it is shaped by his concept of Buddha-nature.

Buddha-Nature

Early in his masterpiece, the *Shōbōgenzō* (Treasury of the True Dharma Eye), Dōgen takes up the question of Buddha-nature (*Busshō*) in a fascicle of the same name. Dōgen's strategy is to begin with classical formulations of Buddha-nature that were well known to his audience.[6] Then, while partially endorsing Buddhist tradition, he also transforms their meanings. As Norman Waddell and Abe Masao have noted, Dōgen often sacrifices grammatical correctness in his translations from Chinese to Japanese for the illumination of an important and original philosophical point.[7]

He begins by quoting from the *Nirvāna Sūtra,* the principal Mahāyāna sutra on Buddha-nature. The passage, in a traditional translation, reads, "All sentient beings without exception have the Buddha-nature. . . ." By quoting the *Sūtra,* he acknowledges tradition.[8] However, he also knew that this formulation is open to the charge of dualism. Saying that all sentient beings *have* Buddha-nature distinguishes Buddha-nature from the beings that have it, treating it as a potential quality of sentient beings.

The traditional formulation also implies a distinction between daily practice and the actualization of enlightenment. Meditation and ordinary, daily practice are maintained, accordingly, not as ends in themselves, but only for the sake of achieving a future end, an end that exists now only as a potentiality.

To remove these hints of dualism, Dōgen twists the expression "All sentient beings without exception *have* the Buddha-nature" to read "All sentient beings without exception *are* Buddha-nature."[9] Buddha-nature, for Dōgen, is not a quality that sentient beings can *have* (or lack); rather, all sentient beings *are* Buddha-nature. Buddha-nature is fundamental reality.

A second feature of Dōgen's nondualism is the scope of Buddha-nature. Buddhist tradition often restricted it to those beings that have the potential for enlightenment, either in this life (humans) or in a future life (other sentient beings that can be reborn as human beings). Nonsentient entities such as rivers and mountains are excluded. Dōgen, however, refuses to accept the sentient/nonsentient distinction as fundamental. He says emphatically:

> Impermanence is in itself Buddha-nature. . . . Therefore, the very impermanency of grass and tree, thicket and forest, is the Buddha-nature. Nations and lands, mountains and rivers, are impermanent because they are Buddha-nature. Supreme and complete enlightenment, because it is the Buddha-nature, is impermanent. Great Nirvana, because it is impermanent, is the Buddha-nature.[10]

Dōgen is both radical and traditional in his treatment of Buddha-nature. To be nondualist, he believes, Buddhist philosophy must commit to the fundamental reality of all beings as Buddha-nature, not just sentient beings. This point is explained, however, by reference to the most traditional of Buddhist commitments: the impermanence of all being.

These ideas are expressed most strikingly and poetically in the "Mountains and Waters Sūtra" (*Sansui-kyō*). There, Dōgen challenges his audience to understand mountains and rivers themselves as *sūtras*, as expressions of the Buddha. He quotes a Chinese source, "The green mountains are always walking; a stone woman gives birth to a child at night," and comments:

> Mountains do not lack the qualities of mountains. Therefore they always abide in ease and always walk. You should examine in detail this quality of the mountains' walking.
> Mountains' walking is just like human walking. Accordingly, do not doubt mountains' walking even though it does not look the same as human walking. The buddha ancestors' words point to walking. This is fundamental understanding. You should penetrate these words.[11]

Taken out of context, these lines might be read as an anthropomorphic projection: "Mountains' walking is *just like* human walking." But instead of implying that the mountains' being should be understood in terms of human being, the metaphor of walking points to a dehomocentric understanding of *all* being. Mountains and humans abide together in their impermanence.

Abe puts this dehomocentric reversal succinctly:

> When Dōgen emphasizes "all beings" in connection with the Buddha-nature, he definitely implies that man's samsāra, i.e., recurring cycle of birth and death, can be properly and completely emancipated not in the "living" dimension, but in the "being" dimension. In other words, it is not by overcoming generation-extinction common to all living beings, but only by doing away with appearance-disappearance, common to all things, that man's birth-death problem can be completely solved. Dōgen finds the basis for man's liberation in a thoroughly cosmological dimension. *Here Dōgen reveals a most radical Buddhist dehomocentrism.*[12]

We fail to understand life and death, the fundamental *human* problem, if we deal with it only in human terms. We fail, as well, if we deal with it in terms of all sentient beings. The life-and-death of human beings is subsumed by the generation-and-extinction (impermanence) of all sentient beings; in turn, the generation-and-extinction of all sentient beings is subsumed by what Abe calls the "appearance-and-disappearance" of *all* beings. There will be no release from human suffering, that is, until human beings experience themselves in the "cosmological dimension" of all beings, until they understand that "mountain's walking is just like human walking."

THE SELF

Dōgen was emphatic in his rejection of two faulty accounts of the self. The self is not an organic entity, like a seed, out of which other things grow. On this metaphor, Buddha-nature stands in a dualistic relation to its "fruit." Dōgen, therefore, rejects a teleological explanation of self in the style of Aristotle. Self does not become real at the end of a long process. Rather, Buddha-nature is completely actual at each moment.

He also rejects an ancient view called the Senika heresy according to which there is a permanent self that is detached from change in the phenomenal world. Of those who espouse this view he says, "... they have not encountered their true self."[13] His charge is phenomenological: such people have not yet had a certain experience; they have not "encountered" their true self as multiple, as interpenetrating other beings.

Dōgen contends that the introspective search for an enduring, autonomous self is futile. To understand the self is to "forget" the Cartesian self. A famous passage from the *Genjōkoan* of Dōgen states this point precisely:

> To study the Buddha way is to study the self. To study the self is to forget the self. To forget the self is to be actualized by myriad things. When actualized by myriad things, your body and mind as well as the bodies and minds of others drop away. No trace of realization remains, and this no-trace continues endlessly.[14]

To "forget" the self is to penetrate the delusion of the Cartesian self. It is to "Know that there are innumerable beings in yourself"[15] and thereby to realize one's true self in the cosmological dimension. Dōgen makes a Humean point: careful phenomenological examination does not reveal a "singular" Cartesian self, but "innumerable beings" present to multiple spheres in which beings exist in relation to other beings.[16]

Dōgen advises that to meet this true self, one must "just sit"; one must practice seated meditation (*zazen*). Zazen is a practice that reveals Buddha-nature through "undivided activity" (*zenki*), activity concentrated right here and right now. It brings one into the "presence of things as they are" (*genjōkōan*). One of Dōgen's most revealing descriptions of this state of direct presence reads:

> When you ride in a boat, your body and mind and the environs together are the undivided activity of the boat. The entire earth and the entire sky are both the undivided activity of the boat.[17]

What exists at that moment is the undivided activity of "the boat." Body, mind, boat, and environs are not separate. Neither are they absolutely identical: "although not one, not different; although not different, not the same; although not the same, not many."[18]

This passage shows that there *is* a self for Dōgen; the self does not disappear or merge into the cosmos. He never denies that there are multiple, provisional, contextually defined borders that shape the sense of self. He maintains difference. Self is always experienced *in relation* to other beings, however, and those relations define what it means to be a self. Indeed, each person's set of defining relations at a given moment are unique.

The realized person, then, is neither a Cartesian unchanging self nor an Aristotelian potentiality. A true self is one that practices undivided activity in the present moment, a practice that reveals the interpenetration (Buddha-nature) of all beings. In each moment there is full and complete realization, unlike the Aristotelian and the Cartesian selves; there is direct experience of the non-substantiality of the self. Thomas Kasulis calls this experience "person as presence."[19]

We are now in a position to connect Dōgen's earlier dogged insistence on the impermanence of Buddha nature with his account of the self. To begin with the distinction between sentience and nonsentience, rather than with the impermanence of *all* beings, is to encourage a delusory understanding of the self in relation to other beings. It moves toward a self that stands apart from "nature," an ideal Cartesian observer that judges rather than participates. It moves away from the ordinary, impermanent self that interpenetrates ordinary beings in daily life. The Senika heresy provides a hierarchical, dualistic picture of self in relation to nature. For Dōgen, this hierarchy is a stairway to delusion, the delusion that permanence is fundamental reality.

Buddha Nature, Self, and Everyday Life

While Dōgen often focuses on seated meditation, and on co-enlightenment with mountains and waters, his nondualism requires that these are never separated from the practice of ordinary, daily life. It has often been noted, for example, that a meeting with a Chinese temple cook was instrumental in Dōgen's view that practice and realization are one. In *Dōgen's Formative Years in China*, Takashi James Kodera relates that during a three-month period when Dōgen was confined aboard ship before being allowed to enter China, he had a conversation with a Chinese temple cook from A-yü-wang Mountain. The monk was sixty-one years old and had traveled a great distance to purchase Japanese mushrooms. Kodera writes:

> Dōgen was deeply impressed with the devotion of the old monk and asked him to stay the night on the ship. The chief cook declined the offer for fear that it might interfere with the normal procedures at his monastery the following day. Dōgen wondered why someone else could not prepare the meal in his place. He asked why a monk as senior as this one remained as chief cook and did not instead engage in sitting in meditation in pursuit of the Way. The old monk laughed loudly and said to Dōgen: "My good man from a foreign land, you still do not comprehend discipline; you still do not know the words."[20]

Dōgen, then a headstrong, young intellectual, misunderstood the old monk because he thought daily chores were in conflict with formal pursuit of enlightenment through seated meditation. His experience in China, however, especially this and other meetings with chief temple cooks, taught him that he was mistaken.

The Mahāyāna claim that nirvāna and samsāra (birth and rebirth) are the same is brashly expressed by Dōgen through the identity of ordinary, everyday activities with nirvāna. Nirvāna is not reached suddenly at the end of a process that leaves daily life behind; it is realized in mindful, everyday action.[21] The fact that vegetarianism has been an important daily commitment in Buddhist philosophy, whereas it has usually been neglected in hierarchical, abstractionist philosophies, is hardly an accident. It reflects a deep difference in the kinds of practices that are regarded as philosophically informative.

Several of Dōgen's most engaging writings concern a reorientation of life toward the ordinariness, the dailiness, of life, which can occur through mindfulness about food, personal hygiene, and care for others. In *Fushuku-hampō* (Mealtime Regulations), he quotes the *Vimalakirti Sūtra:* "When one is identified with the food one eats, one is identified with the whole universe; when we are one with the whole universe we are one with the food we eat." He goes on to comment on this passage: "If the whole universe is the Dharma then food is also the Dharma: if the universe is Truth then food is Truth: if one is illusion then the other is illusion: if the whole universe is Buddha then food is also Buddha."[22] The experience of co-enlightenment, which is expressed paradoxically in talk of "mountains' walking," is here expressed plainly and intuitively. Proper relationship to Buddha-nature—mindful practice of the truth of impermanence—is right before us all the time in ordinary life.

Undivided activity is an "everyday activity" (*Kajō*) for Dōgen. In remarks reminiscent of the co-enlightenment of persons and mountains, he says:

> In the domain of buddha ancestors, drinking tea and eating rice is everyday activity. This having tea and rice has been transmitted over many years and is present right now. Thus the buddha ancestors' vital activity of having tea and rice comes to us. . . . From this you should clearly understand that the thoughts and words of buddha ancestors are their everyday tea and rice. Ordinary coarse tea and plain rice are buddha's thoughts—ancestors' words. Because buddha ancestors prepare tea and rice, tea and rice maintain buddha ancestors. Accordingly, they need no powers other than this tea and rice, and they have no need to use powers as buddha ancestors.[23]

Mindful practice of daily relations with food counteracts the abstractionist tendencies of people (particularly philosophers) to think that only the permanent and abstract are fully real. Food is the dharma because direct presence to the impermanence of food reveals the arbitrariness of borders that we construct when abstracting from immediate experience. Since food becomes the self, and then becomes not-self again (as sayings posted near toilets in Zen monasteries recall), the self must be reconstructed as impermanent and relational.

DŌGEN AND DEEP ECOLOGY

Naess and Fox have argued that the core of deep ecology is the expansion of the Cartesian self to the broader, inclusive, cosmological Self that identifies with all of nature. We have seen that Dōgen speaks of a relational sense of self that experiences interpenetration with nature in seated meditation and in mindful everyday living. The question I wish to address now is whether the fully realized deep ecological Self is the same as Dōgen's self.

Deep ecologists, Spinoza, Jeffers, and Dōgen, all aspire to a nondualistic, nonanthropocentric orientation that makes their work interesting and important to environmental philosophers. However, the connections between Dōgen and deep ecology as they have been made up to this point are simply too broad to be useful. They conceal Dōgen's most distinctive contribution to the philosophy of

self, the centrality of mindfulness about everyday life in formu-
lating an ecological self that is nondualistic, nonhierarchical and
dehomocentric.

Consider what Naess says in his classic article "Identification as a
Source of Deep Ecological Attitudes":

> There is a process of ever-widening identification and ever-narrowing
> alienation which widens the self. The self is as comprehensive as the
> totality of our identifications. Or, more succinctly, our Self is that with
> which we identify. Identification is a spontaneous, non-rational, but not
> irrational, process through which *the interest or interests of another*
> *being are reacted to as our own interest or interests.*

He says clearly that by identification he does not mean identity. Identification, according to Naess, preserves diversity; we identify with
the interests of "another being."

Having acknowledged diversity, however, he amplifies his position
in puzzling ways, puzzling because the holist, hierarchical language
seems to deny what he has just asserted:

> Through identification, higher level unit is experienced: from identi-
> fying with 'one's nearest,' higher unities are created through circles
> of friends, local communities, tribes, compatriots, races, humanity,
> life, and ultimately, as articulated by religious and philosophic
> leaders, unity with the supreme whole, the 'world' in a broader and
> deeper sense than the usual. I prefer a terminology such that the
> largest units are not said to comprise life *and* 'the not living.' One
> may broaden the sense of living so that any natural whole, however
> large, is a living whole.

There is a hierarchy in Naess' construction of the process of identification that moves from parts to "unity with the supreme whole."
(The very distinction between self and Self by means of capitalization indicates this point.) While he grants that there are multiple
ways in which "oneness" can be experienced, including the political
means of Gandhi, he also says, "This way of thinking and feeling
at its maximum corresponds to that of the enlightened, or yogi,
who sees "the same," the *ātman,* and who is not alienated from
anything."[24]

In these passages, Naess commits exactly the error Dōgen warns
against in *Busshō.* He warned against the Senika heresy according to
which the Self is a permanent entity that stands above the manifold
changes of nature. Yet, for similar reasons, Dōgen was emphatically

rejecting the Indian idea of *ātman*, the Hindu permanent self. The Buddhist philosopher David Kalupahana has written:

> The self (*ātman*) . . . is the permanent and eternal reality unsmeared by all the change and fluctuations that take place in the world of experience. In fact, it is the basis of the unity of empirical experience of variety and multiplicity, of change and mutability, of past, present and future. The real self and the unreal or mutable self, the transcendental apperception and empirical consciousness are graphically presented with the parable of the "two birds" perched on one branch, the one simply watching and the other enjoying the fruit.[25]

Kalupahana points out that the distinction between real self and unreal self becomes normatively charged when connected to *brahman* and the caste system. The distinction is both ontological and ethical. The ontological distinction rests on a conceptual hierarchy that is remarkably familiar to Western philosophers, a hierarchy that places the permanent and the eternal above change and mutability, unity above variety and multiplicity. The Self as *ātman* is better (higher) because it experiences the world as, in Naess' terms, "oneness."

Naess frequently distinguishes between the philosophical and popular uses of terms. There is no doubt that he has often been misinterpreted because of his critics' failure to appreciate this point. But it is doubtful whether the distinction is helpful here. It is one thing to choose a term because it carries helpful popular associations; it is another to choose a term whose precise meaning *contradicts* what Naess says about the recognition of diversity. Naess' explanation of the ultimate realization of Self in terms of *ātman* is, therefore, deeply puzzling regardless of whether it is intended to be popular or philosophical.

These troubling connections between the deep ecological self and an eternal self are worsened when other deep ecologists follow Naess in adopting the part/whole model to explain the expansion of self to Self. Freya Mathews is typical of many in distinguishing between atomistic (Cartesian) and holistic (deep ecological) ways of understanding the self. Both understand the relationship as one of "part and whole." However, in contrast to atomism, the holism that Mathews endorses provides that "each element, being logically constituted by its relations with the other elements, is conditioned by the whole."[26]

In spite of casting the two models of self as *distinct* alternatives, it is significant that, in Mathews' own words, they depend on the *same* hierarchical model of part to whole. If they are identical in respect to their model of explanation, where is their difference? This question leads to the suspicion that Self is the Cartesian ego writ large. It would appear that *this* version of the deep ecological Self is still conceptually tied to the old hierarchical project whose goal is to find an entity that is whole, "permanent," "unsmeared by change." The influence of Spinoza weighs heavily here, and like the Hindu *ātman,* moves deep ecology in the direction of a hierarchical, nonrelational Self. Spinoza, Descartes' best critic, clearly saw that Descartes' claim for human minds—that they are independent substances—must fail because, unlike God, human minds are neither epistemically nor ontologically independent. They require a rational explanation in terms of an external "cause," and they are not self-existent.

Descartes' mistake taught Spinoza that only "the whole" can be truly independent in both senses, so that only God, or nature, can qualify as substance. Substances are nonrelational for Spinoza because, by definition, there is nothing else to which they *can* relate. Similarly, Naess and others are in danger of defining the Self nonrelationally. The whole *cannot* relate to anything else just because it is the whole.

I grant that there are many passages in the deep ecology literature that are at odds with this reading. Naess himself has said in an unpublished essay:

> In my outline of a philosophy (Ecosophy T) 'Self-realization!' is the logically (derivationally) supreme norm, but it is not an eternal or permanent Self that is postulated. When the formulation is made more precise, it is seen that the Self in question is a symbol of identification with an absolute maximum range of beings.

With Buddhist philosophy in mind, Bill Devall has written that " . . . all is impermanent. All is changing." Some of his essays can be read as moving in the direction of a recognition of ordinariness as the context in which the ecoself is awakened. Gary Snyder's writings on Dōgen often display an acute sense of the impermanence that is everyday life.[27]

The problem is that the deep ecology literature has endorsed *both* a holist and nonholist, a nonrelational and relational, understanding of Self. There has not been clear, unequivocal recognition that there are (despite Mathews) *three* competing models of self: the Cartesian atomic self, the Spinozist, holist Self expanded to the supreme whole, and Dōgen's relational self. Unlike the Cartesian and Spinozist selves, the relational self cannot be expressed in terms of parts and wholes.

It would be a fundamental misreading of Dōgen's Buddha-nature to say that it is the supreme whole of all impermanent beings, and that the "myriad things" are parts. There is no sense of ascending to higher and higher unities that lead to a "supreme whole" in Dōgen. Abe Masao puts this point succinctly by contrasting Spinoza's understanding of nature with Dōgen's:

> In Spinoza the One God has, in so far as we know, two "attributes" thought (*cogitatio*) and extension (*extensio*); particular and finite things are modifications, being called the "modes" of God, which depend on, and are conditioned by, the divine and infinite being.

But Dōgen's "myriad things" cannot be understood as *modes* of Buddha-nature. They are, rather, fully real as simple (relational) beings. Abe writes:

> A pine tree, for instance, is not a mode of God as Substance, but a mode of "what," namely a mode without a modifier. Therefore, a pine tree is really a pine tree in itself, no more and no less.[28]

Dōgen's Buddha-nature is not a code word for metaphysical unity.

Dōgen's Buddha-nature captures both the unity and diversity of nature without resorting to hierarchical abstractions. The phenomenological description he gives of direct presence speaks as much of diversity as of unity: "although not one, not different; although not different, not the same; although not the same, not many."[29] When Dōgen says "not one," he marks the fact that the direct experience of the everydayness of life is the experience of interpenetration without ultimate, metaphysical unity. An ecological consciousness for Dōgen is not, as for Jeffers or Naess, an experience of "wholeness." It is an experience of interpenetration with a ". . . concrete existence—a 'this.'" "Thus Buddha-nature is a 'what,' a concrete, real being."[30]

DŌGEN AND THE DEEP ECOLOGY-ECOFEMINISM DEBATE

Recently, Fox attempted to extend Naess' work on identification with nature by distinguishing three bases of identification: the personal, the ontological, and the cosmological. Roughly, these coincide with ecofeminism, a Zennist or Heideggerian approach, and deep ecology. We are in a position to see that by driving apart ecofeminism and the

Zen of Dōgen, Fox misrepresents both. In both cases, his implicitly hierarchical thinking does not allow him to appreciate the coincidence of the personal and the public.

Fox charged that Jim Cheney's version of ecofeminism is incoherent because it is anthropocentric. Expansion of self occurs for Cheney through a "personal," gendered context rather than through cosmological identification with the whole. Fox's conclusion is that "The cosmological/transpersonal voice *is* a 'different voice' from the personal voice, but it does not seem to respect gender boundaries."[31] A transformative ecophilosophy is not inherently feminist for Fox.

Dōgen offers an insight into why we should resist Fox's mutually exclusive distinction between the personal and the ontological. There *is* an ontological phenomenology in Dōgen. Through mindfulness about everyday practices, the ecological self is awakened as we immediately experience interpenetration with that pine tree which is "really a pine tree." Everyday mindfulness draws us out of our deluded, narrow selves through the experience of co-enlightenment.

But Dōgen's recommendations are intensely personal as well. Each mindful act is an act of personal ontological commitment, a moment-to-moment reaffirmation of multiple selves in multiple relations to other beings. The movement in Dōgen's thought is to undercut the public/private, personal/impersonal distinctions on which Fox's classification rests.

Similarly, ecofeminism is not merely a personal approach to the self. For feminists, "the personal is the political." Women have been marginalized through the public/private dualism. Women's lives have been constructed as less important than men's lives because they are constructed as merely domestic and private. Feminists do not protest this point by claiming that their lives ought to be constructed as public.[32] To do so would just reinforce the public/private distinction, and further marginalize the domain of the ordinary. Rather, their theoretical aspirations are nondualistic. They argue that the public/private distinction cannot be maintained as it has been espoused by the Western liberal (atomic) self. The kind of self required by the public/private distinction does not exist. In basing his criticism on a version of the public/private split, Fox affirms a dualistic stance when he claims to reject it.

Dōgen would also challenge the way Fox draws the distinction between ontological and cosmological identification. Ontologically based identification "refers to experiences of commonality with all that is that are brought about through deep-seated realization of the fact *that* things are." Though this view, which he associates with Zen Buddhism, cannot be adequately expressed in words, according to Fox, it points toward the experience of "this state of being, this sense of commonality with all that is simply by virtue of the fact *that* it is, at a certain moment. Things *are*! There is something rather than nothing! Amazing!"

In comparison, "cosmologically based identification refers to experiences of commonality with all that is that are brought about through deep-seated realization of the fact that we and all other entities are aspects of a single unfolding reality." Fox confirms that

> the inspiration for this concept derives from Gandhi and Spinoza, both of whom explicated their views within the context of a monistic metaphysics, that is, within the context of a cosmology that emphasized the fundamental unity of existence. Gandhi was committed to Advaita Vedanta (i.e., monistic or, more literally, nondual Hinduism). . . . Spinoza developed a philosophy that conceived of all entities as *modes* of a single substance. . . .

Despite the apparent intellectual distinction, the difference between ontological and cosmological identification is practical rather than theoretical. Fox says that "it would seem to be much easier to communicate and inspire a cosmologically based sense of identification with all that is rather than an ontologically based identification."[33]

It is simply not true, however, that the distinction between the self in Zen literature (at least as represented by the Zen philosopher most often cited by deep ecologists, Dōgen) and the deep ecological, Spinozist, Gandhian (Advaita Vedānta) Self is one of practice rather than theory. Fox does not to recognize that the holist self, which is part of a "monistic metaphysics," is not the relational self.

Fox's characterization of the Zen self reads more like a description of the first premise of the medieval Christian cosmological argument for the existence of a holist God than Dōgen: "Things *are*! There is something rather than nothing! Amazing!" The basic Buddhist commitment to the impermanence of all being, is not the same as the Christian challenge to give a metaphysical explanation for why there is something rather than nothing. The demand for an ultimate metaphysical explanation of existence only makes sense in an abstractionist metaphysics that marginalizes everyday experience. Ordinary things, according to such a metaphysic, "demand an explanation," an explanation that only terminates in the whole.

DŌGEN AND ECOFEMINISM

Feminists, ecofeminists in particular, have criticized deep ecologists for their attempt to find oneness with nature through Eastern philosophy. This attempt is viewed as a maneuver to overcome masculine alienation without confronting the connections between sexism and naturism. I am sympathetic to this charge. In looking to Dōgen for clarification, I am not implying that ecofeminists ought to look to the East. Neither am I suggesting that the ways in which Dōgen is suggestive will be of interest to all ecofeminists. Ecofeminism is a variety of approaches, some of which reject any hint of spirituality, even the "a pine tree is really a pine tree" literalism of Dōgen.

Early on, I said that I was interested in the *particulars* of Dōgen's philosophy, and that a general turn to the East can obscure the individuality of Dōgen. Philosophers ought to be willing to sharpen their views against those of any important philosopher. Dōgen is relevant to the deep ecology/ecofeminism debate because he provides a common ground between deep ecologists and ecofeminists that could result in productive conversation. Those who are familiar with the ecofeminist literature on the ecological self will have noticed already that there are some tempting connections between ecofeminism and Dōgen. Consider only two examples: one from the work of Val Plumwood and the other from the work of Jim Cheney.

Val Plumwood, in an article titled, "Nature, Self, and Gender: Feminism, Environmental Philosophy, and the Critique of Rationalism," concludes:

> Thus it is unnecessary to adopt any of the stratagems of deep ecology—the indistinguishable self, the expanded self, or the transpersonal self—in order to provide an alternative to anthropocentrism or human self-interest. This can be better done through the relational account of the self, which clearly recognizes the distinctness of nature but also our relationship and continuity with it. On this relational account, respect for the other results neither from the containment of the self nor from a transcendence of self, but is an *expression* of self in relationship, not egoistic self as merged with the other but self as embedded in a network of essential relationships with distinct others.[34]

Not a single word of Plumwood's summary requires alteration to describe Dōgen's self: for Dōgen the self is not indistinguishable from nature; nor is it an expanded or transpersonal self that becomes one with the whole. Dōgen's is a relational self that is distinct, but defines itself through mindfulness about its network of essential relationships. Dōgen's relational self resists the abstractionist language of "the whole" by highlighting the provisional, contextual borders of the self in relation to other things: *this* pine tree, and *this* meal.

In a similar fashion, Jim Cheney has written of the differences between the ways self is defined in a gift economy and a market economy: "In a gift economy . . . selves tend to get defined in terms of what I call 'defining relationships'—where our relationships with others are central to our understanding of who we are."[35] The idea that a self is defined, not through relationship with a metaphysical whole, but through defining relationships with specific others, is also deeply reminiscent of Dōgen. The relational self of Dōgen, then, intersects neatly with at least these two ecofeminist accounts of the self.

A second way in which Dōgen coincides with ecofeminist interests is that his radical nondualism leads him to provide a sympathetic account—rare in all the world's philosophical literature—of ordinary, daily practices. It is not accidental that these practices are expected of women in Japan and elsewhere. I conclude by sketching out one possible version of the ecofeminist self that is informed by Dōgen's emphasis on the ordinary.

Dōgen was not a feminist. Early in his career, nevertheless, he was forceful in advocating the view that women and men are equally capable of enlightenment. It is possible he realized that the kinds of ordinary activities through which enlightenment can come—and about which Dōgen wrote in minute detail—are just those sorts of activities that are typically regarded as "women's work."

I see Dōgen as challenging the same kinds of philosophical hierarchies that have plagued and marginalized women. Plato's metaphor of the cave set the tone for Western philosophy by depicting ordinary, daily life as a mere shadowy reflection of the Good and the True. Ways of experiencing the world that are shaped by ordinary, everyday practices are invisible to philosophers trained in these conceptual hierarchies. Practices such as growing and eating food, care for the land, cleaning and maintenance of the home, and daily care for children and others—in short, care for the environment, broadly conceived—are regarded as sub-philosophical, as not worthy of a philosopher's interest.

This dualistic split between the extraordinary and the ordinary has long been gender-based. One need only look at the cosmology of the Pythagoreans for a set of conceptual dualisms that has played a devastating role in marginalizing women's lives: "limit and unlimited, odd and even, one and plurality, right and left, male and female, resting and moving, straight and crooked, light and darkness, good and bad, square and oblong."[36] We have been taught that what is thus defined as "women's work" is "lower," "female," "bodily," "animal," "natural," irrational," "bad," and "dark."

Aristotle and Aquinas are notorious among environmental philosophers for their perpetuation of these hierarchies. As Aristotle put it:

> It is clear that the rule of the soul over the body, and the mind and the rational element over the passionate, is natural and expedient; whereas the equality of the two or the rule of the inferior is always hurtful. The same holds good of animals in relation to men; for tame animals have a better nature than wild, and all tame animals are better off when they are ruled by man; for then they are preserved. Again, the male is by nature superior, and the female inferior; and the one rules, and the other is ruled; this principle, of necessity, extends to all mankind.[37]

For Aristotle, other animals, women, and barbarians are naturally suited to slavery. It is a single issue for him. They form a natural servant class whose purpose is to serve men.

Women have been located at the border between culture and nature. Their "natural" work involves translation of nature into culture: cooking (translation from raw to cooked), agriculture and childbirth. In a culture that naturalizes women it is not surprising that women have been expected to perform caring labor.

Because they have been positioned at the border between nature and culture, women have had no choice but to focus on ordinary, everyday activities. In one sense, then, the ordinary is oppressive to women; it does not necessarily lead to sound environmental practice. Third World women, for example, who are deprived of the right to own land, "ordinarily" may be involved in deforestation for fuel. They have no choice.

Dōgen, in contrast, understands ordinary, daily practices transformatively, as the possibility of *mindfulness* about everyday practices. For ecofeminists, a philosophy that allows us to value the ordinary on its own terms, rather than as a defective reflection of the extraordinary, permit us sympathetically to understand the roles of those who have been expected to mediate men's commerce with the ordinary. Through consciousness of typically women's practices, a new ecological self might develop.

My point is not the essentialist point that women "by nature" are closer to the rhythms of ecological awareness. Many feminists have been clear in pointing out that this association only strengthens sexist categories by reifying them as if they were metaphysical: women then are constructed as bodily, nonrational creatures who *should* be engaged in manual rather than intellectual practices. Nor is my point that all women possess ecological wisdom. Clearly women, as well as men, are implicated in the degradation of nature.

I am, rather, making points about the ways in which *gender* is constructed in sexist cultures (not a point about individuals), and about the kinds of actual *practices* that have been defined by patriarchal and naturist cultures as "women's work" (or "animals' work"). These are the kinds of marginalized practices that such cultures make available precisely to those who are constructed as women (or animals).

The insight provided by ecofeminism is that women, who have engaged in these practices, who have been expected to practice compassionate entrance into others' worlds, have expert knowledge about the ordinary practices through which an ecoself is awakened.[38] As Sara Ruddick has said about the practice of mothering, for example, "Caretakers are immersed in the materials of the physical world." Because of this immersion, "caring labor" is regarded with disdain and marginalized by intellectuals. Yet, its very standpoint as "subjugated knowledge" produces a "superior" version of experience.[39] Because of the practices in which they have engaged, women have firsthand experience with "the presence of things as they are."

Taking daily practices as guides to philosophical reflection reveals that it is not the project of ecophilosophy to connect us to the "environment" (as if we could be disconnected), or to provide abstract rules for our interaction with the "environment" (when we are already environmentally engaged at every moment of our ordinary lives). The ordinary lives of women and men are already grounded in practices that are morally, spiritually, and physically healthy.

The ecological self is not something new, brought into being from nonexistence in an atomic self. The issue is not whether something new can be created, but whether we can become aware of ordinary practices and respond to them mindfully. Activities such as "eating a meal or drinking green tea," or seeing the ordinary everywhere around us—seeing "the donkey's jaw," as Dōgen says—are daily routines that mark the ways in which we are already, and inevitably, ecological beings despite the distortions of dualist, hierarchical, homocentric, and sexist thinking.

Ecofeminism is in a position to reinterpret the idea of a bioregion in terms of ordinariness: a bioregion is that "home" in which we can be our ordinary selves. Warwick Fox has recalled that the word *ecology* is derived from the Greek word *oikos* meaning "the family household and its daily maintenance."[40] A truly transformative ecophilosophy must work to make this original meaning common knowledge.

NOTES

1. Dōgen, "Busshō," *Shōbōgenzō,* trans. Kōsen Nishiyama (Tokyo: Nakayama Shobō, 1988), pp. 12–14.

2. The most detailed argument of this sort occurs in Warwick Fox's *Toward a Transpersonal Ecology: Developing New Foundations for Environmentalism* (Boston: Shambhala, 1990).

3. While Dōgen is not well known in the West, translations of his works are readily available. The complete Japanese text is *Dōgen Zenji Zenshū,* ed. Okubo Dōshu (Tokyo: Chikuma Shobō, 1969–1970). Among the notable translations are: *Flowers of Emptiness: Selections from Dōgen's Shōbōgenzō,* ed. and trans. Hee-Jin Kim (Lewiston, N.Y.: E. Mellen Press, 1985); *How to Raise an Ox,* ed. and trans. Francis Dojun Cook (Los Angeles: Center Publications, 1978); *Moon in a Dewdrop: Writings of Zen Master Dōgen,* ed. and trans. Tanahashi Kazuaki, et al. (San Francisco: North Point Press, 1985); *Shōbōgenzō: Zen Essays by Dōgen,* ed. and trans. Thomas Cleary (Honolulu: University of Hawaii Press, 1986); *Shōbōgenzō,* trans. Kōsen Nishiyama (Tokyo: Nakayama Shobō, 1988); *Sounds of Valley Streams: Enlightenment in Dōgen's Zen,* ed. and trans. Francis H. Cook (Albany: SUNY Press, 1989); *Zen Master Dōgen: An Introduction with Selected Writings*, ed. Yokoi Yuho (New York: Weatherhill, 1976). Norman Waddell and Abe Masao have translated several of the important fascicles from Shōbōgenzō in the *Eastern Buddhist*: "Bendōwa," *Eastern Buddhist* 4, no. 1 (1971): 124–57; "Ikka Myōju," *Eastern Buddhist* 4, no. 2 (1971): 108-18; "Shōbōgenzo Genjokoan." *Eastern Buddhist* 5, no. 2 (1972): 129-40, "Zenki and Shōji," *Eastern Buddhist* 5, no. 1 (1972): 70–80; "Sammai O zammai," *Eastern Buddhist* 7, no. 1 (1974): 118–23; "Shōbōgenzō Buddha-nature," *Eastern Buddhist* 8, no.2 (1975): 94–112; 9, no. 1 (1976): 87–105; 9, no. 2 (1976): 71–87; and Norman Waddell, trans., "Uji," *Eastern Buddhist* 12, no. 1 (1979): 114–29. The notable secondary literature includes: David Appelbaum, "On Turning a Zen Ear," *Philosophy East and West* 33 (1983): 115–22; Steven Heine, *Existential and Ontological Dimensions of Time in Heidegger and Dōgen* (Albany: SUNY Press, 1985); David Loy,

"The Path of No-path: Sankana and Dōgen on the Paradox of Practice," *Philosophy East and West* 38 (1988): 127–46; Carl Olson, "The Human Body as a Boundary Symbol: A Comparison of Merleau-Ponty and Dōgen" *Philosophy East and West* 36 (1986): 107–20; T. P. Kasulis, *Zen Action Zen Person* (Honolulu: The University of Hawaii Press, 1981); Hee-Jin Kim, *Dōgen Kigen: Mystical Realist* (Tucson: University of Arizona Press, 1987); James Takashi Kodera, *Dōgen's Formative Years in China* (Boulder: Prajna Press, 1980); William R. LaFleur, ed., *Dōgen Studies* (Honolulu: University of Hawaii Press, 1985); David Edward Shaner, *The Bodymind Experience in Japanese Buddhism* (Albany: SUNY Press, 1985); David E. Shaner, "The Bodymind Experience in Dōgen's Shōbōgenzō: A Phenomenological Perspective," *Philosophy East and West* 35, no. 1 (1985): 17–35; Joan Stambaugh, *Impermanence is Buddha-nature: Dōgen's Understanding of Temporality* (Honolulu: University of Hawaii Press, 1990); Yasuo Yuasa, *The Body: Toward an Eastern Mind-Body Theory*, trans. Shigenori Nagatomo and Thomas P. Kasulis (Albany: SUNY Press, 1987).

4. See Robert Aitken Roshi, "Gandhi, Dōgen, and Deep Ecology" *Deep Ecology: Living as if Nature Mattered* (Salt Lake City: Peregrine Smith Books, 1985), pp. 232–35; Arne Naess, "Through Spinoza to Mahayana Buddhism, or Through Mahayana Buddhism to Spinoza" in *Spinoza's Philosophy of Man: Proceedings of the Scandinavian Spinoza Symposium, 1977*, ed. Jon Wetlesen (Oslo: Universitetsforlaget, 1978), pp. 136–58, and Fox, *Toward a Transpersonal Ecology*, p. 268. A collection of essays on Buddhism and the environment is *Dharma Gaia: A Harvest of Essays in Buddhism and Ecology*, ed. Allan Hunt Badiner (Berkeley: Parallax Press, 1990). See especially the essays by Joan Halifax, "The Third Body: Buddhism, Shamanism, and Deep Ecology"; Jeremy Hayward, "Ecology and the Experience of Sacredness"; Bill Devall, "Ecocentric Sangha"; Carla Deicke, "Women and Ecocentricity"; and John Seed, "Wake the Dead!"

5. I agree with Thomas Kasulis who has argued that Dōgen's work can be explicated philosophically; he need not be categorized (and dismissed) as a mystic in the popular sense of the word. See "The Zen Philosopher: A Review Article on Dōgen Scholarship in English," *Philosophy East and West* 28 (1978): 353–73.

6. Readers interested in the ways Dōgen connects with and departs from Buddhist tradition can consult Heinrich Dumoulin's two volume *Zen Buddhism: A History* (New York: Macmillan, 1988).

7. Norman Waddell and Abe Masao in introductory comments to their translation of "Shōbōgenzō Buddha-nature," *The Eastern Buddhist* 8 (1975): 94.

8. This idea, however, was not original with Dōgen. See William LaFleur's "Sattva: Enlightenment for Plants and Trees in Buddhism,"

CoEvolution Quarterly 19 (1978): 47–52, for some fascinating background on this issue.

9. Waddell and Abe, "Shobogenzo Buddha-nature," p. 95. Their translation of the second sentence is "All sentient beings-whole being is the Buddha-nature." I have kept the translations parallel here. On the radicalization of Buddha-nature, see Heinrich Dumoulin, *Zen Buddhism: A History.* vol. 2 (Japan), p. 79.

10. "Shōbōgenzo Buddha-nature," pp. 91, 93.

11. "Mountains and Waters Sūtra," in *Moon in a Dewdrop: Writings of Zen Master Dōgen,* pp. 97–98.

12. Abe Masao, "Dōgen on Buddha-nature," *Eastern Buddhist* 4 (1971): 39 (emphasis added).

13. "Shōbōgenzō Buddha-nature," p. 100.

14. "Actualizing the Fundamental Point" (Genjo Koan), *Moon in a Dewdrop,* p. 70.

15. "Undivided Activity" (Zenki), *Moon in a Dewdrop,* p. 84.

16. See "Body and Mind Study of the Way" (Shinjin Gakudo), *Moon in a Dewdrop,* for the two ways of studying the Buddha way. Dōgen accepts the traditional Buddhist understanding of body as "the four great elements" (earth, water, fire, and air) and the five skandhas (form, feeling, perception, impulses, and consciousness). The five skandhas are the mental and physical aggregates into which the phenomenal world is analyzed. The point of the analysis is to show that there is no substantial self.

17. "Undivided Activity" (Zenki), *Moon in a Dewdrop,* p. 85.

18. Ibid., pp. 85–86.

19. See *Zen Action Zen Person,* pp. 87–103. There is no better philosophical introduction to Dōgen's thought than Kasulis's book.

20. Kodera, *Dōgen's Formative Years in China,* p. 37.

21. Nor is there a dualistic preference among everyday activities. Another of the fascicles of the *Shōbogenzō* instructs monks on the dharma of face washing, tooth brushing, and proper use of the toothpick. See "Washing the Face," in Senmen, *Shōbogenzō,* trans. Kosen Nishiyama (Tokyo: Nakayama Shobo, 1988), pp. 370–80.

22. *Fushuku-hampō* (Mealtime Regulations), trans. Roshi Jiyu-Kennett, *Zen is Eternal Life* (Mt. Shasta, Calif.: Shasta Abbey Press, 1987), p. 95. A book that takes Dōgen's writings of food as central to understanding his philosophy is Kosho Uchiyama, *Refining Your Life: From Zen Kitchen to Enlightenment,* trans. Thomas Wright (New York: Weatherhill, 1983).

23. "Everyday Activity" (Kajo), *Moon in a Dewdrop,* p. 125.

24. "Identification as a Source of Deep Ecological Attitudes," *Deep Ecology,* ed. Michael Tobias (San Diego: Avant Books, 1985), pp. 261, 263. Because Gandhi's understanding of self, though political, derives from the Hindu (Advaita Vedānta) idea of self as *ātman,* the alternatives offered by Naess are not really different.

25. David J. Kalupahana, *The Principles of Buddhist Psychology* (Albany: State University of New York Press, 1987), p. 12.

26. Freya Mathews, "Conservation and Self-Realization: A Deep Ecology Perspective," *Environmental Ethics* 10 (1988): 349.

27. Naess is quoted in Fox, *Toward a Transpersonal Ecology*, p. 230, from an unpublished manuscript, "Gestalt Thinking and Buddhism" (1983). See Devall's "Ecocentric Sangha," in *Dharma Gaia*. Among those who have been associated with deep ecology, Gary Snyder's recent writings in *The Practice of the Wild* best express this sense of the everydayness of our relations with nature. Speaking of the passage, Snyder says that "if you doubt mountains' walking you do not know your own walking, Dōgen is not concerned with 'sacred mountains'—or pilgrimages, or spirit allies, or wilderness as some special quality. His mountains and streams are the processes of this earth, all of existence, process, essence, action, absence; they roll being and nonbeing together. They are what we are, we are what they are. For those who would see directly into essential nature, the idea of the sacred is a delusion and an obstruction: it diverts us from seeing what is before our eyes: plain thusness. Roots, stems, and branches are all equally scratchy. No hierarchy, no equality." See Snyder's "Blue Mountains Constantly Walking," *The Practice of the Wild* (San Francisco: North Point Press, 1990), p. 103.

28. Abe Masao, "Dōgen on Buddha-Nature," pp. 41–42.

29. "Undivided Activity" (Zenki), *Moon in a Dewdrop*, pp. 85–86.

30. Dumoulin, *Zen Buddhism: A History*, p 82.

31. Warwick Fox, "The Deep Ecology-Ecofeminism Debate and its Parallels" *Environmental Ethics* 11 (1989): 12–13.

32. This is too broad. Actually, liberal feminists accept these dualistic frameworks and work to be included on the masculine side of the dualism. Other forms of feminism seek to undercut the dualisms altogether. See Alison M. Jaggar, *Feminist Politics and Human Nature* (Totowa, N.J.: Rowman and Allanheld, 1983), especially chaps. 3 to 6, for a discussion of the differences between liberal feminism and other forms of feminism.

33. Fox, *Toward a Transpersonal Ecology*, pp. 250, 251, 252, 259, 260.

34. Val Plumwood, "Nature, Self, and Gender: Feminism, Environmental Philosophy, and the Critique of Rationalism," *Hypatia* 6 (1991): 20.

35. Jim Cheney, "Eco-Feminism and Deep Ecology," *Environmental Ethics* 9 (1987): 122. In *Cooking, Eating, Thinking: Transformative Philosophies of Food* (Bloomington: Indiana University Press, 1992), I argued for just such a feminist sense of self as might arise from mindfulness about our defining relationships to food.

36. *Greek Philosophy: Thales to Aristotle*, ed. Reginald E. Allen (New York: Free Press, 1966), p. 39. Quoted from Aristotle's *Metaphysics* 985b23.

37. Aristotle, *Politics,* bk. 1, chap. 5. See *Animal Rights and Human Obligations,* ed. Tom Regan and Peter Singer (Englewood Cliffs: Prentice-Hall, 1989).

38. In "Toward an Ecological Ethic of Care," *Hypatia* 6 (1991): 60–74, I explore some of the conditions for an ecofeminist ethic.

39. Sara Ruddick, *Maternal Thinking: Toward a Politics of Peace* (New York: Ballantine Books, 1989), pp. 129–30.

40. Fox, *Toward a Transpersonal Ecology*, p. 31.

CHAPTER 15

Conservation Ethics and the Japanese Intellectual Tradition

DAVID EDWARD SHANER AND R. SHANNON DUVAL

One resource for investigating new issues in environmental philosophy and conservation ethics is to consider systematic philosophies that begin with the axiomatic notion of an ecocentric worldview rather than a homocentric or egocentric world view. The Japanese philosophical orientation embodies such a tradition in terms of its longstanding theoretical and practical commitment to an ecocentric worldview. In the Japanese tradition ecocentrism and self-cultivation represent two threads that weave a seamless ethical fabric characterized by developing one's sensitivity to others and nature. It is interesting to note that this philosophical approach is in concert with the worldview of many naturalists. In the body of this essay we explore one such example by unveiling a possible cross-cultural connection between the naturalistic philosophy of Louis Agassiz, a nineteenth-century French-American biologist, and the early writings of Nishida Kitarō, a twentieth-century Japanese philosopher. In the conclusion, we address related issues concerning conservation ethics and the Japanese intellectual tradition.

The connection between Nishida and the ecocentric worldview of Louis Agassiz has already been suggested, albeit unknowingly, by scholars who have discussed the relation between the American philosopher-psychologist William James and Nishida. James represents an often-documented subtle tie between the two diverse cultural communities of Japan and America. In "The Kyoto School and the West," Thomas P. Kasulis documents the connection:

> In the theory of pure experience developed in his first major work, *Study of Good,* Nishida tried to establish a single ground for all kinds of experience whether they be intuitive, empirical, rational, or creative. He sought this ground in the psychological unity, clarity, and presentness of what William James called "pure experience," that is, raw givenness. In short by using James' theory of radical empiricism (philosophy should be based only on what we directly experience, but it should also take into account all that we directly experience) Nishida hoped to reveal the universal source of both empiricism and religious/ ethical/aesthetic intuitionalism.[1]

In his article, "The Range of Nishida's Early Religious Thought: *Zen no Kenkyū,*" David Dilworth states that "'Pure Experience' took off from William James' notion of the same name."[2] In Dilworth's article, "The Initial Formations of Pure Experience in Kitarō Nishida and William James," he develops this connection in greater detail and states: "The concept of 'pure experience' taken from James' 'radical empiricism' was the generative idea which—under Nishida's own pen of course—gave the whole of *A Study of Good* its real interest."[3]

To date Dilworth's work has most satisfactorily explored the connection between James and Nishida. Following Dilworth's lead, Miranda Shaw has recently explored the connection between James and Yogacāra Buddhist philosophy. Being cognizant of the much publicized influence James had upon Nishida, she writes: "There are, however, deeper comparisons that can be made between James and specific Buddhist thinkers. For instance, the concept of 'pure experience' in the philosophies of James and Nishida Kitarō have much in common."[4]

In our discussion of this deeper connection linking the ecocentric orientation of noted American environmentalists and the Japanese philosophical and religious tradition, James' status is effectively reduced to that of a conduit of ideas that nevertheless highlights a deep affinity between the two main characters in this exchange—Agassiz and Nishida. When considering issues relevant to environmental philosophy, the shared ideas of Agassiz and Nishida can be considered to be mutually reinforcing even though Agassiz and Nishida are led to their respective philosophical positions working in entirely different *cultural* contexts. It is our hope that the identification and study of the transcultural *environmental* context that equally inspires both thinkers will further the development of a sound philosophical foundation for environmental concern that can be made attractive to a cross-cultural audience.

Nishida Kitarō (1870–1945) is the most famous Japanese philosopher of the modern era. Nishida was strongly influenced by the ecocentric and empiricist orientation of Japanese Zen Buddhism and was the inspirational leader of the famous Kyoto school of philosophy. In recent years, he has had the distinction of being the sole representative of Japanese philosophy to the youth of Japan. Nishida is the only philosopher whose theories must be studied in preparation for the standardized Japanese college entrance examinations. This is ironic for two reasons. First, the work chosen for study is *A Study of Good (Zen no Kenkyū),* published in 1911, in which the main concept is the doctrine of "pure experience" (*junsui keiken*).[5] Since Nishida later abandoned the centrality of this doctrine in favor of his celebrated "logic of place" (*basho no ronri*),[6] it is ironic that this early work should occupy such a privileged position in the modern educational system.

Second, Nishida borrowed the term *pure experience* from the writings of William James. Although the theme of pure experience highlights indigenous themes already present in the Japanese intellectual tradition, the specific concept had its origins in the intellectual climate of Cambridge, Massachusetts. Early in Nishida's career D. T. Suzuki recommended that he read James' work. James' essays from 1904–1905 (published posthumously as the *Essays in Radical Empiricism*) and *Principles of Psychology* are cited extensively in Nishida's early writings and remained in his personal library.[7] Nishida was sympathetic with James' description of the primacy of a mode of awareness in which the world is experienced as a stream of consciousness prior to making conscious subject-object distinctions. Also attractive to Nishida was James' commitment to radical empiricism, out of which his doctrines of the immediacy of experience and the nondualistic condition of experience arose.[8] Predictably, as radical empiricists, James and Nishida also shared an opposition to the language of Western idealism.

There seems to be agreement by James scholars that his doctrine of pure experience is an original one.[9] The commonality between James and Nishida, however, is too unlikely for there not to be some other meaningful connection. After spending some months reading through the letters of William James, the relevant connection became clear.[10] James' early work at Harvard, as both student and professor, was influenced by America's most distinguished field biologist Louis Agassiz.[11] Indeed, James' letters to his parents reveal that he idolized Agassiz.[12] Agassiz was a radical empiricist par excellence and was famous for his impatience with metaphysical rhetoric. When the young James asked him abstract philosophical questions, Agassiz would tell him to read nature to understand God's mind and works, not books! James' early training in anatomy and physiology and lessons in natural history, delivered personally by Agassiz on the Thayer expedition up the Amazon River,[13] influenced his lifelong commitment to radical empiricism[14] and his work on "pure experience" in particular. In this paper we draw attention to strong circumstantial evidence pointing to the possibility that those features of James' philosophy which Nishida found most attractive were the same features that can be traced to the ecocentric world view held by James' teacher—the celebrated Harvard biologist Louis Agassiz.

In keeping with a grand nineteenth-century tradition, James was a prolific letter writer. In addition, the marginalia he wrote in the pages of his personal books indicate that he often recorded a running "private" dialogue with the authors he was reading. Both resources are most instructive.

On 10 September 1861, James, probably for the first time, wrote to his parents about Louis Agassiz. He said he was going to attend a dozen lectures on "Methods in Natural History." In a letter dated 16 September, he remarked that Agassiz was a favorite with his audiences.[15] In a letter dated Christmas day (1861–63?) he describes Agassiz's method of instruction as one that taught his students to become naturalists by developing *a feel* for their subject matter in the same way artists learn to feel their way into a new medium. For this reason Agassiz preferred new students who were wholly uninstructed. He wanted his students to come to him as if they were blank tablets. Agassiz then molded the students' skills by not letting them "look into a book for a long while," forcing them to "learn for themselves, and be *masters* of it all." James goes on to say that "he makes naturalists of [the students], he does not merely cram them. . . . He must be a great teacher."[16] Later James accompanied Agassiz on a Thayer Expedition to South America and discovered firsthand the rigors of field collecting. James' health proved frail, however, and a series of ailments began in Brazil that persisted throughout his lifetime.

Agassiz's insistence upon empirical verification and collecting left a lasting mark on James' entire career. Although James learned that his temperament was better suited to mineral baths and cool library research, James' pragmatism and methods of scholarship reflect Agassiz's hard-nosed determination and insistence upon collecting respectively. (James' *Varieties of Religious Experience,* for example, can be interpreted as a quasi-inductive argument for the existence of God as revealed by the collected testimonies contained therein.) On the 1865–66 expedition, eighty thousand items of natural history were collected.

William James wrote of his impressions of Agassiz as a man and as a teacher in a letter to his father (12–17 September 1865):

> I have profited a great deal by hearing Agassiz talk, not so much by what he says, for never did a man utter a greater amount of humbug, but by learning *the way of feeling* of such a vast practical engine as he is. No one sees farther into a generalization than his knowledge of details extends, and you have a greater feeling of weight and solidity about the movement of Agassiz's mind, owing to the continual presence of this great background of special facts, than about the mind of any other man I know. . . . I delight to be with him. I only saw his defects at first, but now his wonderful qualities throw them quite in the background. . . . I never saw a man work so hard.

James' observations provide, in fact, an excellent portrayal of the happy and exciting Brazil days:

> The Professor has just been expatiating over the mass of South America, and making projects as if he had Sherman's Army at his disposal. . . . The Prof. now sits opposite me with his face all aglow holding forth to the Captain's wife about the imperfect education of the American people. . . . *Offering* your services to Agassiz is as absurd as it would [be] for a S. Carolinian to *invite* Gen. Sherman's soldiers to partake of some refreshment when they called at his house.

Of more personal contacts between the young man and the older master, James had this to say: "I am getting a pretty valuable training from the Prof. who pitches into me right and left and wakes me up to a great many of my imperfections. This morning he said I was 'totally uneducated.'"[17]

On 30 December 1896, James delivered a testimonial for Louis Agassiz at a reception of the American Society of Naturalists (Agassiz died in 1873). Again, James was quite specific concerning the deeply personal and lasting influence that his teacher had upon him. During the speech James captured Agassiz's love of nature as evidenced by his excitement at just being in the midst of unspoiled natural surroundings. James recalled:

> I had the privilege of admission to his society during the Thayer expedition to Brazil. I well remember at night, as we all swung in our

hammocks in the fairy-like moonlight, on the deck of the streamer that throbbed its way up the Amazon between the forests guarding the stream on either side, how he turned and whispered, "James are you awake?" and continued, "I cannot sleep; I am too happy; I keep thinking of these glorious plans." The plans contemplated were following the headwaters, and penetrating the Andes in Peru. . . . Agassiz's view of nature was saturated with a simple religious feeling, and for this deep but unconventional religiosity he found at Harvard a most sympathetic environment.[18]

As evidenced by James' testimony, Agassiz was one who was truly intimate with nature. *He passed on to James a feeling that an experience of intimacy with the empirical world has religious significance.* However, he also taught him that this religious sensitivity required *cultivating* an inner feeling for one's subject matter.

The present day Nestor of evolutionary biology, Ernst Mayr, similarly emphasizes that mastering the techniques of a skilled cladistic systematist requires developing a feeling for one's subject matter.[19] This feeling reflects the skill of a master professional. Like the guild system of training, true professionalism in the discipline of phyletic classification requires a long time in order to nurture the sensitivity required to collect and properly classify flora and fauna. It is this sort of developed awareness between self and world, personified by Agassiz's example, that James tried to capture through the term *pure experience.* The immediate, intimate, and prereflective character of pure experience is what Nishida found complementary with central themes in the Japanese philosophical and religious tradition. The central theme among Agassiz, James, and Nishida revolves around their shared commitment to cultivating a feeling of sensitive interaction between persons and between persons and their natural environment.

Our comments are not intended to correct any perceived error concerning the often documented connection between James and Nishida (see endnote number four). Rather, our point is that the emphasis placed upon the perceived connection is misdirected. That which Nishida finds attractive in James is pure Agassiz. Nishida's own predilections would have prepared him to appreciate Agassiz the naturalist, who, like central figures in the Japanese philosophical and religious tradition, held an ecocentric world view. Agassiz believed that genuinely appreciating the fact that we are actively involved as actors in a dynamic ecosystem required a quasi-rite of passage. To truly understand this point, its meaning must touch our lives empirically, and Agassiz believed this could only come about through a form of cultivation occasioned by direct experience and scientifically informal field work, not speculative theories. The emphasis upon direct or immediate experience in nature, as described by scholars of the early Japanese tradition, has been characterized as a product of a primitive and archaic worldview. In Japan this emotional and aesthetic attitude provides the basis for becoming sensitive to the *detail* of nature's presence as evidenced by subtle variations of light, shadows, wind, seasonal change, and so on.[20] This so-called primitive quality, however, was what Agassiz purposefully sought in his students. Without preconceptions to clutter the mirror-like "feel" of a working field naturalist, the detailed and subtle differences in nature could be detected and recorded.[21]

The illustrations discussed thus far suggest that cultivating an intimacy between persons and nature requires a clarity and purity of experience in the East as well as the West. James' pure experience, which we suggest is (to a significant degree) an extension of Agassiz's lasting influence,[22] parallels Nishida's own radical empiricism. Nishida's first citation of James in *A Study of Good* occurs early when he discusses his belief that "pure experience can exist only in present consciousness of events."[23] Nishida goes on to suggest that all "psychical phenomena" occur in present consciousness.[24] As an illustrative case in point, Nishida reminds his readers that memory, usually perceived as past consciousness, occurs in the present consciousness. In chapter seven of the first volume of *The Principles of Psychology,* James discusses the manner in which a past state of consciousness is translated into a present state of consciousness. James explains:

> The present conscious state, when I say "'I feel tired,'" is not the direct state of tire; when I say "'I feel angry,'" it is not the direct state of anger. It is the state of *saying-I-feel*-tired, of *saying-I-feel*-angry—entirely different matters.[25]

James' statement coincides with Nishida's claim that "consciousness of the past is not a thing which emerges suddenly, and consequently one does not directly perceive the past."[26]

When Nishida's discussion turns to time and pure experience he writes, "In the present of a conscious event there must be a certain continuation of time."[27] Although scholars of Japanese philosophy will immediately consider the influence of Dōgen (1200–1253), specifically, his distinction between time experienced as "ranging" *(keiraku)* and time as experienced as a series of point instances *(nikon no ima),* one must remain cognizant of James' analysis of the as-experienced character of time in chapter fifteen of *The Principles of Psychology.* Here James discusses the "practical present," not as "knife-edged," but rather as "saddle-back." He calls it a "duration block," saying, "We do not first feel one end and then feel the other after it . . . but we seem to feel the interval of time as a whole, with its two ends embedded in it."[28] James continues to discuss how objects are sometimes experienced as slowly fading out of consciousness:

> If the present thought is of A B C D E F G, the next one will be of B C D E F G H, and the one after that of C D E F G H I—the lingerings of the past dropping successively away, and the incomings of the future making up the loss.[29]

Nishida again refers to *The Principles* when he explores the concept of thought as pure experience. In chapter nine, James lists his five characteristics of thought. Specifically, Nishida is drawn to the fourth of these five characteristics, which states that thought "always appears to deal with objects independent of itself."[30] Later in *The Principles* James elaborates upon this point and explains his belief that thoughts arise from and must ultimately be reconciled with an absolute unity:

> Whatever things are thought in relation are thought from the outset in a unity, in a single pulse of subjectivity, a single psychosis, feeling, or state of mind.[31]

Nishida is interested in this point because it indicates to him that "consciousness of the same content must ever be identical consciousness."[32] Nishida questions this idea saying, "If this kind of meaning too is a function of a great unity, does pure experience in such a case transcend its own sphere?"[33] Developing this concept, he cites James' essay "A World of Pure Experience." Nishida notes James' conclusion that if the consciousness of relationships is included in the term experience, then thought must also be a kind of pure experience.[34] In "A World of Pure Experience," James explains his view:

> *The relations that connect experiences must themselves be experienced, and any kind of relation experienced must be accounted as 'real' as anything else in the system.*[35]

This account by James adds to Nishida's dissatisfaction with what he perceives to be the traditional view that "thought and pure experience were wholly differing kinds of psychical activity."[36] Nishida breaks from this traditional view and concludes, "Pure experience and thought are basically the same event seen from different points of view."[37]

When considering other influences that led Nishida to be sympathetic with radical empiricism, we must remember that both D. T. Suzuki and Nishida had predilections in concert with Zen Buddhism. The radical empiricist orientation of Zen and Agassiz provide an interesting connection warranting further consideration. In this context, the common denominator forged between the Japanese tradition, William James, and people (to be discussed below) like Aristotle, Louis Agassiz, Edward O. Wilson, Ernst Mayr, and Alasdair MacIntyre hinges upon *cultivating* an emotional and aesthetic "feel" for nature that provides the necessary and sufficient condition for an intimate ecocentric interaction with our natural surroundings.

Nishida had been looking for a Western counterpart that would complement indigenous Japanese attitudes toward others and nature.[38] Agassiz's coincidental Japanese predilections are revealed in his *Contributions to the Natural History of the United States,* published in 1857. Agassiz's view is that all species are creations of God's mind. For him, science and religion are brought together beautifully by learning sensitively to understand nature's book as a reflection of God's mind and character. By teaching his students (James included) how to "see" the world from his cultivated perspective, he believed that he was actually teaching courses in theology, environmental ethics, and personal development.[39] The view that nature is endowed with a divine presence (*kami*) that can be more fully appreciated by cultivating one's way of being-in-the-world served as the ideological bridge linking Nishida and Agassiz through James.

James was not able seriously to question the notion of self, ego, or soul that frequently stands in the way of entering fully into an ecocentric, versus egocentric, worldview. The concept of soul was at the heart of James' early religious training. In contrast, Nishida and the entire Buddhist tradition argue that one must abandon egocentric notions of self and accept the doctrine of no-self (*anātman, muga).* In reading James' marginalia written in his personal copy of F. H. Bradley's *Appearance and Reality,* it is apparent that when Bradley discusses a way of being that is without self, James seems utterly incapable of grasping the point. On page 225 of his 1893 edition, he writes, "the Reality is a self-sufficing field of consciousness. (Why then abolish the ego as he does?)." This question is notable for it suggests that James' theological commitments may have created a hermeneutic difference (acting as a barrier) that made it difficult for him to understand Bradley's discussion of no-self. James' comment is not typical here, for his habit is to write counterarguments in the margins of texts. This comment, however, suggests that he is missing Bradley's point concerning the absence of a consciousness of ego in direct experience. (One might argue, given James' theological commitments as argued for in his own texts, that James simply refuses to accept Bradley's position. If this were the case, however, it would be far more characteristic for James to state his position expressly in the form of a marginal counterargument. Rather, James' comment is in the form of an accurate summary of Bradley's point followed by a question.)

James' celebrated stream of thought/consciousness cannot therefore be considered one that rivals Bradley's direct experience without self. The significance of experiencing the world without ego attachments is, of course, crucial for cultivating a mode of being-in-the-world that is intimate. Intimacy requires egolessness such that one's experience is not attached to an intentional frame of reference from subject to object. Intimacy is necessary for an ecocentric awareness of the world. After all, ecocentrism is overcoming, or more accurately, stripping away, the *homo* of homocentrism and the *ego* of egocentrism.

Bradley's thesis in *Appearance and Reality* comes quite close to describing the mutual interpenetration of all things, a position espoused by many Buddhist schools—especially the Hua-yen school. On the inside of the back cover of his copy of *Appearance and Reality,* James summarizes his opinion of Bradley's efforts by stating his own argument. (Incidentally, it was his habit to write such final impressions while frequently developing his own page index of topics to which he may later refer.) James states in this concluding inscription that

> External relations involve internal diversity. Such diversity, being internal, is involved in a *whole.* The whole, thus suggested, is supposed to exist no longer in the finite term whose external relations there implied it, but in absolute whole containing the finite term as a part of its own diversity—Queer Reasoning!

Because James interprets this reasoning as queer, we suggest that Bradley and Agassiz are much closer to the Japanese mind and heart (*kokoro*) than James. On occasions such as this, James' worldview seems out of touch with Buddhist sentimentality. David Dilworth suggests in his article, "The Range of Nishida's Early Religious

Thought: *Zen no Kenkyū,"* that Nishida's pantheistic predilections rendered the conclusions of his work incompatible with James' theistic doctrines.[40] We agree with Dilworth's assessment and suggest that for similar reasons Bradley's orientation toward the self, or lack thereof, is more in concert with some of the basics of Nishida's philosophy, and in general is a more fruitful subject for East-West comparison than, say, James. In "Nishida Kitarō: Nothingness as the Negative Space of Experiential Immediacy," for example, Dilworth compares Nishida's doctrine of pure experience with Bradley's notion of experience as a "felt whole." He states:

> Nishida's style of philosophizing is perhaps also reminiscent of F. H. Bradley, whose notion of the absolute immediacy of experience is elaborated through an endless dialectic of self-negation of the contradictory aspects of subject-object, particular-universal, and so forth.[41]

While Nishida found James' worldview attractive, this point suggests that James may not have reciprocated the sentiment. That is, in consideration of James' attachment to the concept of self, it is not likely that he would have been comfortable in Nishida's world of a *cultivated* selflessness. For Nishida, Bradley, and Agassiz, selflessness facilitates (or is even a prerequisite for) direct, prereflective pure experiences. It is interesting to note that Nishida's understanding of cultivation and selflessness is more in concert with Agassiz's interests relative to James. Agassiz encouraged a cultivated selflessness, insofar as he sought to develop, in himself and his students, an intimacy with nature, because he felt that the acquired skills of a field biologist required the cultivation of a form of pure experience that occasions an intimacy with the environment. Such ecocentric sensitivity can only be made manifest when the ego does not occupy a privileged position in one's experiential encounter with nature.

Let us now consider, albeit briefly, some of these issues and their relation to other prominent figures in both Japanese and Western intellectual traditions. Since Aristotle's concept of *ethos* (character) includes the sense of personal development, it too is in concert with the Japanese Neo-Confucian and Buddhist emphasis upon cultivation (*shugyō*). Accordingly, the classical and modern Aristotelian tradition provides a more fruitful source of comparison than, say, the bulk of rights-based moral theories in the West. Whereas rights-based theories begin with the individual agent as an entity with guaranteed entitlements, the aforementioned developmental approach focuses upon a person as a participant in a more axiomatic relation. According to the parameters of this conceptual and behavioral system, persons are fulfilled by entitlements only because they are in relationships first. Rights have meaning only in ethical contexts; rights implicitly refer to others.

In his celebrated book entitled *After Virtue*, Alasdair MacIntyre develops his own version of a communitarian approach to ethics. MacIntyre shares the Japanese conceptual orientation that our communal life style is indicative of the fact that we are social creatures first and foremost. Our solitary rights prove to be empty when we are forced to live in isolation from others and nature. This axiomatic sense of relatedness, however, is not easy to analyze rationally. Like Nishida and leading environmentalists to be discussed below, MacIntyre believes that our emotions serve as the source of our sense of intimacy. Referring to Aristotle he writes:

> Virtues are dispositions not only to act in particular ways, but also to feel in particular ways. To act virtuously is not, as Kant was later to think, to act against inclination; it is to act from inclination formed by the cultivation of the virtues. Moral education is an "education sentimentale."[42]

The pressing question at this point in our discussion concerns how we might be able to develop greater sensitivity such that we too might experience nature more intimately. If it is not enough to be *told* how to interact harmoniously with nature, then we must ask how we might *be* enlightened regarding our existence in nature. Clearly, there are many ways of fostering this care for the natural world. Although the naturalist and the artist, for example, "see" the world according to a different agenda, their "seeing" is nevertheless made more clear by allowing themselves to participate in nature fully. Whereas the sensitivity of a field biologist may issue from his or her knowledge and habituated appreciation of the elaborate mechanisms sustaining the biosphere, the sensitivity of the Zen priest may issue from cultivating/habituating a more primordial natural experience. Both encounters with nature may be referred to as "biophilia"; both are products of the cultivation of a long and intimate relationship with nature. There is reason cautiously to avoid inferring that the experience of emotional attachments to nature (love of nature) must be indicative of our biological/material bond with organic life. The experience of *biophilia* may in fact be the product of an acquired cultivation process whereby one cultivates a near kinship relationship with the environment. This may be achieved through extensive biological fieldwork or through intentionally cultivating a feeling of oneness with one's environment [as in the practice of *zazen* (seated meditation)].

Today the theme of radical empiricism is alive and well in the personal writings of another celebrated Harvard biologist—sociobiologist, entomologist, and island biogeographer Edward O. Wilson—who uses the term *biophilia* to refer to the cultivated sense of a "love of nature." His book, *Biophilia: The Human Bond with Other Species,* published in 1984, begins as follows:

> On March 21, 1961, I stood in the Arawak village of Bernardsdorp and looked across the white-sand coastal forest of Surinam. For reasons that were to take me twenty years to understand, that moment was fixed with uncommon urgency in my memory. The emotions I felt were to grow more poignant at each remembrance, and in the end they changed into rational conjectures about matters that had only a distant bearing on the original event. The object of reflection can be summarized by a single word, biophilia, which I will be so bold as to define as the innate tendency to focus on life and lifelike processes.[43]

We do not yet know if this tendency is innate or the product of cultural development or both.[44] It can be argued, however, that biologists like Agassiz and Wilson and leading Japanese intellectuals—like the Buddhist Kūkai (774–835), the Neo-Confucian Kaibara Ekken (1630–1714), the Neo-Shintoist Motoori Norinaga (1730–1801), and the Buddhist Nishida—developed a keen emotional sensitivity and empathy with the material environment. Wilson, for example, spent his youth in the Deep South. Since his father's occupation required that the family relocate frequently, he moved from school to school making it difficult to develop long-term classmate friendships. The interesting side consequence of this situation was that it served to enhance young Wilson's intimate friendship with nature. Similarly Agassiz, Kūkai, and the others cultivated an intimacy with nature early in life by renouncing other career plans in favor of time spent in relative natural isolation. It would seem that when it comes to some issues relevant to environmental philosophy, the apparent cultural obstacles of East and West can be overcome by cultivating or acknowledging an emotional attachment to nature. Once this affinity is perceived, it engages a holistic ecocentric view that is characterized by a feeling of an aesthetic and perhaps a material oneness with all things. For Wilson, this feeling serves as the ground of environmental philosophy. Accordingly, the goal of environmental philosophy "is to join emotion with the rational analysis of emotion in order to create a deeper and more enduring conservation ethic."[45]

Because the classical texts of ancient Japan *(Man'yōshu, Tale of Genji,* and *Kojiki* similarly depict the prominence of a deep emotional affinity between persons and nature, perhaps studying the Japanese rationale that describes these feelings can shed light upon our own reflections for, as Wilson says, "a more enduring conservation ethic." The expression of this Japanese emotional and aesthetic attitude is frequently summarized by scholars, especially Norinaga, employing the famous dictum *"mono no aware"* ("sensitivity to things"). From the beginning of recorded history the Japanese worldview seems to have been characterized by an intimate, prereflective, and emotional encounter with the natural world. Emotion thus served as the basis for a type of interspecies awareness. By cultivating one's sensitivity to one's surroundings, one could more effectively intuit feelings of identity with the environment as a whole. For such leading conservationists as Edward O. Wilson and most of the Japanese intellectual tradition, reasoned reflection serves to document and organize more basic feelings that issue from deep within us. The emotions speak to us directly and are unencumbered. When these intimate feelings occur, they are free from moralistic reflection; yet, they serve as a ground for later remembrances and assertive action.

Perhaps the most important link between ecologists, biologists, and the Japanese tradition is a conception of community in which there is no vestige of a Platonic ontological hierarchy of existence. The theme of community has also been important in both modern Japanese philosophy and Neo-Darwinian thinking. While Darwin considered the target of natural selective processes to be the individual, the Neo-Darwinian concept of inclusive fitness allows for competition to be considered a shared phenomenon among relatives, thus providing the axiomatic basis for competing hypotheses regarding altruistic behavior, viz., kin selection, group selection, reciprocal altruism, and so on.[46] Accordingly an entire species' adaptive fitness can be considered in terms of a holistic frame of reference.[47] A species' survival as a whole may thus be considered in accordance with the ability of individual members to participate effectively in a community (thereby enhancing the differential reproductive success of the group). Since much of the Japanese tradition is in concert with the aforementioned ecocentric and communitarian perspective,[48] it would be worth our while to consider aspects of the Japanese Buddhist and Neo-Confucian philosophical tradition as a conceptual resource for environmental philosophy. Perhaps we will be able to piece together attitudes toward nature and communities that the Japanese tradition and modern ecological theory have in common in order to construct a cohesive environmental and conservation ethic.

NOTES

1. Thomas P. Kasulis, "The Kyoto School and the West." *The Eastern Buddhist* n.s. 15, no. 2 (1982): 125–44.
2. David Dilworth, "The Range of Nishida's Early Religious Thought: *Zen no Kenkyū,*" *Philosophy East and West* 19 (1969): 409–21.
3. David Dilworth, "The Initial Formations of Pure Experience in Kitarō Nishida and William James," *Monumenta Nipponica* 24 (1969): 93–111.
4. Miranda Shaw "William James and Yogācāra Philosophy: A Comparative Inquiry," *Philosophy East and West* 37 (1987): 223–44. William James' influence on Nishida has also been mentioned in, for example, Gino K. Piovesana, *Contemporary Japanese Philosophical Thought* (New York: St. John's University Press, 1969), where he states: "Different stages of the conscious process can be distinguished, and Nishida uses many psychologists to support his views, mostly James, Wundt, and G. F. Stout. . . . Furthermore, his [Nishida's] reliance on James' 'pure experience' is more than a question of terminology. For James too, the immediate experience embraces not only the singular content of the terms, but also the relations between them" (pp. 95–96). See also R. Wargo, *The Logic of Basho and the Concept of Nothingness in the Philosophy of Nishida Kitarō*, University of Michigan, Ph.D. dissertation (Ann Arbor, Michigan: University Microfilms, 1972): "The approach which Nishida uses to get at the notion of 'pure experience' is psychological; indeed, the notion as originally propounded by James seems more appropriate to psychological investigation than philosophical inquiry" (p. 66); David A. Dilworth, "Nishida's Early Pantheistic Voluntarism," *Philosophy East and West* 20 (1970): "In a *Study of Good* Nishida showed clear affinities with idealistic and pantheistic thought structures to be found among Western philosophers. These affinities were grounded on his phenomenology of 'pure experience,' a notion he partly derived from William James' 'radical empiricism' but which he ontologized in a way somewhat foreign to James. In his next major work, *Intuition and Reflection in Self-Consciousness*, Nishida returned to the fundamental question of a 'pure experience.' He developed this initial insight via a phenomenology of 'self-consciousness' *(jikaku)* which reaffirmed the ontological priority of subjectivity beyond subject-object distinctions, but stressed especially the fusion of being and value, and the primacy of the will over thought" (p. 36); David A. Dilworth, "Nishida Kitarō: Nothingness as the Negative Space of Experiential Immediacy," *International*

Philosophical Quarterly 13 (1973): *"Zen no Kenkyū* [usually translated as *A Study of Good*] . . . which won him immediate acclaim in the context of the complex spiritual atmosphere of the post-Russo-Japanese war years in late Meiji Japan, took off from William James' notion of 'pure experience' to elaborate an epistemological, metaphysical, ethical, and religious system that was a condensation of his intellectual and spiritual life to that point" (p. 467); and finally, David A. Dilworth, "The Initial Formulations of Pure Experience in Kitarō Nishida and William James," *Monumenta Nipponica* 24 (1969): "Since Nishida himself read and incorporated this concept [pure experience] into his own text, a comparative study of Nishida's and James' formulations should shed light on the directions in which each philosopher was moving" (p. 102), and "There are two sides to James' radical empiricism. The first side is the simpler, and actually the less important aspect of James' position, although it seems to have been the point which most attracted Nishida's attention. This was James' many incisive analyses and metaphors which described a condition of experience prior to subject object distinctions in rational analysis, and which therefore precluded, on empirical grounds, the possibility of reifying 'thought' and 'things.'" (p. 103). The last article is the most comprehensive in developing this theme, since it is fully devoted to exposing the connection between Nishida and James.

5. *"Zen no Kenkyū"* is included in *Nishida Kitarō Zenshū* ["Collected Works of Nishida Kitarō"] vol. I (Tokyo: Iwanami Shoten, 1965–66). For an English translation, see V. H. Viglielmo's *Nishida Kitarō: A Study of Good* (Tokyo: Japanese Government Printing Office, 1960).

6. For a thorough analysis of the logic of *basho* in Nishida's latter work, see Wargo, *The Logic of Basho;* Nishida Kitarō, *Fundamental Problems of Philosophy,* trans. David A. Dilworth (Tokyo: Sophia University, 1970); and David A. Dilworth, "Nishida's Final Essay: The Logic of Place and a Religious World-View," *Philosophy East and West* 20 (1970): 355–68.

7. Dilworth, "Initial Formations," p. 102.

8. Ibid., pp. 103–06 and Miranda Shaw, "William James and Yogācāra Philosophy: A Comparative Inquiry," pp. 225, 227–28.

9. We say that there *"seems to be agreement"* because there is no definitive interpretation (among James scholars) suggesting that the doctrine was adapted from outside sources. In particular, the following list of works critically discuss James' notion of "pure experience." The authors that discuss the development of pure experience do so only from the standpoint of James' earlier ideas on consciousness and stream of thought: Bernard P. Brennon, *William James* (New York: Twayne Publishers, 1978); Gay Wilson Allen, *William James* (New York: The Viking Press, 1967); John J. McDermott, ed., *The Writings of William James* (New York: Random House, 1967); John Wild, *The Radical Empiricism of William James* (New York: Doubleday, 1969); John J. McDermott,

"Introduction to *The Works of William James,*" in *The Works of William James,* ed. Frederick Burdhardt (Cambridge: Harvard University Press, 1982); George E. Myers, *William James: His Life and Thought* (New Haven: Yale University Press, 1986); Eugene Taylor. "The Evolution of William James' Definition of Consciousness," *ReVISION* 4, no. 2 (1981): 40–47; Edward H. Madden and Chandana Chakrabarti, "James' 'Pure Experience' versus Ayer's 'Weak Phenomenalism'," *Transactions of the Charles S. Peirce Society* 12 (Winter 1976): 3–17; Charlene Haddock Seigfried, "The Structure of Experience for William James," *Transactions of the Charles S. Peirce Society* 12 (1976): 330–47; and Robert R. N. Ross, "William James-the Wider Consciousness," *Philosophy Today* 20 (1976): 134–48. There are, however, some James' scholars who, unlike the forementioned, claim that there were sources of inspiration that influenced James' conception of pure experience. For example, in his article "The Doctrine of 'Pure Experience': The Evolution of a Concept from Mach to James to Tolman," *Journal of the History of the Behavioral Sciences* II (1975): 55–66, Paul Tibbits suggests a connection between James' concept or notion of pure experience and Ernst Mach's notion of "pure sensation." Mach developed the idea of pure sensation in his work *Analysis of Sensation* which appeared five years before James' *Principles.* In support of his claim that Mach influenced James, Tibbits cites Ralph Barton Perry's two-volume intellectual history of James, *The Thought and Character of William James* (Boston: Little, Brown, and Company, 1936). After consulting Perry's work, however, it is not clear that Tibbets has correctly ascertained Perry's sentiments. Specifically, Tibbets cites Perry's comment that Mach's *Analysis of Sensation* "was both a contribution to psychology and a precursor of James' doctrine of pure experience" (1:588). An inconsistency develops, however, when one also considers another of Perry's comments: "As to Mach, it is true that his 'sensations' *(Empfindungen),* despite their name, were elements *common* to both minds and bodies, and therefore belonging to neither exclusively. But they were far from composing in themselves that field of reality which James formed in pure experience" (2:389). Perry viewed Mach as "essentially a positivist" and asserted that "James's view of experience . . . was not derived from contemporary positivism. . . . It was in agreement with a *general* tendency of the times" (2:390). Perry concludes that "James's doctrine of the stream of thought was essentially his own" (2:78). Clearly Perry's later interpretation is in strict accord with the bulk of the James scholarship cited above.

10. William James, personal correspondence. 1861–65, William James Collection, Houghton Library, Harvard University, Cambridge.

11. For a good summary of Agassiz's life and distinguished career, see Edward Lurie, *Louis Agassiz: A Life in Science* (Chicago: University of Chicago Press, 1960).

12. Particularly instructive, in this regard, are letters written to his parents dated: 10 September 1861, 25 December 1861–637, Cambridge, 1862 (fragment). 31 March 1865?, 21 April 1865, 23 August 1865?, 12 September 1865, 21 October 1865, November 1865? For a relevant and instructive letter to Alice James, see 6 November 1865. All dated designations are from William James, personal correspondence, 1861–65. William James Collection. Houghton Library, Harvard University, Cambridge.

13. Again, James records his experiences and illnesses in letters to his parents. The Thayer Expedition in which he participated left New York on 1 April 1865. Experiencing first hand the rigors of field work opened James' eyes in a number of ways. First, the great Agassiz became mortal (for James) insofar as living with Agassiz allowed James to perceive weaknesses in his character. Second, James grew to respect Agassiz's energy level and sheer toughness. Third, James learned about developing the patience and keen sensitivity required for productive field work in natural history. Fourth, the illnesses and hardships James experienced taught him something about his own limitations and career plans.

14. An excellent single volume that depicts James' commitment to radical empiricism is *The Works of William James: Essays in Radical Empiricism,* ed. Fredson Bowers (Cambridge. Massachusetts: Harvard University Press, 1976).

15. Enthusiasts of "pragmatism" and "pragmaticism" would be interested to know that in the same letter, James mentions that he suspects the son of Professor Benjamin Peirce (Charles S. Peirce) to be a very smart fellow with a good deal of character and independence. Benjamin Peirce was an eminent Harvard mathematician.

16. A text of the letter is provided in Gay Wilson Allen, *William James, A Biography* (New York: Viking Press. 1967), p. 84.

17. From Edward Lurie, *Louis Agassiz: A Life in Science* (Chicago: University of Chicago Press, 1960), pp. 347–48 (emphasis added).

18. American Society of Naturalists reception speech, William James Collection, Houghton Library, Harvard University, Cambridge.

19. Personal communication.

20. See, for example, E. G. Seidensticker, "'In Praise of Shadows: A Prose Elegy of Tanizaki," *Japan Quarterly* 1 (1954): 16–52.

21. Learning to see detail is the trademark of a great scientist. Consider the following examples. On 23 August 1865, during the Thayer expedition, James writes that Agassiz found forty-six new species of fish in four days! Likewise Edward Wilson uses his monocular vision to great advantage when classifying ants; he can detect, without a magnification aid, subtle morphological differences, even hairs, in individual specimens. Developing an eye for detail is also important for excavations of fossil remains. Stephen Jay Gould describes this acquired skill in "Empire of the Apes," *Natural History* 96, no. 5 (May 1987): 20–25.

Although field detection and field collection require some hermeneutic act, informed as they necessarily are by some methodological framework, the metaphor of the polished mirror can still be meaningfully employed in order to convey the primacy of clarity, sensitivity, and intimacy.

22. Although we have documented this relationship in the text above, it is possible to distinguish two distinct empirical orientations expressed by James and Agassiz. Using Jungian phraseology, we can consider James an introvert and Agassiz an extrovert. James' interest in empiricism clearly reflects his proto-phenomenological leanings. He is interested in intentionality, perspective, reflexivity, and shared cognitive features. Analysis of these phenomena requires turning one's attention inward, as it were, in an effort to better understand the "knower." Agassiz, on the other hand, is interested in empiricism as it relates to a scientific analysis of the "known." For Agassiz experience does not usually entail analysis of internal cognitive states; rather, it is a vehicle for investigating a more interesting and objective outer world just waiting to be discovered and collected by this energetic systematist. Thus, the lasting influence of Agassiz upon James refers to James' attempt to develop an empirical scientific analysis of internal states of consciousness-psychology.

23. V. H. Viglielmo, trans., Nishida Kitarō, *A Study of Good* (Tokyo: Japanese Government Printing Office, 1960), p. 2.

24. Ibid.

25. William James, *The Principles of Psychology,* vol. 1 (New York: Dover Publications, 1950; Henry Holt and Company, 1890), pp. 189–90.

26. Nishida, *A Study of Good.* p. 2.

27. Ibid., p. 3.

28. James, *The Principles of Psychology.* 1:609.

29. Ibid., p. 606.

30. Ibid., p. 225.

31. Ibid., p. 278.

32. Nishida. *A Study of Good.* p. 9.

33. Ibid.

34. Ibid., p. 11.

35. William James. "A World of Pure Experience:" in *Essays in Radical Empiricism.* ed. Frederick Burkhardt (Cambridge: Harvard University Press, 1976), p. 22.

36. Nishida. *A Study of Good,* p. 11.

37. Ibid., p. 17. The final reference to James' texts in *A Study of Good* is to James' "deck of cards" illustration in "The Stream of Thought." James analyzes the thought processes involved as a person makes the statement, "a pack of cards is on the table:" in order to demonstrate. "What a thought *is* and what it may be developed into, or explained to stand

for, and be equivalent to, are two things, not one" *(The Principles of Psychology,* 1:278). Nishida is intrigued by James' idea that when the subject is thought of, the predicate is, in some sense, assumed.

38. Thus far we have focused upon Nishida's connection with William James. However, it must be mentioned that he was also influenced, perhaps to a greater extent, by the tradition of German idealism. The sources cited in footnote five also develop this connection. In particular, Nishida was influenced by the breadth of Hegel's global philosophy. Hegel was not only cognizant of foreign philosophical traditions, but he also attempted to articulate what he considered to be the relative merits of each tradition within his scheme. In this sense, Hegel was engaged in the systematic discipline of comparative philosophy. Nishida was motivated by Hegel's global spirit and attempted to further the cause by creating a more detailed analysis of philosophical presuppositions East and West. Ultimately, Nishida not only attempted to situate different philosophical traditions, but he also sought to create an original perspective whereby the limitations of particular traditions could be transcended. Since Nishida was very well read in the Western philosophical tradition, as well as his own tradition, his work represents some of the earliest and most insightful analysis in comparative (East/West) philosophy.

39. Actually this perspective was not uncommon among nineteenth-century biologists. In particular, taxonomy and systematics were considered by many to be fields that held significant theological value. Given the popularity of the proof for the existence of God by the argument of design (a la Arch-bishop Paley), the work of collectors and field biologists was frequently discussed in terms of theories concerning the nature of God's mind as revealed by His vast creation. Each new species discovered and classified added splendor to the vast diversity of God's creation. Much of the original opposition to Darwin's *On the Origin of Species,* including Agassiz's opposition, centered upon the non-teleological character of explanations for the transmutation of species contained therein. Without positing the fixity of species, which also implied their simultaneous creation, doubt would be cast upon God's direct "design" and perpetual involvement in the natural world. Recent study of Darwin's personal notebooks suggest that Darwin's famous "delay" in writing the *Origin* was due to his being wholly cognizant of the radical philosophical and theological ramifications that his thesis implied. For a commentary upon Agassiz's theological commitments, see Edward Lurie, *Louis Agassiz: A Life in Science* (Chicago: University of Chicago Press, 1960); Edward O. Wilson, *Biophilia* (Cambridge: Harvard University Press, 1984), p. 45; Stephen Jay Gould, "Uniformity and Catastrophe," in *Ever Since Darwin* (New York: W. W. Norton & Co., 1977), pp. 147–52; Stephen Jay Gould, "Agassiz in the Galapagos,"

in *Hen's Teeth and Horse's Toes* (New York: W. W. Norton & Co., 1983), pp. 107–19; Ernst Mayr, "Agassiz, Darwin, and Evolution," in *Evolution and the Diversity of Life* (Cambridge: Harvard University Press, 1976), pp. 251–76; and Louis Agassiz, *Contributions to the Natural History of the United States of America,* vol. 1 (Boston: Little, Brown, 1857). For discussions of Darwin's delay and readings of his notebooks, see Stephen Jay Gould, "Darwin's Delay," *Ever Since Darwin,* pp. 21–27; Sihran S. Schweber, "The Origin of the *Origin* Revisited," *The Journal of the History of Biology* 10 (1977): 229–316; Frank J. Sulloway, "The *Beagle* Voyage and Its Aftermath," *Journal of the History of Biology* 15 (1982): 325–96; Charles Darwin, *Metaphysies, Materialism, and the Evolution of Mind: Early Writings of Charles Darwin* (Chicago: University of Chicago Press, 1974); and Michael Ruse, *The Darwinian Revolution* (Chicago: University of Chicago Press, 1979).

40. Dilworth, "The Range of Nishida's Early Religious Thought," p. 419.

41. David Dilworth, "Nishida Kitarō: Nothingness as the Negative Space of Experiential Immediacy." *International Philosophical Quarterly* 13 (1973): 481.

42. Alasdair MacIntyre, *After Virtue* (Notre Dame: University of Notre Dame Press. 1981). p. 140. For another communitarian perspective, see Michael J. Sandel, *Liberalism and the Limits of Justice* (Cambridge: Cambridge University Press, 1982).

43. Edward O. Wilson, *Biophilia* (Cambridge: Harvard University Press, 1984), p. 1. Wilson first used the term in the *New York Times Book Review,* 14 January 1979, p. 43.

44. For a discussion of themes related to this point, see David Edward Shaner's "The Cultural Evolution of Mind," Edward O. Wilson's "The Evolutionary Origin of Mind," and Marvin Minsky's "The Society of Mind," in *The Personalist Forum* 3, no. 1 (Spring 1987): 33–69; 11–18; 19-32.

45. Wilson, *Biophilia,* p. 119.

46. See for example W. D. Hamilton, "The Genetical Evolution of Social Behavior," *Journal of Theoretical Biology* 7 (1964): 1–52; Edward O. Wilson, *Sociobiology: The New Synthesis* (Cambridge: Belknap Press of Harvard University Press, 1975); and Charles J. Lumsden and Edward O. Wilson, *Genes, Mind, and Culture* (Cambridge: Harvard University Press, 1981).

47. It should be noted that the seeds of this conceptual approach in post-Darwinian biology, contrary to Thomas Henry Huxley's more popular interpretation of a Darwinian world "red in tooth and claw," are at least as old as the work of the Russian Prince Kropotkin. See P. Kropotkin, *Mutual Aid: A Factor of Evolution* (New York: McClure Phillips and Company, 1903), and P. Kropotkin, *Ethics: Origin and Development* (New York: Benjamin Blom, 1924). Interestingly, the position of

Huxley's grandson is in accord with Kroptkin; see Sir Julian Huxley, "Cultural Process and Evolution," in A. A. Roe and G. G. Simpson, eds., *Behavior and Evolution* (New Haven: Yak University Press, 1958), pp. 437–54, and Sir Julian Huxley, "The Emergence of Darwinism," in Sol Tax, ed., *The Evolution of Life*, vol. I (Chicago: University of Chicago Press, 1960), pp. 1–21. For a representative essay of T. H. Huxley's position, see an excerpt from a larger work published in 1896 entitled "Evolution and Ethics," in Arthur L. Caplan, ed., *The Sociobiology Debate: Readings on Ethical and Scientific Issues* (New York: Harper and Row Publishers, 1978), pp. 27–34. Recent contributions to this important theme include Stephen Jay Gould, "Caring Groups and Selfish Genes," in *The Panda's Thumb* (New York: W. W. Norton and Co., 1980); Stephen Jay Gould, *The Flamingo's Smile* (New York: W. W. Norton and Co., 1985), pp. 64–95, and Louis A. Fourcher, "A View of Subjectivity in the Evolution of Communicative Behavior," *Journal of Social and Biological Structures* 1 (1978): 387–400; J. Hill, "The Origin of Socio-cultural Evolution," *Journal of Social and Biological Structures* I (1978): 377–86; David Layzer, "Altruism and Natural Selection," *Journal of Social and Biological Structures* 1 (1978): 297–305; David Layzer, "On the Evolution of Intelligence and Social Behavior," in Ashley Montague, ed., *Sociobiology Examined* (Oxford: Oxford University Press, 1980), pp. 220–53; Mary B. Williams, "Species are Individuals: Theoretical Foundations for the Claim," *Philosophy of Science* 52 (1985): 578–90; Vernon Pratt, "Functionalism and the Possibility of Group Selection," *Studies in the History of Philosophy of Science* 5 (1975): 371–72; Mihaly Csikszentmihalyi, "Sociocultural Speciation and Human Aggression," *Zygon* 8 (1973): 96–112; Clara Mayo, "Man: Not Only an Individual but a Member," *Zygon* 3 (1968): 21–31; Philip Hefner, "Toward a New Doctrine of Man: The Relationship of Man and Nature," *Zygon* 2 (1967): 127–51; Philip Hefner, "Survival as a Human Value," *Zygon* 15 (1980): 203–12; Philip Hefner, "Sociobiology, Ethics, and Theology," *Zygon* 19 (1984): 185–212; A. L. Rheingold and D. F. Hay, "Prosocial Behavior of the Very Young," in Gunther S. Stent, ed., *Morality as a Biological Phenomenon* (Los Angeles: University of Califomia Press, 1980), pp. 93–108; Michael Ruse, "Definitions of Species in Biology," *The British Journal for the Philosophy of Science* 20 (1969): 97–119; Michael Hammond, "Emile Durkheim's 'The Division of Labor in Society' as a Classic in Human Biosociology," *Journal of Social and Biological Structures* 6 (1983): 123–34; Charles J. Lumsden, "Cultural Evolution and the Devolution of Tabula Rasa:" *Journal of Social and Biological Structures* 6 (1983): 101–14; T. K. Pitcaim and F. F. Strayer, "Social Attention and Group Structure: Variations on Schubert's 'Winterreise'," *Journal of Social and Biological Structures* 7 (1984): 369–76.

48. It may be interesting to note that the concept of group selection does have a Japanese counterpart, albeit issuing from an entirely different context. See Watsuji Tetsurō, *Rinrigaku (Ethics),* vols. 10 and 11 of *Zenshū* [Complete Works], 2d ed. (Tokyo: Iwanami Shoten, 1978), chap. 1, "Ningen no gaku to shite no Rinrigaku no igi" [The Significance of Ethics as the Study of Man"], trans. David Dilworth, *Monumenta Nipponica* 26 (1971): 389–413; Tanabe Hajime, "The Logic of the Species as Dialectics," trans. David Dilworth and Taira Sato, *Monumenta Nipponica* 24 (1969): 273–88; Watsuji Tetsurō, "Yōkyoku ni arawareta rinri shisō: Japanese Ethical Thought in Noh Plays of the Muramachi Period," trans. David Dilworth, *Monumenta Nipponica* 24 (1969): 467–98; Richard B. Pilgrim, "Intervals (Ma) in Space and Time: Foundations for a Religio-Aesthetic Paradigm in Japan," a paper delivered at the "Interpreting Across Boundaries" Conference, sponsored by the Society for Asian and Comparative Philosophy, Honolulu, Hawaii, 1984; and Imanishi Kinji, "'A Proposal for *Shizengaku:* The Conclusion to the Study of Evolutionary Theory," *Journal of Social and Biological Structures* 7 (1984): 357–68.

CHAPTER 16

From Symbiosis (*Kyōsei*) to the Ontology of "Arising Both from Oneself and from Another" (*Gūshō*)[1]

HIROSHI ABE

What kind of questions should philosophers inquire into these days? In the first section, I will attempt to resolve this issue by analyzing main problem of this paper.

1. MAIN PROBLEM

Questions regarding the being of human beings would previously take forms such as, 'What is man?'[2] or 'What is man's place in the nature of things [*Sein*]?'[3] The purpose of these questions was to find a definition of the *essentia* of human beings, in order to obtain 'a unified idea of man'[4], which could integrate an enormous variety of information concerning the being of human beings in philosophy, theology, human science, etc. Moreover, according to Scheler, this purpose could be accomplished by determining the uniqueness of the being of human beings in which it differs from other ways of being (e.g., the principle of 'spirit' (*Geist*)) and by demarcating a location for the domain of the being of human beings in *Sein* (i.e., the entire system comprising all the existents that consists of different fields of being).

Needless to say, even approximately eighty years after Scheler's death, such a question continues to be of great importance. In fact, it can be further said that the question has much more relevance now than it did in his times, because in all the sciences, even in the field of philosophy itself, there currently exists an incredible level of specialization as compared to the situation eighty years ago.

Nevertheless, as mentioned above, this question has undergone a complete change at present, at the onset of the twenty-first century.

With global environmental issues becoming increasingly serious in recent times, the question regarding the being of human beings is compelled to undergo a transformation. What kind of transformation does this question experience as a result of these issues and why?

In his book *The Imperative of Responsibility*, Hans Jonas states the following: '*The presence of man in the world* had been a first and unquestionable given, from which all idea of obligation in human conduct started out. Now it has itself become an object of obligation: the obligation namely to ensure the very premise of all obligation'.[5] I would like to reply to the question under consideration by further elaborating upon this statement by Jonas.

Concerning the being of human beings, questions such as that by Scheler are, thus far, sufficient for our inquiry. Naturally, when we ask this traditional question, we presume the existence of an entire system comprising all the existents (Scheler's concept of *Sein*) and human beings—if we could not presuppose the *exsistentia* of all the existents including human beings as a given, it would be impossible for us to inquire into the traditional question. Nevertheless, the current situation of human beings is such that both the being of human beings and that of other existents can no longer be considered an indubitable foundation because of the increasing menace of global environmental issues. In the face of such a situation, it is very likely that the question pertaining to the being of human beings must inevitably change. For, if we wish to ask the above-mentioned traditional question today, it is crucial for us to engage ourselves, first and foremost, in inquiring into how the presupposition can be secured on the basis of which the inquiry concerning the traditional one itself is possible.

In this way, the question regarding the being of human beings has now changed from its traditional version to a modern one, for instance, *how the existence of both human beings and the entire system of all the existents can be secured*, which enables us to inquire into the former question itself. Along with this change, the original question's characteristics also undergo a transformation—the uniqueness of the being of human beings is no longer under consideration. Therefore, on what aspect of the being of human beings does this new question focus?

As everybody knows, every organism selectively draws matter and energy out of the environment for its own use, which it subsequently synthesizes or transforms for the purpose of self-preservation, reproduction, etc. (anabolism). In return, it discharges useless matter and heat, which are the products of anabolic activity, into the environment (catabolism). These two activities (i.e. metabolism) of the organism depend on the cyclic flow of matter and energy in its own ecosystem, which is based on a metabolic system consisting of producer, consumer, and decomposer. Further, this cycle of matter in the ecosystem is itself dependent upon a larger system, such as the water cycle between the earth's surface and the atmosphere and that of mineral nutrients between the land and the sea. Thus, the cycle of matter on earth forms the ultimate basis of being for all animate beings, who exist only because they have been cast into this worldwide circulation in nature from the beginning.

We human beings, who live by means of both metabolism and Marx's 'social metabolism' (a series of activities such as the development of resources, production, consumption and abandonment), are not exempted from this fundamental condition of being. Whether or not we are conscious of it, our existence requires being cast into the above-mentioned cycle of nature. It is impossible for us to deny this fact, since we cannot even make a denial of it without being based on such thrownness of the being of human beings. Therefore, the present-day question concentrates on the facticity of the being of human beings, who have been passively involved in the global circulation of nature from the outset. The moot question, as we have already seen, now inquires into the means by which the existence of human beings can be secured.

Before proceeding further, it is necessary to ask again the above-mentioned question: What kind of question should philosophers inquire into today? My answer to this is as follows: contemporary philosophers should inquire into how the existence of both human beings and the entire system of existents can be secured, focusing on the fact that human beings have been cast into the cycle of nature. Thus, this paper aims at considering this new question pertaining to the being of human beings. In such a scenario, how should we begin this consideration?

In his final years, Georg Picht devoted himself to discussing a similar question, whereby he instituted a science called 'human ecology' that deals with 'the conditions of human life on this planet'.[6] The present-day global ecological crisis caused by modern science motivated him to conceive of this new science. Faced with this difficult problem, he established a new standard of truth, which stressed that 'what is useful to life is "fruitful"'[7] and attempted to make 'a revision of the fundamental concepts and methods which have carried the science up to now'.[8] Therefore, at the onset, human ecology raises the following question concerning science and the logos on which it is based:

> If humankind makes itself the object of its science, that is, if it will apply the universal model of ecology to itself and build a 'human ecology'. . . . Now, with its knowledge, it no longer stands beyond and outside the domain of the object which it investigates. It can no longer ignore the recognition that *the projections of logos—the projections performed through technology—upon the biosphere change and often destroy this and that the logos itself is, therefore, an ecological first-rate determinative.* This experience must lead to a revolution in the self-understanding of the science. Namely, we can now no longer avoid the question *whether the science itself, its theoretical model, its axioms and the attitude of humankind toward the nature which is sketched in them beforehand have a structure that is in harmony with the life conditions of humankind in this same nature or whether the word 'science' indicates a thought form which cannot be integrated into our ecosystem because of its structure.*[9]

The first purpose of human ecology is this critical consideration of both science and the nature of its logos. Its second purpose lies in 'the integration of human beings' "logos" into the constitution of their ecosystem'[10], that is, the conception of a new logos that can unite with the structure of the human ecosystem, since 'human beings will only be able to survive in their ecosystem if they succeed in harmonizing their "logos" with the fact that they are living things'.[11]

Addressing these two purposes as our own tasks, which are, according to Picht himself, 'a reflection on the structure of the model of world which is presupposed when we build theories and on its relation to the structure of our biosphere'[12], we will endeavor to investigate the above question, namely, how can the existence of both human beings and the entire system of existents be secured?

Thus, in this paper, we will first focus upon biological and ecological research on symbiosis in order to clarify the *logos* on which it is based, along with critically considering the nature of this *logos* itself. Second, instead of this *logos*, we intend to present the idea of an alternative *logos*, which corresponds with the real fact of symbiosis as 'the structure of our biosphere', and ontology, which is founded on this new concept of *logos* and which, therefore, can potentially secure the existence of both human beings and the entire system of existents (Picht writes: 'If human beings should contribute to their self-preservation, then they must acknowledge that an ecosystem lies in the balance of symbiosis, which permits no population to regard itself as the center of the whole system.'[13] This is why symbiosis is thematized in this paper as 'the structure of our biosphere').

However, for achieving the above aim, it would be necessary to survey the history of biological (and ecological) research on symbiosis from the second half of the nineteenth century to the present day, in order to determine its fundamental trend, and from the research, learn about various concrete cases of symbiotic phenomena occurring in nature. We will perform such a survey in section two.

2. HISTORICAL DEVELOPMENT OF THE STUDY OF SYMBIOSIS AND VARIOUS ASPECTS OF SYMBIOTIC PHENOMENA

Let us provide a brief outline of the study of symbiosis in biology and ecology before describing its historical development. The term *symbiosis* can be roughly defined in three ways. For future discussion, we will refer to these three definitions as (a) 'symbiosis' (as its literal meaning—living together), (b) 'mutualism in the narrow sense of the term' and (c) 'mutualism in the broad sense of the term'. Considering these definitions of the word, the history of symbiotic study can be understood as the process of change in the concept of symbiosis, to be more precise, the process of change from (a) to (b) to (c). What is implied by each of these three definitions? How and why has the change of definition occurred?

(a) It is said that the study of symbiosis in biology was triggered by the publication of *Die Erscheinung der Symbiose* (1879) by Anton DeBary, a German researcher of plant pathology. DeBary took into account examples of organisms of different species living together while maintaining close relationships with each other—physically and physiologically. (The best-known examples of this phenomenon are the relationships between the *Actinia* and the *Paguroidea* and between the *Leguminosae* and the *leguminous bacterium*). He coined the term *Symbiose* to refer to the relationship of organisms of different species living (*bios*) together (*sym*). The first definition of the term *symbiosis* (i.e., 'symbiosis') is 'the living together of two organisms in close association'[14], in the above sense. It should be noted here that the required conditions for a symbiotic relationship, according to his definition, are as follows: (1) the 'close association' should be *invariant* and (2) the two species concerned should be 'living together', that is, the two species should be *physically close to each other.*

(b) It would not be difficult for careful observers, however, to recognize that the two conditions presented above are not always necessary for two species to maintain a close physiological or behavioral relationship. For instance, although the entomophilous flowers and the insects that visit them maintain a 'close association' and depend upon each other regarding issues of vital importance such as propagation for the former and the main source of food for the latter, literal constancy is not regularly observed in their interaction, nor is physical closeness in a strict sense found between their respective habitats, with the exception of those that have established a so-called runaway co-evolutional relationship only with particular species, as seen in that of the fig and the fig wasp. In that case, what could be the factor that contributes to generating these 'close associations' between organisms of different species? At this stage, the perspective of cost and benefit is incorporated in the consideration of interspecific relationships (in present-day biology, such cost and benefit, in terms of the fitness of individuals or increase in population, are to be evaluated from the viewpoint of gene fitness). Following this, the above-mentioned factor can be identified as the reciprocal relationship between species, and the meaning of the term *symbiosis* is transformed into that pertaining to 'an interaction between species that is beneficial to both.'[15] This becomes the second definition of the concept *symbiosis*, that is, mutualism in the narrow sense of the term, as presented in *Les Commensaux et les Parasites* (1875), written by Pierre van Beneden, a Belgian zoologist, four years before the publication of DeBary's book.

At the same time, an interesting fact has been pointed out regarding van Beneden's presentation of mutualism in the narrow sense of the term in his book. While discussing mutual phenomena in the natural world, van Beneden deliberately capitalized the word 'mutualists'. The reason behind this is thought to be that 'the capitalization of "Mutualists" is probably an indirect reference to the "Mutualite" societies organized by workers in France and Belgium to support each other financially.'[16] Van Beneden played an active role in the 1830 revolution to win Belgian independence. It is supposed that this political experience in his youth made him sympathetic towards the labor movement. Therefore, the concept of mutualism in the narrow sense of the term, when it was first presented, was associated with socialism in a broad sense. This association was reinforced by

Mutual Aid: A Factor in Evolution (1902), a representative book by Pyotr Alekseyevich Kropotkin, a famous Russian anarchist. As is generally known, Kropotkin attempted to illustrate in his book that Darwin's theory of evolution did not theoretically justify the necessity of the struggle for existence in nature; however, it scientifically proved the importance of mutual aid, that is, mutualism in the narrow sense of the term, which was exclusive of any competitive factors.

Despite this attempt by Kropotkin, 'mutualism has been avoided [among biologists and ecologists] during most of the twentieth century because of its association with left-wing politics (perhaps especially with Kropotkin)'[17]: It was not until the 1970s that mutualism was a subject for their consideration. However, this should not be understood merely as the consequence of the discrepancy between the freedom of the scientific stance from any dogma and a particular political ideology. In my opinion, the main factors leading to such a consequence should be noted as follows:

1. Dogma stating that it is competition that determines biological existence, such as that underlying Darwin's theory of natural selection concerning inter-individual relationships in a population, was also applied to the study of interspecific relationships in the biotic community (typical examples of this are the Lotka-Volterra model and 'the competitive exclusion principle' of C. F. Gause, which were both advocated in the 1920s and 1930s) and formed the basis of the above study (for instance, the theory of 'ecological niche', which used to occupy a central position in the field of biocenology, is based on the competitive exclusion principle).

2. Furthermore, due to the anarchist connotation mentioned above, symbiosis as mutualism in the narrow sense of the term was understood to exist in a paradoxical—and therefore incompatible—relationship with competition, which is the negative interaction between two species. The transition between mutualism and competition was considered to be impossible.

It is speculated that taking into account only these two factors, biological and ecological researchers were able to continue regarding mutualism as an exceptional phenomenon.

(c) In contrast, a new trend of symbiotic study that first appeared in the field of ecology in either the 1970s or 1980s can be considered as having resulted from skepticism concerning the very factors mentioned above. According to the first factor, a synecological paradigm showing that the interspecific relation in the biotic community is established mainly through competition; these days, the counterargument for this is generally supported by means of a variety of experimental manipulations as follows: 'Ecologists have made significant advances in understanding community structure and function by focusing on negative interactions such as predation, competition, and physical disturbance. . . . However, *positive interactions, such as facilitation and mutualism, also play pivotal roles in organizing communities*, and incorporating positive interactions into ecological theory can fundamentally alter our understanding of the processes and mechanisms that shape communities.'[18]

One interesting example providing evidence that 'mutualisms have large effects on community structure and function'[19] is the interaction between marine fishes such as salmonids and terrestrial trees lining the banks of rivers and streams.

> Juvenile salmonids spend up to two years feeding in freshwater streams and rivers before migrating to marine waters, where they mature and gain nearly all of their biomass, after which they return to their natal habitats to spawn and die. Trees subsidize production in these streams with the input of nutrients, leaf litter, and woody debris that supports higher populations of aquatic invertebrates, the main food source for juvenile salmon. . . . At the landscape scale, forested streams typically support up to three times more salmon than unforested streams. . . . Salmon, thus, benefit from living in streams surrounded by trees, but the benefit is not unidirectional. Spawning salmon migrations inject huge amounts of marine-derived nitrogen, carbon, and phosphorous into relatively nutrient-starved systems. . . . As a result, annual forest growth per unit area can be up to three times higher in forests adjacent to salmon spawning sites. . . . Furthermore, this subsidy of nutrients may alter the competitive balance among tree species.[20]

With respect to the second factor, the following skepticism is presented regarding one of its underlying assumptions—the impossibility of inter-transition between mutualism and competition (a similar skepticism is also presented regarding another assumption, the antinomy of mutualism and competition, as is shown later): 'Mutualists in one ecological setting can be adversaries in another setting . . . conversely, interactions traditionally viewed as antagonistic can be mutualistic, depending on environmental and community settings.'[21] The reason for this is as follows:

> Most ecology textbooks devote much space to the classification of species interactions. Regarding the interactions of two species, if we

symbolize as '+' the case in which the effect caused by one of the species increases the proliferation rate of population and fitness of individual in the other species, the opposite case as '-', and the case which is neither as 'o', . . . then, according to this classification, each interaction corresponds to only one combination of symbols, for example, competition is (- -) and predation is (+ -). While such a classification based on a one-to-one correspondence is clear and straightforward, *it often ignores the variability of interactions by emphasizing their average consequences.* However, *because the consequence of interactions is determined by the balance between cost and benefit, it can be reversed when the cost and the benefit change according to the ecologic condition. . . .* What should be noted here is that a *classification based on average consequences is in danger of overestimating one aspect of the interspecific relationship and that, therefore, the greater the variability becomes, the more unreliable such a classification becomes.*[22]

In other words, 'interspecific relationships are not always invariant but can change dynamically according to changes in time or space.'[23] The classification of interspecific relationships is nothing more than an abstraction used by biologists. Due to such variability, an interspecific relationship is competitive when the benefit for the two species concerned is lower than the cost, while it becomes mutualistic when the former exceeds the latter[24]. Thus, the third definition of the term symbiosis emerges, that is to say, 'interspecific interactions in which the benefits exceed the costs for both participants.'[25]

To understand this third definition, it should be noted that 'interspecific interactions in which the benefits exceed the costs for both participants' are 'the relationships in which the two species concerned use each other's existence for their respective benefit, not those in which each of the species gains the identical benefit or cost.'[26] Based on this explanation, agriculture, for example, can be perceived as mutualism because it involves 'a mutualistic interaction between humans and domesticated plants'[27], and similar relationships are also found in cultivation, stockbreeding, aquaculture, etc. Considering the various interspecific relationships of this type in nature, it could certainly be said that 'the earth is full of mutualistic relationships.'[28] This is why we describe the third definition as mutualism in the *broad* sense of the term.

As shown in the examples of 'apparent competition' and 'apparent mutualism'[29], the effects that one species can have on the other solely through an intermediary in the form of a third species (like A in the previous example) or a fourth or fifth plays an important role in the species interaction pertaining to mutualism in the broad sense of the term (as seen in the relationship between B and C in the previous example). The effects that 'require the presence of intermediary species in order to arise'[30] are named 'indirect effects' by ecologists. An indirect effect is different from a 'direct effect', which is 'a result of a physical interaction between two species'[31]: the former arises only in multi-species assemblages, while the latter 'would occur between a pair of species both in isolation and within multi-species communities of varying composition.'[32]

After studying such indirect effects, present day ecologists have discovered definite evidence against the second assumption mentioned above, the antinomy of mutualism and competition. Natural communities demonstrate competitive interactions between two species that 'are still antagonistic from a pairwise perspective but become mutualistic when imbedded within the nexus of community interactions.'[33]

A good example of such interactions is included in Michio Hori's research concerning scale-eating cichlids.

> Congeneric species of scale-eating cichlids may benefit each other even though they share the same prey. These predatory fishes consume the scales of other living fish using a species-specific approach and attack sequence. In two congeneric species, attack success was greater when in the presence of the congeneric, but not conspecific, scale eaters. . . . Presumably, prey fish were unable to be as vigilant against multiple attack strategies. Thus, two species using a similar resource (scales on a given fish) facilitated, rather than interfered with, each other's success.[34]

While tracing the process of change in the concept of symbiosis, we have briefly surveyed the history of symbiotic study in biology and ecology. It can be summarized as follows:

1. In nature, not only two species that are physically close to each other or whose physiological or behavioral relationships can be easily recognized but also two *apparently unrelated* species that are *far from each other*, such as trees in the forest and the salmon in the sea, can have indirect mutualistic relationships. As implied by this, 'all of the species in the global ecosystem are, after all, in direct and indirect mutualistic relationships.'[35] Furthermore, 'because matter circulates in the ecosystem, indirect effects reach throughout the earth through the inorganic environment'[36],

all living things on earth (including human beings) are in such mutualistic relationships.

2. The mutualistic relationships stated above arc not invariable and fixed, determined solely between the two species concerned. As suggested in the example regarding apparent competition and apparent mutualism, the mutualistic relationships can easily change *according to the context of the whole interspecific interactions of the two species, which are multiple because each can have mutual relationships with any other species.*

3. In addition, this interaction between the two species is not merely limited to a dichotomy such as 'either competition or mutualism' or 'either friend or foe'; it can principally *transcend such an 'either-or' relationship,* as is clearly shown in the above instance of scale-eating fish. In other words, it is a relationship that can be both competitive and mutualistic.

As elucidated thus far, indirect effects enable the occurrence of the above-mentioned interactions (from 1 to 3) between species. It can be said, therefore, that these very indirect effects are quite essential for the occurrence of symbiotic phenomena in nature.

This is well-demonstrated in the fact that the present research on symbiosis in ecology focuses on the indirect effects. In such a situation, how can indirect effects be explained at present? Can the *logos,* which underlies ecology and the real fact of symbiosis, and the indirect effects that are studied in ecology correspondent with each other? These questions will be examined in the next section.

3. The "logos" of Ecology

With regard to the first question, Masahiko Higashi, a Japanese ecologist, explains the method of research regarding indirect effects as follows:

> The term *indirect effect* generally refers to whatever "effect" that is transmitted from one to another through a mediator. . . . Recognized only through the logical chain which traces that of cause and effect, indirect effect is essentially invisible. . . . One of the clues to solve this problem is, paradoxically, found in the very characteristic of the indirect effect that "it is recognized only by tracing the chain of logic". In other words, it can be said that *an understanding of the indirect effect is essentially a theoretical problem and that indirect effects within a certain system can be defined and elucidated only by means of the theoretical model of the causal network.* . . . However, because each phenomenon requires its

own formulation based on the corresponding type of theoretical model, it is necessary to use a mathematical method to investigate indirect effects in every different type of model.[37]

In the above citation, it is stated that in ecology, an inquiry regarding the indirect effect is a 'theoretical problem' that should be clarified 'mathematically', based on a 'theoretical model of the causal network'. However, would it be possible to estimate the indirect effects of interspecific interactions as they exist in nature by means of such a mathematical method? Would we not risk distorting a phenomenon in the natural world by imposing a *logos* upon it that is fundamentally different from that of the very phenomenon, even if we happened to succeed in explaining it by applying the theoretical model, for example, the hypothesis preformed through experimental manipulations? Such questions will acquire a greater degree of significance if we consider the history of human errors that have led to unexpectedly adverse effects. Such effects have resulted from our intervening with the ecosystem, while aiming at achieving certain desired effects based on simulations of theoretical models, as shown in *Silent Spring* by Rachel Carson. To quote from Picht once again, we 'can no longer ignore the recognition that the projections of logos—the projections performed through technology—upon the biosphere change and often destroy this, and that the logos itself is, therefore, an ecological first-rate determinative'.

After considering the above problem, we will critically examine two representative methods of research pertaining to indirect effects in current biomathematics.

First, we will consider a method using a matrix as follows: 'There is a popular and useful basic theory which enables us to evaluate indirect effects through the evaluation of direct effects. . . . Arrange all species having direct effects vertically and all of those that are affected horizontally, in order to draw a chart (matrix) of direct effects produced by respective pairs. From the inverse matrix of this, you can evaluate indirect effects.'[38] Naturally enough, however, this method of calculating indirect effects is based on the assumption that all direct effects existing in the interactions of every organism in the biotic community have been evaluated. In addition, if '*it is theoretically necessary to evaluate the direct effects of the interactions of the entire species on the earth* because all of the species in the community have indirect effects not only on one another but also on the whole earth'[39], it is 'virtually impossible'[40], as Matsuda himself states, to reveal the actual nature of indirect effects by means of this method.

The second method under examination is 'path analysis', which is 'a statistical approach that estimates the degree to which changing a causal variable will affect a dependent variable through both direct and indirect pathways.'[41] A detailed explanation of this method is given below:

> The path analysis approach is a method which allows us to understand direct and indirect effects quantitatively by distributing correlations among variables in the multivariate system, the causal relations of which have been clarified. . . . In this method, a model named 'path diagram' should be made before beginning analysis. In making the model, we connect one variable to another by drawing arrows (paths) which indicate causal relations or temporal successions. The magnitude of the direct effect of a path is expressed as a standardized partial regression coefficient of multiple regression, which is called 'path coefficient'. A path which leads from one variable to another variable through various arrows shows the indirect effect of the former on the latter and its magnitude is calculated by multiplying all of the path coefficients of the respective arrows.[42]

However, as long as the basic premise is that the causal relationships among variables, the objects of analysis, 'have been clarified', path analysis contains a problem which is similar to that of the first method: 'As the complexity of a causal model increases, sample sizes must also increase. This may limit the application of this approach in complex systems.'[43] Moreover, a more serious problem of this method has been pointed out: 'Because path analysis is related to traditional linear regression techniques, which assume unidirectional causality, it is unclear whether it can adequately handle reciprocal effects.'[44] It is evident, therefore, that this approach is also inappropriate for understanding the reality of indirect effects among organisms.

Why are these mathematical analyses unable to show us the indirect effect as it occurs? It is because, in our opinion, both of these methods basically follow a procedure in which (1) initially, the indirect effect is reduced to the direct effects between two species, which are understood only as linear and unilateral effects between species in other words, as those picked out of an entire context of linked interactions between all species in the community and (2) the indirect effect is reconstructed by summing up these direct effects.

(This can be regarded as a method based on the 'four rules of logic' advocated by Descartes in his *Discourse on Method.*)

In that case, why do ecologists adopt such methods? As indicated by Higashi's above-mentioned comment that an indirect effect is 'recognized only through the chain of logic which traces that of cause and effect', ecologists adopt such methods in an attempt to understand all kinds of interspecific relationships by solely considering *the model of the causality* of two species as a *linear and unidirectional interaction.* This view held by ecologists is based on the hidden premise that the cause exists independently of the effect. This is because, if the cause and the effect in the causality were not different from each other but were identical and continuous, the effect of the cause would plainly be the same as the cause itself; in other words, no differing effect would arise from the cause, and therefore, no causality would exist. If we define an autogenous occurrence as 'arising from oneself' and a heterogenous one as 'arising from another', then we can give another interpretation to the above-mentioned premise of ecologists— causality should be arising from another, not arising from oneself.

This, however, suggests that the above premise is located in the logical space dominated by binaries such as 'either arising from another (i.e., the existence of causality) or arising from oneself (i.e., the non-existence of causality)'. In accordance with Tokuryū Yamanouchi, a Japanese philosopher of the Kyoto school, we name this bivalence of either affirmation or negation "logos". Subsequently, we can say that *the logos that underlies ecology is none other than "logos" as a binary logic.*

Now that the *logos* of ecology has been clarified in this manner, we should consider the second question: does "logos" correspond to the indirect effect'?

We already have the answer to this question. Although "logos" is equivalent to the above-mentioned causal relationship between the two species (i.e., the abstract direct effect that is separated from the linked interactions among all the species in the community for the purpose of adapting to the "logos"), it does not correspond to the interrelationships among organisms in nature, which are controlled by indirect effects. This is because such relationships cannot be linear and one-way causal relationships—for example, the causalities of a case in which species A (which is the cause) has existed independently of species B (which is affected) before A has any effect on B.

Let us reformulate our discussion thus far. As shown in the above-mentioned ecological studies of symbiosis, when species Y has an effect on species Z, more precisely, when Y has an influence on every species in the community, and ultimately, on the earth through its effect on Z, Y is constantly affected either directly or indirectly by every other species, including Z. Otherwise, it would be impossible for Y to exist in nature. (This manner of existence also underlies the above-stated characteristic of thrownness of the being of human beings). If Y depends on Z to such a degree that Y cannot have any effect on Z until Z exists, the causal relationship between Y and Z can be regarded as an effect of Z on itself. In this sense, this causality can be said to be arising from oneself. Nevertheless, as long as Y and Z are different from each other, any effect of the former on the latter should be thought of as arising from another. In such a case, is the effect of Y on Z arising from oneself or arising from another?

If we attempt to answer this question by strictly adhering to reality, we have to say that the effect neither arises from oneself nor from another or that it arises both from oneself and from another. This means that the above interaction of Y and Z, which is controlled by the indirect effect (i.e. relationship between the two species in nature), cannot be understood by means of a "logos" based on binary logic.

In that case, what kind of *logos* can be appropriately applied to the indirect effect, the reality of symbiotic phenomena in nature, and new ontology founded on this alternative *logos*? We will answer this question in the subsequent concluding section.

4. The Logic of *Lemma* and the Ontology of "Arising Both from Oneself and from Another" (*GŪSHŌ*)

First, we shall inquire into why "logos" cannot correspond with indirect effects. If we recall the example of the effect of Y on Z or the above instance of scale-eating cichlids, this question can be easily answered: it is because "logos" has only two values—'x' and 'non-x'—and therefore, it is impossible to acknowledge the existence of an intermediate between them (i.e., the law of the excluded middle). However, since indirect effects rule in nature, there can also be something which is 'both x and non-x' (e.g., to arise both from oneself and from another) or 'neither x nor non-x' (e.g., to arise neither from oneself nor from another).

If this is so, then the suitable *logos* for indirect effects would undoubtedly be based, not on the law of the excluded middle which is the basis for the "logos" but, neologically speaking, on 'the law of the *included* middle'. In the following consideration of the characteristics of such a new *logos*, we can derive a clue from T. Yamanouchi's interpretation of Nāgārjuna's *Mūlamadhyamakakārikā* (*Treatise Concerning the Middle*, in Japanese, 中論). In his study, Yamanouchi writes as follows:

> The law of contradiction forbids strictly both affirmation and negation from being valid at the same time. Therefore, [Western] *logos* declares not only that judgment should be either affirmative or negative but also that it cannot be otherwise, for example, the intermediate and the third. But Nāgārjuna's philosophy, in contrast, dares to posit 'the middle' and advocates the middle way [of logical thinking]. This is the reason why his main work is entitled 'Treatise Concerning the Middle' or 'Treatise Concerning the Intuition of the Middle'. . . . Obviously, the thought of 'the middle' is central to his position. It may be probably sage to acknowledge that this means *the reverse of the law of the excluded middle*.[45]

In such a context, how does such logic as can be found in 'the reverse of the law of the excluded middle' appear in this *Treatise Concerning the Middle*?

In general, the type of statement that consists of four phrases is called 'tetra-lemma' (in Japanese, 四句分別 or 四論). It is well-known that the *Treatise Concerning the Middle* contains a number of odes in the tetra-lemma form.[46] In essence, however, we can divide them all into two ideal types.[47]

(A) S is (1) neither P (2) nor non-P (3) nor both 'P and non-P' (4) nor 'neither P nor non-P'.
(B) S is (1) either P (2) or non-P (3) or 'both P and non-P' (4) or 'neither P nor non-P'.

Thus, this typical example of Nāgārjuna's argument, in accordance with tetra-lemma, refers to 'the cases of (1) affirmation, (2) negation, (3) both affirmation and negation, and (4) neither affirmation nor negation.'[48] According to Yamanouchi, such an argument can be regarded as an expression of 'the logic which does not exclude but includes the middle, if we classify these [i.e., the third and fourth eases] into 'the middle.'[49]

However, the following question arises at this point: what kind of reasoning justifies the reverse of the law of the excluded middle in Nāgārjuna's logic, which is composed of four lemmas—affirmation, negation, both affirmation and negation, and neither affirmation nor negation? Concerning this aspect, Yamanouchi explains: 'I transpose the third and fourth [lemmas], in order to take "neither affirmation nor negation" as the third lemma and "both affirmation and negation" as the fourth one. I think that *"neither affirmation nor negation" is at the core of the whole logic [of Nāgārjuna]. . . . It is "neither affirmation nor negation" that opens up the viewpoint of "the middle"*. Without grounding on this lemma, "both affirmation and negation" would be impossible.'[50] If this is so, how does the third lemma of 'neither affirmation nor negation' render the standpoint of 'the middle' possible?

Needless to say, a remarkable characteristic of 'neither affirmation nor negation' is that this lemma is not only a negation of affirmation but also a negation of negation. In fact, it is easy for us to understand what is implied by 'negation of affirmation', but what could 'negation of negation' possibly mean? Yamanouchi replies as follows:

> The answer to this question is that this negation [of negation] alone is meaningless and that it cannot be meaningful without its close relation to other lemmas. . . . Seemingly, it may be nothing but a duplication of negation. But in substance, it turns the second lemma toward the first one and combines them. . . . Because 'negation of negation', which is no simple negation, makes negation approach affirmation and relieves it from being hopeless denial. If there is neither affirmation nor negation, what remains? Common sense appears to indicate that there is nothing but pure nihility. Nevertheless, or rather therefore, *there arises a world where both affirmation and negation are negated: it can be not only affirmation but also negation because it is neither. It is nothing but the world of the fourth lemma.*[51]

The crux of Yamanouchi's explanation is that 'negation of negation' means a denial of the very dichotomy inherent in 'either affirmation or negation' and that only the abandonment of bivalence in 'neither affirmation nor negation' makes 'both affirmation and negation' possible, which is none other than the standpoint of 'the middle', because it builds bridges between affirmation and negation and enables both of them to coexist.

According to Yamanouchi, Nāgārjuna's logic is the tetra-lemma to which the third lemma is central, which is 'not mere negation but lies at least in a complex connection between affirmation and negation and enables negation itself to evoke a new affirmation.'[52] In reference to this, we will use the term 'the logic of *lemma*', in Yamanouchi's words. Therefore, we can regard the *lemma* itself as a form of logos which is capable of corresponding to the indirect effect.

In such a situation, based on this logic of *lemma*, what should we consider 'the ontology of life' that corresponds to the reality of symbiosis? In conclusion, I would like to outline my own opinion pertaining to this problem.

In projecting such ontology (*logos* of being), our fundamental aim is not to elucidate the being of human beings and of living things within the framework of the existing principle of explanation but to see the structure (*logos*) of the reality of life on earth (including human beings) as it exists.

If we recognize that all natural organisms mutually depend on one another in direct or indirect relationships, presented above in the ecological research on symbiosis and in the example regarding the effect of Y on Z, then it would be impossible to find an organism in nature that could have arisen from itself. This is because it is impossible for A to exist in nature independently of B, in other words, to be as *substantia*. Without B, A would not be as A itself. Correspondingly, does every living thing in nature exist in such a manner of arising from another as is seen in the above-mentioned linear and one-way causality? The answer would be in the negative when A is dependent on B, it would be incorrect to think that B already exists as *substantia* before A, that is, without any relation to A, for it is only when B also is reliant upon A that B exists as itself.

In short, the being of life in nature is neither arising from oneself nor from another. In other words, A and B do not exist in a way similar to *substantia*; therefore, the mutual relationship between both does not correspond with the relationship between *substantiae* either. Hence, as long as we accept the ontology of *substantia*, we can provide no other expression to describe the being of living things apart from '[arising] from a non-cause'[53] in Nāgārjuna's words.

In contrast, Nāgārjuna raises the following query: 'Whatever existent that is established through contingence, how can that, if it is not yet established, be contingent?'[54] As mentioned by Nāgārjuna, without the substantial being of each organism, the above-stated mutual relationships in nature would not be possible. If A did not exist before B, it would be impossible for B to exist as *dependent* on A and vice versa. That is to say, as its own condition of possibility, the mutual dependence of A and B necessarily requires the substantial being of the two. Seen from this perspective, the interaction between A and B is such that one is as *substantia* (in other words, one has arisen from itself), and then, by depending upon this fact (that is, by the fact of having arisen from another), the other also exists. Given this condition, it is necessary to regard the being of living things as arising both from oneself and from another.

Even if, as mentioned above, the interaction between A and B in nature is based upon the being of the two, which implies arising both from oneself and from another, it is obvious that this kind of being of A and B prevents their mutual dependence from being realized. This is because their mutual dependence is made possible by their existence as arising from a non-cause. Thus, we can conclude that *the being of every organism in nature is arising both from oneself and from another, even though or rather just because it is arising from a non-cause*, and that the ontology of life corresponding with the reality of symbiosis is, therefore, none other than that of arising both from oneself and from another—which aims to elucidate the structure (*logos*) of being, namely, that of arising both from oneself and from another combined with arising from a non-cause.

Without doubt, in order to arrive at the concrete content of this new ontology, it is important for us to learn a great deal from not only the latest ecological research pertaining to different symbiotic phenomena in nature but also the latest theoretical analysis of biomathematics (e.g. the theory of a complex adaptive system[55]), which attempts to explain the mechanism of symbiotic phenomena as it occurs. From such a study, we could formulate a perfect answer to the question regarding the being of human beings, or how the existence of both human beings and the entire system of existents can be secured.

Notes

1. In Japanese, both *kyōsei* and *gūshō* are written using the same Chinese character (i.e., 共生).
2. Max Scheler (tr. by Hans Meyerhoff), *Man's Place in Nature* (New York: The Noonday Press, 1969), p. 3.
3. *Ibid.* (The information within brackets is mine).
4. *Ibid.*, p. 6.
5. Hans Jonas (tr. by H. Jonas in collaboration with David Herr), *The Imperative of Responsibility—In Search of an Ethics for the Technological Age* (Chicago & London: The University of Chicago Press, 1984), p. 10.
6. Georg Picht, 'Ist Humanokologie moglich? [Is Human-ecology Possible?]' in *Humanokologie und Frieden* [*Human-ecology and Peace*], ed. Constanze Eisenbart (Stuttgart: Klett-Cotta, 1979), p. 17.
7. *Ibid.*, p. 32.
8. *Ibid.*, p. 27.
9. *Ibid.*, p. 21f. (italics mine).
10. *Ibid.*, p. 66.
11. *Ibid.*
12. *Ibid.*, p. 30.

13. *Ibid.*, p. 66.
14. *Ibid.*, p. 66.
15. *Ibid.*
16. *Ibid.*, p. 317.
17. *Ibid.*, p. 318. (The information within brackets is mine).
18. Mark E. Hay et al., 'Mutualisms and Aquatic Community Structure: The Enemy of my Enemy is my friend' in *Annual Review of Ecology, Evolution, and Systematics* 35, 2004, p. 175f. (italics mine).
19. *Ibid.*, p. 176.
20. *Ibid.*, p. 190f.
21. *Ibid.*, p. 176.
22. Takayuki Ōgushi, 'Kotaigun kara shukankankei he [From Population to Interspecific Relationship]' in *Chikyūkyōseikei to wa nanika [What is Global Symbiotic System?]* ed. Masahiko Higashi and Takuya Abe (Tokyo: Heibonsha, 1992), p. 202. (italics mine).
23. *Ibid.*, p. 201.
24. For instance, we can postulate a circumstance in which A, a predator, preys on two species, B and C. B and C are eventually involved in a relation wherein either one's increase in population results in an increase in that of A, the predator, which leads to a higher predation pressure, thus causing a decrease in the other's population. In this situation, the relation between B and C is competitive, because both of the species suffer a loss by being victims to the predation. This is, in turn, because their indirect interactions promote the propagation of the common predator. Such a relationship is referred to as 'apparent competition' by ecologists.

    This apparent competition between B and C, however, changes into a mutualistic relationship as soon as A's 'switching' of the food preference occurs in such a way that it preferentially preys on only the species that has a larger population. This means that A preys only on B when B's population increases. Consequently the predation pressure for C decreases, which results in an increase in its proliferation rate. Thereafter, the switching occurs again, prompting A to prey exclusively on C, this time, while the reproductive rate of B increases. In this situation, therefore, B and C develop a mutual relationship through their alternate self-sacrifice for each other. This relationship is called 'apparent mutualism' in ecology.
25. Hay et al., *op. cit.*, p. 176.
26. Hiroyuki Matsuda, *Kyōsei to wa nanika—sakushu to kyōsō wo koeta seibutsudoshi no daisan no kankei [What is Symbiosis?—the third relationship of organisms which is beyond exploitation and struggle]* (Tokyo: Gendaishokan, 1995), p. 23.
27. *Ibid.*, p. 57.
28. Makoto Katō, 'Seibutsu no kyōsei kara mita shizen [Nature Viewed from Symbiosis of Organisms]' in *Kankyō toshiteno shizen, shakai,*

bunka [*Nature, Society and Culture as Environment*] ed. Kōgaku Arifuku (Kyoto: Kyoto University Press, 1997) p. 61.

29. Cf. fn. 24.

30. J. Timothy Wootton, 'The Nature and Consequences of Indirect Effects in Ecological Communities' in *Ann. Rev. Ecol. Syst.* 25, 1994, p. 444.

31. *Ibid.*

32. *Ibid.*

33. Hay et al., op. cit., p. 185.

34. *Ibid.*, p. 189. Hori also reported other interesting observations: 'Mutualism also may occur among individuals within a species, as exemplified by frequency-dependent selection in the scale eater *Perissodus microlepis*. Individual *P. microlepis* have asymmetrical mouthparts and corresponding attack strategies: "right-handed" individuals have mouthparts oriented to the right and attack the left side of their prey; "left-handed" individuals have mouthparts oriented to the left and attack the right side of their prey. Deviations from an even ratio of morphs within a population resulted in lower attack success in the dominant morph. . . . These observations suggest that these two morphs act mutually to increase attack success by decreasing prey-fish alertness for attacks from one side or the other' (*Ibid.*).

35. Matsuda, *op. cit.*, p. 125.

36. *Ibid.*

37. M. Higashi, 'Kansetsukoka—shukankankei no hukuzatsusa, jyunansa wo umidasu kakureta sayo [Indirect Effects—Hidden Effects Producing Complexity and Flexibility of Interspecific Interactions]' in Higashi and Abe, *op. cit.*, p. 223. (italics mine).

38. Matsuda, *op. cit.*, p. 127.

39. *Ibid.* (italics mine).

40. *Ibid.*

41. Wootton, *op. cit.*, p. 457f.

42. Izumi Washitani, 'Shokubutsu no hanshoku to seibutsukan sōgosayō [Plant Propagation and Biotic Interactions]' in *Samazamana kyōsei— seibutsushukan no tayōna sōgoriyō [Various Symbiosis—Diversified Interspecific Interactions*] ed. T. Ohgushi (Tokyo: Heibonsha, 1992), p. 126f.

43. Wootton, *op. cit.*, p. 459.

44. *Ibid.*

45. Tokuryū Yamanouchi, *Rogosu to renma [logos and Lemma]* (Tokyo: Iwanami, 1974), p. 86. (The information within brackets and italics are mine).

46. Among all the odes in *Treatise Concerning the Middle*, which are approximately 450 in number, over 80 have a tetra-lemma form (including those that are abridged and imperfect). Cf. Musashi Tachikawa, *Kū no kōzō—Chūron no ronri [The Structure of Sunyata—The Logic of Mūlamadhyamakakārikā*] (Tokyo: Daisanbunmeisha, 1986), p. 132.

47. Cf. *ibid.*, p. 131.
48. Yamanouchi, *op. cit.*, p. 71.
49. *Ibid.*, p. 70. (The information within the brackets is mine). Naturally, in contrast to Yamanouchi's interpretation, there exists another version that states, 'fundamental laws of formal logic, such as that of contradiction and that of the excluded middle are obeyed in the tetra-lemma of *Mūlamadhyamakakārikā*' (Tachikawa, *op. cit.*, p. 132.). However, it is no necessary for us to determine which argument is correct. As stated above, the main intention of this paper is to conceptualize the *logos* in such a way as to transcend the dichotomy resulting from the law of the excluded middle. This is why our present consideration focuses on Yamanouchi's interpretation.
50. Yamanouchi, *op. cit.*, p. 71. (The information within the brackets and italics are mine).
51. *Ibid.*, p. 190f. (The information in the brackets and italics are mine).
52. *Ibid.*, p. 191. On the contrary, the above logic cannot be directly found in *Treatise Concerning the Middle*. 'Nāgārjuna's logic of *sunyata* primarily implies radical negation of the fourth lemma [i.e. "neither P nor non-P"]' (Akiyoshi Tanji, 'Gangyo no 'kishinron'-chūshaku no ichikōsatsu [A Study of Wonhyo's Commentary on *Discourse on the Awakening of Faith in the Mahayana* (大番起信論)]' in *Indogaku-Bukkyōgaku-Kenkyū* [*Journal of Japanese Society for Indian and Buddhist Studies*] vol. 51 num. 1, 2002, p. 10.). In other words, Nāgārjuna himself gives no explicit explanation of how 'both affirmation and negation' in the third lemma is deduced from 'neither affirmation nor negation' of the fourth one. According to Tanji, the first person to express 'the logic of *sunyata*' (*ibid.*), which shows the ground of the transition from the latter to the former, is Wonhyo, a priest in the seventh century Silla Kingdom who was known as a representative of early Korean Buddhism. In his commentary on *Discourse on the Awakening of Faith in the Mahayana*, Wonhyo 'argues that absolute negation is absolute affirmation by interpreting "one soul [i.e., the soul of all sentient beings]" as the fourth lemma [i.e., "neither affirmation nor negation"] and "two aspects of the soul [i.e., 'the soul as suchness" and "the soul as birth-and-death"]" as "both suchness and birth-and-death", which corresponds to the third lemma, and then understanding that one soul and its two aspects are one and the same' (*ibid.*, p. 10f. The information within brackets is mine).
53. Nāgārjuna, (tr. by David J. Kalupahana), *The Philosophy of the Middle Way—Mūlamadhyamakakārikā* (Albany: State University of New York Press, 1986), p. 105. (The information within brackets is mine).
54. *Ibid.*, p. 202.
55. Cf. Simon A. Levin, *Fragile Dominion: Complexity and the Commons* (Cambridge, Mass: Perseus Books, 1999).

CHAPTER 17

The Confucian Environmental Ethics of Ogyū Sorai: A Three-Level, Eco-Humanistic Interpretation

"A Confucian ethic might be described as a form of social ecology because a key component is relationship in the human order against the background of the natural order. A profound sense of the interconnectedness of the human with one another and with nature is central to Confucian thinking. The individual is never seen as an isolated entity but always as a person in relation to another and to the cosmos."

—Mary Evelyn Tucker[1]

"Given the success of the Japanese people in intensively using and densely inhabiting a limited and fragile environment over many centuries without destroying either its beauty (albeit partly marred by the devastating postwar industrialization) or its productivity, they may be exceptionally well qualified to take the lead in conserving an analogously small and fragile planet."

—J. Baird Callicott[2]

Introduction

While it is the natural environment that sustains human society, it is human society that can destroy or protect the natural environment. So, in order to cope with the coming ecological age, our ethics must include sound social ethics and sound environmental ethics at the same time. In the main trend of traditional Western anthropocentric ethics, there are beliefs in objective values that are supposed to be absolute, eternal, universal, unchanging, and applicable to all human beings and their cultures. The ethical system based on such beliefs is so strong, monolithically rigid, and not even partly concessional that it tends, when confronted with different kinds of cultural and ethical views, to reject them entirely. The merits of different social ethics backed by sound views of nature have historically been beyond the sight of Western anthropocentric ethics. Thus, traditional Eastern ethical systems have been severely criticized and undeservedly neglected by modern thinkers in both the West and Japan.

There occur, however, in contemporary societies many moral conflicts between excessive evaluation of human values and excessive underestimation of natural values to the extent that human viability itself is at stake.[3] Population explosion, excessive industrialization, factory farming on a global scale, and other causes of environmental degradation (to give but a few instances), would not have arisen if people were much more aware of the symbiotic welfare of all humans and nature. The more people are imbued with Western modern cultures, the harder it is to depart from human-centered principles to which they have adhered and by which they have been nourished. Yet, in today's climate of ecological crisis, it is of the utmost importance to let human-centered principles be overridden by ecology-oriented principles in order to be impartial between human and natural values.

Traditional Western ethical theorists such as Plato, Kant, Mill, and Hare have highly developed social ethics, yet problematic views of nature. On the other hand, the emerging environmental ethics represented by such environmental thinkers as Leopold, Naess, Vandana Shiva, and Callicott have replaced the modern Western worldview with an ecological worldview that is revolutionary enough to challenge traditional Western ethics.[4] While the Eastern ethical and religious traditions have presupposed a respect for nature (or an eco-holistic view of nature in today's terms), Western social ethics have been traditionally backed by a human-centered view of nature. This has resulted in a dichotomy between modern Western systems, which have rich social ethics and flawed views of nature, and traditional non-Western systems, which have poor social ethics characterized by sound ecological views of nature. Callicott once criticized Singer's sentientism as merely an expansion of the traditional Western human-centered view, to which Singer responded that environmental ethics has not developed to cope with today's threat yet.[5] If a sound social ethic grounded in a sound view of nature is only a utopian dream, then there can be no ethic to save the global village from its current ecological crisis. So, it is necessary—even urgent—that social ethics and environmental ethics are somehow combined. In order to preserve our natural environment, it is imperative that we create a society that exists in symbiosis with nature. Both environmental and social ethics must not be considered separately, since environmental ethics must, I think, be supported by social ethics and social ethics must be based on the sound environmental ethics. This type of moral thinking will create a new ethic to cope with our environmental crisis for the sustainable future.

In post-war Japan, politics, economy, education, and other institutions backed by Western modern thoughts have prevailed and replaced the traditional ecological worldviews and ideas. It is only in recent years that the environmental ethics embedded in traditional Japanese thought have been given a fresh look by Western environmental thinkers, as exemplified by Callicott's monumental work, *Earth's Insights*.[6] If a sound environmental philosophy could be found in traditional Japanese thought, there would be a foundation upon which the Japanese people could build a sustainable society. Confucianism is one of the most influential philosophical systems in Japan and has contributed to that country's ecology-oriented traditional society. While Japanese Confucianism was started by Kaibara Ekken and practiced by Ninomiya Sontoku, its greatest thinker was Ogyū Sorai.[7]

This essay will sketch Sorai's traditional framework of social and environmental ethics from the perspective of contemporary ethics, including the holistic environmental ethics of Naess and Callicott and the analytical methodology of Mackie and Hare.[8] Sorai offers a three-level, eco-humanistic philosophy that offers a sound social ethic grounded on a firm environmental ethic.

1. SORAI'S TWO-LEVEL UTILITARIANISM

Ogyū Sorai (1666–1728) was born in Edo, the scion of a samurai family. His father served Tsunayoshi, the fifth Shōgun, as a physician and was exiled to Kazuma (now in Chiba prefecture) from 1679 to 1690. These years of exile were hard, though living among and watching common fishermen and farmers influenced Sorai's thinking thereafter. Upon his return to Edo, he set himself up as a Confucian teacher, and later served as an advisor to Tokugawa Yoshimune, the seventh Shōgun. His interests included poetry and music, politics, military science, linguistics and philosophy. In the Japanese scholarly tradition, Chinese was the equivalent of classical Latin, and Sorai mastered Chinese mainly by studying the Six Classics.[9] In his school, conversations were in Chinese, and he left many volumes of philosophy and poetry written in classical Chinese verse. He devoted himself to philological analysis and, using his linguistic methodology, attacked Chu Hsi and other Neo-Confucians on the grounds that their usage of key words was mistaken. His commentary on *The Analects* was quite original. He had a vast number of followers and his influence on the Japanese scholarly tradition, culture, and education was profound. He was so original that Sorai-learning has been as influential as Chu Hsi-learning and Yang-ming-learning in the Japanese Confucian tradition.

Sorai drew from Confucian thought to create a philosophy that was distinctly utilitarian. The purpose of Sorai's ethico-politics is to make people happier (安民 "an-min"), as evidenced in the following passages:

> The way of Confucius is the way of early kings . . . The way of the early kings is the way that provides for the peace of the realm below heaven (安天下 "an-tenka").[10]

This ancient passage suggests the importance of stabilizing the realm below heaven and the future world.

> The intention of the early kings was simply to pacify people.[11]

Here we can clearly see that the main criterion of Sorai's ethico-politics lies in the happiness and peace of people and society (a sort of social happiness ethics.) The way of the ancient sage kings can provide a model or paradigm for rulers of later ages. In this process, the ultimate purpose of our morals and politics could be seen to be synonymous with the utility principle of the greatest happiness for the greatest number.

Another similarity between Sorai's ethics and Western utilitarianism is the indirect application of the utility principle (of general happiness). In Hare's two-level utilitarianism, simple general principles for everyday practical usage—called intuitive principles—derive from the utility principle.[12] Thus, practical rules, political and legal institutions, and other kinds of systems are chosen, and justified, by the criterion of contributing to the increase of people's interests (or the general happiness). Intuitive principles—such as those that are widely accepted in each society—should lead to the maximization of people's interests. In this regard, people do not need to constantly think critically which course of action would lead to the general happiness. Rather, they need only obey the accepted, simple, general principles that would make society better and people's character upright. This rough sketch of the division of the fundamental utility principle and secondary, derivative intuitive principles should be sufficient for our purpose of comparing modern Western ethics with Sorai's system.

For Sorai, the ultimate purpose of ethico-politics is the happiness and peace of the people and society (安民、安天下 *an-min, an-tenka*). For that purpose to be realized, political, legal, and educational institutions (said to have been made by sage kings) are needed. Subjects of educational institutions are poetry, literature, ritual propriety, and music (詩書礼楽 *shi-sho-rei-gaku*). Thus, Sorai's theory corresponds to Hare's two-level utilitarianism, although it was not as analytic and sophisticated as its Western equivalent.

Ritual propriety (礼 *li*, or rites) can be roughly formulated as "the manner of communication amongst humans, and between humans and nature," and is important in understanding people's desire to return to the "origin of the whole," that is, to be united with the whole.[13] Music (楽) is associated, in Confucian traditions, with rites: "Music expresses the harmony of the universe, while rituals express the order of the universe. Through harmony all things are influenced and through order all things have a proper place."[14] This is reminiscent of the Pythagorean idea of cosmic music. The education of people in music, literature, and rites corresponds well with Plato's notion of primary education in the ideal state.[15]

The ideal society, as Sorai considers it, would be quite holistic and organic in contrast with our modern individualistic, democratic society. In his time, the state was considered to be a closed world and Sorai did not need to think about international politics or the sovereignty of the state. So, when he spoke about "peace under Heaven" (安天下 *an-tenka*), he meant both the whole society and the natural environment. In his ideal society, people took part in social activity according to their abilities and temperaments (in this point his ideal society is surprisingly similar to the Platonic ideal state). He preferred the independent, feudalistic Han to a prefectural system under centralized government. The special and important role of rulers is to know people well and appoint able and suitable people as supporters of government. Moreover, ruling samurai should settle on their own lands, which would obviate the necessity of residing in Edo every other year, where they were required to hold a residence and leave hostages to prevent rebellion against the Shogunate.[16] He was keen that local industry be based on agricultural production, and recommended that rulers or leaders lead simple and frugal lives. The development of a monetary economy would encourage the ruling samurai to adopt extravagant lifestyles that would ultimately lead to economic corruption and decay. Frugality (by staying in one's own land) and the system of ritual propriety (*li*) would lead to socio-economic stability and save people from poverty and distress. Rulers, as the father and mother of the people, must be frugal and impartial judges, enforcing sound institutions and striving for the contentment and peace of the people. It may not be far-fetched to say that the aim of Sorai's ideal ruler is the creation of a sustainable society.

2. SOLVING MORAL CONFLICTS

Loyalty to one's spouse was an important duty in Confucianism, yet over time it became so extreme that a wife's loyalty to her late husband would prohibit her from remarrying. Ch'eng I, one of fore-runners of Chu Hsi, said that the widowed wife should not marry, even when she is in poverty and starving.[17] The general principle of loyalty to the dead spouse clashes here with another general principle that one should take care of one's own life. In the same way, the general principle of samurai loyalty clashed with another general Confucian principle of loving people. Such moral conflicts were favorite themes in samurai dramas and other tragedies. The problem of such moral conflicts could not be resolved easily until one divided moral thinking into two levels, which we shall deal with soon.

Generally, in traditional Japanese morality, one's obligations (義理 *giri*), which originated from relationship ethics, very often clashed with humane affections (人情 *nin-jō*). Filial piety often conflicted with loyalty or spousal affection, creating a moral dilemma with no clear solution. For example, in the story of forty-seven *rōnin*, samurai were caught between a duty to avenge their lord on one hand and the illegality of their actions on the other.[18] The solution offered by contemporary utilitarian philosophers may be summarized as follows: the moral agent could choose the right course by comparing the alternative courses of action, putting himself in the shoes of all participants as a sort of impartial spectator that weighs all the participants' preferences. The course that is weightier in preferences will be the right (or universalizable) course to take. Such utilitarian solutions are based on the interests (or preferences) of the people concerned, solutions that will ostensibly lead to an increase in the total welfare of a society. Their methods depend on the notion of impartiality (or universalizability). Because of this, their judgments become kinds of moral principles that are applicable to similar people in similar situations, however specifically the principle might be formulated. Thus, the decision becomes the right utilitarian solution insofar as it contains the notion of *impartiality* and the *interest* (or *welfare)* of participants. If one lets such ethical methods become embodied as a virtue, it will take the shape of *impartial benevolence.*

The solution to these conflicts is found in the two-level utilitarianism elaborated by Hare. The argument can be summarized as follows. There are two sorts of principles. One is the ready-made principle that is given in education, as customary morality, or via the rules of society. The second are those principles created in concrete situations where it is difficult for general principles to be applied. The former is called *the intuitive level* of moral thinking by Hare while the latter is known as *the critical level.* We are governed in most situations by intuitive moral principles. However, when general principles clash with each other we need to set aside intuitive principles and use critical moral thinking to obtain the right answer. That is, when conflicts occur among intuitive moral principles or rules, it becomes necessary to think critically and weigh the interests of participants in alternative courses of action. We would then choose the weightier course (in terms of interests, preference satisfactions, or happiness) as the right course. After the conflict is resolved in this way, the general principles (such as loyalty or filial piety), that were shelved temporarily, will be revived again for everyday usage since they ordinarily promote general happiness and moral education.[19]

Next, let us see how Sorai's solution to moral conflict is related to Hare's two-level utilitarianism. The main moral problem for Sorai was the conflict between loyalty (the supreme imperative of morality backed by Chu Hsi's philosophy) and the impartial benevolence in the ethico-politics (*jin-sei*) of *jen* (仁, pronounced "*jin*" in Japanese). Sorai said that the five relationships and division of social classes was not the natural way but the Way created by the "sage-kings"[20] that contains the relationship ethics of loyalty, filial piety and other virtues (as general principles).[21] He also emphasized that *jen* is a generic virtue that is above all virtues and consistently governs them.[22] *Jen* is, in a narrow sense, one of many virtues such as righteousness, ritual propriety and others. Yet in a wider sense, *jen* is an inclusive virtue that subsumes all other virtues at the critical level. On this point, Sorai's *jen* has much in common with utilitarian "impartial benevolence." Both are aimed at general happiness via the utility principle and both are located at the critical level of moral thinking. This differs from the principles that govern the other special virtues such as loyalty and filial piety, which are not self-sustainable and can cause conflicts with other principles.

This interpretation of Sorai's ethico-politics according to contemporary ethics could be meaningful for environmental ethics because separating moral thinking into two levels could be useful for solving some of the grave ethical problems we confront today. For example, there are the conflicts of human and natural values, the values of different cultures, and the values of Western modernism and the emerging ecological worldview. Before we proceed toward Sorai's eco-holistic Confucian views concerning social and environmental ethics, we must first explain Sorai's revisionist views on traditional Confucianism.

3. The Absence of Objective Value

Sorai's Japanization of Confucianism involved a criticism Chu Hsi's notion of objective value that parallels Mackie and Hare's criticism of Platonic objective value.[23] For Chu Hsi, objective value was The Way (道 *tao*, in Jp. *michi* or *dō*) or "Heaven's Principle" (天理 *tenri*) in Neo-Confucian terms:

> Since every individual thing must have a Principle, it is inevitable that the organization of the state and society must also have its own Principle. The ruler's accordance with the Principle will therefore result in good government, whereas failure to do so will lead to political disorder. Thus, the Principle becomes equivalent to the Way or moral order (*Tao*), much stressed in early Confucianism—stressed as an important means for bringing good government to the state and peace to the world. The Tao, as conceived by Chu Hsi, has an eternal objectivity.[24]

The Principle (理 *li*) means here both the law of nature and the moral law at the same time. The Principle is considered the origin of all order in the cosmos, society, and between individuals. Hence, it was considered that if one attains the Heavenly Principle, one becomes a sage and society will become ordered.

In this rough sketch, one can make out the highly idealistic picture of Confucian ethico-politics. Various questions emerge from this position. How can the principle of nature that is factual (saying that something *is* a certain way) be at the same time a prescriptive force (demanding that people *should do* something)? How can descriptive judgment be at the same time prescriptive and imperative? If rulers embody the Way, then they should rule themselves harmoniously since the Way is the origin of harmony for both humans and nature. But even supposing a ruler can become a sage, there remains the question: how would social order be brought forth without institution or legislation that would guarantee and enforce the benevolence of the ruler and the obedience of the people? Sorai's version of Confucianism is largely revisionist and practical enough to answer this question. According to Sorai, the Way is not a set of eternal, objective values; it is something artificial, that is, man-made. The Way was, Sorai believed, created by the ancient sage kings in the shape of rites (*li*), music, legal enforcement and political administration (礼楽刑政 *"rei-gaku-kei-sei"*). Rites and music are considered "teachings" and legal enforcement and political administration are considered "institutions." Hare reminds us that not only moral principles but also some laws and institutions are located at the intuitive level, including rights and substantial justice. Thus, Sorai's thinking corresponds to Hare's general moral principles at the intuitive level.[25]

Chu Hsi's and Plato's philosophies can be considered a kind of universalism. Three characteristics that Hare attributes to Plato's philosophy can be found in Chu Hsi: (1) there are objective values, (2) the natural law and the moral law coincide, and (3) the moral law is universally applicable. What Hare achieved was the refutation of these Platonic theses. He did this by challenging each of the three points above: (1) there are no objective values, (2) the moral law is different from natural law, (i.e., no "ought" can be derived from "is"), and (3) there are no substantial moral laws that are universally applicable. In elaborating on this final point, Hare argues that there are only artificial, simple and general moral principles at the intuitive level and that the morally justifiable (or universalizable) course of action is to be chosen in each special situation at the critical level. Hare replaced, in this sense, Platonic objective values with artificial institutions and moral principles.

In this way, both Hare and Sorai pull morality from the celestial world of objective value down to terrestrial, secular world. Making the earthly happiness of people the primary moral criterion, Hare created, instead of the eternal Forms (*eidos* or *idea*), a system of simple and general moral principles for everyday and educational usage. Sorai created, instead of Way as an eternal Heavenly Principle, temporal earth-bound ways, institutions and teachings for people. Ethical universalism cannot help but cause irreconcilable clashes with other kinds of ethical universalism. In considering the global environment, what matters is not universalism as such, but creating a new criterion concerning right and wrong—a new moral standpoint for choosing the right course in concrete situations in the real world. In this sense, environmental ethics must be situational, or contextual, the most important precept being to judge from an impartial standpoint and consider the whole welfare of humans and nature.

4. DIFFERENTIATING LEVELS

Sorai's philosophy seems to endorse two distinct perspectives that need to be clarified in order to understand his ethics. To better articulate these two competing aspects of Sorai's philosophy, let us divide his name into two characters, *Sora* and *Sori*, each of which will clearly show a contrasting aspect of Sorai's ethics. *Sora* is a sort of traditionalist who believes in the universal value of ancient teachings by the earlier Chinese sage kings. *Sori* is a decisive utilitarian whose ultimate criterion is the welfare principle, happiness and peace of people (安民 an-min). These two aspects of Sora-ism and Sori-ism seem difficult to reconcile.[26]

According to Sora-ism, the Way was created by the ancient sage kings who were acquainted with Heaven-Earth-Nature (including human nature.) Therefore the Way is universal, normative, paradigmatic, and unchangeable. After the Way was created by ancient sage kings, it was changed by other kings. Yet the Way itself should, once created, be always followed by rulers of later ages. Tradition was held in high esteem, like the worship and celebration of Heaven and ancestors.[27] According to Sori-ism, the way is created for the ultimate purpose of making people happy and the world peaceful. Therefore, the way should be considered as a set of rules or principles derived from the primary, ultimate principle of welfare (including the welfare of nature). In this view, the way must be changed if it is adverse to the social interests or worse than other institutions or rules. Customs, laws and rites in Japan in the age of the historical Sorai were different from those of ancient China. What was created in the past could be revised or reformed by critical moral thinking. In fact, Sorai, in his *Discourse on Government (Seidan)* and *Policy for Great Peace (Taihei-saku)*, offers political and institutional reforms in various ways. Let us next try to find a way to reconcile Sora-ism and Sori-ism.

If *Sora* insists on the eternal validity of the way of the ancient sage kings, the way would become something like an objective value that should be universally applicable irrespective of the differences between societies, time-periods, and natural environments. People would then fall again into the spell of the objective value of Chu Hsi's kind. Therefore, *Sora* could not stick to this interpretation. On the other hand, if *Sori* insists on the validity of welfarism, the Way would have only instrumental value, useful for the purpose of social happiness and peace. Then, the Way that is supposed to have a supreme, objective value would tend to deteriorate into a descriptive word used only customarily without any prescriptive force.

Sorai himself might have reconciled this difference as follows: the Sora-ist way that consists of rules and principles could be based on the Sori-ist consideration of the whole welfare of humans and nature. The gap between *Sora* and *Sori* could, according to this two-level utilitarian interpretation, be bridged; that is, Sora-ism could be located on the institutional and educational level (which corresponds with Hare's intuitive level), and Sori-ism on the social happiness level (Hare's critical level). The later criticism of Sorai's tended to separate *Sori* from *Sora* so that Sorai's politics were considered separate from his ethics. Yet, if we have succeeded in combining *Sori* with *Sora*, then our conclusion is that Sorai had not separated both; rather, he had, like modern utilitarian thinkers, founded politics on the basis of ethics.

Sorai's scheme of reforming politics can be summarized in this way: the four classes of ruling samurai, farmer, artisan, and merchant were not decided by nature, but by the ancient sages: "class society is acceptable because it is useful for social stability." The special role of rulers is to read people well and choose able advisors or bureaucrats for public offices: "there is limit to the product that heaven and earth bring forth."[28] Without people leading frugal lives, the economy will decay. Sorai was so anxious for the state to dissolve the distinction between the rich and the poor that he argued for banning luxuries, especially for the ruling samurai class. His concerns regarding the suffering of people encouraged him to enforce a political system that relied on a ruler's paternalism. In this sense, his utilitarianism of increasing the interests of the people was not based on increasing the total pie, but by saving the poorer people from distress (via equal distribution) and by making rich people lead frugal lives. This measure is reasonable, as far as one sees that the pie is limited because of the restrictions nature imposes upon human lives, and the whole welfare of humans and nature should override the promotion of the interests of only a few humans. This is instructive in answering today's problem concerning the huge, global differences between the rich and the poor.

If Sorai were confronted with modern ideologies such as individualism, human rights, freedom, equality, and democracy, he might have said that they were not the eternal, celestial Way given by Heaven, but rather the temporary, terrestrial way created by the modern Western sage-emperors for the purpose of making people happier. If Sorai had known today's representative democracy, and the effects of that system in promoting people's welfare, he would have agreed with democracy, or at least, its principles. If he found, however, that the democratic system was not workable for the restoration of the environment, he would say that the system must be changed and revised, not only by social, but environmental ethical considerations. Yet for Sorai, moral thinking is, as we will shortly see, much more than the social ethics.

When Hare's two-level utilitarianism is only concerned with increasing human interests (whether or not it includes the interests of other sentient beings), it tends to cause the neglect of the welfare of nature, since human interests are often considered independent of natural welfare. It is this neglect of natural welfare that causes environmental degradation. The utilitarian social/ethical principle of increasing human interests is destined to cause conflicts with other, more eco-centered principles, and therefore it is not self-supporting. On the other hand, eco-centered environmental ethics is critical of human-centered social ethics, and in the case where natural value is considered superior to human values, it is criticized as eco-fascism.[29] If we interpret environmental ethics simply from the perspective of Hare's two-level utilitarianism, it would seem that there is no way of bridging the gap between both social and environmental ethical views. However, further examination of Sorai's ethics will yield a solution to this dilemma.[30] When Sorai says that the Way was created by the ancient sage kings (or rather saint kings), he means that Creation held a goal that went beyond social welfare. In other words, creation began in accordance with *tian* (天, *ten* in Japanese) or with our faith in *tian*: "The Way of ancient kings is based on respecting tian."[31]

Confucian respect for tian could be interpreted for environmental ethics as a concern for the whole welfare of humans and nature. Furthermore, only the sage (聖人 *seijin*) can master the principle (*li*); no other people after Confucius could reach the wisdom of the sage, which "could never be attained by learning."[32] This statement suggests that only the ancient sage can approach *tian*; other people can only follow the way of the sages.

Heaven was, for Sorai, something unfathomable and unreachable. If one takes Heaven as something that symbolizes the natural environment, no one living today, with all the amount of up-to-date and precise knowledge about the globe, would be able to know the whole truth about it. People could use their knowledge about the globe in order to further their own self-interest. No one could predict today's global ecological crisis seventy years ago, even though a myriad of knowledge had already been made available at that time. The ancient saints were so impartial and wise that they could, beyond the social/ethical level, reach an eco-holistic view that was seen clearly on the small-scale. This eco-holistic view could be attained only by saints who were wise and virtuous enough to reach the comprehensive knowledge of the supposed whole of humans and nature. The moral agent, qualified as the creator of the way, should be a critical thinker who can, based on logic and facts, impartially prescribe the way (i.e., the universal prescriber of Hare). Sorai might have thought that only the ancient saint kings were competent enough to become such moral agents who could, being impartially benevolent for *all under heaven*, create the way.

This Confucian eco-holism belongs to a different level of moral thinking than Hare's two levels of social ethics. Once we recognize the difference between these levels, we can solve some of those problems that stem from today's sharp opposition between social ethics and environmental ethics by locating each problem on a different level. As we saw earlier, two levels of social ethics are embedded in Sorai's main philosophical works, *Benmei* and *Bendo*. In these and other works by him, however, he seldom emphasizes a relationship between human beings and nature. Sorai's environmental thesis is so overshadowed by his socio-political ethics that it has escaped the eyes of later thinkers, who have interpreted his social ethics according to a modern Western dualistic view (which separates humans from nature) similar to contemporary utilitarianism. Yet from the perspective of today's advanced environmental ethics there lurks in Sorai's view an environmental thesis based on the ecological worldview of traditional Confucianism. If we can find evidence in his writings that he endorses a traditional Confucian view of nature, we can find another level of environmental (or eco-holistic) ethical thinking that is different from the social/ethical level.

Let us see next if this level of environmental ethics is reflected in the Confucian key-word of *"jen"* (following Sorai's method of examining the usage of words). Ch'eng Hao, a neo-Confucian thinker and forerunner of Yang-ming, says that "The man of *jen* regards heaven and earth and all things as one body."[33] Also Yang-ming's catchphrase was "*Jen* of embodying heaven and earth" (*tenchi-ittai-no-jin*).[34] *Jen* is, then, the virtue that consists in the deep ecological unity of humans and nature. *Jen* is, however, more than that; it is also the virtue of humans as *the moral agents* who are concerned about eco-holistic welfare.

It is said in the *Doctrine of the Mean,* "If they [those who are absolutely sincere] can fully develop the nature of things, they can then assist in the transforming and nourishing process of Heaven and Earth (贊天地之化育). If they can assist in the transforming and nourishing process of Heaven and Earth, they can thus form a trinity with Heaven and Earth."[35] Confucian virtues are Heaven-centered rather than human-centered, and help humans to assist the productive processes of Heaven and Earth for the welfare of humans and nature as a whole. This is the most important virtue for human service to nature and it is diametrically opposed to modern anthropocentric dominion over nature.[36] The point of Confucian environmental ethics is that the eco-holistic view of nature, together with the service for nature, is the basis of social ethics. Therefore, the increase of the whole welfare of humans and nature can be the very aim and the ultimate criterion of Confucian ethics.

Sorai considers the universe to be a living organism (活物 *katsu-butsu*).[37] Moreover, Sorai writes in the first paragraph in *Bemmei* as follows:

> Humaneness (*jen*) refers to the virtue that provides for the prosperity of everyone and the peace and stability of the people. It is the great virtue of the sages. The great virtue of heaven and earth is creative production. The sages modelled themselves on this virtue. For this reason humaneness is also known as "the virtue that favours creative production." The sages were rulers of all under heaven in antiquity. Thus, of the virtues of a ruler, none is more revered than humaneness. Accordingly, a commentary [*the Great Learning*] observes. "To be a ruler, one must abide in humaneness."[38]

We can see from this passage that Sorai, in spite of his criticism of Chu Hsi's Way, inherited the Neo-Confucian theme of the human virtue to assist the producing virtue of Heaven and Earth. This virtue is what is called *jen* (Jp. *"jin"*). *Jen* is translated here into English as "humaneness." Yet, while "humaneness" (or "humanity") covers only humanistic virtues at the social/ethical levels, "*jen*" is more than just a humanistic virtue. Being biased by this translation, the modernist understanding of the Confucian social/ethical aspects of *jen* as humanity is liable to be separated from the ecological worldview. Rather, the Confucian social/ethical aspect of *jen* must be somehow combined with the more environmentally basic eco-holistic aspect of *jen*. It is said in *The Book of Change* that "Change means production and reproduction."[39] According to Shimada Kenji, "*Jen* is the Heaven's virtue itself of producing and reproducing."[40] Here we can see clearly that Sorai is an orthodox Confucian in his belief in Heaven. The reason why he did not mention much about the ecological (or eco-holistic) aspect of *jen* may be that Sorai, who was so much concentrated in linguistic analysis of the Way, did not need to mention a basic precondition of society.

Each aspect of *jen* so far stated roughly corresponds with (1) Sorai's respect for Heaven, which is often expressed as bringing peace to the realm below heaven (*an-tenka*), (2) Sori-ism on the social/ethical level, and (3) Sora-ism on the institutional and educational level. If this is right, all three aspects could be considered as different levels of the integral whole of the Confucian ethico-religious system. Thus interpreted, social and environmental ethics could be combined as parts of an organic, integrated whole. Here we can see that the social/ethical level of *jen* must be based on and limited/regulated by the more basic, eco-holistic *jen* that originates from the Confucian notion of Heaven.

Sorai's three-level system can be used to solve contemporary moral problems as follows. When conflict occurs between human interest and natural welfare, we shift the arena to another level of moral inquiry where the whole welfare of humans and nature governs our environmental ethical thinking. We can make this eco-holistic ethics embedded in Confucianism an ultimate criterion. In the event that conflict occurs among moral principles originating from various views, we can find a solution by using this eco-holistic criterion and by asking which course of action will lead to the whole welfare of humans and nature (i.e., that which is more useful for restoring nature). This might be called an earth-based (or earth first) ethic.[41] We might call thus-interpreted Soraian ethical framework three-level eco-humanism, each level tentatively being called "*eco-holistic level*," "*separated level*" (since human society tends to be separated from nature on this level), and "*institutional level*" (connected with moral teachings and other practices). This three-level interpretation of Soraian ethics could explain the ideological background of Edo-society; that is, the reason why Edo society could create a green society, retaining and enriching nature. For *jen* rulers (仁君 *jin-kun*) of Edo-era, it was rather easy to build a peaceful society symbiotic with nature, since their ethico-politics were based on the ecological worldview.[42]

While Western academics developed into specific disciplines characterized by analytic clarity, Confucian philosophers have historically been well-rounded thinkers acquainted with a variety of disciplines such as religion, ethics, politics, economics, aesthetics, and education. Each field of learning is based on the ecological worldview (that is, on the eco-holistic level), with knowledge being practical and general rather than specific. In Confucianism, the scientific method had not yet been developed and people were often governed by superstitions and irrationalism, both of which have been mocked by modern critics. While modern Western sciences developed in each of their specified fields with great analytic clarity, they seem to have lost a holistic perspective; Confucian learning, on the other hand, although not specialized, kept the view of the whole, since it is not separated from nature. Here, the loss of analytic clarity is compensated by synoptic imagination. If we separate Sorai's thought into the distinct academic fields of politics (i.e., institutions and teachings), ethics (i.e., the general happiness of the people), and religion (i.e., respect of heaven), then each would become almost meaningless compared with its modern equivalents. However, once they are combined into an integral system grounded in an ecological worldview, they become viable.

Peace and stability of people could not be attained without the sustainable natural environment. Thus, the eco-holistic welfare of humans and nature as a whole should override purely human interests or the natural welfare alone. Since human interests are related to the natural welfare, the people of Edo Japan had to limit or decrease human interests to prevent the deterioration of the natural environment. Technologies were not advanced; people preferred physical work and skill over mechanisms. Thus, Edo was renowned as a society that did not know pollution. Such a symbiotic system between humans and nature had made it easier for *jen*-rulers helped by Confucian scholars with synoptic views to carry out their *jen*-rules (仁政 *jin-sei*).

5. Bringing Peace to the Realm below Heaven

In the Confucian ethico-political system, in contrast with Western individualist systems, one of the cardinal points is to retain order among individuals, family, the state, and the world. This means that, in this eco-holistic system, the whole family is considered more important than individuals, the state as a whole is considered more important than the individual family, and (possibly) the world is considered more important than the sovereign state. The ideal of Confucian ethico-politics was expressed in the *The Great Learning* by the motto, "Cultivate yourself, regulate your family, rule your country well, and bring great peace" (修身、斉家、治国、平天下). If we compare this ideal with the modern Western ideology of individualism, state sovereignty, and anthropocentrism, we will find that the Confucian eco-holistic way is more effective than the modern Western way for attaining the welfare of the whole and world peace. Confucian *jen*-politics is, in this sense, more effective than the sovereign state government with its self-interest-oriented economy. In line with his own ethico-politics, which critically inherited neo-Confucian *jen*-politics (or moral-politics), Sorai's economical thinking can be called a *jen*-economy, diametrically opposed to the individualistic interest-oriented economy.

When quarrels occurred in Edo society, both sides were punished. Citizens of Edo, therefore, had to yield self-interest to the greater good. This means that "peace and harmony" (平和 *hei-wa*) among all under Heaven, a sort of pacifist principle, overrides other ethical principles. The rulers would, under ideal conditions, be able to embody people's desire to preserve or restore nature in the shape of the mandate of Heaven, since Heaven was thought to be the symbol of the natural environment. In order for this system to be workable, the rulers must be sufficiently impartial and considerate of the welfare of humans and nature as a whole.

When Sorai says: "bringing peace to the realm below Heaven" (安天下 *an-tenka*), it means "bringing peace within the state," but it includes the will for "world peace," because world peace is the supreme aim of traditional Confucian *jen* ethico-politics. "Great peace under Heaven" (天下泰平 *tenka-taihei*) was the catch phrase of the age throughout Edo-era Japan. Sorai's variety of eco-holism urges us to take the whole of humans and nature into consideration. Certainly, world peace is today the very prerequisite of sustainability of the global village.

In his *Bendō*, Sorai writes that "Now the way of the early kings is the way that produces peace to the realm below heaven. The way that produces peace to the realm below heaven (*tenka*) consists in humaneness (*jen*). Therefore, Confucius said, "Our way is penetrated with unity." Why did he say that our way is "penetrated" with unity?

Humaneness is the unifying virtue. Moreover, it is the greatest virtue. For that reason, it can well penetrate many virtues thereby."[43] The phrase "to bring (or provide) peace to the realm below heaven" appears repeatedly (at least ten times) in this short essay. This means that the aim of Sorai's ethical thinking is not only to increase the general happiness of people but also to maintain, or make sound, the whole welfare of all humans and nature under heaven. He was concerned with the welfare of people based on the ecological world-view. For Sorai, the world is not only a human world but also a natural world: it is "Heaven-Earth-Nature." Sorai's world can mean the whole world as well as Japan as a state, although his knowledge about his contemporary world was limited to the scope of East Asia.

People in Edo-era Japan did not know such human-centered values as human rights or liberty; what they knew is that they should accepted death as a fate and that they should not fear poverty. They knew Confucius' sayings:

> I have heard that those who administer a state or a family do not worry about there being too few people, but worry about unequal distribution of wealth. They do not worry about poverty, but worry about the lack of security and peace on the part of people. For when wealth is equally distributed, there will not be poverty; when there is harmony, there will be no problem of there being too few people; and when there are security and peace, there will be no danger to the state . . .
>
> With coarse rice to eat, with water to drink, and with a bent arm for a pillow, there is still joy. Wealth and honour obtained through unrighteousness are but floating clouds to me.[44]

Although people were generally poor and short-lived, they knew how to enjoy life without consuming energy. They developed flower arrangement, natural foods, tea ceremony, visual art, crafts, bonsai, haiku, all of which emerged from their love of nature.

In today's real politics of modern democracy, human rights and interests seems to be prior to the good of nature, and state sovereignty superior to the welfare of the world. On the eco-holistic level, however, the increase of human interest often means the decrease of natural welfare, and thus the increase of human interests beyond a certain limit (to the neglect of natural welfare) will destroy the basis of human society. The ecology-conscious Confucian rulers in the Edo era were highly concerned about the mutual welfare of people and nature on the eco-holistic level, more so than the leaders of modern democratic states whose anthropocentric concerns outweigh the welfare of people and nature as a whole. If there is anything to be learned from Japanese Confucian ethico-politics practiced in the Edo-era, one of the central themes must be this: restoring nature in this critical age depends on the balancing of human interests against the natural welfare.[45]

NOTES

1. Mary Evelyn Tucker, "Ecological Themes in Taoism and Confucianism," in Mary Evelyn Tucker and John A. Grim eds., *Worldviews and Ecology: Religion, Philosophy, and the Environment* (Maryknoll: Orbis Books, 1994) 157.

2. J. Baird Callicott, *Earth's Insights: A Multicultural Survey of Ecological Ethics from the Mediterranean Basin to the Australian Outback* (Berkeley: University of California Press, 1994) 107.

3. Thomas Berry, 'Ecological Geography', in Mary Evelyn Tucker and John A. Grim eds., *Worldviews and Ecology: Religion, Philosophy, and the Environment* (Maryknoll: Orbis Books, 1994).

4. See J. Baird Callicott, *Beyond the Land Ethic: More Essays in Environmental Philosophy* (Albany: State University of New York Press, 1999) and Alan Drengson & Yuichi Inoue, eds., *The Deep Ecology Movement: An Introductory Anthology* (Berkeley: North Atlantic Books, 1995).

5. J. Baird Callicott, 'The Search for an Environmental Ethics' in Tom Regan, ed., *Matters of Life and Death: New Introductory Essays in Moral Philosophy,* (New York: Random House, 1980) 395–401 and Peter Singer, *Practical Ethics,* Second Edition (Cambridge: Cambridge University Press, 1993) 285.

6. See Callicott, *Earth's Insights.*

7. See Mary Evelyn Tucker, *Moral and Spiritual Cultivation in Japanese Neo-Confucianism: The Life and Thought of Kaibara Ekken* (1630-1714) (Albany: State University of New York, 1989) and T. Yamauchi, 'Sontoku's Environmental Ethics,' *Hotoku Studies*, No.1, International Ninomiya Sontoku Association, 2004.

8. See J. Mackie, *Ethics: Inventing Right and Wrong* (New York: Penguin, 1977) and R.M. Hare, *Moral Thinking: Its Levels, Method and Point* (Oxford: Clarendon Press, 1981).

9. See Wing-Tsit Chan, trans. and ed., *A Source Book in Chinese Philosophy,* (Princeton: Princeton University Press, 1963) 715 n. 84.

10. Ogyū Sorai, '*Benmei'* in K. Yoshikawa et. al., eds., *Ogyū Sorai, Nihon Shisō Taikei* Vol. 36, (Tokyo: Iwanami-shoten, 1973) 12, 44. See also John A. Tucker, *Ogyū Sorai's Philosophical Masterworks, The Bendō and Benmei* (Honolulu: University of Hawaii Press, 2006) 139.

11. Sorai, *Benmei* 44 and John A.Tucker, *Ogyū Sorai's Philosophical Masterworks* 176.

12. See R.M. Hare, *Moral Thinking: Its Levels, Method and Point*, Chaps. 2, 3.

13. Xinzhong Yao, *An Introduction to Confucianism* (Cambridge: Cambridge University Press, 2000) 200.

14. Yao 171.

15. See T. Yamauchi, "The New Aims of Primary Education: In Search for a Moral Education" (in Japanese), *Study Reports of Higashi Osaka Junior College,* Vol. 27 (2002).

16. Ogyū Sorai, *Seidan,* in Masahide Bitō, ed., *Ogyū Sorai,* (Tokyo: Chūo-Kōron-Sha, 1983) 351 f., 326.

17. Shimada Kenji, *Shushi-gaku to Yōmei-gaku* (Tokyo: Iwanami-shoten, 1967) 62.

18. Shimada 96–98.

19. See Hare, *Moral Thinking*, Chap. 6.

20. Ogyū Sorai, *Taiheisaku (A Policy for Great Peace),* in K. Yoshikawa et. al. eds., *Ogyū Sorai,* 467.

21. Ogyū Sorai, *Tōmonsho,* in Masahide Bitō, ed., *Ogyū Sorai,* 351.

22. Ogyū Sorai, *Bendo,* 33. See Ogyū Sorai, *Benmei* 54.

23. See Mackie 15. Also see Chapters 5-6 in H.M. Hare's *Plato* (Oxford: Oxford University Press: 1982).

24. Fung Yu-lan, *A History of Chinese Philosophy,* Vol. II (Princeton: Princeton University Press, 1953) 562.

25. See Hare, *Moral Thinking*, Chapter 9.

26. See Ogyū Sorai, *Benmei* 44, 66, and 96.

27. See Ogyū Sorai, *Tōmonsho* 301.

28. Ogyū Sorai, *Seidan* 437.

29. See J.Baird Caliicott, 'Holistic Environmetal Ethics and the Problem of Ecofascism,' in his book, *Beyond the Land Ethic.*

30. See T. Yamauchi, "Wang Yang-ming" in A. J. Palmer & P. B. Corcaran (eds.), *Fifty Key Thinkers on the Environment* (New York: Routledge, 2002).

31. Ogyū Sorai, *Benmei* 120. Tian (天 'ten') is considered to mean "the inherent order of the natural world." In Japanese Confucianism, tian is often synonymous with 'heaven-earth-nature' (天地自然 ten-chi-jizen), which means that 'tian' includes 'the natural environment'.

32. Ogyū Sorai, *Benmei* 68.

33. Wing-Tsit Chan, *A Source Book in Chinese Philosophy,* 524, 530. See also T. Yamauchi, "Wang Yang-ming," in Joy Palmer, ed., *Fifty Key Thinkers on the Environment* (New York: Routledge, 2001) 27–32.

34. Y. Kondō, *Denshūroku* (Tokyo: Meiji-shoin, 1961) 367. Also see Wing-Tsit Chan (translated with notes), *Instructions for Practical Living and Other Neo-Confucian Writings by Wang Yang-ming,* (New York: Columbia University Press, 1963) 170. See also Shimada Kenji, *Shusi-gaku to Yomei-gaku,* 44, 133–317.

35. Wing-Tsit Chan, *A Source Book in Chinese Philosophy* 108.

36. See Tu Wei-ming, *Centrality and Commonality: An Essay on Confucian Religiousness* (Albany: State University of New York Press, 1989) 77, 86.

37. J.R. McEwan, *The Political Writings of Ogyū Sorai* (Cambridge: Cambridge University Press, 1962) 6, 10. Also see Ogyū Sorai, *Tōmonsho,* 303, 308, and 333.

38. John A. Tucker, *Masterworks* 186. See also Sorai *Bennmei* 53.

39. Wing-Tsit Chan, *A Source Book in Chinese Philosophy* 266, 735.

40. Shimada, Kenji, *Shusi-gaku to Yomei-gaku,* 45, 52. See also Wing-Tsit Chan, *A Source Book in Chinese Philosophy,* 594, and Fung Yu-lan, *A History of Chinese Philosophy,* Vol. II, 52.

41. The relation of the separated level to the eco-holistic level would be similar with that of institutional level with humanistic social ethics. However, this problem is beyond the scope of this paper. See T. Yamauchi, "Animal Liberation, Land Ethic, and Deep Ecology," *Journal of Kyoto Seika University,* No. 29 (2005).

42. See John A. Tucker, *Masterwork* 163.

43. Ogyū Sorai, *Bendō* 33.

44. *Analects,* 16:1, and 7:15. See Wing-Tsit Chan, *A Source Book in Chinese Philosophy* 32, 44–45.

45. My thanks to J. Baird Callicott, James McRae, Shunichi Noguchi, and Karen Mather, who helped me in preparing this paper.

CHAPTER 18

Triple-Negation: Watsuji Tetsurō on the Sustainability of Ecosystems, Economies, and International Peace

JAMES McRAE

INTRODUCTION

Environmental security is a branch of environmental studies that explores how national security issues are affected by ecosystem sustainability and the demands placed upon the natural world by human populations. The pursuit of consumer interests can often place stress on the environment, which can lead to a collapse of both ecosystems and economies, which in turn promotes political instability. For this reason, the fields of environmental ethics, business ethics, and international relations are ultimately intertwined. This essay draws from the philosophical anthropology of Watsuji Tetsurō's *Fūdo* to explain why human culture, economics, and the politics of warfare are so intimately tied to sustainability issues. The ethical principles of Watsuji's *Rinrigaku* are then used to articulate a normative framework that could be used to promote sustainability—and thereby maintain peace—on an international scale. By developing a relational understanding of environmental and business ethics that emphasizes roles and responsibilities over individual autonomy and rights, we can regulate business practices in a manner that is both environmentally and socially conscious. Because mismanagement of the environment leads to socio-economic problems that provoke global conflicts, the promotion of sustainability according to Watsuji's ethics can contribute to both a healthy economy and international security.

I. The Ethics of Watsuji Tetsurō

The Japanese word for ethics, *rinri* (倫理), consists of the characters for "fellows" and "principle," and thus ethics is the discipline that determines the principles for properly ordering human relationships.[1] Watsuji's philosophy of the person is deliberately opposed to Western ideas of ethical individualism and metaphysical dualism. He argues that the human mind and body are completely inseparable, and that the "field of human relationships is superior to the individual."[2] This is clearly demonstrated in the terminology that he uses to discuss the idea of the person. In Japanese, there are two common terms used to designate the concept of "person": *kojin* and *ningen*:

1. 個人 Kojin (Individual): This word consists of the character *hito* (人)[3] preceded by the character *ko* (個), which is a counter used for enumerating random, inanimate objects. The word as a whole refers to an individual, a being set apart from the world "for the purposes of enumeration."[4] Watsuji thinks this has a decidedly lonely connotation: a person as *kojin* is fundamentally separated from other people and is, as a result, less than fully human. When used in this respect, the term "individual" has a cold and impersonal meaning. A focus on individual autonomy rather than social interrelation can easily degenerate to individualism, which leads to selfish, lonely despair. The only solution is social interaction.[5]

2. 人間 Ningen (Human Being): *Ningen* is a combination of the words *nin* (人, also read *hito*), or "person," and *gen* (間, also read *aida/ma*), which means "the space in between things."[6] *Ningen* can be literally translated as "the space between persons" or "a person as in between." Thus, the "human being" as *ningen* is a person fundamentally defined by his or her relationship to a particular spatio-temporal context and the other beings within that context. *Ningen* thus refers to the inter-relational nature of human beings.

Whereas *kojin* represents an individual self that is set apart from a particular context, *ningen* describes a person as a human being who is defined by his or her presence within space and who defines that space in return. Since we, as human beings, cannot avoid living in a certain portion of space-time, we must look to this spatio-temporal context as one of the essential defining factors of ourselves. As a result of this interpretation of the person, we must "abandon the modern European idea of seeing the world from the standpoint of self-consciousness. Instead, we must grasp the individual from the totality of human relationships."[7]

For Watsuji, in order to understand the human being, "we must first take note of the 'betweenness' *(aidagara)* in which people are located."[8] *Aidagara* (間柄) refers to the relationships that connect us to one another and allow us to interact with other persons in our contexts (our *particular* environments).[9] All beings exist within a "*basho*" (場所, life-field, place, or context) in space, such that "to exist *within a body* in a spatial *basho* is the most fundamental mode of human being."[10] A person's mind exists within his/her body (the first ground of context) and that body exists within the spatio-temporal world (the final ground of context). Other people naturally form an essential part of one's environment. Thus, one's relationship with one's *basho* (context) is characterized by the "betweenness" that one shares with one's natural environment and the other people that exist within that *basho*.

Watsuji argues that climate (風土, *fūdo*) plays an essential role in the development of the person. He describes the person as defined by the two factors of climate and history:

> Here the space- and time-structure of human existence is revealed as climate and history: the inseparability of time and space is the basis of the inseparability of history and climate . . . The human duality, of the finite and the infinite, is most plainly revealed as the historical and climatic structure.[11]

The history of an individual includes not only one's genealogy, but the history of the culture in which one lives. The climate in which one exists is the medium for self-discovery.[12] From the concept of *climate* springs Watsuji's theory of intersubjectivity: it is within the life-field (*basho*) that we find "the interconnected meanings of the life-world."[13] *Basho* is the ultimate ground of existence that fundamentally connects a human being to his or her environment through the vehicle of the body. It is this "betweenness" that unites human to human and allows one to be defined by the term "*ningen*," as a person within a context.[14] The only way for a person to truly exist as an individual in relation to the natural world is through this betweenness with one's environment as an extension of one's body. Any attempt to define oneself as an individual separate from this context results in *kojin*, a lonely being removed from the world and incapable of achieving authentic person-hood. This is because *kojin* is a fictitious "self" that attempts to exist independent of the environment that defines all true selves. It is only by casting off the egoistic illusion of *kojin* and immersing oneself in one's *basho* that one can shape one's true identity as a person.[15]

It might be argued that Watsuji's definition of the person is overly anthropocentric and does not focus enough upon mankind's relation-ship to nature. This interpretation of Watsuji's philosophy of the person fails to take into account the emphasis that he places on the effects of nature upon the person in his book, *Fūdo*. One's natural surroundings play an essential role in the development of the person, to the extent that the different cultures of the world owe their distinct characters to the unique natural climates in which they make their homes. *Ningen* exists not only in the space between all persons, but in the space between those persons and the natural world. In order to develop oneself, one must cultivate one's relationship with the totality of one's environment, not simply with selected parts of that environment.

Watsuji states that all human beings have a "double structure" of self in relation to their context: as *ningen* we are *individuals* completely defined by our *relationship* with our climate.[16] One is a fully developed human being only when one realizes this double structure and embraces one's context as an essential part of oneself. Yet in order to realize *ningen*, one must first make a movement from the individualism of *kojin* through a process of self-negation in which one denies the illusion of one's "individual" self:

> What is at stake here is the taking of a first step toward self-awareness. Apart from the self-awareness of an individual, there is no social ethics. The other moment is the individual's surrender to the totality. This is what has been called the *demand of the superindividual will,* or of total will. Without this surrender, there is also no social ethics.[17]
>
> An individual who does not imply the meaning of negation, that is, an essentially self-sufficient individual, is nothing but an imaginative construction . . .[18]

Many people, in an attempt to develop and define their selves, seek to do so by cutting that self off from its environment and constructing what they consider to be an autonomous self. However, because the individual is essentially defined by his or her environment, this fictitious, "individual" self is nothing more than an illusion, and the person becomes isolated from his or her environment. For Watsuji, the concept of the self as a lone individual that rises above or separates itself from its context is completely empty.

Here one might object: does this view of anti-individualism mean that we do not exist apart from the larger "herd" of humanity? Not at all. Watsuji's betweenness implies that there is a space (*aida*) that exists between human beings, such that "we *can* come to meet in the between *and* that we are at a distance from one another."[19] We exist in this space and this space exists between us. Steve Odin states:

> [Watsuji] goes on [to] explain this twofold character of *ningen* in terms of a dialectic of "self-other" (*jita*) relations, arguing that while both the self and the other are absolutely other, they are nevertheless one in communal existence (1937, 12). According to Watsuji it is precisely this dialectical unity between the "self" (*ji*) and the "*other*" (*ta*) which constitutes the double character of *ningen* in its essential wholeness as an individual-society relationship.[20]

To exist in the world as *ningen* is to be completely defined by one's experiences in the world. Yet, because each person has a different web of interpersonal relations (betweenness) within a particular context, each individual has characteristically different experiences within his or her unique context that lead to a distinctively different person in each case. Each person is still a function of his or her betweenness with other people; it is simply that this betweenness is different for each person because of his or her different relations with different other persons as a function of the first ground of context, the body. Everyone is defined by context; what makes a person unique is the particular way in which he or she chooses to actively influence that context.

In his *Rinrigaku*, Watsuji defines ethics in terms of *ningen sonzai* (人間存在): "human beings existing":

> By the way, our question was "what is ethics?" and we found that this question asks about the fundamental structure of the *sonzai* of *ningen*.[21]

> [*Sonzai*] means "the maintenance or subsistence over against loss" . . . If it is tenable to hold that the *son* is the self-sustenance of the self and *zai* means to remain within human relations, then *son-zai* is precisely the self-sustenance of the self as betweenness. That is, it means that *ningen* possesses herself. We could also simply say that *sonzai* is "the interconnection of the acts of *ningen*."[22]

The ethical, for Watsuji, is the totality of actions within a particular context that allow the person as *ningen* to thrive and positively interrelate with his or her context. "Right" refers to those actions particular to an individual context that promote harmonious interrelation between *ningen* and the environment. "Wrong" refers to those relationships that hinder harmonious contextual interrelation. When Watsuji says that ethics is "the interconnection of the acts of *ningen*," he means it is the relationship of the good of all persons within a given context. Every act is "an interactivity between subjects."[23] No one can commit an action on a purely individual basis. Every action, via "betweenness," affects other persons. Thus, the personal good immediately translates to the good of other persons and the environment.

II. ENVIRONMENTAL SECURITY

Environmental security studies the effects that environmental changes have upon human conflict, which threatens the social, physical, and economic well-being of humans.[24] Figure 18.1 illustrates a hybrid theoretical model that explains the causal relationship between human activity, environmental impact, and violent conflict.[25] The arrows that point to the right show the causal relationship between human activity, environmental impact, negative social effects, and promotion or avoidance of violent conflict. Since the 1970s, the environmental impact of human beings has been understood according to the simple equation of I=PAT: environmental impact is a function of population, affluence, and technology.[26] Current theoretical models in environmental

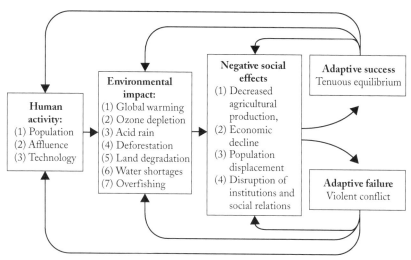

Figure 18.1: Environmental Impact and Violent Conflict: A Hybrid Theoretical Model.

security are substantially more complex, expanding upon the core
idea of the I=PAT equation to explain how environmental degradation
promotes violent conflict. Population growth leads to scarcity because
it divides limited resources among more people. This is exacerbated
by the fact that these resources are typically not equally distributed
among the members of a society; the poor are impacted more quickly
and significantly than those with money and power.[27] Affluence amplifies the impact of population because consumer societies expect a
higher standard of living, which places a greater strain on food, water,
and energy sources. Technology refers to the processes used to obtain
energy and resources from the natural environment. This can have
either a negative effect (e.g., coal, oil, and nuclear power) or a positive effect (e.g., solar and wind energy). Taken together, population,
affluence, and technology produce an environmental impact that can
have negative results for human beings and other living things.

The term "environmental impact" or "environmental change" refers
to a "human-induced decline in the quantity or quality of a renewable
resource that occurs faster than it is renewed by natural processes."[28]
Thomas F. Homer-Dixon argues that seven major environmental
effects contribute to human conflict: global warming, ozone depletion, acid rain, deforestation, the degradation of arable land, water
shortages, and overfishing.[29] These environmental pressures lead to
conflict as a result of four interrelated social effects: decreased agricultural production, economic decline, population displacement, and
the disruption of institutions and social relations. As natural resources
and food become scarcer, the economy begins to decline. Environmental refugees are created as people move away from areas where
there is no employment, few resources, and extensive environmental
degradation. Large population movements lead to group identity
conflicts, which disrupt social relations. Unequal resource distribution
intensifies the disparity between social classes, which promotes socio-
political conflict. Poor countries are more vulnerable to environmental
change and thus the developing world is more likely to suffer from
conflicts due to environmental problems.[30] If left unchecked, these
negative social effects ultimately promote violent conflict.

While Homer-Dixon suggests that the negative social effects of
environmental change necessarily lead to violent conflict once they
have reached a critical threshold, Matthew, Gaulin, and McDonald
have suggested that there is a certain amount of adaptivity that can
potentially mitigate the use of force. As the environment is progres-
sively degraded by human activity, negative social effects begin to

accumulate. If human beings are able to regulate their activity to minimize conflict and adapt to environmental change, they can achieve a tenuous equilibrium in which violence is averted. If they fail to adapt, violent conflict will be inevitable.[31] Homer-Dixon argues that environmental security is a feedback loop: population and activity per capita can stress vulnerable ecosystems, leading to negative environmental effects, which influence social effects, which can lead to conflict. The arrows in Figure 18.1 that loop from right to left represent this feedback loop. Social effects and conflict affect human preferences, beliefs, social relations, and institutions, which in turn influence population and activity per capita.[32] Matthew, Gaulin, and McDonald echo this idea in their notion of adaptivity: successful adaptation has a positive effect upon politics, the economy, and the environment, while unsuccessful adaptation leads to conflict, which has a deleterious effect upon human beings, their institutions, and the natural world.

When interpreted from a Watsujian framework, the lessons of environmental security are not surprising: human beings affect and are profoundly affected by their environments. Because personhood and culture are a function of the natural and social environment in which one is radically contextualized, one should expect that harm inflicted upon the environment will ultimately manifest itself socio-politically. While human beings have the ability to adapt to environmental pressures—a process that Watsuji explains at length in regard to the volatile climates of Japan and India—extreme, human-inflicted changes such as global warming or overfishing are likely to stress ecosystems beyond the critical threshold of adaptation. At this point, conflict becomes almost inevitable; even if we can temporarily avert disaster by reaching a tenuous adaptive equilibrium, the negative effects of human-induced environmental change produce a feedback loop that can disrupt this delicate balance.

III. Triple-Negation: Watsuji, Environmental Ethics, and Security

Watsuji's understanding of ethics as the relationship between *ningen* (contextualized human beings) and *fūdo* (the natural and social environment) provides a normative framework that can help to promote both sustainability and peace. Watsuji's understanding of the person accurately reflects the biological reality of the human species. J. Baird Callicott, the leading interpreter of Aldo Leopold's land ethic, describes the ecological view of human beings:

> Ecology is the study of relationships of organisms to one another and to the elemental environment . . . The ontological primacy of objects and the ontological subordination of relationships characteristic of classical western science is, in fact, reversed in ecology. Ecological relationships determine the nature of organisms rather than the other way around. A species is what it is because it has adapted to a niche in the ecosystem. The whole, the system itself, thus, literally and quite straightforwardly shapes and forms its component parts.[33]

Human beings, both as individuals and as a species, are defined by their relationships with each other and with the natural environment. Humans are a distinct species, but we are shaped by our environments in terms of morphology, diet, culture, etc. The anthropocentric worldview is characterized by a belief that human beings are separate from and superior to the rest of the planet, which makes the earth little more than raw material to be exploited for human benefit. Watsuji's understanding of the person seems to anticipate Leopold's idea that human beings are merely plain citizens of the biotic community: instead of conquering the land as an "other" that can be used for our own benefit, we should strive to preserve the land as part of the interdependent process that is the ground for our very existence.[34]

Watsuji's understanding of *aidagara* (betweenness) is also reflected in the land ethic. The characters for *ningen* literally mean "person" (人) and "field" (間) in the sense of an electro-magnetic field. Thus, one's notion of self is defined by concentric circles of interdependence that incorporate one's family, friends, community, and culture as well as one's local and global environment. This parallels Callicott's interpretation of Leopold's land ethic:

> Since individual organisms, from an ecological point of view, are less discrete objects than modes of a continuous, albeit differentiated, whole, the distinction between self and other is blurred. . . . As one moves, in imagination, outwardly from the core of one's organism, it is impossible to find a clear demarcation between oneself and one's environment. . . . The world is, indeed, one's extended body and one's body is the precipitation, the focus of the world in a particular space-time locale.[35]

Once human beings acknowledge their radical contextualization, they will be moved to revise their ethical systems to reflect the intrinsic value of the environment. Callicott argues that humans have evolved an "affective moral response to perceived bonds of kinship and community membership and identity."[36] If moral sympathy is, as Nitobe Inazo says, "sensitivity to the distress of others," humans can learn to be sensitive to the distress of the environment, even if it is not a person (since it has an objective well-being that ultimately affects our own).[37]

So how can human beings learn to live in harmony with the environment? One dominant paradigm that has been used extensively in business ethics is *kyōsei* 共生, or symbiosis. Surprisingly, this paradigm has received little attention in environmental ethics, even though it is grounded in the biological and ecological sciences. Japanese philosopher Abe Hiroshi has helped to pioneer the application of this concept to environmental ethics. Literally, symbiosis refers to different species "living together" for extended periods of time. While symbiotic relationships can be parasitic (in which one species benefits at the other's expense) or commensal (one species benefits while the other is neither harmed nor benefitted), *kyōsei* refers to mutualism, in which both species benefit from their interaction. Drawing from Matsuda Hiroyuki, Abe defines mutualistic symbiosis as "interspecific interactions in which the benefits exceed the costs for both participants."[38] Abe stresses that *kyōsei* should be understood as mutualism in the broadest sense. It is not necessary for both species to gain an identical benefit from the relationship for it to be mutualistic, so long as the well-being of both species is enhanced. Even species that are not directly related to one another can interact in a mutually beneficial manner. Because matter is constantly circulated throughout an ecosystem, all living things are, to some extent, interdependent. While some species—like the classic example of the clownfish and sea anemone—form explicitly mutualistic symbiotic relationships, all species in an ecosystem affect one another to some extent.[39] Historically, human beings have acted in a manner that more closely resembles parasitism or commensalism, using the environment as raw material to satisfy strictly anthropocentric ends with little concern for the welfare of the other species affected. However, environmental security suggests that injury to the environment causally contributes to social destabilization and conflict, which means that even from an anthropocentric perspective, the good of human beings is closely tied to the good of the environment.

Kyōsei is not only a term that applies to cross-species interrelation; in business ethics, it has been used as a paradigm to promote harmonious relationships between human beings and nonliving entities such as corporations. It is the key paradigm in the Caux Roundtable

Principles for Business, which have been voluntarily adopted by many of the world's largest corporations as a normative framework to guide international business. Within the context of the Caux Principles, *kyōsei* is broadly defined as "'symbiosis,' which means 'different creatures living together'" or "living and working together for the common good."[40] The Caux Principles were first proposed by Kaku Ryūzaburō (Chairman of Canon, Inc.) who argued that in business, there must be a harmony between profit and ethical principles: "the common good is a necessary condition to make the world better, and kyosei is the sufficient condition."[41] These principles are grounded in stakeholder theory, a normative approach to business ethics that reconceptualizes the roles and relationships that define corporate obligations. Traditional shareholder theory argues that corporate executives have obligations only to those who have a financial share of the company and thus stand to profit from its success. Stakeholder theory expands upon this limited model to incorporate all those who have a stake in the outcome of the company's actions. While managers are responsible to stockholders, these are not the only people to whom they have moral obligations. The firm is at the hub of a wheel, the spokes of which are the stakeholders: financiers, suppliers, employees, communities, customers, and other groups that are affected by the actions of the business.[42] As Chester I. Barnard argues, the purpose of a corporation is to serve society, not vice versa.[43] All stakeholders must play a role in the solution of problems that affect the entire community: sub-system goals that actualize the good of a part of the community should only be pursued if they are consonant with overall system goals that promote the good of all stakeholders.[44]

Watsuji's ethics allows us to apply the notions of *kyōsei* and stakeholder theory to environmental ethics to create a set of normative principles like the Caux Roundtable Principles that can promote environmental sustainability and security. Watsuji recognizes human beings as radically contextualized. Ethics is designed to mitigate and minimize human conflict, so we need to recognize the connection between environmental change and scarcity if we wish to prevent warfare. Watsuji argues that ethics occurs in the tension between two poles, the "I" (or individual) and the "we" or social (see Figure 18.2).

| I-Pole | Ningen 人間 | We-Pole |
| Individualism | **Ethics** | Conformism |

Figure 18.2: Watsuji's Double-Negation.

On one hand, we exist as individual human beings with goals that we wish to actualize and rights that we wish to protect. On the other hand, we are defined by our social, historical, and environmental context in which individuality is subsumed. Ethics is created through a process of double-negation, which involves two distinct movements: (1) the individual negates the community, which is necessary for normative concepts such as individual rights, then (2) the individual negates himself or herself to return to the community, which is essential for the creation of ethical notions such as the common good, generalizable goals, roles, and responsibilities.[45] Individuality is only possible by virtue of our relationships, which in turn can only exist because of individuality. This is what Watsuji means when he defines *ningen* as "persons in between." A guitar string only functions when it is placed under tension between the bridge and the nut; attaching the string at only one end makes it impossible to play. Similarly, human beings can only function ethically in the tension between the individual and the community; embracing then negating both egoistic individuality on one end and empty conformism on the other makes ethics impossible.[46]

A similar process of negation needs to take place for environmental ethics to be possible. Watsuji argues that human beings are defined not only by their relationships with other people, but also the natural environment in which their culture has developed. While the ethics of *ningen* is created by the double-negation of the individual human and the collective, environmental ethics is created by a process of triple-negation in which the individual and society both negate themselves in relation to the natural environment (see Figure 18.3).[47] The good of the individual and the good of human society must be balanced with

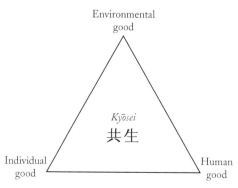

Figure 18.3: Triple-Negation

the good of the environment because these goods are all ultimately interdependent. The paradigm through which this balance can occur is *kyōsei*: the good of the individual is maximized when one strives to live in a mutually symbiotic relationship with other people and with the environment. Focusing only on the individual good leads to egoism, which is problematic because it prizes the good of one person (or a select few) over the good of others. Purely anthropocentric environmental ethics are problematic because they fail to take into account the full range of stakeholders that stand to either benefit from a healthy ecosystem or suffer from negative environmental changes. True symbiosis is only attained through an ecocentric ethic that values the environment itself and other living beings as stakeholders. While human beings should act from a fundamental respect for the intrinsic value of other humans and the natural environment, there is also a benefit to the self-interest of the agent in the sense that the maintenance of a healthy environment minimizes the negative social effects that lead to violent conflict.

CONCLUSIONS

Watsuji argues for a fundamental reevaluation of the philosophical anthropology that grounds our understanding of ethics. By reconceptualizing the notion of the autonomous, rational agent as *ningen*, a radically contextualized being, it is evident that one's natural environment plays a critical role in the promotion of one's well-being. Humans are ultimately defined through a process of triple-negation between the individual, community, and natural environment: the good of all three entities is promoted only through the harmonious interrelation of *kyōsei*. This means that we must view other human beings and the natural world as stakeholders in the common good rather than as raw material for the satisfaction of self-interest. The practical advantage of this view is that it promotes environmental security. By regulating human activity according to *kyōsei*, we can minimize our environmental impact and thereby reduce the negative socio-economic effects that promote violent conflict.

Ultimately, human beings need to adopt a set of moral principles that promote *kyōsei* on a local, national, and international scale. As indicated above, the Caux Roundtable Principles have been immensely successful at promoting stakeholder theory in international business ethics, and it might be possible to create a set of environmental ethical principles that could be voluntarily adopted by businesses and governments to promote sustainability and thereby minimize the negative social effects that generate conflict. It is beyond the scope of this paper to generate an exhaustive set of principles; ideally, these principles should be determined in an international dialogue like the one that generated the Caux Principles. However, there are several principles that would be essential to any environmental ethic that is designed to promote both sustainability and security. All human beings are stakeholders in the welfare of the environment, socio-economic stability, and international security. It is morally irresponsible to profit at the expense of other individuals or the environment upon which we all depend for natural resources. Poor countries are more likely to suffer from the negative environmental impact of unchecked population growth, consumerism, and unsustainable technologies. This means that poor countries are at a greater risk of the negative social effects that lead to violent conflict, which threatens the security and economic stability of other nations. It is thus in the interest of each nation to promote the economic and environmental sustainability of other countries. In the final analysis, it is only by protecting the environment that we can protect ourselves.

NOTES

1. Robert Carter, *Encounter with Enlightenment: A Study of Japanese Ethics* (Albany: State University of New York Press Press, 2001), 130.

2. Yasuo Yuasa, *The Body: Towards an Eastern Mind-Body Theory*, trans. Nagatomo Shigenori and T.P. Kasulis (Albany: State University of New York Press, 1987), 24.

3. This is simply the generic term for "human" that one would use when saying "who is that *person* over there?" See T.P. Kasulis, *Zen Action, Zen Person* (Honolulu: The University Press of Hawaii, 1981), 5.

4. Kasulis, 5–6.

5. Carter, *Encounter with Enlightenment,* 125.

6. Tetsurō Watsuji, *Watsuji Tetsurō's Rinrigaku: Ethics in Japan*, trans. Yamamoto Seisaku and Robert E. Carter (Albany: State University of New York Press, 1996), 18–19.

7. Yuasa, 23.

8. Yuasa, 37.

9. Carter, *Encounter with Enlightenment,* 130.

10. Yuasa, 45.

11. Tetsurō Watsuji, *Climate and Culture: A Philosophical Study*, trans. Geoffrey Bownas (New York: Greenwood Press, 1988), 9–10.

12. Watsuji, *Climate and Culture,* 14.

13. Watsuji, *Rinrigaku,* 38.

14. Watsuji, *Rinrigaku*, 37–38.

15. Watsuji, along with the rest of the Kyōto School, is sometimes interpreted as fascist because he ostensibly downplays the role of the individual and over-emphasizes the importance of the collective. However, this is based on a misrepresentation of Watsuji, who emphasizes the simultaneous negation of *both* individualism *and* conformism (this concept of double-negation is discussed at length later in this chapter). The Japanese government selectively appropriated Watsuji's work for political ends during the Second World War, but we can no more indict Watsuji for this than we can criticize Nietzsche for being misused by Hitler. As Robert Carter argues, "it must be kept in mind that his [Watsuji's] intent was not to advocate tyranny or fascism, but to seek out an ethical and social theory whereby human beings as human beings could interact easily and fruitfully in the space between them, creating as a result a society, and a world-wide association of societies which selflessly recognized the value of the individual and the crucial importance of the well-being of the whole" ("Watsuji Tetsurō", *The Stanford Encyclopedia of Philosophy* (Spring 2011 Edition), ed. Edward N. Zalta, <http://plato.stanford.edu/archives/spr2011/entries/watsuji-tetsuro/>). For a detailed discussion of Watsuji's philosophy in the context of *nihonjinron* studies and World War II politics, see Graham Parkes, "The Putative Fascism of the Kyoto School and the Political Correctness of the Modern Academy," *Philosophy East and West*, 47:3 (1997): 305–336.

16. Watsuji, *Rinrigaku*, 22.

17. Watsuji, *Rinrigaku*, 23.

18. Watsuji, *Rinrigaku*, 22.

19. Robert Carter, "Interpretive Essay: Strands of Influence," *Watsuji Tetsurō's Rinrigaku: Ethics in Japan*, trans. Yamamoto Seisaku and Robert E. Carter (Albany: State University of New York Press, 1996), 338.

20. Steve Odin, *The Social Self in Zen and American Pragmatism* (Albany: State University of New York Press, 1996), 54–55.

21. Watsuji, *Rinrigaku*, 31.

22. Watsuji, *Rinrigaku*, 20–21.

23. Watsuji, *Rinrigaku*, 235.

24. Thomas F. Homer-Dixon, "On The Threshold: Environmental Changes as Causes of Acute Conflict," *International Security* Vol. 16 No. 2, Fall 1991, 76–116, <http://www.library.utoronto.ca/pcs/thresh/thresh1.htm>.

25. Figure 18.1 represents a synthesis of the theoretical models of several leading theorists in environmental security. Homer-Dixon's analysis of the causal relationship between environmental stress, negative social effects, and violent conflict has been modified by Matthew, Gaulin, and McDonald's explanation of the role that adaptation plays in mitigating conflict. The details of these theories will be explained below.

26. Paul R. Ehrlich and John P. Holdren pioneered this concept in their article, "Impact of Population Growth," *Science* 171 Jan. 1971: 1212–17.

27. Thomas F. Homer-Dixon, "Environmental Scarcities and Violent Conflict: Evidence from Cases," *International Security*, Vol. 19, No. I, Summer 1994, 5–40, <http://www.library.utoronto.ca/pcs/evidence/evid1.htm>.

28. Homer-Dixon, "Environmental Scarcities and Violent Conflict."

29. Homer-Dixon, "On The Threshold" and "Environmental Scarcities and Violent Conflict: Evidence from Cases."

30. Homer-Dixon, "Environmental Scarcities and Violent Conflict."

31. Richard A. Matthew, Ted Gaulin, and Bryan McDonald, "The Elusive Quest: Linking Environmental Change and Conflict," *Canadian Journal of Political Science* Vol. 36 No. 4, Sep. 2003, 857–878.

32. Homer-Dixon, "On the Threshold."

33. J. Baird Callicott, "The Conceptual Foundations of the Land Ethic," *In Defense of the Land Ethic* (Albany: State University of New York Press, 1989), 87.

34. Aldo Leopold, "The Land Ethic," *A Sand County Almanac* (New York: Random House, 1990), 239–240.

35. J. Baird Callicott, "The Metaphysical Implications of Ecology," *In Defense of the Land Ethic* (Albany: State University of New York Press, 1989), 112–113.

36. Callicott, "The Conceptual Foundations of the Land Ethic" 83.

37. Nitobe Inazo, *Bushido: The Soul of Japan* (Rutland: Tuttle, 1969), 47. Nitobe is specifically talking about the way that *bushidō*, the ethic of the Japanese samurai, interprets the Confucian virtue of *jin* (仁), which is often translated as "benevolence," "compassion," or "humaneness."

38. Hiroshi Abe, "From Symbiosis (Kyōsei) to the Ontology of 'Arising Both from Oneself and from Another'," *Interdisziplinäre Phänomenologie* 4 2007: 109–129. Abe's article appears as Chapter 16 of this anthology.

39. Abe, 119–120.

40. Henri-Claude de Bettignies, Kenneth E. Goodpaster, and Toshio Matsuoka, "The Caux Roundtable Principles for Business: Presentation and Discussion," *International Business Ethics: Challenges and Approaches*, Ed. Georges Enderle (Notre Dame: University of Notre Dame Press, 1999), 133.

41. Kenneth E. Goodpaster, "Bridging East and West in Management Ethics: Kyosei and the Moral Point of View," *International Business Ethics: Challenges and Approaches*, Ed. Georges Enderle (Notre Dame: University of Notre Dame Press, 1999), 150–151.

42. Thomas M. Jones, Andrew C. Wicks, and R. Edward Freeman, "Stakeholder Theory: The State of the Art," *The Blackwell Guide to Business Ethics*, Ed. Norman E. Bowie (Malden: Blackwell, 2002), 19–20.

43. Jones et al., 22.

44. Jones et al., 23.
45. Watsuji, *Rinrigaku* 114–115. Bernard Bernier addresses Watsuji's concept of double-negation in his essay, "Transcendence of the State in Watsuji's Ethics," *Frontiers of Japanese Philosophy 2: Neglected Themes and Hidden Variations*, Ed. Victor Sōgen Hori and Melissa Anne-Marie Curley (Nagoya: Nanzan University Press, 2008), 94–100.
46. Japanese business practices are sometimes criticized for promoting the good of the whole at the expense of individuality and dissent. Watsuji would condemn such practices because they would favor the we-pole over the I-pole, negating the individual while embracing the collective. It is only when there is a balance between the two that ethics can exist.
47. Watsuji only discusses the double-negation that occurs between the individual and the community. This concept of triple-negation is my own extension of his philosophy to environmental ethics.

Afterword

Recontextualizing the Self in Comparative Environmental Philosophy

J. Baird Callicott

The first East-West Philosophers Conference occurred in 1939. It was held in Honolulu Hawai'i, aptly situated midway between the East (Asia) and the West (North America and westward points beyond). One of the participants, Wing-tsit Chan, recalls that

> It was a very small affair. There were only five of us: Charles A. Moore, the organizer, and Filmore S. C. Northrop from Yale representing the West; George P. Conger of Minnesota, representing India; Takakusu Junjiro, the eminent Buddhist scholar, representing Japan; and I, representing China. We dealt with generalities and superficialities and lumped Brahman, Tao, and Buddhist Thusness together. We hardly went beyond Spinoza in Western philosophy. . . . We saw the world as two halves, East and West.[1]

One may suppose, from Chan's mention of Spinoza that these five sages lumped in Spinoza's Substance (aka God) together with Brahman, the Dao, and Buddhist Thusness and concluded that they were all just different names for the same thing expressed in different cultural modalities. All roads lead to Rome and all philosophical thought, no matter where cogitated or in what cultural context, eventually leads to the one ultimate reality. But all roads do not, as a matter of fact, lead to Rome and all philosophical thought does not, as a matter of fact, converge on one and the same general (and superficial) idea. Let me hasten to say that I mean no disrespect to the giants on whose shoulders we comparative philosophers stand today—to Moore, Northrop, Conger, Takakutsu, and Chan. Gerald James Larson reminds us that in 1939

> Hitler unleashed his Blitzkrieg into Poland; Japan had become a militarized state and was devouring China; and the British viceroy, without consulting the Indian National Congress, had declared India a participant in the incipient war. We are aware, furthermore, that two years later there was to be a devastating bombing attack on the very venue of the First East-West Philosophers Conference in which it had been decided that Brahman, Tao, and Buddhist Thusness could be "lumped together."[2]

In the geopolitical context of 1939, cross-cultural philosophical ecumenicism may have been a necessary antidote to the cross-cultural hegemonical (and megalomaniacal) violence that was then rising to full fury. This book, in any case, manifests, embraces, and celebrates irreducible difference and philosophical pluralism. There is no concept of God in Chinese philosophy—in neither Confucianism nor Daoism (as Mary Evelyn Tucker here notes). Buddhist philosophy may well be regarded as the deconstructive antithesis of Hindu philosophy; and, accordingly, the concept of *śūnyatā* at the heart of Buddhist metaphysics may well be regarded as precisely the negation of the concept of *Brahman*. Further, Buddhism in Japan, leavened with Japanese Shintoism, had evolved, after ten centuries of northeastward migration, so far from the original Buddhism of India, now more or less surviving as Theravada Buddhism, to share with it little more than a name and an iconic founding figure.

In the Introduction to this book, we identified three main reasons for the pursuit of comparative environmental philosophy: (1) the inherent charm of the subject itself—to study comparative environmental philosophy is a pleasant intellectual activity that one might well undertake for its own sake; (2) the environmental crisis no more respects cultural and intellectual boundaries than it respects geographical and political boundaries—and environmental ethics are as badly needed in Asia as anywhere else in the world; (3) the comparative study of very different ways of viewing the world and different values concerning the world can reveal deep assumptions in one's own worldview that might escape critical reflection in the absence of *alternative* assumptions.

Reviewing the many diverse essays focused on very different traditions of Asian thought through the lens of this third rationale for the pursuit of comparative environmental philosophy reveals an unexpected unity in them, after all. They do indeed lump together in a surprising way: they all expose the parochialism and ultimately the bankruptcy of the Western concept of the self, originating in ancient Greek philosophy and, if anything, becoming even more deeply ensconced in the modern Western tradition of thought. We can call that deeply ensconced concept of the self the *atomic* or *monadic* concept of the self. Or we can call it Rational Individualism— "rational" here meaning, as in neoclassical economics, exclusively self-interested as well as calculating.

In the dualistic tradition of Pythagoras, Empedocles, and Plato, the true self is the spritely *psychē* that has "fallen" into the alien material world of earth, air, fire, and water. It is imprisoned or entombed in a foreign organic body as punishment for some unspecified sin—perhaps violence born of Hate (or Strife), if we can trust Empedocles. In the *Cratylus*, Plato provides this "etymology" of the word *sōma*:

> [S]ome people say that the body (*sōma*) is the tomb (*sēma*) of the soul, on the grounds that it is entombed in its present life; . . . I think that it is most likely the followers of Orpheus who gave the body its name, with the idea that the soul is being punished for something, and that the body is an enclosure or prison in which the soul is securely kept (*sōzetai*)—as the name *sōma* suggests—until the penalty is paid; for on this view, not even a single letter [vowel] of the word needs to be changed.[3]

Thus, are life and death inverted. This bodily, entombed existence of the soul, in a worldly vale of tears, is actually death. Pure and bodiless is the true life of the once and future god that is the soul. According to Plato, doubtless following Pythagoras, the "place" of that pure and bodiless existence of the soul is the realm of the Ideal Forms or Numbers (which, according to Aristotle, were for Plato, as for Pythagoras, one and the same). Adopted, it seems, by many strains of Christianity, this monadic notion of the self is drunk in with their mother's milk when little American children are taught to recite their first nursery rhyme and bedtime prayer: "Now I lay me down to sleep/I pray the Lord my soul to keep/If I should die before I wake/I pray the Lord my soul to take."

We typically think of the Platonic soul as tripartite, which is the way it is portrayed in the early books of the *Republic*. But in the tenth book of the *Republic*, Plato asserts that the appetitive and spirited parts of the soul are not its true nature and did not exist before it was entombed in the body. The body-sullied aspects of the soul are sloughed off when the soul is no longer associated with a body. The soul may dissociate itself entirely from the bodily realm by ascetic habits and mathematical research. That of course makes the rational part of the soul—"rational" here meaning logical, as in traditional philosophy—the true soul and the soul itself monadic, not triadic.

In the other great tradition of ancient Greek moral philosophy—the materialistic tradition of the sophists, following the atomism of Leucippus and Democritus—the self is portrayed *by analogy* with material atoms. The Greek word *átomos* is formed from *temnō*, meaning *cut,* and the alpha-privative, *á-*, and means *uncuttable* or *indivisible*. If we were to assume the same playful license that Plato does in the *Cratylus*, we might derive the word *individual* from *indivisible*, requiring only a change of the last few letters, and thus etymologically connect *individualism* with *social atomism*. Playful "etymology" aside, the prevailing concept of the self in Western thought is, as it were, a social atom, an individual. Each egoistical social atom is on an unwavering inertial course driven by the psychological forces of desire and aversion—and thus on a collision course with other egoistic social atoms in a lawless social vacuum or void. Only by means of a social contract are man-made laws devised to enable civilized life to emerge from an otherwise ceaseless and debilitating war of each against all.

Descartes adopted and intensified the Pythagorean-Platonic concept of the self as the *psychē logikē* in the *sōma*, the rational ghost in the machine. The Cartesian self, on the one hand, and its mechanical body, on the other, exist in entirely separate ontological realms—the *ego* in the *res cogitans*, the *corpus* (or *automaton*) in the *res extensa*. In its essence, the Cartesian self is rational, but confused and confounded by the deceptive bodily senses, which somehow impinge upon it. Only by doubting the reliability of sense data and trusting just innate, rational, clear-and-distinct ideas can the mind attain certain knowledge. Leibniz attempted to reconnect the *res cogitans* and the *res extensa* by endowing each dimensionless (unextended) point in the latter with some degree of consciousness, transforming Descartes unthinking points in space into psychic monads.

Hobbes adopted and intensified the materialist tradition of Protagoras, Antiphon, and Thrasymachus. Together, Descartes, Leibniz, and Hobbes helped create the hyper-individualism we find today in Western thought and culture, culminating in *Homo economicus* and contemporary rational choice theory and (remember the quotation from Plato's *Cratylus* here) prisoner-dilemma game theory (in myriad permutations) as its ultimate expression. The Western self is a psyche inhabiting a body, just as our bodies inhabit our houses. The only consciousness to which we have access is our own. We look fearfully out the portals of the senses onto an alien and threatening material world. Other human (and perhaps animal) bodies—we surmise, but cannot know for sure—are also inhabited by egos similar to our own. Our individuality is primarily numerical; each of us is one, whole, and complete in ourselves. We strive to distinguish ourselves from other individuals by cultivating one or another of our psychic or somatic endowments or, more sadly still, by the brands of the commercial products we consume. Our relationships with other egos are altogether external, as they too, like ourselves, are isolated by a bodily cladding. We are independent and our peculiar mix of psychic endowments are either God-given, or, after the death of God, existentially self-made. As rational beings we are interested only in our own interests, especially as we are utterly insensible of the interests of others.

Most contemporary Westerners think that their atomic or monadic self is simply given, a brute fact, as implacably real and natural a fact as that the sky is blue or that their material bodies are subject to the law of gravity. That is the way they experience it—so deeply imbued is this idea of self in the Western worldview. But from the perspective of Asian traditions of thought, the atomic or monadic concept of the self—in other words, Rational Individualism—is a socially constructed concept; there are alternative ways of conceiving the self. All of the essays in this collection touch on those alternatives; and, indeed, for many, one or another of those alternative ways of conceiving the self is a central theme. Moreover, many of the authors of the essays in this anthology argue that one or another alternative conception of the self is more consonant with ecology and more in tune with an environmental consciousness and conscience.

Indeed, the affinity of environmental consciousness and conscience with the sense of self in one Asian tradition of thought was at the heart of the environmental philosophy, "Ecosophy T," developed by Arne Naess, one of the founders of the field.[4] Prior to helping found environmental philosophy and Deep Ecology, more particularly, Naess had developed an interest in the Indian nonviolent resistance

movement theorized and actively led by Mohandas Gandhi. His
interest in Gandhi's work led him to classical Indian Advaita Vedanta
and its equation of *ātman* (the self) with *Brahman* (the one universal
Being, manifested in every finite being). At the core of Naess's
Ecosophy T is the doctrine of Self-realization, which phrase Naess
claimed to have borrowed from Gandhi's own writings.[5] (Mindful
of Wing-tsit Chan's mention of the prominence of Spinoza at the
first East-West Philosophers' Conference, it might be illuminating
as well to mention that Naess also invoked Spinoza's metaphysics
as a source and inspiration for his own Ecosophy T.[6]) The phrase
"self-realization" conjures up images in the modern American mind
of thousands of books by "life coaches" and pop psychologists on how
to win friends (and lovers), influence (and manipulate) people, and
make oodles and oodles of money. The self to be realized would be,
of course, this culturally constructed inner, isolated soul, so deeply
ensconced in the Western worldview. And this poor, lonely little self
is realized—cultivated and made to shine forth, flourish, and triumph
over other poor, little lonely selves—by one or another technique
(take your pick, there are thousands on offer, for a median book price
of $29.99). To avoid the inevitable confusion with this ubiquitous
Western-style sense of self-realization, Naess always capitalized it
thus: Self-realization. And he metaphysically grounded the distinction between self- and Self-realization in the Sanskrit distinction
between the *jīva* (the narrow self) and the *ātman* (the universal Self).
Practically speaking, Self-realization in Ecosophy T is attained when
one realizes that oneself (or perhaps better oneSelf) is embedded
in one's environment and continuous with it. The paper on Hindu
environmental philosophy in this volume by George James provides
an especially clear and sustained discussion of this notion of the Self
and of Gandhi's environmental philosophy, while Framarin, and
Gruzalski each carry forward—in one way or another, both critically
and developmentally—the line of thought in environmental ethics
inaugurated by Arne Naess in 1973.

Naess's younger contemporary, human ecologist Paul Shepard,
anticipated Naess in relating an alternative concept of the self to
ecology in a way more informed by ecology; (Naess himself was not
particularly well versed in ecology.):

> In one aspect, the self is an arrangement of organs, feelings,
> and thoughts—a "me"—surrounded by a hard body boundary:
> skin, clothes, and insular habits. . . . The alternative is a self as a

center of organization, constantly drawing on and influencing the surroundings, whose skin and behavior are soft zones contacting the world instead of excluding it. . . . Ecological thinking . . . requires a vision across boundaries. The epidermis of the skin is ecologically like a pond surface or a forest soil, not a shell so much as a delicate interpenetration. It reveals the self ennobled and extended rather than threatened as part of the landscape and the ecosystem, because the beauty and complexity of nature are continuous with ourselves.[7]

The Australian environmental activist, John Seed, applied Naess's Ecosophy T to his own endeavors and extended Shepard's eco-spatial expansion of the Self to the evolutionary temporal dimension:

When humans investigate and see through their layers of anthropo-centric self-cherishing, a most profound change in consciousness begins to take place. Alienation subsides. The human is no longer an outsider, apart. Your humanness is then recognized as being merely the most recent stage of your existence . . . you start to get in touch with yourself as mammal, as vertebrate, as a species only recently emerged from the rainforest. As the fog of amnesia disperses, there is a transformation in your relationship to other species, and in your commitment to them. . . . "I am protecting the rainforest" develops to "I am part of the rainforest protecting myself. I am that part of the rainforest recently emerged into thinking."[8]

One might well dispute the claim that the evolutionary-ecological self as conceived by Paul Shepard and John Seed have anything in common with the concept of *ātman/Brahman* in Hindu philosophy. Despite explicitly connecting it with Hindu metaphysics via Gandhi and with the similarly totalizing metaphysics of Spinoza (which Moore, Northrop, Conger, Takakutsu, and Chan apparently lumped together with Hindu metaphysics) Naess's *original* characterization of the ecological Self is quite different from the *ātman/Brahman* concept. According to Naess, among other things Deep Ecology involves,

Rejection of the man-in-environment image in favor of the *rela-tional, total-field image*. Organisms as knots in the biospherical net or field of intrinsic relations. An intrinsic relation between two things A and B is such that the relation belongs to the definitions or basic constitutions of A and B, so that without the relation, A and B are no longer the same things. The total field model dissolves not only the man-in-environment concept, but every

compact thing-in-milieu concept—except when talking at a superficial or preliminary level of communication.⁹

Here Naess succinctly sketches a very different concept of the self
than the Self that Gandhi sought to realize. Like the Pythagorean-
Platonic-Cartesian self that is dominant in Western thought, Gandhi's
Hindu Self is also internal and essential. The crucial difference is that
in the dominant Western tradition the self is particulate—monadic
or atomic—while in Advaita Vedanta, the Self is universal. The
Self in me is identical with the Self in you and in everyone else.
This concept of an internal, essential, but universal Self invites
two alternative moral responses: Withdrawal in disgust from the
world of appearances (phenomena, *maya*) as not only illusory but
also as macabre—the Self divided against itSelf in ceaseless mortal
combat, In Eastern-influenced Western philosophy, this was Arthur
Schopenhauer's response. The other response is compassionate
loving-kindness expressed toward the Selfsame Self in unenlightened
others. In Eastern-influenced Western philosophy, this was Albert
Schweitzer's response.

In his first foray into Deep Ecology, Naess sketches a relational,
not an essential, concept of self. He also succinctly outlines the
general philosophical concept at its core—that of "internal relations."
That is, oneself may be conceived as a node or nexus in a skein or
web of relationships. One's relationships—both socio-cultural and
environmental—constitute oneself. Apart from the skein or web of
relationships that constitute oneself, oneself would no longer be the
self that one finds oneself actually to be. Were one born in a different
socio-cultural-environmental milieu, oneself would be significantly
different from the self one actually is.

Let us contrast what we might call the Eco-relational sense of self
with Rational Individualism as here defined. At the core of Rational
Individualism is the general philosophical concept of "external relations." Externally related things are what they are independently of
their relationships with other things. Good examples of externally
related things are the proverbial billiard balls on a pool table. The
Eight Ball remains the Eight Ball irrespective of its relationships
with all the other balls on the table and irrespective of its state of
motion and location on the table. By contrast, let us compare the skein
or web or relationships that compose the Eco-relational self to the
proverbial seedless (selfless) onion; and compare stripping the self of

its relationships to peeling the proverbial onion. As the relationships are peeled away, one by one, what do we finally reach at the core of the onion/self? Nothing. *Śūnyatā*.

Stephanie Kaza quotes this verse from the famous ninth-century Zen master, Dōgen: "To study the Buddha way is to study the self/To study the self is to forget the self/To forget the self is to be actualized by the myriad things." Epitomized by the haiku and kōan, quite central to Zen Buddhist teachings is that a single terse verse may have many layers of meaning. Kaza explores one layer of meaning in these lines composed by Dōgen: "experiential knowing." I offer another: Apart from the myriad things coming uniquely together just here, just now, the self is nothing. Or put positively, as does Dōgen, to study the self is to realize that the self just is to be actualized (realized) by the myriad things. Perhaps better yet, Simon James puts my point with both clarity and authority:

> [W]hatever exists cannot do so on account of its possessing a non-relational essential nature: things, as Buddhists say, are empty (*śūnya*) of 'self-existence' or 'own-being' (*svabhāva*). Instead, it is said that any particular thing is what it is because of the coincidence of certain conditioning factors[;] . . . it is imbued with an inherent nature . . . because of the relations it bears . . . to other things.

But my understanding of the sense of self that Dōgen is getting at and Kaza's differ only in matters of small detail as both she and I, in her words, seek to "to break through delusions that generate and perpetuate a sense of an independent and separately existing self" and cultivate "relational perception."

Many of these Indian philosophical themes are echoed in the section on Chinese thought. In the opening essay, Mary Evelyn Tucker contrasts the Confucian sense of self-cultivation with that of the West and along the way observes, as I before mentioned, that there is no God in Chinese traditions of thought. Rather there are, in Confucianism, the realms of Heaven, Earth, and Humanity. Self-cultivation involves attuning oneself to the Heaven-Earth axis of order and thus attaining a nobility of character or virtue. And the principal task of the noble person is attuning the human social order to the natural Heaven-Earth order. The Greek term for the natural order is *kosmos*. According to Tucker, Confucianism provides not an anthropocentric but an "anthropocosmic" environmental ethic.

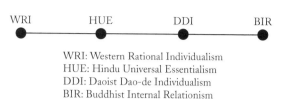

WRI: Western Rational Individualism
HUE: Hindu Universal Essentialism
DDI: Daoist Dao-de Individualism
BIR: Buddhist Internal Relationism

Figure 19.1: Spectrum of Alternative Concept of Self.

The Buddhist sense of self (ultimately empty and purely internally related) and the Western Rational Individualistic sense of self (externally related and essentialist) lie at extreme ends of a spectrum (see Figure 19.1). Upon further consideration, neither seems to fully capture our reflective experience of selfhood. On the one hand, Western rational individuals are not as indistinguishable as hydrogen atoms. On the other, no matter how similar the early-childhood conditioning, intensive enculturation, and metaphysical and religious indoctrination, such relational uniformity never produces clones. Careful reflection on who we are places the actual self somewhere on that spectrum between these extremes. On the part of the relational extreme, we cannot deny that who we are is conditioned by who our parents were, what biome and what society we grew up in, how we were educated, and all the other myriad things that actualize ourselves. On the part of the monadic extreme, any parent of a child knows that children come into the world with a unique personality. Two children—fraternal twins, for example—born to the same parents in the same biophysical milieu, enculturated into the same religio-philosophical weltanschauung, and given the same schooling and, in general, exposed to more or less the same myriad things turn out to be different—often markedly different—persons.

In Daoism we find such a concept of the self that lies between the extremes of the ultimately empty, purely internally related Buddhist sense of self and the externally related, essentialist Western Rational Individualistic sense of self. In addition to the *Dao* there is, in Daoism, also the *de*—which is of co-equal importance, but which, as Karyn Lai points out, has been given short shrift in most casual philosophical discussions of Daoism. The title of the earliest Daoist classic is, after all, the *Dao**de**jing*. In reviewing the more serious philosophical discussions of Daoism, Lai finds various interpretations of the *de* that penetrate more deeply into the concept than that it just means "virtue." Ignoring subtle differences in the more serious interpretations, *de* appears to be just that non-empty core of the self that is the non-relational component of one's distinctiveness or individuality.

To affirm, honor, and cultivate one's *de* is to achieve integrity (and thus virtue), according to Lai. However, she stresses that *Dao* and *de* are complementary, not oppositional, and that one's *de* is expressed within the relational context of the *Dao*. In the *Daodejing*, she writes,

> there is strong suggestion of an intrinsic relatedness between individuals within the framework of the *dao*. Relations are intrinsic [i.e., internal] rather than extrinsic [i. e., external] in that individuals are determined in part by their respective places in the *dao*. . . . [D]e seems to provide the specifications for an individual's *integrity* in the context of its relations with other individuals. Within an environment where interdependence is emphasized, the integrity of individuals is important as it is necessary to prevent the obliteration of individual distinctiveness, interests, and needs, which might too easily be subsumed under the rubric of the whole. These two features—interdependence and integrity—are held in a finely tuned balance. The individual seeks and attains meaning *within* contextual and relational boundaries and affiliations. However, if these are overly restrictive, the integrity of the individual will be diminished or eradicated. Hence, *de* is important in setting the extent of self-determination. *De* refers to (a development or cultivation of) the distinctive characteristics of individuals. Yet, the sense of integrity is far removed from any suggestion of independent, separate existence.

In the opening essay of the section on Japanese Traditions of Thought, Steve Odin expounds on the way that the philosophers of the Kyoto School have taken Buddhist Internal Relationalism to extraordinary levels of philosophical sophistication, especially by Watsuji Tetsurō. According to Odin, in Watsuji's ethics,

> the "person" as *ningen* does not mean simply the individual (*hito*), but the "relatedness" or "betweenness" (*aidagara*) in which people are located. . . . Watsuji develops as his main philosophical theme the embodied spatiality of human existence in various social environments, so that the individual both influences and is influenced by the family, the community, and ultimately the natural environment of a *fūdo* or "climate". . . . [B]oth self and nature are grounded in a common field of reality as the subjective and objective aspects of a single continuum or relational matrix.

Of all the essays in this collection, that by Deane Curtin focuses on an alternative concept of the self—alternative to that ensconced in the Western worldview—not as *a* central theme, but as *the* central theme.

He makes explicit what was only implicit in my foregoing discussion, that the Deep Ecology tradition in environmental philosophy, spawned by Arne Naess, has exhibited a greater affinity for Buddhist Internal Relationalism than to Hindu Universal Essentialism and its Western analogue in the philosophy of Spinoza, despite Naess's claims to the contrary. But in appropriating Buddhist thought, especially that of Dōgen, Deep Ecologists may have distorted it. Ironically, as Curtin interprets him, Dōgen seems to betray the origins of Buddhism as the antithesis of Hindu essentialism, for, according to Curtin, Dōgen thought that "Buddha-nature is fundamental reality." In other words, Curtin seems to read Dōgen as a Universal Essentialist. Stephanie Kaza would quite disagree, as she reads Dōgen as finding nothing, *śūnyatā*, at the core of the self. Quoting the same lines from Dōgen as Kaza, Curtin concludes that they enable oneself "to realize one's true self in the cosmological dimension." He might as well have substituted *ātman* for "one's true self" and *Brahman* for "the cosmological dimension." Curtin, however, goes on to deny this very Hinduization of Dōgen— claiming that such a heresy is committed by the Deep Ecologists and not by him—and to reaffirm Buddhist Internal Relationalism. Piling more irony on top of all this, both Curtin and Kaza approach Dōgen and a Buddhist concept of the self informed by contemporary feminism. Curtin's polemical essay shows itself to be a kind of protracted kōan, for there is much to ponder in its twists and turns.

In their contribution to this collection, David Shaner and R. Shannon Duval are not concerned centrally and hardly even peripherally with the concept of self in Japanese philosophy. But it does come up in their discussion and in a most interesting and revealing way. According to Shaner and Duval, the Pythagorean/Platonic concept of the soul-self was so deeply ingrained in the mind of one Western philosopher, William James (who was in many other ways a radical thinker) that he was unable to even entertain any alternative to it: "James was not able," they write, "seriously to question the notion of self, ego, or soul that frequently stands in the way of entering fully into an ecocentric, versus egocentric, worldview. . . . In contrast, Nishida and the entire Buddhist tradition argue that one must abandon egocentric notions of self and accept the doctrine of no-self (*anātman, muga*)." To even entertain "a way of being that is without self"—so fundamental to "the entire Buddhist tradition," as they note—"James seems utterly incapable of grasping the point." Although James, as Shaner and Duval point out, influenced his Japanese contemporary, Nishida Kitarō, James's blindness to any alternative to the monadic Western sense of self prevented any meaningful mutuality, any meaningful influence of Nishida or any other Japanese philosopher on James: "While Nishida found James' worldview attractive, this point suggests that James may not have reciprocated the sentiment. That is, in consideration of James' attachment to the concept of self, it is not likely that he would have been comfortable in Nishida's world of a *cultivated* selflessness." It should be noted, however, that Arne Naess found a quite different and indeed relational—though hardly in a Buddhist—sense of self articulated by James in his *Principles of Psychology*.[10]

Need I go on essay-by-essay to the last of those in the last section of this anthology? Haven't I proved my point that there is a common theme running through them all—an alternative to the atomic or monadic concept of the self in the Western worldview, Rational Individualism? While there seems to be a decided tilt in favor of Buddhist Internal Relationalism "they all expose," as I began by saying, "the parochialism and ultimately the bankruptsy of the Western concept of the self, originating in ancient Greek philosophy and, if anything, becoming even more deeply ensconced in the modern Western tradition of thought." And that negative, deconstructive function of these essays is more important than any affirmative case to be made for any one of the alternatives. If Shaner and Duval are correct, *pace* Naess, that James's incapacity to even comprehend some other notion of the self than that which every factor in his experience had inculcated and reinforced—his religious upbringing, philosophical training, the capitalist economy and liberal democratic polity that he inhabited—indicates that the lynchpin which must be pulled before an ecological worldview can coalesce is this insidious monadic individualism and social atomism.

Not only is this idea an impediment to an ecological worldview, it threatens to undermine the very society, economy, polity, and culture that fosters it. A conception of society as an aggregate of independent individuals is insensible to the reality—and fragility—of the collective whole, upon which deluded believers in independent individualism so deeply depend, whether they realize it or not. The notion that our economy is all about the private creativity of risk-taking entrepreneurs, is to ignore both the social and educational capital that entrepreneurs appropriate, largely as a public subsidy, and the public transportation and communications infrastructures that they rely on to get their messages out to consumers and their goods to market. A polity of social atoms, some winners and others losers, becomes unlivable for the winners when the losers reach a critical mass and begin to sicken and starve, homeless on the streets. Even if the private militias of the haves protect them from attack by the have-nots, such a dystopia is no place to live a fully human life. Some relational sense of self—be it Buddhist, Daoist, Hindu, or evolutionary-ecological—is necessary if we are to meet the social, economic, and political challenges we face as well as the environmental challenges. That's what these essays—all of them—can teach us.

NOTES

1. Wing-Tsit Chan, "Chu Hsi and World Philosophy," in Gerald James Larson and Elliot Deutsch, eds., *Interpreting Across Boundaries* (Princeton, N. J.: Princeton University Press, 1988), p. 230.

2. Gerald James Larson, "Introduction: The 'Age-Old Distinction between the Same and the Other'" in Gerald James Larson and Elliot Deutsch, eds., *Interpreting Across Boundaries* (Princeton, N. J.: Princeton University Press, 1988), p. 6.

3. Plato, *Cratylus* 400c, C. D. C. Reeve, tr., *Plato, Complete Works*, John M. Cooper, ed. (Indianapolis, Ind.: Hackett Publishing Company, Inc., 1997), pp. 118–119.

4. For a full discussion, see the essay by Deane Curtin in this collection.

5. See Arne Naess, "Identification as a Source of Deep Ecological Attitudes," in Michael Tobias, ed. *Deep Ecology*, Revised (San Marcus, Cal.: 1988): 256–270; and Arne Naess, *Ecology, Community, Lifestyle*, David Rothenberg, tr.& ed. (Cambridge: Cambridge University Press, 1989).

6. For example, Arne Naess, "Spinoza and Ecology," *Philosophia* 7 (1977): 45–54.

7. Paul Shepard, "Ecology and Man: A Viewpoint," in Paul Shepard and Daniel McKinley, eds., *The Subversive Science: Essays Toward an Ecology of Man* (Boston: Houghton Mifflin, 1969), p. 2.

8. John Seed, "Anthropocentrism," Appendix E in Bill Devall and George Sessions, *Deep Ecology: Living as if Nature Mattered* (Layton Ut.: Peregrin Smith Books, 1985), p. 243.

9. Arne Naess, "The Shallow and the Deep, Long-range Ecology Movements: A Summary," *Inquiry* 16 (1973): 95–100, p. 96 (emphasis in original).

10. Arne Naess, "Identification."

Contributors

Hiroshi Abe holds a Ph.D. in Philosophy and is an Associate Professor in the Graduate School of Human and Environmental Studies at Kyoto University. His publications on the subject of Japanese philosophy and environmental ethics include "On Symbiosis with Nature" in *Intellectual Problems in the 21st Century—A Reconstruction of Intelligence from an Ethical Point of View* (edited by Yoshihiko Ishizaki, Nakanishuya-Shuppan Publishing, 2001) and a chapter in *The Legacy of the Kyoto School of Philosophy: Life, Death and Environment* (edited by Tagashi Ogawa, Kōyō-Shobō Publishing, 2008).

J. Baird Callicott is Distinguished Regents Professor of Philosophy at the University of North Texas. He is the co-Editor-in-Chief of the *Encyclopedia of Environmental Ethics and Philosophy* and author or editor of a score of books and author of more than one hundred and fifty journal articles, encyclopedia articles, and book chapters in environmental philosophy and ethics. Callicott has served the International Society for Environmental Ethics as President and Yale University as Bioethicist-in-Residence. His research goes forward simultaneously on four main fronts: theoretical environmental ethics, comparative environmental ethics and philosophy, the philosophy of ecology and conservation policy, and biocomplexity in the environment, coupled natural and human systems (sponsored by the National Science Foundation). Callicott is perhaps best known as the leading contemporary exponent of Aldo Leopold's land ethic and is currently exploring an Aldo Leopold Earth ethic in response to global climate change.

Deane Curtin is a Professor and Chair of the Philosophy Department at Gustavus Adolphus College. He has also served as a visiting professor of philosophy at Kansai Gaidai University, Cambridge University, and Kings College. His books include *Environmental Ethics for a Postcolonial World* (Rowman and Littlefield, 2005) and *Chinnagounder's Challenge: The Question of Ecological Citizenship* (Indiana University Press, 1999).

R. Shannon Duval is a professor of philosophy at Mount Mary College and worked as a Charles A. Dana Foundation Research and Teaching Assistant at Furman University. Her publications include *The Encyclopedia of Ethics* (Facts on File, 1999).

Alan Fox is an Associate Professor in the Department of Philosophy at the University of Delaware. He has published numerous scholarly articles, including "Concrete Ethics in a Comparative Perspective: Zhuangzi meets William James," (in *Varieties of Ethical Reflection*, ed. Michael Barnhart, Lexington Books, 2002), and "Reflex and Reflectivity: *Wuwei* in the *Zhuangzi*" (*Asian Philosophy*, 6:1 (1996): 59–72).

Christopher Framarin earned his M.A. in philosophy from the University of Hawai'i at Mānoa in 2001 and his Ph.D. in philosophy from the University of New Mexico in 2005. He is currently an associate professor in philosophy and religious studies at the University of Calgary. His publications include the book, *Motivation in Indian Philosophy* (Routledge, 2009) and the article, "Environmental Ethics and the Mahabharata: The Case of the Khandava Forest" (forthcoming in the journal, *Sophia*).

Bart Gruzalski earned his Ph.D. from the University of Maryland in 1974. After serving for almost two decades as a professor of philosophy at Northeastern University, he chose to leave academia to help found the Pacific Center for Sustainable Living in Humboldt County, California. His numerous publications on Asian and comparative philosophy include *On the Buddha* (Wadsworth, 1999) and *On Gandhi* (Wadsworth, 2001).

Ian Harris is a Professor of Buddhist Studies at the University College of St. Martin and is the co-founder of the UK Association for Buddhist Studies. His publications include *Buddhism and Politics in Twentieth Century Asia* (Continuum, 2001), *Cambodian Buddhism* (University of Hawai'i Press, 2008), and *Buddhism, Power and Political Order* (Routledge, 2009).

George James is Associate Professor of Philosophy and Religion Studies at the University of North Texas. Over the past twenty years he has been exploring the relationship between religious ideas and practices and environmental activism in India. His published works include *Interpreting Religion* (Catholic University of America Press, 1995),

Ethical Perspectives on Environmental Issues in India (APH Publishing Corporation, 1999) and his forthcoming *Ecology is Permanent Economy: The Activism and Environmental Philosophy of Sunderlal Bahuguna* (SUNY, 2013).

Simon P. James is a Lecturer in Philosophy at Durham University and holds degrees in environmental ethics (Ph.D.), philosophy of science (M.A.), and biology (B.A.). His publications include *Buddhism, Virtue and Environment* (with David E. Cooper, Ashgate, 2005) and *Zen Buddhism and Environmental Ethics* (Ashgate, 2004).

Karyn Lai is a Senior Lecturer and the Philosophy Discipline Coordinator in the School of History and Philosophy at the University of New South Wales in Sydney, Australia. Her publications include *An Introduction to Chinese Philosophy* (Cambridge University Press, 2008) and *Learning from Chinese Philosophies: Ethics of Interdependent and Contextualized Self* (Ashgate, 2006).

Stephanie Kaza is an interdisciplinary scholar with expertise in a variety of academic areas. She holds a Ph.D. in Biology from the University of California, Santa Cruz and a M.Div. from Starr King School for the Ministry, and she is currently a Professor of Environmental Studies at the University of Vermont. Dr. Kaza serves as the President of the Society of Buddhist-Christian Studies and is a member of the Religion and Ecology group of the American Academy of Religion. Her extensive publishing record includes the following books: *Hooked! Buddhist Writings on Greed, Desire, and the Urge to Consume* (Shambhala, 2005), *Sources of Buddhist Environmentalism* (co-edited with Kenneth Kraft, Shambhala, 2000.), and *The Attentive Heart: Conversations with Trees* and *Dharma Rain* (Ballantine, 1993).

James McRae earned his Ph.D. in comparative philosophy from the University of Hawai'i at Mānoa in 2006, specializing in ethics and Japanese thought. He is currently an Associate Professor of Asian Philosophy and Religion and the Coordinator for Asian Studies at Westminster College in Fulton, Missouri. His publications include the book, *The Philosophy of Ang Lee* (with Robert Arp and Adam Barkman, University Press of Kentucky, 2013) and chapters in *Rethinking the Nonhuman* (edited by Neil Dalal and Chloe Taylor, forthcoming), *Value and Values* (edited by Roger T. Ames and Peter Hershock, forthcoming from University of Hawai'i Press), and *Introducing*

Philosophy Through Pop Culture (edited by William Irwin and David Kyle Johnson, Blackwell Press, 2010).

James Miller earned his Ph.D. from the Division of Religious and Theological Studies at Boston University in 2000 and his M.A. in Theological and Religious Studies from Cambridge University in 1997. He is currently a professor of Religious Studies and Cultural Studies at Queen's University in Ontario, Canada. His publications include the books *The Way of Highest Clarity: Nature, Vision and Revelation in Medieval China* (Three Pines Press, 2008), *Chinese Religions in Contemporary Societies* (ABC-CLIO, 2006), and *Daoism: A Short Introduction* (Oxford, 2003).

Steve Odin is a Professor of Philosophy at the University of Hawai'i at Mānoa and has served as a Visiting Professor at Boston University and Tohoku University in Sendai, Japan. His published works on Japanese philosophy include *Artistic Detachment in Japan and the West: Psychic Distance in Comparative* Aesthetics, (University of Hawai'i Press, 2001) and The *Social Self in Zen and American Pragmatism* (SUNY Press, 1996).

R.P. Peerenboom holds both a Ph.D. in comparative philosophy from the University of Hawai'i and J.D. from Columbia Law School. He has practiced law in both the United States and China, has served as a professor at both the UCLA School of Law and La Trobe University, and is the Director of the China Rule of Law Programme at the Oxford Foundation for Law, Justice and Society. His publications include *China's Long March Toward Rule of Law* (Cambridge University Press, 2002) and *Law and Morality in Ancient China: The Silk Manuscripts of Huang-Lao* (SUNY Press, 1993).

David Shaner served as the Gordon Poteat Professor of Philosophy at Furman University until his retirement in 2012. In addition to a Ph.D. in comparative philosophy from the University of Hawai'i at Mānoa, he holds a seventh-degree black belt in the Japanese martial art of Ki-Aikido and is the chief instructor for the Eastern Ki Federation. His numerous publications include *Science and Comparative Philosophy* (with Shegenori Nagatomo and Yuasa Yasuo, Brill, 1990) and *The Bodymind Experience in Japanese Buddhism: A Phenomenological Perspective of Dōgen and Kukai* (SUNY Press, 1985), and he is the editor of SUNY's *Philosophy and Biology* book series (SUNY Press, 1988 to present).

Mary Evelyn Tucker holds a Ph.D. in the History of Religions from Columbia University and serves as a Senior Lecturer and Senior Research Scholar at Yale University in the School of Forestry and Environmental Studies, Divinity School, and Religious Studies Department. She has also been a member of the faculties of Harvard Divinity School, The University of California at Berkeley, and Bucknell University. Her many publications on Confucian philosophy include *Confucian Spirituality, Volumes I and II* (Crossroad Publishing Company, 2003–2004), *Confucianism and Ecology: The Interrelation of Heaven, Earth, and Humans* (with John Berthrong, Harvard University Press, 1998), and *Moral and Spiritual Cultivation in Japanese Neo-Confucianism: The Life and Thought of Kaibara Ekken (1630–1714)* (SUNY Press, 1989).

Sandra Wawrytko is an Associate Professor of Philosophy at San Diego State University. Her scholarly publications include *Dao Companion to Chinese Buddhist Philosophy: Dharma and Dao* (Springer, 2009) and *The Undercurrent of Feminine Philosophy in Eastern and Western Thought* (University Press of America, 1981).

Tomosaburō Yamauchi is a Professor Emeritus at Osaka University of Education and has served as a visiting lecturer and research fellow at numerous institutions, including Kyoto University, Kobe University, and Monash University. His publications on ethics include *A History of Western Ethics* (Gakujutsu Tosho, 1983), *Putting Oneself in Another's Shoes: The Moral Philosophy of R.M. Hare* (Keiso-Shobo, 1991), and *Reading Singer* (Showado, 2008).

Index